Complete Estonian

Mare Kitsnik and Leelo Kingisepp

Complete Estonian

Mare Kitsnik and Leelo Kingisepp

First published in UK in 2008 as *Teach Yourself Estonian* by Hodder Education.
An Hachette UK company.

First published in US in 2008 by The McGraw-Hill Companies, Inc.

This edition published in 2019 by John Murray Learning.

British Library Cataloguing in Publication Data: a catalogue record for this title is available from the British Library.

ISBN 978 1 5293 2501 0

1

Printed and bound in Great Britain by CPI Group (UK) Ltd., Croydon, CR0 4YY.

John Murray Learning policy is to use papers that are natural, renewable and recyclable products and made from wood grown in sustainable forests. The logging and manufacturing processes are expected to conform to the environmental regulations of the country of origin.

John Murray Learning

Carmelite House

50 Victoria Embankment

London EC4Y 0DZ

www.hodder.co.uk

Contents

Meet the authors

Mare Kitsnik

I was born in Elva, southern Estonia, and graduated from high school there. My education continued in Tartu. I live and work in Tallinn.

I have two masters' degrees: in linguistics from Tallinn University and in psychology from the University of Tartu. In 1990, I knew that I wanted to teach Estonian as a second language. I have taught in schools, universities, language courses, researched into how people learn Estonian as a second language and worked as an expert in my field and as a teacher trainer. I am currently freelance, mostly developing language materials and learning methodologies for students. I am interested in how non-Estonians view Estonian as a language, in development of language skills at different levels, and in communicative teaching of grammar and vocabulary. I have had several articles published and have been involved in writing professional handbooks on these subjects.

I love creating teaching materials. I have authored or shared in the writing of twelve full-length textbooks of Estonian as a second language including *Complete Estonian* in the Teach Yourself series; *Avatud uksed* ('Open Doors'), a textbook for more advanced learners, and *Naljaga pooleks* ('Just for Laughs') for beginners (all co-authored with Leelo Kingisepp); a ninth-grade textbook for general schools; a textbook for upper secondary schools; and professional language textbooks for employees in service and security fields.

Developing the teaching of Estonian has helped me make friends worldwide.

Leelo Kingisepp

I come from Tartu in southern Estonia.

I acquired my master's degree in Estonian and Finnish language and literature at the University of Tartu. Soon after graduation in 1991, I developed an interest in teaching foreign languages and taught Finnish, English and Estonian to adults and children. In 1997 I spent a year in Canada at the University of New Brunswick studying the methodology of second language teaching.

I then moved to Tallinn, the capital of Estonia, and worked at developing study materials for teaching Estonian as a second language. This has become a source of real fun and has involved me in groups of authors producing handbooks for teachers, sets of textbooks for schools and adults, language-learning CD-ROMs, websites and various study aids such as language learning games, illustrated maps, etc.

With Mare Kitsnik I have co-authored three textbooks of Estonian as a second language: *Avatud uksed* ('Open Doors') (2002), *Naljaga pooleks* ('Just for Laughs' for beginners) (2006) and *Complete Estonian* in the Teach Yourself series. I have lectured on material development internationally; have been a consultant to groups of authors; and worked as a teacher trainer in Moldova, Georgia and Latvia. Over the years the compilation of teaching resource material has become a true passion which I try to combine with bringing up my small son, doing teacher training and running a small farm in southern Estonia.

Credits

Only got a minute?

Estonia is located in northern Europe and is the most northerly of the three Baltic states (Estonia, Latvia and Lithuania). Estonia is south of Finland (separated from it by the Gulf of Finland), west of Russia, north of Latvia and east of Sweden (with the Baltic Sea in between). Estonia's capital, Tallinn, with its medieval city centre, is situated on the Baltic coast.

The Estonian language is spoken as a mother tongue by about 1.1 million people. It is the only state language in Estonia. Outside Estonia there are Estonian speakers in America, Australia, Canada, Russia and Sweden.

Estonian belongs to the Finno-Ugric group of languages and is similar to Finnish. The Finno-Ugric languages are very different from English, so learning Estonian can seem strange at first.

To start with, you have to learn some new letters like 'õ', 'ä', 'ö' and 'ü'. You also need to learn to read in a new way as in Estonian, unlike in English, every letter corresponds to a sound.

Making meanings in Estonian is a process of attaching letters to the end of words. For instance **Eesti** means *Estonia*, **Eestis** means **in** *Estonia*. Logical, isn't it? Also, the large number of international loan words in Estonian makes it easier to understand the language. Look at the following words: **hotel**, **telefon**, **buss**, **takso**, **sport**, **bioloogia**, **restoran**, **teater**, **info**, **kontsert**, **baar**, **kohv**, **rumm**, **viski**, **kokteil**. Yes, they mean *hotel*, *telephone*, *bus*, *taxi*, *restaurant*, *theatre*, *info*, *concert*, *bar*, *coffee*, *rum*, *whisky*, *cocktail*!

Learning an exclusive language is a unique experience which will impress your friends and, certainly, all Estonians.

Only got five minutes?

What's Estonia like?

Estonia is a small northerly country about the size of the Netherlands. Estonia's long coastline is bathed by the Gulf of Finland to the north and the Baltic Sea to the west. Estonia has lots of islands, the biggest of which are Saaremaa and Hiiumaa. The Estonian landscape is, quite literally, flat. The highest mountain of Estonia – Munamägi – is in fact a hill no higher than 318 metres. However, from it you will see the beauty of Estonia at its best – mystical green forests stretching in the distance, interspersed here and there by deep blue forest lakes.

The population of Estonia is just over a million, so the country is not densely populated. A third of the population lives in the capital city Tallinn; the other big towns are Tartu, Narva, Pärnu, Viljandi and Haapsalu. Distances are not great. You can travel the length of Estonia in almost half a day provided you don't stop for a coffee in small idyllic towns or walk the nature trails which lead you through fragrant swamps, meadows and forests where elk, deer or wild boar are to be seen.

Modern life in Estonia provides high level IT services such as internet banking, mobile coverage in even the most remote areas and free Wifi in most shopping centres, restaurants and petrol stations. Cultural activities include jazz and film festivals, all types of theatre and musical events, and sport activities.

What's the Estonian language like?

Estonian belongs to the Finno-Ugric language group, along with such languages as Finnish and Hungarian. Reading Estonian is easy, as a letter corresponds to a sound. To pronounce Estonian, you need to learn some new letters like **õ**, **ä**, **ö** and **ü**. For instance, in the word **sõber** *friend*, you pronounce 'õ' like the 'o' in the English word *cold*. To say **Aitäh!** *Thank you*, the 'ä' is pronounced like the 'a' in the English word *cat*.

Öö means *night* and you pronounce it like 'er' in the word *herd* but longer. The word **üks** means *one* and you pronounce the 'ü' like 'ur' in the word *bureau*.

Once you know how to read the different letters, you might find that Estonian words are sometimes very long. The trick is that **vahukoorekook** *whipped cream cake* in Estonian is written as one word instead of three **vahu/koore/kook**.

The structural logic of the Estonian language is also different from English. To understand grammatical meanings you have to look at the *end* of the word. For instance in English you can just say *I love*, *you love*, etc., and nothing much changes within the word but in Estonian, you have to have different endings: **armasta<u>n</u>** *I love*, **armasta<u>d</u>** *you love*, **armasta<u>me</u>** *we love*.

To say *in Estonia* or *from Estonia*, you also add endings to the word **Eesti** *Estonia*. For instance **Eesti<u>sse</u>** means *to Estonia*, **Eesti<u>s</u>** means *in Estonia*, **Eesti<u>st</u>** means *from Estonia*.

Sometimes adding endings is not straightforward. What makes learning Estonian fun, is that some words change completely. For instance, **tuba** means *room*, but in order to say *in the room*, you don't just add 's' but you change the whole word and say **toas** *in the room*. Fortunately, most words are not so complicated.

Estonian can be a little confusing in that both 'he' and 'she' (and by extension 'his' and 'her') are indicated by one word **ta/tema**. The sentence **Ta on tema sõber** can be translated into English in four different ways: *He is his friend. He is her friend. She is his friend. She is her friend.* Fortunately context enables you to understand who the subject of the sentence is.

A similar problem occurs when you want to indicate the future, which is not grammatically possible in Estonian. One only needs to use words like **homme** *tomorrow*, **varsti** *soon*, etc.

Estonians are sometimes very proud of the complexity of their language, but you should not let this discourage you as you try to learn Estonian, which like any other language, is designed to convey universal meanings and is no more complicated to learn than any other language.

Introduction

Hakkame eesti keelt õppima!
Let's start learning Estonian!

Is this the right course for me?

If you are an adult learner trying to learn Estonian for the first time and you want to learn in order to communicate in everyday situations, this is the course for you. Perhaps you would like to brush up your language after a break or some previous studies? Again, you might find this course very well suited to your purposes.

Complete Estonian has been compiled to suit the needs of an English-speaking independent learner and the methodology used does not presume an instructor's explanations. And even if you are intending to learn with the support of a language class, the material can also be used for that purpose. You don't need to have previous language-learning experience or the knowledge of linguistic terminology as the language content is presented in simple everyday language and illustrated with lots of examples.

Structure of the course

The course consists of a book divided in to 14 units, each concentrating on a certain topic (or topics), and two recordings, which are essential to get the maximum benefit from the course.

All units follow the same structure and consist of six parts:

▶ **Dialogues** or texts presenting everyday situations accompanied by key words and expressions and exercises
▶ **Language patterns** that follow a logical order for a beginner's level
▶ Cultural and useful **information about Estonia**
▶ **Exercises** for practising language patterns and vocabulary
▶ **Speaking exercises**
▶ **Test yourself**

At the end of the book, you will find a key to the exercises and diagnostic tests, Estonian–English and English–Estonian vocabularies, a taking it further section with advice on how to carry on after you have completed the course, a grammar glossary, which explains some of the terms used, and six appendices, with slightly more complex information about aspects of Estonian grammar.

Symbols

 Listening practice

 Vocabulary

 Speaking practice

 Test yourself

How to use the course

All units start with a listening task. Before you start to listen, however, it might be useful to go through the key words and expressions that follow each dialogue or text. To make learning easier, words that change when used are presented with so-called main forms. You should listen to the text several times. It would then be quite useful to read and translate the text with the help of the key words and expressions. Each listening task also has comprehension exercises that should be completed *after* you have listened. Do take your time; perhaps work out the exercises out loud – the recording will help you. This way you will easily acquire some phrases and questions that you will find useful in conversation. As there are several listening tasks in every unit, don't try to do them all at one go. Work with one text only until you feel comfortable with the new vocabulary and expressions.

When you have done this it is time to move on to the language patterns. You will see that the headings in these sections are given as sample sentences, with the grammatical term underneath. The language patterns are chosen to help a beginner learn more easily and we have tried to present them in an order which will allow you to start feeling the inner logic of the Estonian language and how best to use it for conversation. Some grammar topics are dealt with over several units in order to make them more 'digestible'. The course touches on most topics that occur in everyday conversation but the learner is not expected to acquire everything in detail.

First, read through the grammar explanation and then complete the exercise that (usually) follows. Sometimes the exercise can be quite long and demanding, asking you, for instance, to form certain constructions of words you might not know. The idea is that you follow the given examples and then construct your own, following the analogy. Later on, such tables serve as a tool to which you can always return if you are not sure how a certain form is constructed. Please do not frustrate yourself by trying to learn these tables by heart! In some of the units, several language patterns are presented one after the other, so, if you feel it is too much to take at once, it's quite alright to move on to the Speaking section, which is more relaxing and allows you to use ready 'chunks' of language.

After most grammar sections, there are more exercises in the 'Practice' part. The exercises here graduate from less demanding tasks to more complicated ones. You might find it is helpful if you try to work out what is asked of you orally first and then write your answers, only after this checking in the key to the exercises at the end of the book.

The last part of each unit is called 'Speaking'. Here you are expected to produce the language yourself. Each task guides you through a certain conversation situation in which you have to react adequately. If you are not sure, you can always go back to the corresponding dialogue or text at the beginning of the unit as all these communication tasks are built around the dialogue you have worked with in that unit. The answers to the Speaking exercises are also on the recording so after completing an exercise you can listen to see if you got it right.

The cultural texts that you will find at various points in a unit are constructed such that, in addition to learning about Estonia, its culture and everyday life, you will also learn some more useful vocabulary that is not included in the listening texts.

Each unit ends with a 'Test yourself', which helps you to see how well you have understood the key points of the unit.

Tere!

Hello!

In this unit you will learn:
- ▶ *The most common Estonian greetings*
- ▶ *How to say please and thank you*
- ▶ *How to tell the time*
- ▶ *How to apologize*

Listening 1

You will hear some typical Estonian greetings. Listen to the dialogues and then complete Exercise 1. The vocabulary list that follows will help you to understand what the people are saying.

 01.01

a	**Mees**	Tere!
	Naine	Tere-tere!
b	**Naine**	Tere hommikust!
	Mees	Hommikust!
c	**Mees**	Tere päevast!
	Naine	Tere!
d	**Naine**	Tere õhtust!
	Mees	Tere õhtust!

mees	*man*
naine	*woman*
Tere!	*Hello!*
Tere-tere!	*Hello-hello!*
Tere hommikust!	*Good morning!*
Hommikust!	*Good morning!*
Tere päevast!	*Good afternoon!*
Tere õhtust!	*Good evening!*

EXERCISE 1

Now listen to the dialogues again and decide in which dialogue people say **1** good evening, **2** good morning, **3** good afternoon, **4** hello.

GREETINGS IN ESTONIAN

Tere! *Hello!* is the most neutral greeting, which can be used any time of the day with anyone. The words **hommik** *morning*, **päev** *day* and **õhtu** *evening* in greetings indicate the time of day they should be used. Say **Tere hommikust!** from daybreak to midday; **Tere päevast!** from midday until dark; then switch to **Tere õhtust!** until daybreak. Answer the greeting by either repeating the whole expression or just part of it **Tere õhtust! – Tere õhtust!/Tere!/Õhtust!**

Listening 2

You will hear how Estonians say *goodbye*. Listen to the dialogues and complete Exercises 2 and 3.

 01.02

a	**Mees**	Nägemist!
	Naine	Nägemist!
b	**Neiu**	Noh, nägemist!
	Noormees	Tšau!
c	**Naine**	Head aega!
	Mees	Head aega!
d	**Neiu**	Homseni!
	Noormees	Nägemiseni!
e	**Neiu**	Nägemiseni!
	Noormees	Reedeni!
f	**Mees**	Head ööd!
	Naine	Head ööd!

neiu	*young lady, girl*
noormees	*young man*
Nägemist!	*Goodbye!*
Noh!	*Well!* (interj. expressing resignation, understanding, etc.)
Tšau!	*Bye! (informal)*
Head aega!	*Goodbye!*
Homseni!	*Till tomorrow!*
homme	*tomorrow*
Nägemiseni!	*So long!, see you!*
Reedeni!	*Until Friday!*
reede	*Friday*
Head ööd!	*Good night!*

EXERCISE 2

Which expression is used in which dialogue? Listen and tick the box(es) for each dialogue. One expression is not used in any of the dialogues.

Expression	a	b	c	d	e	f
1 Head ööd!						
2 Nägemiseni!						
3 Head aega!						
4 Nägemist!	✓	✓				
5 Tere päevast!						
6 Tšau!						
7 Homseni!						
8 Reedeni!						

EXERCISE 3

What are the appropriate greetings for each time of day?

1 10.00

2 15.00

3 22.00

PARTING WORDS

For saying goodbye **Head aega!** or **Nägemist!** are the universal expressions, which can be used anytime with anyone. Some expressions used when saying goodbye can only be said at certain times like **Head päeva!** during the day, **Head õhtut!** during the evening and **Head ööd!** during the night.

Tšau! *bye* is very informal in tone used by younger people, mostly when saying goodbye but it can also be used as a greeting.

If you know the time at which you will meet the person again you may wish to say **Homseni!** *till tomorrow* (**homme** *tomorrow*) or **Ülehomseni!** *till the day after tomorrow*. If you know the specific day you will meet again you can use the special form of the name of the day, for instance.

esmaspäev	*Monday*	Esmaspäeva**ni**!	*till Monday*
teisipäev	*Tuesday*	Teisipäeva**ni**!	*till Tuesday*
kolmapäev	*Wednesday*	Kolmapäeva**ni**!	*till Wednesday*
neljapäev	*Thursday*	Neljapäeva**ni**!	*till Thursday*
reede	*Friday*	Reede**ni**!	*till Friday*
laupäev	*Saturday*	Laupäeva**ni**!	*till Saturday*
pühapäev	*Sunday*	Pühapäeva**ni**!	*till Sunday*

Very common parting words are **Nägemiseni!** *see you*, or **Kuulmiseni!** *will hear from you* (the latter is used especially on the phone).

Note that the names of the days are not written with capital letters, unlike in English.

EXERCISE 4

 01.03

Listen and repeat.

EXERCISE 5

 01.04

Put the names of the days in the correct order. Listen and check.

a esmaspäev ____1____
b kolmapäev ____
c laupäev ____
d neljapäev ____
e pühapäev ____
f reede ____
g teisipäev ____

EXERCISE 6

Find the right translation.

1	Goodbye!	**a**	Tere päevast!
2	Good night!	**b**	Nägemist!
3	Good morning!	**c**	Homseni!
4	Good afternoon!	**d**	Tere!
5	Good evening!	**e**	Head ööd!
6	See you tomorrow!	**f**	Tere õhtust!
7	Bye!	**g**	Tere hommikust!
8	Hello!	**h**	Tšau!

EXERCISE 7

You are parting from a colleague who tells you the following. When does he indicate you will meet again?

1	Homseni!	**a**	You will meet again on Friday.
2	Reedeni!	**b**	You will meet again on Monday.
3	Esmaspäevani!	**c**	You will meet again tomorrow.

Listening 3

You will hear how Estonians say *please* and *thank you*. Listen to the dialogues and then complete Exercise 8.

 01.05

a	**Mees**	Palun!
	Naine	Aitäh!
b	**Naine**	Palun!
	Mees	Oi, suur tänu!
c	**Neiu**	Suur aitäh!
	Noormees	Pole tänu väärt!

palun	*please*
aitäh	*thank you*
oi	*oh*
suur tänu	*many thanks*
suur aitäh	*thanks a lot*
pole tänu väärt	*don't mention it* (lit. *not worthy of thanks*)

EXERCISE 8

Which expression is used in which dialogue? Listen and tick the box(es) for each dialogue.

Expressions	a	b	c
1 Oi, suur tänu!			
2 Pole tänu väärt!			
3 Suur aitäh!			
4 Palun!			
5 Aitäh!	✓	✓	

HOW TO SAY PLEASE AND THANK YOU

Aitäh means *thank you*. Saying **Suur aitäh!** (lit. *big thank you*) or **Suur tänu!** means *thank you very much*. You can also say **Suur-suur aitäh!** or **Suur-suur tänu!** if you want to express your gratitude more emotionally.

Tänu can't be used on its own like **aitäh**. It comes from the verb **tänama** *to thank* and you can say **Tänan!** *I thank*. Then it is a synonym for **Aitäh!**

Palun is used in the same way as English *please* or *here you are* when you pass something to someone, for instance, or just to add politeness to the sentence.

Palun can also be used for saying *don't mention it* or *you are welcome* but more commonly **Pole tänu väärt!** is used. For instance:

Suur-suur aitäh!	**Palun!**
Suur tänu!	**Pole tänu väärt!**

Listening 4

You will hear some more useful expressions. Listen to the dialogues and then complete Exercise 9.

 01.06

a	**Mees**	Palun vabandust.
	Naine	Pole midagi.
b	**Naine**	Oi, vabandust!
	Mees	Pole viga.
c	**Mees**	Head isu!
	Naine	Aitäh.
d	**Mees**	Terviseks!
	Naine	Terviseks!

palun vabandust	*excuse me please, I'm sorry*
pole midagi	*it's OK, it's nothing*
vabandust	*sorry*
pole viga	*it's OK*
Head isu!	*I hope you'll enjoy your meal!*
Terviseks!	*Cheers!*

MORE USEFUL EXPRESSIONS

For apologizing the most common expression is **palun vabandust** *I'm sorry*. To say *it's OK* use **pole midagi**, or **pole viga**.

Before starting to eat it is common to express the wish that other people at the table enjoy their meals by saying **Head isu!** (lit. *have a good appetite*). The response to that is either **Head isu!** or **Aitäh!** *Thank you*.

Terviseks! is the equivalent of English *Cheers!*, said when drinking to someone's health. **Tervis** means *health* and **terviseks** is also said if someone sneezes. Be careful not to mix up **Tervist!** *hello* and **Terviseks!**

EXERCISE 9

 01.07

Which expressions belong together? Listen to the dialogues and choose **a**, **b** or **c**. Then listen to the correct answers.

1 Palun vabandust!
   a Aitäh.
   b Pole midagi.
   c Head isu!

2 Oi, vabandust!
   a Terviseks!
   b Pole viga.
   c Nägemist!

3 Head isu!
   a Aitäh.
   b Terviseks!
   c Pole midagi.

4 Terviseks!
   a Aitäh.
   b Terviseks!
   c Pole midagi.

EXERCISE 10

What is the right response if you hear the following expressions? There are two correct answers to each question.

1 Tere!   **a** Terviseks! **b** Tere! **c** Tere-tere!

2 Tere hommikust!   **a** Tere hommikust! **b** Tere! **c** Tere õhtust!

3 Head aega!   **a** Nägemiseni! **b** Tšau! **c** Aitäh!

4 Palun!   **a** Pole midagi. **b** Aitäh. **c** Suur tänu.

5 Suur tänu!   **a** Palun. **b** Aitäh. **c** Pole tänu väärt.

6 Head isu!   **a** Aitäh. **b** Pole midagi. **c** Head isu!

7 Oi, vabandage palun!   **a** Pole midagi. **b** Pole viga. **c** Oi, suur tänu.

Listening 5

You will now hear how Estonians tell the time. Listen to the dialogues and then complete Exercise 11.

01.08

a	**Noormees**	Mis kell on?
	Neiu	Kell on üks.
b	**Noormees**	Mis kell on?
	Neiu	Kell on kaks.
c	**Noormees**	Mis kell on?
	Noormees	Kell on kolm.
d	**Naine**	Kui palju kell on?
	Mees	Üks hetk. Kell on pool üks.
e	**Mees**	Kui palju kell on?
	Naine	Veerand üks.
f	**Mees**	Mis kell on?
	Naine	Kolmveerand üks.

kell	*clock*
Mis kell on?	*What's the time?* (lit. *What's the clock?*)
Kell on üks.	*It's one o'clock.*
Kell on kaks.	*It's two o'clock.*
Kell on kolm.	*It's three o'clock.*
Kui palju kell on?	*What's the time?* (lit. *How much is the clock?*)
Üks hetk.	*Just a moment.* (lit. *one moment*)
Kell on pool üks.	(It's) *half past twelve* (lit. *It's half towards one.*)
veerand üks	(It's) *quarter past twelve* (lit. *quarter towards one*)
kolmveerand üks	(It's) *quarter to one* (lit. *three quarters to one*)

EXERCISE 11

In which dialogue are these times given?

1 12.45 _____

2 14.00 _____

3 12.15 _____

4 13.00 a

5 15.00 _____

6 12.30 _____

> **INSIGHT**
>
> You need to practise pronunciation a lot! Please find time to read the texts aloud along with the audio. Just listening to Estonian music on YouTube will help you to get used to how Estonian sounds.

Language patterns

PRONUNCIATION OF VOWELS

There are nine vowels in Estonian: **a, e, i, o, u, õ, ä, ö, ü**. All vowels occur in either short or long forms. In written text, short vowels are indicated by a single letter and long ones by a double letter, for instance k**e**ll *clock*; m**ee**s *man*; pal**u**n *please*; s**uu**r *big* etc. The long vowel is a continuous sound, in which the two vowels are pronounced as one long sound without a pause.

We will take a closer look at the pronunciation of vowels now. If possible, an approximation of the sound in English is given. The sounds do not correspond one to one so take these explanations as guidelines only.

Note that the stress of Estonian words is usually on the *first syllable*.

EXERCISE 12

 01.09

First read the explanations. Then listen to the words and repeat them. Do this several times.

A is pronounced like the 'u' in *but* p**a**lun *please*, t**a**kso *taxi*, k**a**ks *two*, k**a**heks**a** *eight*, p**a**nk *bank*

Aa is pronounced like the 'ar' in *dark* but slightly longer b**aa**r *bar*, m**aa** *land, country*, j**aa**nuar *January*, ban**aa**n *banana*, r**aa**dio *radio*

E is pronounced like the 'e' in *pet* t**e**r**e** *hello*, k**e**ll *clock*, n**e**li *four*, s**e**its**e** *seven*, t**e**lefon *telephone*

Ee is pronounced like the 'e' in *pet*, but with double length v**ee**rand *quarter*, m**ee**s *man*, **Ee**sti *Estonia*, v**ee**bruar *February*, t**ee** *tea, road*

I is pronounced like the 'i' in *kit* **i**su *appetite*, **i**lm *weather*, m**i**nut *minute*, k**i**no *cinema*, n**i**m**i** *name*

Ii is pronounced like the 'ee' in *keep* v**ii**s *five*, s**ii**s *then*, telev**ii**sor *TV set*, s**ii**n *here*, m**ii**nus *minus*

U is pronounced as 'u' in *put* pal**u**n *please*, b**u**ss *bus*, t**u**lema *to come*, nei**u** *young lady, girl*, a**u**to *car*

Uu is pronounced as 'oo' in *room* s**uu**r *big*, k**uu**s *six*, j**uu**ni *June*, j**uu**li *July*, j**uu**ksur *hair-dresser*

O is pronounced like the 'o' in *hot* h**o**mmik *morning*, k**o**lm *three*, k**o**hv *coffee*, f**o**to *photo*, h**o**tell *hotel*

Oo is pronounced like the 'au' in *caught* p**oo**l *half*, okt**oo**ber *October*, **oo**per *opera*, k**oo**l *school*, s**oo**vima *to wish*

Õ is pronounced like the 'o' in *cold* **õ**htu *evening*, s**õ**ber *friend*, s**õ**na *word*, **õ**nn *happiness*, **õ**de *sister*

Õõ is pronounced like the 'o' in *cold*, but longer v**õõ**ras *stranger*, Kr**õõ**t *female name*, p**õõ**sas *bush*, r**õõ**m *joy*, r**õõ**mus *glad, joyful*

Ä is pronounced like the 'a' in *cat* p**ä**ev *day*, n**ä**gemist *goodbye*, ait**ä**h *thank you*, m**ä**rts *March*, **ä**ri *business*

Ää is pronounced like the 'a' in *cat*, but double length Pole t**ä**nu v**ää**rt. *Don't mention it*, Otep**ää**, a town in southern Estonia, **ää**dikas *vinegar*, s**ää**sk *mosquito*, r**ää**kima *to speak*

Ö is pronounced as 'er' in *stronger* r**ö**stima *to toast*, k**ö**ha *cough*, l**ö**rts *slush*, *sleet*, **ö**konoomia *economy*, **ö**kosüsteem *ecosystem*

Öö is pronounced as 'er' in *herd* but longer **öö** *night*, t**öö** *work*, t**öö**tama *to work*, k**öö**k *kitchen*, m**öö**bel *furniture*

Ü is pronounced like the 'ur' in *bureau* **ü**ks *one*, **ü**heksa *nine*, k**ü**mme *ten*, **ü**llatus *surprise*, k**ü**lm *cold*

Üü is pronounced like the 'ur' in *bureau* but longer m**üü**ma *to sell*, m**üü**k *sale*, n**üü**d *now*, t**üü**piline *typical*, t**üü**tu *annoying*

Numbers 1–12

These are the numbers you need for talking about time.

1	**üks**	*one*	7	**seitse**	*seven*
2	**kaks**	*two*	8	**kaheksa**	*eight*
3	**kolm**	*three*	9	**üheksa**	*nine*
4	**neli**	*four*	10	**kümme**	*ten*
5	**viis**	*five*	11	**üksteist**	*eleven*
6	**kuus**	*six*	12	**kaksteist**	*twelve*

EXERCISE 13

 01.10

1 Listen to the numbers 1–12 and repeat.

2 Listen and write the number you hear in figures.

In order to practise this grammar topic further, do Exercises 15–17 in the Practice section.

TALKING ABOUT TIME

You ask the time by saying **Mis kell on?** or **Kui palju kell on?** or **Palju kell on?** All three mean *What time is it?* The word **kell** *clock* is used as the English equivalent *o'clock*.

The common answer is **Kell on** + corresponding number, for example **Kell on üks.** *It's one o'clock.*

It is also possible to shorten the answer by saying just the number, for example: **Mis kell on? Üks.**

NB! Saying *It's half past three* is different from how you say it in English. In Estonian, we say **Kell on pool neli.** lit. *It's half to four*, i.e. we say **pool** *half* and then the next hour.

For instance:

Kell on pool kuus.	*It's half past five.*
Kell on pool seitse.	*It's half past six.*

NB! Saying *It's quarter past …* is also different from English. For example, in Estonian we say *It's quarter past six* **Kell on veerand seitse** lit. *It's quarter towards seven*, i.e. we say **veerand** *quarter* and then the next hour.

For instance:

Kell on veerand kuus.	*It's quarter past five.*
Kell on veerand seitse.	*It's quarter past six.*
Kell on veerand üks.	*It's quarter past 12.*

It's quarter to six is **Kell on kolmveerand kuus** in Estonian (lit. *It's three quarters to six*).

The 12-hour clock is used in everyday talking. Sometimes we add to the time word **hommikul** *in the morning*, **õhtul** *in the evening*, **päeval** *in the daytime*, **öösel** *at night* if it is otherwise unclear what time exactly we are talking about.

For instance:

Kell on üks päeval.	**Kell on 13.00.**
Kell on üks öösel.	**Kell on 01.00.**
Kell on seitse hommikul.	**Kell on 07.00.**
Kell on kuus õhtul.	**Kell on 18.00.**

Opening hours

A normal working day in Estonia starts at eight and finishes at five. Lunch hours are from 12 to two. Dinnertime is usually between six and eight pm.

The 24-hour clock is used in official contexts, for example at bus terminals, ports, airports and railway stations and also on the radio and television.

EXERCISE 14

Match the pictures and sentences.

    a Kell on üks.
    b Kell on pool kaks.
    c Kell on kolmveerand kaks.
    d Kell on kaks.
    e Kell on veerand kolm.
    f Kell on pool kolm.
    g Kell on kolmveerand kolm.
    h Kell on neli.

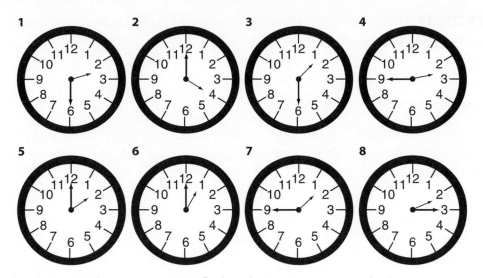

In order to practise this grammar topic further, do Exercises 18–19 in the Practice section.

Practice

EXERCISE 15

What is the Estonian for these numbers?

1 eight *kaheksa* _____

2 eleven _____

3 five _____

4 four _____

5 nine _____

6 one _____

7 seven _____

8 six _____

9 ten _____

10 three _____

11 twelve _____

12 two _____

EXERCISE 16

What are the missing numbers?

Üks, kaks, neli, viis, seitse, kaheksa, kümme, üksteist, kaksteist.

EXERCISE 17

Put the numbers in ascending order.

kaheksa	☐
kaks	☐
kaksteist	☐
kolm	☐
kümme	☐
kuus	☐
neli	☐
seitse	☐
üheksa	☐
üks	1
üksteist	☐
viis	☐

EXERCISE 18

What's the time? Choose the correct answer.

1	Kell on pool neli.	**a** 15.30	**b** 16.30
2	Kell on pool seitse.	**a** 19.30	**b** 18.30
3	Kell on pool kümme.	**a** 9.30	**b** 10.30
4	Kell on pool kaks.	**a** 14.30	**b** 13.30
5	Kell on veerand kaksteist.	**a** 12.15	**b** 11.15
6	Kell on veerand kaheksa.	**a** 7.15	**b** 8.15
7	Kell on veerand kolm.	**a** 15.15	**b** 14.15
8	Kell on veerand üks.	**a** 12.15	**b** 13.15

EXERCISE 19

 01.11

What's the time? Compare your answers with the recording.

1 11.00 *Kell on üksteist hommikul.*

2 16.15

3 18.30

4 14.45

5 17.00

6 9.15

7 13.30

8 12.15

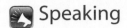 Speaking

EXERCISE 20

Here are some situations for you to practise. You are having a supper with some friends. Read and answer the questions.

1 The food is served and you all are starting to eat. Someone says **Head isu!** How do you respond?

2 You are passing a dish of food to someone. Say *Here you are.*

3 You are given something. Would it be correct to say **Tänan** or **Aitäh**?

4 You bump into your neighbour. How do you say *I'm sorry?*

5 You want to raise a glass to everybody's health. What do you say?

6 It's late and you are leaving to go home. How do you say *Good night* to the others?

EXERCISE 21

 01.12

Do the following. After you have completed the dialogue, listen to the recording and check.

1 Say *Good morning!*

2 Ask *What's the time?*

3 You are told *It's eight o'clock.*

4 Say *Thank you.*

EXERCISE 22

Take Sina's part in the dialogue below. When you have finished, listen to the recording and check.

 01.13

Mees	Tere!
Sina	Say *Hello!*
Mees	Kui palju kell on?
Sina	Say *It's half past three.*
Mees	Aitäh!

⍰ Test yourself

1 **Tere õhtust!** means
   a Good evening!
   b Hello!
   c Till evening!

2 **Nägemist!** means
   a Good night!
   b Until Friday!
   c Goodbye!

3 *Saturday* and *Sunday* in Estonian are
   a neljapäev ja reede
   b teisipäev ja kolmapäev
   c laupäev ja pühapäev

4 **Vabandust!** means
   a Cheers!
   b Sorry!
   c Thank you!

5 Someone says **Suur aitäh!** What is the correct answer?
   a Pole tänu väärt!
   b Terviseks!
   c Homseni!

6 The correct answer to **Terviseks!** is
   a Head isu!
   b Terviseks!
   c Tere!

7 The numbers two and nine in Estonian are
   a kaheksa ja üks
   b kaks ja üheksa
   c kuus ja kolm

8 What is the correct answer to question **Mis kell on?**
   a Veerand üks.
   b Pole viga!
   c Oi, suur tänu!

9 How do you say *It's eight o'clock?* in Estonian?

   a Kell on kaks.

   b Kell on veerand kaheksa.

   c Kell on kaheksa.

10 How do you say in Estonian *It's half past nine?*

   a Kell on pool üheksa.

   b Kell on pool kümme.

   c Kell on pool üks.

2 Saame tuttavaks!
Let's get acquainted!

In this unit you will learn:
▶ *How to introduce yourself*
▶ *How to ask and answer questions about languages you speak*
▶ *How to say 'How are you?'*

Listening 1

You will hear people introducing themselves. Listen to the dialogues and then complete Exercise 1 correctly according to the dialogues.

🎧 02.01

a	**Peeter**	Tere! Mina olen Peeter.
	Maarika	Väga tore. Maarika.
b	**Erki Kuusk**	Tere! Erki Kuusk.
	Jaan Mägi	Väga meeldiv. Mina olen Jaan Mägi.
c	**Kristjan Saar**	Tere! Mina olen Kristjan Saar.
	Kristjan Jõgi	Kuidas palun?
	Kristjan Saar	Kristjan Saar.
	Kristjan Jõgi	Selge. Mina olen ka Kristjan. Kristjan Jõgi.

mina olen	*I am*
ole/ma, -n	*to be*
väga tore	*pleased to meet you* (lit. *very pleasant*, slightly informal)
väga meeldiv	*pleased to meet you* (lit. *very pleasant*)
Kuidas palun?	*Excuse me?*
selge	*OK; I see, It's clear*
ka	*also, too*

> **INSIGHT**
>
> The explanation about the words like **olema** to be and its forms etc. can be found in 'Mina olen *I am* – the verb to be' after Exercise 10, below.

EXERCISE 1

Which names are used in the dialogues? Listen and tick the box(es) for each dialogue.

Names		a	b	c
1	Kristjan Jõgi			
2	Maarika			
3	Jaanika			
4	Kristel			
5	Jaan Mägi			
6	Kristjan Saar			
7	Peeter	✓		
8	Erki Kuusk			

EXERCISE 2

 02.02

Although there are many international **eesnimed** *first names* used in Estonia there are also lots of typical Estonian names. You can't tell from the endings of Estonian names whether they're men's or women's names.

Here is a selection of common Estonian names. Listen to and repeat them to practise your pronunciation.

Female names: Mare, Maarika, Ene, Leelo, Hille, Tiina, Elo, Tuuli, Ulvi, Krõõt, Õie, Anneli, Kärt, Heli, Ülle, Merike, Sirje, Piret

Male names: Alo, Margus, Henn, Teet, Indrek, Siim, Ott, Urmas, Sulev, Kaarel, Tõnis, Jaanus, Pärtel, Tiit, Ülo, Meelis, Tanel, Erki

EXERCISE 3

 02.03

Here are some international names and their equivalent in Estonian. Some of them are written as in English, but are pronounced differently. Listen to and repeat them to practise your pronunciation.

Female names: *Maria* – Maarja; *Laura* – Laura; *Christina* – Kristiina; *Ann* – Anne; *Catherine* – Katrin; *Margarethe* – Reet; *Christy* – Kristi; *Elisabeth* – Liisa

Male names: *Thomas* – Toomas; *Michael* – Mihkel; *Tony* – Tõnu; *John* – Jaan; *George* – Jüri; *Peter* – Peeter; *Andrew* – Andrus; *Paul* – Paul

ESTONIAN SURNAMES

If you lack questions for small talk when meeting Estonians, ask what their name means **Mida teie perekonnanimi tähendab?** *What does your surname mean?* (pl, formal). You'll be surprised, as a lot of Estonian surnames (and also some first names) have concrete meanings. For instance, there are more than 5,000 people called **Tamm** *oak*, which is the most common surname in Estonia, and thousands more named after other types of tree, like **Kuusk** *spruce*, **Kask** *birch*. Names of animals are also very common in surnames, for example **Ilves** *lynx*, **Rebane** *fox*, **Karu** *bear*; or birds like **Luik** *swan*, **Kurg** *stork*, **Pääsuke** *swallow*. Another big group of surnames come from professions **Sepp** *blacksmith*, **Mölder** *miller*, **Rätsep** *tailor*; and geographical locations **Saar** *island*, **Jõgi** *river*, **Mägi** *mountain*, **Järv** *lake*, **Meri** *sea*, etc.

Listening 2

You will hear people saying what their names are. Listen to the dialogues and then complete Exercises 4 and 5.

 02.04

a	**Noormees**	Tere! Mina olen Karl. Ja mis sinu nimi on?
	Neiu	Minu nimi on Kristel.
	Noormees	Ilus nimi.
	Neiu	Aitäh.
b	**Mees**	Kuidas on teie nimi?
	Naine	Piret Luik.
	Mees	Väga meeldiv.
c	**Naine**	Mis on teie perekonnanimi?
	Mees	Rätsep.
	Naine	Ja eesnimi?
	Mees	Rain.

V

ja	*and*
mis	*what*
sinu nimi	*your name* (singular, informal)
Mis sinu nimi on?	*What is your name?* (singular, informal)
minu nimi	*my name*
minu nimi on	*my name is*
ilus	*beautiful*
nimi	*name*
Kuidas on teie nimi?	*What is your name?* (formal; can also be plural)
teie nimi	*your name* (plural, formal)
perekonnanimi	*surname*
eesnimi	*first name*

EXERCISE 4

Which expressions are used in the dialogues? Listen and tick the box(es) for each dialogue. Not all expressions are used.

Expression	a	b	c
1 Pole viga!			
2 Aitäh!			

3	Väga meeldiv!			
4	Mis sinu nimi on?	✓		
5	Kuidas on teie nimi?			
6	Mis on teie perekonnanimi?			

EXERCISE 5

Find a sentence that has the same meaning.

1 **Mis on teie eesnimi?**
   a Mis on teie perekonnanimi?
   b Kuidas on teie eesnimi?

2 **Minu nimi on Siiri.**
   a Siiri on ilus nimi.
   b Mina olen Siiri.

3 **Väga meeldiv.**
   a Väga tore.
   b Selge.

Saame tuttavaks! *Let's get acquainted!*

The standard expression to start a conversation with the aim of introducing yourself is **Saame tuttavaks!** *Let's get acquainted!* You can either say just your first name or the full name, depending on the level of formality. It is not necessary to say your surname if the situation is informal, especially with younger people and children. The surname only without the first name is called, for instance, at the doctor's or in other formal situations.

On very formal occasions you can say **Kas ma tohin ennast tutvustada?** *May I introduce myself?* or when introducing two people to each other **Kas ma tohin tutvustada ...?** *May I introduce ...?* More formality can be added by using the words **proua** *madame* or **härra** *mister*. The abbreviations **hr** for **härra** and **pr** for **proua** are very common in letterheads and addresses. The word **preili** *miss* for an unmarried woman is hardly ever used when making introductions as it unnecessarily stresses the marital status.

BODY LANGUAGE

Estonians do not kiss when greeting and they definitely do not kiss when introduced to someone they do not know. Instead they shake hands, especially when first introduced to someone. On formal meeting, people can still shake hands even if they know each other well. For instance on formal business meetings it is quite common that the chairman shakes hands with everybody to make them feel welcome. If in doubt as to whether to shake hands or not, it is usually better to offer your hand for shaking as it is viewed as a friendly act. Younger Estonians have more or less dropped the habit of the handshake but among the Russian-speaking population of Estonia handshaking for greeting is very common even among the younger generation.

Listening 3

In these dialogues people ask about languages that they speak. Listen and then complete Exercises 6 and 7 correctly according to the dialogues.

 02.05

a	**Turist**	Vabandage, kas te räägite saksa keelt?
	Kohalik	Räägin küll.
b	**Turist**	Vabandage, kas te oskate inglise keelt?
	Kohalik	Ei, kahjuks ei oska.
c	**Turist**	Kas te räägite prantsuse keelt?
	Kohalik	Vabandust, ma ei saa aru.
d	**Kohalik**	Kas te oskate eesti keelt?
	Turist	Natukene.

turist	*tourist*
kohalik	*local (person)*
vabandage	*excuse me* (formal, can also be plural)
kas te räägite …?	*do you speak …?* (plural, formal)
saksa keelt?	*German* (lit. German language)
inglise keelt?	*English*
prantsuse keelt?	*French*
eesti keelt?	*Estonian*
rääki/ma, räägi/n	*to speak*
räägin küll …	*Yes, I do speak …*
Kas te oskate …?	*Can you speak …?* (plural, formal)
oska/ma, -n	*to know, to be able* (can)
Kahjuks ei oska.	*Unfortunately I can't.*
Keel	*language*
kahjuks	*unfortunately*
ei räägi	*don't speak*
Ma ei saa aru.	*I don't understand.*
aru saa/ma, saa/n aru	*to understand*
natukene	*a little*

EXERCISE 6

What names of languages do you hear in the dialogues? Listen and tick the box(es) below for each dialogue. The first one is done for you.

Languages		a	b	c	d
1	eesti				
2	saksa	✓			
3	prantsuse				
4	inglise				

EXERCISE 7

Here are some question for you to answer. Tell the truth!

1 Someone asks you **Kas te räägite eesti keelt?** How do you answer?

   a Kahjuks ei räägi.

   b Natukene räägin.

   c Räägin küll.

2 Someone asks you **Kas te räägite inglise keelt?** How do you answer?

   a Kahjuks ei räägi.

   b Natukene räägin.

   c Räägin küll.

3 Someone asks you **Kas te oskate saksa keelt?** How do you answer?

   a Kahjuks ei oska.

   b Natukene oskan.

   c Oskan küll.

Talking about languages

Foreigners often complain that it is very hard to practise Estonian in Estonia as the local people usually can speak some foreign language that they want to practise themselves. It is somewhat true because all Estonians have learnt at least two foreign languages at school starting in early grades. The most commonly learnt languages are English, German, Russian and French but some schools also offer classes of Finnish, Swedish, Spanish, Japanese and other languages. The mentality is that being such a small nation one has to know other languages and therefore it's a norm that you know some languages other than your own.

Note that names of languages in Estonian, unlike in English, are spelled with no capital letters and also the word **keel** *language* has to be used.

Listen to and repeat the names of the languages.

 02.06

vene keel	*Russian (language)*	**jaapani keel**	*Japanese (language)*
hiina keel	*Chinese (language)*	**soome keel**	*Finnish (language)*
hispaania keel	*Spanish (language)*	**rootsi keel**	*Swedish (language)*
itaalia keel	*Italian (language)*	**läti keel**	*Latvian (language)*
portugali keel	*Portuguese (language)*	**leedu keel**	*Lithuanian (language)*

The question **Kas te räägite eesti keelt?** means *Do you speak Estonian?* It is also correct to ask **Kas te oskate eesti keelt?** meaning *Can you speak Estonian?*

Listening 4

In these dialogues people ask *How are you?* Listen to the dialogues and then complete Exercise 8.

 02.07

a	**Naine**	Tere! Kuidas läheb?
	Mees	Tänan. Pole viga.
b	**Õpetaja**	Tere hommikust. Kuidas elate?
	Õpilane	Tere. Väga hästi. Aga teie?
	Õpetaja	Mina ka.
c	**Õpetaja**	Tere päevast. Kuidas läheb?
	Õpilane	Tänan küsimast. Normaalselt.
d	**Jaan**	Kuidas läheb?
	Peeter	Hästi. Aga sul?
	Jaan	Ka hästi.

Kuidas läheb?	*How are you?*
Tänan.	*Thank you.*
Pole viga.	*Not too bad.*
Õpetaja	*teacher*
õpilane	*student*
Kuidas elate?	*How are you?* (lit. *How are you living?*) (plural, formal)
ela/ma, -n	*to live*
väga hästi	*very well*
Aga teie?	*What about you?* (plural, formal)
mina ka	*me too*
tänan küsimast	*thank you* (lit. *Thank you for asking.*)
normaalselt	*OK* (lit. *normally*)
hästi	*nicely, well*
Aga sul?	*What about you?* (singular, informal)

EXERCISE 8

What expressions do you hear in the dialogues? Listen and tick the box(es) for each dialogue. The first one is done for you.

	Expressions	a	b	c	d
1	Normaalselt				
2	Kuidas elate?				
3	Hästi				
4	Natukene				
5	Kuidas läheb?	✓			
6	Väga hästi				

7	Aga teie?				
8	Aga sul?				
9	Tänan küsimast				
10	Pole viga				

Asking How are you?

The question **Kuidas läheb?** *How are you?* is not used as a short greeting in Estonian (as it can sometimes be used in English). It is quite normal to give a short overview of what you have been up to lately rather than just answering **Hästi!** *Very well!* and walking away. So if you ask **Kuidas läheb?** be prepared to exchange a few words.

If you want to ask the other person how they are you can ask:

Kuidas läheb?	*How are you?*
Kuidas elate?	*How are you?* (plural, formal)
Kuidas elad?	*How are you?* (singular, informal)
Kuidas käsi käib?	*How are you?* (lit. untranslatable phrase)

The last is a little old fashioned, but you will still hear it said.

If you are fine, you answer **Tänan, hästi!** *Fine, thank you!* or **Väga hästi!** *Very well!*

Pole viga *not too bad* or **normaalselt** *OK* also mean you are doing well. If you want to ask how the other person is doing then the phrase depends on the question you were asked:

Kuidas läheb?	*How are you?*	**Aga sul?**	*What about you?* (singular, informal)
		Aga teil?	*What about you?* (plural, formal)
Kuidas elate?	*How are you?*	**Aga sina?**	*What about you?* (singular, informal)
		Aga teie?	*What about you?* (plural, formal)

If you don't remember what exactly the question was, it is safest to ask back **Aga kuidas sul läheb?** (singular) **Aga kuidas teil läheb?** (plural).

EXERCISE 9

 02.08

Choose the correct answer. Listen and check.

1 **Kuidas läheb?**
   a Normaalselt.
   b Natukene.

2 **Kuidas elad?**
   a Hästi.
   b Mina ka.

3 Mina olen Maarika.
   a Pole viga. Mina olen Piret.
   b Väga meeldiv. Mina olen Piret.

4 Kuidas elate?
   a Tänan küsimast. Hästi.
   b Tere hommikust. Hästi.

5 Kuidas läheb?
   a Hästi. Aga sina?
   b Hästi. Aga sinul?

6 Kuidas elad?
   a Hästi. Aga sina?
   b Hästi. Aga sinul?

INSIGHT

Unless you learn the new words your progress will be very slow. Please take at least 15 minutes a day to learn new vocabulary. If you manage to learn 5 words a day, by the end of a year you will know almost 2,000 words which is enough to communicate in everyday situations.

Language patterns

PRONUNCIATION OF CONSONANTS

We will now take a closer look at the pronunciation of the Estonian consonants. As you will see, many of them are similar to the English ones.

Consonants, just like the vowels, can appear in short or in long form. The short form is usually represented by one consonant and the long form by two consonants.

EXERCISE 10

 02.09

In the following list you will find Estonian first names. Listen to the names and repeat them. Do this as many times as you need.

h as in *Hello!*, not pronounced at the beginning of a word.

Helle (f*), Ri**h**o (m*), E**h**a (f), A**h**to (m), **H**elve (f)

hh the same as **h** but longer. Occurs in very few words.

j as yin *yes*
Jaan (m), **J**uhan (m), Ka**j**a (f), **J**uta (f), **J**aanus (m)

jj the same as **j** but longer. Occurs in very few words.

l is softer than the English **l**
Lembit (m), A**l**o (m), A**l**ar (m), Ka**l**ju (m), Ka**l**ev (m)

ll the same as **l** but longer
Ü**lle** (f), **Ill**imar (m), Ve**ll**o (m), He**lle** (f), Ma**lle** (f)

m is the same as in English
Mare (f), Sii**m** (m), Ur**m**as (m), **M**art (m), **M**argit (f)

mm the same as **m** but longer
Le**mm**i (f), I**mm**o (m), Ti**mm**o (m), To**mm**i (m)

n is the same as in English
Naima (f), E**n**e (f), Lii**n**a (f), A**n**u (f), Sve**n** (m)

nn the same as **n** but longer
He**nn** (m), A**nn**e (f), Le**nn**a (f), A**nn**eli (f), Õ**nn**e (f)

r is a rolling sound in Estonian, quite different from English, you need to practise a lot!
K**r**istjan (m), Kaa**r**el (m), A**r**di (m), Kau**r** (m), P**r**iit (m)

rr the same as **r** but longer
Ha**rr**i (m), Ha**rr**iet (f)

s as in *school*
Tõni**s** (m), Joo**s**ep (m), E**s**ta (f), **S**irli (f), **S**iiri (f)

ss the same as s but longer
Sa**ss** (m), Ju**ss** (m), Ka**ss**andra (f), Ja**ss** (m)

v as in *video*
Valve (f), Ul**v**i (f), Sule**v** (m), I**v**o (m), E**v**elin (f)

vv the same as **v** but longer. Occurs in very few words

g as in *goat*
A**g**o (m), Si**g**ne (f), In**g**e (f), **G**ert (m), **G**reete (f)

gg does not occur in Estonian words

b as in *boat*
Lem**b**it (m), Im**b**i (f), Mai**b**i (f), Tam**b**et (m), El**b**e (f)

bb does nor occur in Estonian words

d as in *door*
Rai**d**o (m), Lin**d**a (f), E**d**a (f), Ka**d**i (f), **D**iana (f)

dd does not occur in Estonian words

k as in English but without aspiration
Hei**k**i (m), **K**ärt (f), U**k**u (m), **K**erli (f), **K**oidu (f)

kk the same as **k** but longer. Does not occur in common first names but occurs in many other words like
lu**kk** *lock*, pa**kk** *packet*, nu**kk** *doll*, ku**kk**uma *to fall*, pa**kk**umine *offer*

p as in English but without aspiration
Piia (f), **P**aavo (m), **P**ille (f), Aa**p** (m), Kau**p**o (m), Joose**p** (m)

pp the same as **p** but longer

E**pp** (f) and also in many other words like li**pp** *flag*, su**pp** *soup*, hü**pp**ama *to jump*, va**pp**er *brave*

t as in English but without aspiration

Taavi (m), **T**erje (f), Ri**t**a (f), **T**oivo (m), Ma**t**i (m)

tt the same as **t** but longer

O**tt** (m), Ru**tt** (f), O**tt**o (m) and also in many other words like ko**tt**, *bag* pa**tt** sin, ra**tt**ur *biker*

*f and m given in brackets indicate whether it is a woman's (f) or a man's (m) name.

MINA, SINA *I, YOU – PERSONAL PRONOUNS*

'I', 'you', 'he', 'she', 'it', 'we' and 'they' are called 'personal pronouns'. There are six of them in Estonian. Personal pronouns in Estonian have a long form (the first in the following table) and a short form (the second one). We tend to use the short forms in ordinary speech. If we use the long form we're showing that we want to give special emphasis to the person we're talking about. The short forms are used more often.

mina (ma)	*I*	**meie (me)**	*we*
sina (sa)	*you*	**teie (te)**	*you*
tema (ta)	*he/she (can also mean it)*	**nemad (nad)**	*they*

The **sina/sa** is used to mean *you* when you are speaking informally to someone you know well; **teie/te** is used to mean *you* in more formal situations. There is more about this later. Estonian doesn't make a grammatical distinction between 'he' and 'she', so there is only one personal pronoun for **tema** *he/she*.

MINA OLEN *I AM – THE VERB TO BE*

Just like the English *to be*, the Estonian olema changes its form according to who we're talking about.

ma ole**n**	*I am*	me ole**me**	*we are*
sa ole**d**	*you are*	te ole**te**	*you are*
ta **on**	*he, she is*	nad **on**	*they are*

If we want to make *I am* into the negative we place the word **ei** *no* before the verb, which changes to **ole** for all the different persons. If you prefer you can think of **ei ole** as the negative of all the forms of *to be*: *am not*, *are not* and *is not*. Easy!

ma **ei ole**	*I am not*	me **ei ole**	*we are not*
sa **ei ole**	*you are not*	te **ei ole**	*you are not*
ta **ei ole**	*he/she is not*	nad **ei ole**	*they are not*
NB! ei ole = pole			
Note that **ei ole** can be replaced by **pole**, which has exactly the same meaning.			

Let's see how to use the verb **olema** *to be* in these sentences.

Ma olen Peeter Kuusk.	*I am Peeter Kuusk.*
Ma ei ole Peeter Kask.	*I am not Peeter Kask.*
Sa oled Kristel.	*You are Kristel.*
Sa ei ole Tiina.	*You are not Tiina.*
Ta on õpilane.	*He/She is a student.*
Ta ei ole õpetaja	*He/She is not a teacher.*
Me oleme õpetajad.	*We are teachers.*
Me ei ole õpilased.	*We are not students.*
Te olete turistid.	*You are tourists.*
Te ei ole kohalikud.	*You are not local people.*
Nad on kohalikud.	*They are local (people).*
Nad ei ole turistid.	*They are not tourists.*

We don't have to use personal pronouns, because the ending of the verb indicates the person of the verb.

For instance:

Ole**n** üliõpilane. = Ma olen üliõpilane.

Ole**me** turistid. = Me oleme turistid.

EXERCISE 11

Find the right translation.

1	We are teachers.	**a**	Ta on õpetaja.
2	You (singular) are not a teacher.	**b**	Ma ei ole õpetaja.
3	They are teachers.	**c**	Me oleme õpetajad.
4	He is a teacher.	**d**	Teie olete õpetajad.
5	I am not a teacher.	**e**	Sa ei ole õpetaja.
6	You (plural, formal) are teachers.	**f**	Nad on õpetajad.
7	She is a teacher.		

In order to practise this grammar topic further do Exercise 15 in the Practice section.

MINA RÄÄGIN *I SPEAK – PRESENT TENSE*

Verbs, i.e. words like 'speak', 'run', 'see', have different endings in Estonian according to who is doing the action. This is different from English, where (usually) the only time the verb ending changes is when 'he', 'she' or 'it' is doing the action: I speak, he speaks.

Note that the present tense **mina räägin** in Estonian means *I speak, I'm speaking, I will speak* and *I do speak.*

ma räägi**n**	*I speak*		me rääg**ime**	*we speak*
sa rääg**id**	*you speak*		te rääg**ite**	*you speak*
ta rääg**ib**	*he, she speaks*		nad rääg**ivad**	*they speak*
ma **ei** rääg	*I do not speak*		me **ei** rääg	*we do not speak*
sa **ei** rääg	*you do not speak*		te **ei** rääg	*you do not speak*
ta **ei** rääg	*he, she does not speak*		nad **ei** rääg	*they do not speak*

In the dictionary you will find verbs in the 'I-form' (first person singular); from this you will be able to work out the forms for the other persons.

From this unit on, the 'I-form' of all verbs will be given. Note that the forms of the word **ole/ma**, -**n** *to be* are read the following way: drop the ending -**ma** and to **ole** add -**n** = so *I am* reads **ole/n**. The same system will be used throughout the book for all verbs.

In order to practise this grammar topic further, do Exercises 16–17 in the Practice section.

KAS SA OLED PEETER? *ARE YOU PETER?* – QUESTIONS

To ask questions in Estonian, we usually use a question word, for example 'who' or 'how': **Kes** sina oled? *Who are you?* **Kuidas** elate? *How are you?*

When we want to ask a question such as *Are you Peeter?* or *Do you speak Estonian?* we use the question word **kas?** which acts like a marker warning you that what's coming next is a question:

Kas te olete Peeter?	*(Question) you are Peter?*
Kas te räägite eesti keelt?	*(Question) you speak Estonian language?*

When we answer *yes*, we say:

Jah, olen küll.	*Yes, I am.*
Jah, räägin küll.	*Yes, I speak.*

The word **küll** is untranslatable but it adds stress to your answer, for instance

Kas te räägite saksa keelt?	Räägin **küll**. *Yes I do speak.*
Kas nad räägivad inglise keelt?	Räägivad **küll**. *Yes, they do speak.*

When you answer *no¸* you say

Kas teie olete Peeter?	**Ei ole. Ma olen Alexander.** *No, I am not. I am Alexander.*
Kas te räägite vene keelt?	**Ei räägi.** *No, I don't speak.*

EXERCISE 12

Translate into Estonian. Use formal address.

1 Are you Jaan Mägi?

2 Are you the teacher?

3 Are you a local person?

4 Yes, I am Jaan Mägi.

5 No, I am not Kristjan Saar. I am Jüri Kask.

In order to practise this grammar topic further do Exercises 18–19 in the Practice section.

MINU, SINU *MY, YOUR* – POSSESSIVE PRONOUNS

When we want to say that something belongs to me, we use the word for *I*, **mina** or **ma**, but we change its ending to show that it means *of me*, **minu** or **mu**. The words for *you* and *they* also change. Note that the words **tema**, **meie**, **teie** do not change.

mina/ma	*I*	**minu/mu**	*my (of me)*
sina/sa	*you* (singular)	**sinu/su**	*your* (singular) *(of you)*
tema/ta	*he, she or it*	**tema/ta**	*his, her or its* (of him, her or it)
meie/me	*we*	**meie/me**	*our (of us)*
teie/te	*you* (plural)	**teie/te**	*your* (plural) *(of you)*
nemad/nad	*they*	**nende**	*their (of them)*

Some examples of usage:

Kuidas on **teie** nimi?	*What is your name?*
Minu nimi on Sille.	*My name is Sille.*
Minu nimi on Sille Soo.	*My name is Sille Soo.*
Kuidas on **sinu** eesnimi?	*What is your* (singular, informal) *first name?*
Mis on **teie** eesnimi?	*What is your* (plural) *first name?*
Minu eesnimi on Siim.	*My first name is Siim.*
Mis on **sinu** perekonnanimi?	*What is your* (singular, informal) *surname?*
Kuidas on **teie** perekonnanimi?	*What is your* (formal) *surname?*
Minu perekonnanimi on Luik.	*My surname is Luik.*

EXERCISE 13

Find the right translation.

1	our teacher	**a**	tema õpetaja
2	your (singular, informal) teacher	**b**	teie õpetaja
3	their teacher	**c**	meie õpetaja
4	his teacher	**d**	sinu õpetaja
5	your (plural, formal) teacher	**e**	nende õpetaja
6	her teacher		

In order to practise this topic further, do Exercise 20 in the Practice section.

FORMAL AND INFORMAL FORMS OF ADDRESS

Estonian has two ways of saying 'you': formal and informal. You use the informal, or familiar, form when talking to a friend or a child. Young people use it when talking to one another.

You use the formal form to address a person whom you have not previously met, or a person who stands in a senior position in relation to yourself (such as in student–teacher or patient–doctor relationships). In Estonian society, the rule of using formal address is quite strict and you stand a good chance of being considered rude if you are informal. It is always safest to use the polite form first and if the other person allows or suggests, switch to the informal form.

Kas sa oled Peeter?	*Are you Peeter?* (informal)
Kas teie olete Peeter Soo?	*Are you Peeter Soo?* (formal)
Mis sinu nimi on?	*What is your name?* (informal)
Mis teie nimi on?	*What is your name?* (formal)

The Estonian word for the informal address is **sinatamine** and for the formal address **teietamine**. If you do not want the other person to use the formal address with you, you can say: **Mind võib sinatada.** lit. *You can say 'you' to me.*

In order to practise this grammar topic further do Exercise 21 in the Practice section.

KAS SA SAAD ARU? *DO YOU UNDERSTAND? – COMPOUND VERBS*

In Estonian, there are a lot of compound verbs like **aru saama** *to understand*, which is made up of two words, the main verb (**saama**) and the auxiliary verb (**aru**). These types of verb change their endings as you can see in the table.

ma saa**n aru**	*I understand*	me saa**me aru**	*we understand*
sa saa**d aru**	*you understand*	te saa**te aru**	*you understand*
ta saa**b aru**	*he/she understands*	nad saa**vad aru**	*they understand*
ma **ei** saa **aru**	*I do not understand*	me **ei** saa **aru**	*we do not understand*
sa **ei** saa **aru**	*you do not understand*	te **ei** saa **aru**	*you do not understand*
ta **ei** saa **aru**	*he/she does not understand*	nad **ei** saa **aru**	*they do not understand*

As you can see, the verb (**saama**) comes first and it changes. The auxiliary (**aru**) comes second place and it does not change. Sometimes the two parts of a compound verb aren't next to each other in the sentence, for instance: Ma **saan** kõigest **aru** *I understand everything.*

EXERCISE 14

Fill in the gaps with the word **tuttavaks saama** *to get acquainted*.

1 Ma *saan* Kauriga *tuttavaks*.

2 Sa _____ Kauriga _____

3 Ta _____ Kauriga _____

4 Me _____ Kauriga _____

5 Te _____ Kauriga _____

6 Nad _____ Kauriga _____

Practice

EXERCISE 15

Fill in the blank with the verb **olema** in its correct form.

1 Ma *olen* Kristel.

2 Te _____ õpetajad.

3 Ta ei _____ kohalik.

4 Me _____ õpilased.

5 Sa _____ Jaak.

6 Nad ei _____ turistid.

7 Ta _____ õpetaja.

8 Nad _____ õpetajad.

EXERCISE 16

Fill in the right word (*I, you* etc.).

1 *Ma* oskan eesti keelt.

2 _____ oskad eesti keelt.

3 _____ oskab eesti keelt.

4 _____ oskame eesti keelt.

5 _____ oskate eesti keelt.

6 _____ oskavad eesti keelt.

EXERCISE 17

Choose the correct form.

1 Mina **olen/on** Jaan.

2 Meie **oleme/oled** turistid.

3 Sina **on/oled** Peeter.

4 Ta **räägib/räägin** eesti keelt.

5 Te **räägite/räägib** inglise keelt.

6 Nad **oskame/oskavad** prantsuse keelt.

7 Ta **räägib/räägite** vene keelt.

EXERCISE 18

Answer the questions. Give both positive and negative answer.

1 Kas sa räägid vene keelt? *Räägin küll. Ei räägi.*

2 Ka te (*pl*) räägite vene keelt?

3 Kas nad räägivad vene keelt?

4 Kas tema räägib vene keelt?

EXERCISE 19

 02.10

Translate into Estonian. Listen to the correct answers.

1 Do you (pl, formal) speak Estonian? No, I don't.

2 Does she speak French? Yes she does.

3 Do they speak Spanish? Yes they do.

4 Do they speak English? No they don't.

5 Do you (sing, informal) speak German? No I don't.

EXERCISE 20

Choose the correct form.

1 Kuidas on **sina/sinu** nimi?

2 **Minu/mina** nimi on Piret.

3 Kuidas on **sina/sinu** perekonnanimi?

4 **Mu/ma** perekonnanimi on Sepp.

5 Härra Jõgi on **nad/nende** õpetaja.

6 Härra Jõgi on ka **mina/minu** õpetaja.

EXERCISE 21

Translate as formal questions. Translate as informal questions.

1 Are you Peeter Pääsuke?

2 Do you speak English?

3 What is your name?

4 What is your surname?

🗣 Speaking

EXERCISE 22

Here are some situations for you to practise. You are a tourist and the conversations take place at your hotel.

1   You are asked something in Estonian but you don't understand. What would you say?

2   Someone approaches you and asks **Kas teie olete härra Põder?** What do you say?

3   The person at the registration desk needs to fill in a registration form and asks you **Kuidas on teie perekonnanimi?** How do you answer?

4   Then she asks **Kas te räägite eesti keelt?** What do you say?

5   You see the same person the next morning and she asks **Kuidas läheb?** How do you answer?

6   You are sharing a breakfast table with an Estonian lady who introduces herself by saying her first name. How do you respond?

EXERCISE 23

 02.11

You are asked the following questions. Answer them. Listen to the correct answers.

1   **Kas te räägite inglise keelt?**   Answer *Yes, I do.*
2   **Kas te räägite saksa keelt?**   Answer *Unfortunately, I don't.*
3   **Kas te räägite eesti keelt?**   Answer *Sorry, I don't understand.*
4   **Kas te räägite itaalia keelt?**   Answer *A little.*
5   **Kas te räägite jaapani keelt?**   You didn't quite hear what was said. Say *Excuse me?*

EXERCISE 24

Complete the dialogue. You are meeting Mihkel for the first time. Listen to the completed dialogue.

 02.12

Sina	Say *Good morning.*
Mihkel	Tere!
Sina	Say your name.
Mihkel	Väga meeldiv. Mina olen Mihkel.
Sina	Say *Very pleasant*, and ask if Mihkel speaks English.
Mihkel	Ei, kahjuks ei räägi.
Sina	Ask if Mihkel speaks German.
Mihkel	Räägin küll. Natukene.

EXERCISE 25

Do the following.

1 Say hello.

2 Say that you are Anna/Peter.

3 Ask politely what is the other person's name you don't know.

4 You didn't hear very well. Say *Excuse me?*

5 You heard the name this time. Say *Very pleasant.*

EXERCISE 26

 02.13

Do the following. Listen to the completed dialogue.

1 You meet a friend on the street. Say *Hello.*

2 Ask how she is.

3 She is very well. Now she wants to know how you are.

4 Say *Thank you* (i.e. thank you for asking) and say you are OK.

❓ Test yourself

1 How do you say in Estonian *I am a tourist?*
- **a** Ta on turist.
- **b** Nad on turistid.
- **c** Ma olen turist.

2 How do you say in Estonian *My name is …?*
- **a** Minu nimi on …
- **b** Ilus nimi …
- **c** Väga meeldiv …

3 In Estonian what is the German language?
- **a** soome keel
- **b** rootsi keel
- **c** saksa keel

4 What does this sentence mean: **See on meie õpetaja.**
- **a** I am your teacher.
- **b** This is our teacher.
- **c** This is my student.

5 If you talk to someone in English and he answers **Vabandust, ma ei saa aru**, what does it mean?
- **a** Yes, I speak English.
- **b** Sorry, I don't understand.
- **c** Pleased to meet you.

6 What would be correct answer to question **Kas te räägite eesti keelt?**
- **a** Natukene.
- **b** Väga tore.
- **c** Selge.

7 Someone asks you how you are and you want to say that you are very well. What do you say?
- **a** Mina ka.
- **b** Pole viga.
- **c** Väga hästi.

8 You are meeting someone formally. How do you ask *What's your name?*
- **a** Mis sinu nimi on?
- **b** Kuidas on teie nimi?
- **c** Kuidas on sinu nimi?

9 How do you say in Estonian *He speaks English?*

    a Teie räägite inglise keelt.

    b Tema räägib inglise keelt.

    c Meie räägime inglise keelt.

10 How do you ask in Estonian *Do you understand?*

    a Kas sa saad aru?

    b Kuidas elate?

    c Kuidas läheb?

3 Vabandage, kus on …?

Excuse me, where is the …?

In this unit you will learn:
- ▶ *How to ask where something is located*
- ▶ *How to ask about city transport*
- ▶ *How to tell the taxi driver where you want to go*
- ▶ *How to name vehicles and places in town*
- ▶ *How to say the cardinal numbers (11–1 million)*

Listening 1

You will hear people asking where something is located. Listen to the dialogues and complete Exercises 1–2 below.

 03.01

a	**Turist**	Tere! Vabandage, kus on kohvik?
	Võõras	Kohvik on siin.
b	**Turist**	Tere! Vabandage, kus on bussipeatus?
	Võõras	Vaadake, see on seal.
c	**Turist**	Vabandage, kus on väljapääs?
	Võõras	Vist seal, sealpool.
d	**Turist**	Vabandage, kus on infopunkt?
	Võõras	See on seal, suures saalis.
e	**Turist**	Vabandage, kus on tualett?
	Võõras	Vaadake, see on seal trepi juures.
f	**Turist**	Vabandage, kas te teate, kus on taksopeatus?
	Võõras	Ma tõesti ei tea. Võib-olla sealpool.

turist, -i	*tourist*
võõras, võõra	*stranger*
vabanda/ma, -n	*to apologize*
vabandage	*excuse me (plural, formal)*
kus	*where*
kohvik, -u	*café, coffee shop*
siin	*here*
bussipeatus, -e	*bus stop*
see, selle	*it*

seal	*there*
väljapääs, -u	*exit*
vist	*probably*
sealpool	*in that direction*
infopunkt, -i	*information desk, information office*
suur, -e	*big*
saal, -i	*hall*
suures saalis	*in the big hall*
tualett, tualeti	*toilet, WC*
vaata/ma, -n	*to look*
vaadake	*look*
trepp, trepi	*stairs*
trepi juures	*at the stairs, near the stairs*
tead/ma, tea/n	*to know*
taksopeatus, -e	*taxi stop*
tõesti	*really*
võib-olla	*maybe*

NB! The explanation about the words like **turist**, **-i** *tourist* and its forms etc. is described in 'Language patterns' after Exercise 9, below.

EXERCISE 1

Listen to the dialogues and underline the places you hear.

apteek, bussipeatus, infopunkt, hotell, kohvik, suur saal, taksopeatus, tualett, väljapääs

EXERCISE 2

Choose the right translation.

1 See on siin.
   a It is here.
   b It is there.

2 Vaadake, kohvik on seal.
   a Look, the coffee shop is over there.
   b Maybe the coffee shop is in that direction.

3 See on suures saalis.
   a It's near the stairs.
   b It's in the big hall.

4 Ma tõesti ei tea.
   a It is here.
   b I really don't know.

Listening 2

You will hear people asking for directions. Listen to the dialogues and complete Exercises 3–5 according to the dialogues.

 03.02

a	**Turist**	Vabandage, kas see buss läheb lennujaama?
	Bussijuht	Jah, läheb küll.
b	**Turist:**	Vabandage, kas see buss läheb sadamasse?
	Bussijuht	Ei lähe. Sadamasse lähevad trammid number üks ja kaks.
c	**Turist**	Öelge palun, mis bussid lähevad kesklinna?
	Võõras	Ma arvan, et kaheksa ja kaheksateist ja vist kakskümmend kaheksa ka.
d	**Turist**	Tere! Vabandage, kuidas ma kesklinna saan?
	Võõras	Minge trolliga number kolm.

bussi/juht, -juhi	*busdriver*
buss, -i	*bus*
mine/ma, lähe/n	*to go*
lennujaam, -a	*airport*
Kas see buss läheb lennujaama?	*Does this bus go to the airport?*
Läheb küll.	*Yes, it does.*
sadam, -a	*harbour*
tramm, -i	*tram*
number, numbri	*number*
ütle/ma, -n	*to say, to tell*
öelge palun	*please tell (pl, formal)*
mis bussid	*what buses*
kesklinn, -a	*city centre*
arva/ma, -n	*to guess*
vist	*probably, perhaps*
kuidas	*how*
Kuidas ma kesklinna saan?	*How do I get to the city centre?*
saa/ma, -n	*here: to get to*
minge	*go (imperative, pl, formal)*
troll, -i	*trolleybus*
trolliga	*by trolleybus*

EXERCISE 3

Listen and choose the right answer.

1   Lennujaama läheb   **a** buss,   **b** tramm,   **c** troll
2   Sadamasse läheb   **a** buss,   **b** tramm,   **c** troll
3   Kesklinna läheb   **a** buss,   **b** tramm,   **c** troll

EXERCISE 4

Choose the correct translation.

1 **Vabandage, kas see buss läheb lennujaama?**
   a Excuse me, does this bus go to the airport?
   b Excuse me, does this bus go to the harbour?

2 **Kesklinna lähevad bussid number üks ja kaks.**
   a Buses number 1 and 2 go to the city centre.
   b Buses number 11 and 12 go to the city centre.

3 **Minge trolliga number viis.**
   a Go by trolleybus no 5.
   b Go by bus no 5.

EXERCISE 5

Decide which one of the responses is not correct. Three responses are correct for each question.

1 **Vabandage, kas see buss läheb kesklinna?**
   a Selge.
   b Ei lähe.
   c Jah, läheb küll.
   d Ma arvan, et läheb küll.

2 **Sõidame palun kesklinna.**
   a Kohe.
   b Selge.
   c Jah, läheb küll.
   d Jah.

3 **Vabandage, kus on kohvik?**
   a Vist seal, sealpool.
   b Jah, läheb küll.
   c Ma tõesti ei tea.
   d See on siin.

Listening 3

You will hear dialogues between a taxi driver and a client. Listen to the dialogues and complete Exercises 6–7 according to the dialogues.

 03.03

a	**Klient**	Tere! Sõidame palun kesklinna.
	Taksojuht	Selge.
b	**Klient**	Tere! Pärnu maantee üheksa palun.
	Taksojuht	Pärnu maantee kaheksa, jah?
	Klient	Ei, Pärnu maantee üheksa.
	Taksojuht	Selge. Vabandust.
c	**Klient**	Tervist. Hotell Viru juurde palun.
	Taksojuht	Jah.
	Klient	Kui palju see maksab?
	Taksojuht	Sada krooni.
d	**Klient**	Tere! Sõitke palun Kumu Kunstimuuseumi juurde.
	Taksojuht	Kohe.
	Klient	Kui palju see maksab?
	Taksojuht	Umbes kaheksakümmend krooni.

 TIP
Please note since 1 January 2011 the Estonian currency has been the Euro.

V

klient, **kliendi**	*client, customer*
takso, -	*taxi*
takso/juht, -juhi	*taxi driver*
sõit/ma, sõid/an	*to drive, to go*
selge	*OK, clear*
maantee, -	*road, highway*
Pärnu maantee	*Pärnu highway*
hotell, -i	*hotel*
hotell Viru juurde	*to the hotel Viru*
kui palju	*how much*
maks/ma, -an	*to cost, to pay*
sada, saja	*hundred*
kroon, -i	*crown*
sõitke	*drive, go (imperative, pl, formal)*
kunstimuuseum, -i	*art museum*
Kumu kunstimuuseumi juurde	*to (the) Kumu art museum*
kohe	*at once, immediately*
umbes	*about*
kaheksakümmend	*eighty*

EXERCISE 6

Listen and answer the questions.

1 Where does the client want to go in dialogue **a**?

2 Does the client want to go to Pärnu maantee 9 or 8 in dialogue **b**?

3 Where does the client go in dialogue **c** and how much does it cost?

4 Where does the client go in dialogue **d** and how much does it cost?

EXERCISE 7

Here are some situations to practise. There are two correct answers for each situation.

1 **You would like to go to the town centre. What do you say?**

    a Tervist. Kesklinna palun.

    b Tere. Sõidame palun kesklinna.

    c Tere. Palun öelge, kus on kesklinn.

2 **You would like to go to Pärnu maantee 9. What do you say?**

    a Tere. Pärnu maantee kaheksa palun.

    b Tere. Pärnu maantee üheksa palun.

    c Tere. Sõitke palun Pärnu maantee üheksa juurde.

3 **You would like to ask about the price of the service. What do you say?**

    a Kas see maksab sada krooni?

    b Kas see on Pärnu maantee?

    c Kui palju see maksab?

Listening 4

You will hear dialogues that take place in town. Listen and then complete Exercises 8–9.

 03.04

a	**Mall**	Oi, vaata, seal on loomaaed!
	Martin	Ohhoo!
	Mall	Ja siin on kaubanduskeskus.
	Martin	Tõesti? Nii väike!
b	**Tõnu**	Kas see on teater?
	Erki	Ei, see on turg. Teater on seal.
	Tõnu	Ahah.
c	**Jaan**	Vabandage, kus siin on apteek?
	Võõras	Apteek on seal. Aga see on juba kinni.
	Jaan	Ahah. Aitäh.

looma/aed, -aia	*zoo*
Ohhoo!	*Oh!*
kaubanduskeskus, -e	*department store, (Am.) mall*
Tõesti?	*Really?*
väike, väikse	*small*
Nii väike!	*So small!*
ahah	*OK, I see (informal)*
apteek, apteegi	*chemist's*
aga	*but*
juba	*already*
kinni	*closed*

EXERCISE 8

Which places do you hear in the dialogues? Listen and tick the box(es) for each dialogue

Places	a	b	c
1 teater			
2 turg			
3 kaubanduskeskus			
4 kunstimuuseum			
5 loomaaed	✓		
6 sadam			
7 apteek			
8 lennujaam			

EXERCISE 9

Answer the questions. There are three correct answers to each question.

1 Kas see on kunstimuuseum?

   a Ei, see on hotell.

   b Ahah.

   c Jah, on küll.

   d Kunstimuuseum on seal.

2 Oi, vaata, seal on teater!

   a Ahah.

   b Ohhoo!

   c Ma tõesti ei tea.

   d Nii väike!

3 Vabandage, kus on loomaaed?

   a Ohhoo!

   b Siin, aga see on juba kinni.

   c Vaadake, see on seal.

   d Vabandust, ma tõesti ei tea.

Language patterns

KUS ON ...? *WHERE IS ...? – INESSIVE CASE, ADESSIVE CASE*

In English, words like *zoo*, *shop*, *new*, *old* etc. do not usually change in the sentence. Different meanings are indicated with prepositions like *with*, *in*, *at*, *near* etc. In Estonian instead of prepositions bits of info are added to the end of the word (they are called case endings) and it is written as one word, for instance **teatris** means *in the theatre*. Estonian also has postpositions that are written as separate words, for instance **teatri juures** means *near the theatre*.

All case endings and postpositions are added not to the first form that is found in the dictionary but usually to the so-called second form (called genitive as a grammatical term), which always ends with either **i**, **e**, **a**, or **u** and can also otherwise differ from the first form; for instance, **turg** market is the first form, but if you want to say *near the market* or *at the market* you have to know the second form, which is **turu**, correspondingly **turu juures** *near the market*, **turul** *at the market*. It may seem rather complicated but there's no need to worry as mostly what you will see in text is the second form and you will just have to remember it. It is useful, however, when starting to learn Estonian always to learn both the first and second forms, both of which you will find in dictionaries.

From this unit on second forms are also presented in the vocabulary lists.

Note how the second form of the words **turist** *tourist*, **kohvik** *coffee shop* etc. are read: the ending given after the comma is just added to the end of the word, so, for instance, the second form of the word **turist** reads turisti etc. If some sound changes take place within the word, the second form will be given as a full word, for instance **trepp**, trepi. The same system will be used throughout the book for all such types of word.

Note how the forms for the words made of two words (like **bussijuht**) are given: if the second part of the word has sound changes, it will be written out and you should read it like this **bussi/juht**, **-juhi** = **bussijuhi**.

Now we will learn some case endings which indicate where something or someone is located. When we want to say where something or someone is, we can use either the ending **-s**, the ending **-l** or a postposition (for instance **juures** *near*).

The ending **-s** usually indicates that the location is *inside* something. In English, the prepositions *in*, *inside*, or *at* are used in this case.

The ending **-l** usually indicates that the location is **on** something. It corresponds to English *on* or *at*.

Note that the meaning of **-s** *inside* and **-l** *on* is not always so straightforward, since with some words it just depends on tradition which ending is used, for instance we always say koolis *at school*, loomaaias *in the zoo*, suvilas *in the summerhouse*, teatris *in the theatre*, kinos at the cinema etc. but kontserdil *at the concert*, turul *at the market*, näitusel *at the exhibition*; koosolekul *at the meeting* etc.

The postposition **juures** shows that something is **near** something or somebody.

Here are some examples.

Mis? What?	Kus? Where?	Kus? Where?
buss, -i *bus*	bussi**s** *in the bus*	bussi **juures** *near the bus*
hotell, -i *hotel*	hotelli**s** *in/at the hotel*	hotelli **juures** *near the hotel*
teater, teatri *theatre*	teatri**s** *in/at the theatre*	teatri **juures** *near the theatre*
jaam, -a *station*	jaama**s** *in/at the station*	jaama **juures** *near the station*
apteek, apteegi *chemist's*	apteegi**s** *in/at the chemist's*	apteegi **juures** *near the chemist's*
suur saal, suure saali *big hall*	suure**s** saali**s** *in the big hall*	suure saali **juures** *near the big hall*
turg, turu *market*	turu**l** *at the market*	turu **juures** *near the market*
laud, laua *table*	laua**l** *on the table*	laua **juures** *near the table*
maantee, - *road*	maantee**l** *on the road*	maantee **juures** *near the road*
trepp, trepi *stairs*	trepi**l** *on the stairs*	trepi **juures** *near the stairs*

Note that the adjective and noun have the same endings, for instance **suur saal** – suure**s** saali**s** *in the big hall*.

EXERCISE 10

Answer the questions.

Mis? *What?*	**Kus?** *Where?*	
1 tramm, -i	*tram*	*trammis*
2 muuseum, -i	*museum*	_____
3 sadam, -a	*harbour*	_____
4 kesklinn, -a	*city*	_____
5 suur, -e hotell, -i	*big hotel*	_____
6 tualett, tualeti	*toilet, WC*	_____
7 väljak, -u	*square*	*väljakul*
8 tänav, -a	*street*	_____
9 sein, -a	*wall*	_____
10 tee, -	*road*	_____

In order to practise this grammar topic further do Exercise 15 in the Practice section.

KUHU TE LÄHETE? *WHERE ARE YOU GOING TO? – ILLATIVE CASE, ALLATIVE CASE*

Mees läheb hotelli. *A man goes to the hotel.*

Mees on hotellis. *A man is in the hotel.*

We have learnt how to indicate location and now we will have a closer look at how to indicate movement towards a certain location, i.e how to answer the question **kuhu?** *where to?* In Estonian, different types of case ending are used, which all translate into English as **to** or **into**.

If you remember the case endings for the question **kus?** *where?*, then you will find it easy to work out the right endings for question **kuhu?** *where to?*

If the case ending for **kus?** *where?* was **-l**, then for **kuhu?** *where to?* it is **-le**.

If the case ending for **kus?** *where?* was **-s**, then for **kuhu?** *where to?* it is **-sse** or there is no case ending at all and the so-called short form is used instead.

Here are some examples.

Kus? *Where?*	**Kuhu?** *Where to?*
-l	**-le**
Olen turu**l**. *I am at the market.*	Lähen turu**le**. *I go to the market.*
Olen töö**l**. *I am at work.*	Lähen töö**le**. *I go to work.*
Olen näituse**l**. *I am at the exhibition.*	Lähen näituse**le**. *I go to the exhibition.*
-s	**-sse**
Olen kohviku**s**. *I am in the coffee shop.*	Lähen kohviku**sse**. *I go to the coffee shop.*
Olen bussipeatuse**s**. *I am at the bus stop.*	Lähen bussipeatuse**sse** (bussipeatu**sse**). *I go to the bus stop.*
Olen teatri**s**. *I am at the theatre.*	Lähen teatri**sse**. *I go to the theatre.*
-s	short form (without ending)
Olen infopunkti**s**. *I am at the info desk.*	Lähen infopunkti. *I go to the info desk.*
Olen lennujaama**s**. *I am at the airport.*	Lähen lennujaama. *I go to the airport.*
Olen apteegi**s**. *I am at the chemist's.*	Lähen apteeki. *I go to the chemist's.*
Olen kodu**s**. *I am at home.*	Lähen koju. *I go home.*

Note that the ending **-sse** is used less than the short form.

The list of different types of the short form can be found in Appendix 4.

LÄHEN HOTELLI JUURDE *I WILL GO BY THE HOTEL*

When we want to express that we go near something, we can use the postposition **juurde**, in English *up to, towards, by something*.

Mees läheb hotelli juurde. *A man goes by the hotel.*   **Mees on hotelli juures.** *A man is near the hotel.*

Kus? *Where?*	Kuhu? *Where to?*
Olen hotelli **juures**. *I am near the hotel.*	Lähen hotelli **juurde**. *I go by the hotel.*
Olen trepi **juures**. *I am near the stairs.*	Lähen trepi **juurde**. *I go by the stairs.*
Olen muuseumi **juures**. *I am near the museum.*	Lähen muuseumi **juurde**. *I go by the museum.*

EXERCISE 11

 03.05

Answer the questions. Listen to the correct answers.

Kus? *Where?*	**Kuhu?** *Where to?*
1 Olen Pärnu maanteel.	Lähen *Pärnu maanteele.*
2 Olen võistlusel.	Lähen _____
3 Olen Vabaduse väljakul.	Lähen _____
4 Olen sadamas.	Lähen *sadamasse.*
5 Olen kaubanduskeskuses.	Lähen _____
6 Olen taksos.	Lähen _____
7 Olen muuseumis.	Lähen _____
8 Olen kaupluses.	Lähen _____
9 Olen kesklinnas.	Lähen *kesklinna.*
10 Olen infopunktis.	Lähen _____
11 Olen kohviku juures.	Lähen *kohviku juurde.*
12 Olen kaupluse juures.	Lähen _____

In order to practise the last two grammar topics further do Exercises 16–18 in the Practice section.

Travelling to Estonia

The best landmark for Estonia is **Läänemeri** *the Baltic Sea*, which washes its northern and western coasts.

The capital of Estonia, Tallinn, with its medieval city centre is situated on the northern coast. **Helsingi** *Helsinki* is located, a distance of 85 km away on the opposite shore of **Soome laht** *the Gulf of Finland*. The other bigger cities close to Tallinn are **Riia** *Riga* (307 km), **Peterburi** *St Petersburg* (395 km) and **Stockholm** *Stockholm* (405 km).

All international flights to Estonia use Tallinn airport. **Lennujaam** *the airport* is about 3 km from the city centre, not quite walking distance but easily accessible by either taxi or by bus. There are direct flights to Estonia from western Europe and Scandinavia (**Frankfurt** *Frankfurt*, **Berliin** *Berlin*, **London** *London*, **Pariis** *Paris*, **Amsterdam** *Amsterdam*, **Barcelona** *Barcelona*, **Milaano** *Milan*, **Oslo** *Oslo*, **Stockholm** *Stockholm*, **Helsingi** *Helsinki*) and from **Balti riigid** *the Baltic States* (**Riia** *Riga*, **Vilnius** *Vilnius*), **Venemaa** *Russia* (**Moskva** *Moscow*), **Ukraina** *Ukraine* (**Kiiev** *Kiev*) and **Valgevene** *Belarus* (**Minsk** *Minsk*).

Bus is the cheapest mode of transport to and from Estonia and Euroline links Tallinn with western Europe and Scandinavia. **Bussijaam** *the bus station* in Tallinn is about 20 minutes' walk from the city centre and is easily accessible by taxi, bus or tram.

Raudteejaam *the railway station* is next to **vanalinn** *the old town*. A train runs each night between Tallinn and Moscow.

The busiest means of transport between Tallinn and the Scandinavian Europe is **laev** *the ferry* as over 2 million passengers a year travel across the Gulf of Finland between Helsinki and Tallinn. It is also possible to take a boat directly to **Rootsi** *Sweden* and **Saksamaa**

Germany. **Sadam** *the harbour* consists of several **terminal** *terminals*, some of which are only a 10-minute walk from the old town.

CONSONANT CHANGES

As you saw earlier, the consonants (k, p, t, g, b, d) within the first and the second form sometimes also differ. Now we will have a look at some of the most typical changes.

	first form	**second form + case ending**
kk – k	te**kk** *blanket*	te**k**il *on the blanket*
pp – p	tre**pp** *stairs*	tre**p**il *on the stairs*
tt – t	ko**tt** *bag*	ko**t**is *in the bag*
k – g	aptee**k** *chemist's*	aptee**g**is *at the chemist's*
p – b	vai**p** *carpet*	vai**b**al *on the carpet*
t – d	tor**t** *(fancy) cake*	tor**d**il *on the cake*
g – g disappears	tur**g** *market*	turul *at the market*
d – d disappears	poo**d** *shop*	poe**s** *in the shop*
b – b disappears	tu**b**a *room*	toa**s** *in the room*

Note that in words such as **pood** *shop* and **tuba** *room* it is not only the consonants that change. Fortunately, there are not too many words like this in Estonian.

PALUN ÜTLE, PALUN ÖELGE *PLEASE TELL – IMPERATIVE*

When we want to tell or ask somebody to do something, specific language forms called imperatives are used. There are two such forms: the singular and plural. When talking to one person who is a good friend or child, the singular is used. When talking to several people and in formal situations the plural is used. It is always polite to add the word **palun** *please* to the sentence.

Now we will have a look at how to make the forms of imperative.

To make the singular form just leave off the ending like **räägin** *I speak* **Räägi!** *Speak!* In the negative, we add the word **ära** – **Ära räägi!** *Don't speak!*

Imperative singular

tee**n** *I do*	Tee! *Do!*	**Ära** tee! *Don't do!*
vaata**n** *I look*	Vaata! *Look!*	**Ära** vaata! *Don't look!*
vabanda**n** *I apologize*	Vabanda! *Apologize!*	**Ära** vabanda! *Don't apologize!*
ütle**n** *I say*	Ütle! *Say!*	**Ära** ütle! *Don't say!*
maksa**n** *I pay*	Maksa! *Pay!*	**Ära** maksa! *Don't pay!*
sõida**n** *I drive*	Sõida! *Drive!*	**Ära** sõida! *Don't drive!*
NB! lähe**n** *I go*	Mine! *Go!*	**Ära** mine! *Don't go!*

The plural form is a little more complicated to make and we will look at it in more detail later.

For the moment note that plural (or polite form) ends with **-ke** or **-ge** and to say the request negatively we add the word **ärge**.

Imperative plural

Teh**ke**!	*Do!*	**Ärge** teh**ke**!	*Don't do!*
Vaada**ke**!	*Look!*	**Ärge** vaada**ke**!	*Don't look!*
Vabanda**ge**!	*Apologize!*	**Ärge** vabanda**ge**!	*Don't apologize!*
Öel**ge**!	*Say/tell!*	**Ärge** öel**ge**!	*Don't say/tell!*
Maks**ke**!	*Pay!*	**Ärge** maks**ke**!	*Don't pay!*
Sõit**ke**!	*Drive!*	**Ärge** sõit**ke**!	*Don't drive!*
Min**ge**!	*Go!*	**Ärge** min**ge**!	*Don't go!*

EXERCISE 12

Fill in the blanks with imperative singular forms. The first one is done for you.

1 tee**n**	Tee!	Ära tee!
2 sõida**n**		
3 vaata**n**		
4 räägi**n**		

In order to practise this grammar topic further do Exercises 19–20 in the Practice section.

SÕITKE BUSSIGA NUMBER 2 *TAKE BUS NUMBER 2 – COMITATIVE CASE*

When talking about driving by different means of transport in Estonian the ending **-ga** is added to the end of the means of transport, for instance ma sõidan bussi**ga**. Literally, it means *I drive **with** the bus*. In English the preposition **by** is used instead.

mis? *what?*	**sõidan millega?**	*drive/go by what?*
buss, -i *bus*	bussi**ga**	*by bus*
tramm, -i *tram*	trammi**ga**	*by tram*
troll, -i *trolleybus*	trolli**ga**	*by trolleybus*
takso, - *taxi*	takso**ga**	*by taxi*

Note that *I go by foot* in Estonian is **lähen jala** or **lähen jalgsi**, i.e the case ending **-ga** is not used.

EXERCISE 13

Answer the questions.

mis? what?		**sõidan** *millega?* go by what?	
1	laev, -a	*ferry*	laeva**ga**
2	lennuk, -i	*aeroplane*	_____
3	jalg/ratas, -ratta	*bike*	_____
4	auto, -	*car*	_____
5	metroo, -	*metro*	_____
6	rong, -i	*train*	_____
7	marsruuttakso, -	*minibus*	_____

In order to practise these grammar topics further do Exercises 21–22 in the Practice section.

Transport in cities

Public transport in Estonia means **buss** *bus*, **takso** *taxi* or **marsruuttakso** *minibus*. In Tallinn, **tramm** *tram*, **troll** *trolleybus* and **elektrirong** *electric train* also run. **Peatus** *the stops* are marked with blue and white signs indicating the means of transportation and corresponding numbers for different routes. There is no **metro** *metro* in Estonia. **Pilet** *the ticket* can be purchased at any **kiosk** *kiosk* (unless they have put up a sign **Pileteid ei ole** *There are no tickets for sale*) or from the driver, but this costs slightly more. **Kuupilet** *monthly tickets* are also sold, which are useful to have in case you have to travel many times a day.

Once you have the ticket you should punch it after entering the means of transportation. In Tallinn, the tram rails often run in the middle of the road, so passengers wait on the pavement and when the trams stop on these tracks, the rest of the traffic will stop to allow passengers on or off, and then move on with the tram. **Ekspressbuss** *express bus* involves a slightly more expensive ticket and there are fewer bus stops; mostly they run to the outskirts of towns, just like the **elektrirong** *electric train* in Tallinn.

KAKSTEIST, KAKSKÜMMEND *TWELVE, TWENTY – CARDINAL NUMBERS*

The rules for constructing numbers above 10 in Estonian are quite simple. First, you have to know the basic numbers (1–10). For 11–19 the word **-teist** (English *-teen*) is added to the first digit and for all tens **-kümmend** is added.

11	üks + **teist**	=	**üksteist**
12	kaks + **teist**	=	**kaksteist**
13	kolm + **teist**	=	**kolmteist**
14	neli + **teist**	=	**neliteist**
15	viis + **teist**	=	**viisteist**
16	kuus + **teist**	=	**kuusteist**
17	seitse + **teist**	=	**seitseteist**

18	kaheksa + **teist**	=	**kaheksateist**
19	üheksa + **teist**	=	**üheksateist**
20	kaks + **kümmend**	=	**kakskümmend**
30	kolm + **kümmend**	=	**kolmkümmend**
40	neli + **kümmend**	=	**nelikümmend**
50	viis + **kümmend**	=	**viiskümmend**
60	kuus + **kümmend**	=	**kuuskümmend**
70	seitse + **kümmend**	=	**seitsekümmend**
80	kaheksa + **kümmend**	=	**kaheksakümmend**
90	üheksa + **kümmend**	=	**üheksakümmend**

The numbers from 21 up are formed in the same way as in English. Note that the number is written as two separate words. For example: **21** kakskümmend üks, **32** kolmkümmend kaks.

The hundreds from 100 up are formed in the following way (*hundred* is **sada**):

100		=	**sada**
200	kaks + **sada**	=	kaks**sada**
300	kolm + **sada**	=	kolm**sada**
400	neli + **sada**	=	neli**sada**
500	viis + **sada**	=	viis**sada**
600	kuus + **sada**	=	kuus**sada**
700	seitse + **sada**	=	seitse**sada**
800	kaheksa + **sada**	=	kaheksa**sada**
900	üheksa + **sada**	=	üheksa**sada**

The thousands are formed in the same way as hundreds but written as two separate words (*thousand* is **tuhat**).

1000	**tuhat**	6000	kuus **tuhat**
2000	kaks **tuhat**	7000	seitse **tuhat**
3000	kolm **tuhat**	8000	kaheksa **tuhat**
4000	neli **tuhat**	9000	üheksa **tuhat**
5000	viis **tuhat**	10,000	kümme **tuhat**

The millions are formed in the following way (*million* is **miljon**):

1 million	miljon
2 million	kaks miljonit
3 million	kolm miljonit

EXERCISE 14

03.06

1 Listen to the cardinal numbers from the previous grammar section and repeat.

03.07

2 Write the numbers in words.
   a 12 *kaksteist*
   b 16 _____
   c 20 _____
   d 28 _____
   e 37 _____
   f 70 _____
   g 100 _____
   h 3000 _____

In order to practise this grammar topic further do Exercises 23–24 in the Practice section.

Estonian currency

Since 1 January 2011 the Estonian currency has been the euro. The country's currency used to be the **kroon** *crown*, which was broken down into 100 cents (100 **senti**). The abbreviation for Estonian crown was **kr** (internationally EEK). The Estonian crown was fixed against the euro at 1 EUR = 15,6466 EEK. **Paberraha** (the notes, lit *paper money*) came in eight denominations: **1 kroon** *1-crown note*, **2 krooni** *2-crown note*, **5 krooni** *5-crown note*, **10 krooni** *10-crown note*, **25 krooni** *25-crown note*, **50 krooni** *50-crown note*, **100 krooni** *100-crown note* and **500 krooni** *500-crown note*.

All notes had a prominent Estonian figure on one side and a significant place or building on the other side, i.e.:

1-crown note	Estonian artist **Kristjan Raud** (1865–1943); Toompea castle in Tallinn with the tower of Tall Hermann
2-crown note	Estonian/German anthropologist, naturalist and geographer **K. E. von Baer** (1792–1876); Tartu University (founded in 1632)
5-crown note	Estonian chess player and International Grand Master **Paul Keres** (1916–75); Narva stronghold on the Narva River
10-crown note	folklorist, theologian and linguist **Jakob Hurt** (1839–1907); Tamme-Lauri oak at Urvaste
25-crown note	Estonian writer **Anton Hansen-Tammsaare** (1878–1940); rural log construction farm at Vargamäe
50-crown note	Estonian composer **Rudolf Tobias** (1873–1918); Estonia Opera House in Tallinn
100-crown note	first Estonian female poet and playwright **Lydia Koidula** (1843–86); north Estonian limestone cliff
500-crown note	politician and journalist **Karl Robert Jakobson** (1841–82); Estonian national bird, barn swallow (*Hirundo rustica*) in flight against a landscape background

The 10-crown note was, in spoken language, often called **kümnekas** and the 25-crown note **kahekümneviiekas**. For 100-crown note, people said **Koidula** and for 500 crowns **Jakobson**.

Estonian **mündid** *coins* (**münt** *coin*) were small and lightweight and come in six denominations: **viis senti** *5 cents*, **kümme senti** *10 cents*, **kakskümmend senti** *20 cents*, **viiskümmend senti** *50 cents*, **1 kroon** *1-crown*, **viis krooni** *5-crowns*.

Parkimisautomaat *the parking meter* took 1-crown and 5-crown coins, although in bigger cities paying for parking by mobile phone is more widely used. All public phones are card operated but they are hard to find as most people have mobile phones nowadays.

Practice

EXERCISE 15

Divide the words into two groups depending on whether they take the ending **-s** or **-l** in a sentence of the type **Ma olen muuseumis**.

kesklinn, näitus, sadam, turg, tramm, väljak, tualett, teater, maantee, lennujaam, laud, trepp

EXERCISE 16

Choose the right form.

1 Olen **sadamas/sadamasse**.

2 Olen **lennujaama/lennujaamas**.

3 Olen **kesklinna/kesklinnas**.

4 Olen **Pärnu maanteel/Pärnu maanteele**.

5 Olen **kunstimuuseumi juurde/kunstimuuseumi juures**.

6 Olen **hotell Viru juures/hotell Viru juurde**.

EXERCISE 17

Choose the right form.

1 Sõidan **teatrisse/teatris**.

2 Lähen **turul/turule**.

3 Sõidan **apteegis/apteeki**.

4 Lähen **kaubanduskeskuses/kaubanduskeskusse**.

5 Sõidan **lennujaamas/lennujaama**.

6 Lähen **muuseumi juures/muuseumi juurde**.

7 Lähen **trepi juures/trepi juurde**.

EXERCISE 18

Write down where you would go to in order to do the things you want.

	You want	Kuhu?
1	a cup of coffee	Lähen kohvikusse.
2	some medicine	Lähen _____
3	to travel by plane	Lähen _____
4	to ask for some info	Lähen _____
5	to buy some vegetables	Lähen _____
6	to see a play	Lähen _____
7	to take a bus	Lähen _____
8	to do some work	Lähen _____

teater, kohvik, apteek, töö, bussipeatus, infopunkt, lennujaam, turg

EXERCISE 19

Choose the correct form.

1 **Vabandan/vabanda**, kus on tualett?

2 **Vaata/vaatan**, seal on loomaaed!

3 **Sõida/sõidan** palun kunstimuuseumi juurde!

4 **Maksan/maksa** sada krooni!

5 **Ära sõidan/sõida** hotelli juurde!

6 **Ära maksa/maksan** 100 krooni!

EXERCISE 20

Make the requests formal.

1 Sõida palun hotelli juurde. *Sõitke palun hotelli juurde.*

2 Vaata, seal on loomaaed! _____

3 Mine apteeki! _____

4 Ütle, kus on bussipeatus! _____

EXERCISE 21

Which of these words are not a means of transport?

auto, buss, infopunkt, jalgratas, kaubanduskeskus, kohvik, laev, lennuk, loomaaed, rong, sadam, takso, tramm, troll, turg

EXERCISE 22

Form sentences according to the example.

1 teater, sõitma, *laev Teatrisse sõidame laevaga.*

2 turg, sõitma, rong _____

3 töö, sõitma, lennuk _____

4 apteek, sõitma, auto _____

5 infopunkt, sõitma, jalgratas _____

EXERCISE 23

Find the correct match.

1	kuuskümmend üheksa	**a**	15
2	viisteist	**b**	28
3	kolmkümmend	**c**	46
4	üheksateist	**d**	69
5	viissada kuuskümmend üks	**e**	71
6	kolmkümmend kaheksa	**f**	30
7	kaheksakümmend kaks	**g**	82
8	üksteist	**h**	19
9	nelikümmend kuus	**i**	11
10	seitsekümmend üks	**j**	38
11	tuhat kakssada kaheksakümmend üheksa	**k**	561
12	kakskümmend kaheksa	**l**	1289

EXERCISE 24

 03.08

What numbers do you hear? Write them down in figures.

 Speaking

EXERCISE 25

 03.09

You are asked the following questions. Answer them, then listen to the correct answers.

1 Vabandage, kus on infopunkt? Say *It's here.*

2 Vabandage, kus on väljapääs? Say *It's there.*

3 Vabandage, kus on apteek? Say *It's probably in that direction.*

4 Vabandage, kus on kohvik? Say *I really don't know.*

EXERCISE 26

Complete the dialogue. You are talking to the bus driver. After you have completed the dialogue, listen to the recording and check.

 03.10

Sina	Say *Hello!*
Bussijuht	Tere!
Sina	Apologize and ask if this bus goes to the airport.
Bussijuht	Ei lähe.
Sina	Ask which buses go to the airport.
Bussijuht	Lennujaama läheb buss number kaks.
Sina	Say *Thank you.*

EXERCISE 27

Do the following. You want to take the bus to the town centre.

  a Say *Hello.*

  b Ask politely where the bus stop is.

  c The person you asked tells you it's over there. Say *Thank you.*

  d The bus comes. Ask the driver if this bus goes to the town centre.

  e He tells you it goes and gives you the ticket. Ask how much it costs.

  f It costs 15 crowns. Say *Thank you.*

EXERCISE 28

Do the following. You are standing at the bus stop and you want to go to the art museum.

a Say *Hello!*, and ask what buses go to the art museum.

b You are told that it's buses no. 18 and 61. You are not quite sure if you heard right. Repeat the numbers of the buses for clarification.

c Your bus arrives and you start driving off. Soon you see a building that looks like a museum. Ask the driver if this is the art museum.

d The driver says it is. Say *OK* and *thank you*.

Test yourself

1 **Kohvik on seal** means
   a The coffee-shop is here.
   b The coffee-shop is there.
   c The coffee shop is near the stairs.

2 You would like to know where the exit is. What do you say?
   a Vabandage, kas see buss läheb kesklinna?
   b Vabandage, kus on väljapääs?
   c Vabandage, kas see on kunstimuuseum?

3 What is the translation of question *Where?*
   a Kus?
   b Kes?
   c Kas?

4 You want to say that you are at the airport. What do you say?
   a Olen lennujaamas.
   b Olen lennujaama juures.
   c Sõidan lennujaama.

5 The numbers **12** and **19** in Estonian are
   a Kaheksateist ja üksteist
   b Kuusteist ja üheksakümmend
   c Kaksteist ja üheksateist

6 How is correct to say *I will go to the museum*?
   a Lähen muuseumisse.
   b Olen muusemis.
   c Mine muuseumisse.

7 **Bussiga** means
   a by bus
   b in the bus
   c near the bus

8 Find the correct match to number **1892**.
   a Tuhat üheksasada kaheksakümmend kaks.
   b Tuhat kaheksasada üheksakümmend kaks.
   c Tuhat kakssada kakskümmend kaks.

9 Which one is the polite form to ask the taxi driver to go to the airport?

    a Sõida palun lennujaama.

    b Sõitke palun lennujaama.

    c Mine palun lennujaama.

10 You want to ask how much the ticket costs. What do you say?

    a Mis bussid lähevad kesklinna?

    b Kas see on turg?

    c Kui palju see maksab?

Mida teile?

What will you have?

In this unit you will learn:
▶ *How to order food and drinks in a bar*
▶ *How to clarify your order*
▶ *How to ask questions about food*

Listening 1

In this dialogue a customer is ordering food and drink in a coffee shop. Listen to the dialogue and complete Exercise 1.

 04.01

Klient	Tere hommikust!
Baaridaam	Tere!
Klient	Palun üks must kohv.
Baaridaam	Palun. Kas see on kõik?
Klient	Ei. Palun veel üks kartulisalat.
Baaridaam	Palun. Kakskümmend viis krooni.
Klient	Palun.
Baaridaam	Aitäh.

> **TIP**
>
> Please note since 1 January 2011 the Estonian currency has been the Euro.

klient, kliendi, klienti	*client, customer*
baaridaam, -i, -i	*bar tender* (female)
palun üks …	*one … please* (lit. *please one …*)
must, -a, -a	*black*
kohv, -i, -i	*coffee*
see, selle, seda	*this*
kõik	*all, everything*
Kas see on kõik?	*Is this all?*
Palun veel üks …	*One … more please.* (lit. *please more one …*)
kartulisalat, -i, -it	*potato salad*

Note that from this unit on three main forms are given for nouns (see also 'Palun kaks salatit *Two salads please* – partitive singular case', below).

EXERCISE 1

Listen to the dialogue and choose the correct answers.

1 The dialogue took place **a** in the evening, **b** during the day, **c** in the morning.

2 The client bought **a** a black coffee, **b** two black coffees, **c** a black coffee and an orange juice.

3 The client **a** didn't buy anything else, **b** bought a potato salad **c** bought a sandwich.

4 The client paid **a** 20 kroons, **b** 15 kroons, c 25 kroons.

Listening 2

Urmas is ordering a drink at the bar. Listen to the dialogue and then complete Exercises 2–3.

 04.02

Baarman	Tere!
Urmas	Üks õlu palun.
Baarman	Kas suur või väike?
Urmas	Väike.
Baarman	Kohe. Nelikümmend krooni.
Urmas	Palun.
Baarman	Ma toon teie õlle lauda.
Urmas	Väga tore.

baarman, -i, -i	*bar tenderer* (male)
õlu, õlle, õlut	*beer*
suur, -e, -t	*big*
väike, -se, -st	*small*
Kas suur või väike?	*A big or a small one?*
kohe	*right away*
too/ma, -n	*to bring*
laud, laua, lauda	*table*
Ma toon teie õlle lauda.	*I will bring your beer to the table.*
väga tore	*very good*

EXERCISE 2

Listen to the dialogue and choose the correct answers.

1 Urmas is ordering **a** juice, **b** beer, **c** water.

2 He wants to have **a** a small glass, **b** a medium glass, **c** a big glass.

3 He has to pay **a** 20 kroons, **b** 30 kroons, **c** 40 kroons.

4 He will have his drink **a** at the bar, **b** at the table, **c** at home.

EXERCISE 3

What do these questions mean? Choose the correct translation.

1 Kas suur või väike salat?
   a Would you like a big or a small salad?
   b Would you like one or two salads?

2 Ma toon teie õlle lauda.
   a I will give you your beer now.
   b I will bring your beer to the table.

3 Kohe.
   a Immediately.
   b We don't have it.

Listening 3

In this dialogue a client is choosing and buying pies. Listen to the dialogue and complete Exercise 4 below.

 04.03

Ettekandja	Tere! Mida teile?
Klient	Tere! Üks pirukas palun.
Ettekandja	Mis pirukat te soovite?
Klient	Aga mis pirukad teil on?
Ettekandja	Meil on liha- ja kohupiimapirukad.
Klient	Aga mis pirukad need on?
Ettekandja	Need on seenepirukad. Väga head.
Klient	Olgu. Võtan siis kaks seenepirukat.
Ettekandja	Kas veel midagi?
Klient	Aitäh, see on kõik.

ettekandja, -, -t	*waitress*
Mida teile?	*What will you have? (lit. What for you?)*
pirukas, piruka, pirukat	*small pie, pasty*
soovi/ma, -n	*to wish*
Mis pirukat te soovite?	*What pie do you wish?*
aga	*but*
Mis pirukad teil on?	*What pies do you have?*
meil on	*we have*
liha/pirukas, -piruka, -pirukat	*meat pie*
kohupiima/pirukas, -piruka, -pirukat	*curd pie*
need, nende, neid	*these*
Mis pirukad need on?	*What pies are these?*
seene/pirukas, -piruka, -pirukat	*mushroom pie*

väga	*very*
hea	*good*
kahjuks	*unfortunately*
olgu	*OK*
siis	*then*
võt/ma, -an	*to take, get*
Kas veel midagi?	*anything else?* (lit. *more something?*)
See on kõik.	*That's all.*

EXERCISE 4

Listen to the dialogue and decide if the following sentences are **a** true or **b** false.

1 The client wants to buy 10 pies.

2 There are three types of pie on sale.

3 The client wants to buy meat pies.

4 Eventually the client bought two mushroom pies.

Listening 4

Kristel is ordering a drink. Listen to the dialogue and then complete Exercise 5.

 04.04

Kelner	Mis ma teile toon?
Kristel	Palun üks mineraalvesi.
Kelner	Kas gaasiga või ilma?
Kristel	Ilma gaasita palun. Aga jääga kui võimalik.
Kelner	Üks hetk.

kelner, -i, -it	*waiter*
too/ma, -n	*to bring*
mineraal/vesi, -vee, -vett	*mineral water*
gaas, -i, -i	*gas*
gaasiga	*with gas*
ilma	*without*
Kas gaasiga või ilma?	*With gas or without?*
Gaasita	*without gas*
jää, -, -d	*ice*
jääga	*with ice*
kui võimalik	*if possible*
üks hetk	*just a moment* (lit. *one moment*)

Listen to the dialogue and decide if the following sentences are **a** true or **b** false.

1 Kristel wants to have mineral water.

2 She wants to have mineral water with gas.

3 She wants to have ice in her mineral water.

Listening 5

Two friends are at the bar. Pille is asking Helle what she wants to have. Later on she gets the drinks from the bar. Listen to the dialogue and then complete Exercises 6–7.

 04.05

Pille	Mis ma sulle võtan?
Helle	Võta üks tee. Must tee sidruniga.
Pille	Ahah. Kas sa tahad veel midagi?
Helle	Kas joome konjakit ka?
Pille	Miks mitte! Mina maksan.
...	
Pille	Kaks teed sidruniga ja kaks konjakit.
Baarman	Kui palju ma konjakit panen?
Pille	Pange 5 cl.
Baarman	Kas veel midagi?
Pille	Ei, see on praegu kõik.

sulle	*for you*
tee, -, -d	*tea*
must, -a, -a	*black*
sidrun, -i, -it	*lemon*
sidruniga	*with lemon*
ahah	*OK*
taht/ma, taha/n	*to wish, want*
veel midagi	*anything else*
joo/ma, -n	*to drink*
konjak, -i, -it	*cognac*
ka	*also*
miks mitte	*why not*
maks/ma, -an	*to pay*
kui palju	*how much*
pane/ma, -n	*to give, to pour*
Kas veel midagi?	*Anything else?*
praegu	*at the moment*
kõik	*all*

EXERCISE 6

Listen to the dialogue and decide if the following sentences are **a** true or **b** false.

1 Helle would like to have a cup of green tea.

2 Helle and Pille decide to have a cognac, too.

3 Pille wants to pay for the drinks.

   …

4 Pille orders two cups of tea with lemon.

5 Pille also orders one cognac.

EXERCISE 7

 04.06

Choose the correct answer. Listen to the recording and check.

1 **Kas see on kõik? a** Väga head. **b** Aitäh, see on kõik.

2 **Kas suur või väike? a** Väike. **b** Jääga.

3 **Ma toon teie õlle lauda. a** Väga tore. **b** Tere!

4 **Kas joome konjakit ka? a** Miks mitte! **b** Üks hetk.

5 **Kas gaasiga või ilma? a** Jääga. **b** Ilma.

> **INSIGHT**
> When you read the language pattern section don't try to take in too much at once. Just read and practise one topic at a time. This way you will not be overwhelmed with new information.

Language patterns

KOHV KOOREGA, AGA ILMA SUHKRUTA *COFFEE WITH CREAM, BUT WITHOUT SUGAR – COMITATIVE CASE, ABESSIVE CASE*

As we have seen previously, many meanings in Estonian can be expressed with case endings, i.e. bits of info added to the end of the word. Often the case endings have the same meaning as English prepositions.

While ordering drinks and food in a bar or coffee shop, you will need to know how to say with and without, which in Estonian can be expressed with case endings.

The case ending **-ga** means *with*, thus suhkru**ga** means *with sugar*. The case ending **-ta** means *without*, therefore suhkru**ta** means *without sugar*. As you remember, the case ending is added to the second form of nominal words.

As you can see, the ending of the question can indicate the case ending, for example: Mille**ga**? *with what?* – koore**ga** *with cream*.

Note that the meaning **-ta** *without* can be emphasized with the word **ilma** (which also means *without*), therefore both sentences are correct: kohv suhkru**ta** as well as kohv **ilma** suhkru**ta**.

Note also that it doesn't matter if you say **kohv koorega** or **koorega kohv** – the meaning is the same.

EXERCISE 8

Divide the expressions into two groups depending whether the meaning is *with* or *without*.

Translate the expressions.

1 kohv koorega +

2 kooreta kohv –

3 suhkruga kohv

4 suhkruta kohv

5 gaasiga vesi

6 gaasita vesi

7 mahl jääga

8 mahl ilma jääta

9 tee ilma sidrunita

10 kohv konjakiga

In order to practise this grammar topic further do Exercise 15 in the Practice section.

ANNA MULLE MENÜÜ *GIVE ME A MENU – ALLATIVE CASE*

With verbs **andma** *to give*, **ütlema** *to say* etc. that express the transfer of information or things from one person to another, we use the allative case. In English, it corresponds sometimes to the use of the prepositions *to* or *for*, but very often there is no direct equivalent in English. For example Ettekandja annab kliendi**le** menüü – *The waitress gives the customer the menu*. Urmas ütleb ettekandja**le** tere. – *Urmas says hello to the waitress*.

Sometimes, the verb is dropped altogether, for example:

Mida (ma) teile (annan)?	*What for you?*
Palun (andke) mulle …	*For me please …*

It would be useful if you were to remember the forms of the allative case of the personal pronouns. As usual with the personal pronouns, there are longer forms (the first ones) and the short forms (the second ones). In colloquial language we tend to use the shorter forms.

Kelle**le**? *to whom?*	
minu**le** / mul**le** *to me*	mei**le** *to us*
sinu**le** / sul**le** *to you*	tei**le** *to you*
tema**le** / tal**le** *to him/her*	nende**le** / nei**le** *to them*

Some examples using the allative case

Palun anna mul**le** menüü.	*Please give me the menu.*
Kas ostan sul**le** ka kohvi?	*Shall I buy coffee for you too?*
Palun andke tal**le** üks pirukas.	*Please give him/her a pie.*
Palun tooge mei**le** kaks õlut.	*Please bring us two beers.*
Mida tei**le**?	*What will you have?*
Palun mul**le** üks kartulisalat.	*Please give me a potato salad.*
Mis ma sul**le** võtan?	*What shall I get for you?*

EXERCISE 9

Translate the following sentences into English.

1 Palun osta mulle üks kohv.

2 Mida sulle?

3 Mis ma talle võtan?

4 Palun andke meile üks õlu.

5 Palun andke mulle menüü.

6 Palun mulle üks sidruniga tee.

7 Palun tooge meile kaks lihapirukat.

In order to practise this grammar topic further do Exercise 16 in the Practice section.

PALUN ÜKS ÕUNAMAHL *ONE APPLE JUICE PLEASE – COMPOUND NOUNS*

One very typical feature of the Estonian language is compound nouns. They can be compiled of two or more words and look quite long. When you see a long and possibly incomprehensible word, it would be useful to see if you could divide it up to separate words, for instance mineraal/vesi – *mineral water*.

EXERCISE 10

 04.07

Listen and repeat the examples of some compound nouns.

mahlad	**juices**
õunamahl, -a, -a	*apple juice*
tomatimahl, -a, -a	*tomato juice*
apelsinimahl, -a, -a	*orange juice*
ploomimahl, -a, -a	*plum juice*
ananassimahl, -a, -a	*pineapple juice*
jõhvikamahl, -a, -a	*cranberry juice*
kirsimahl, -a, -a	*cherry juice*

võileivad	**sandwiches**
juustuvõileib, -leiva, -leiba	*cheese sandwich*
vorstivõileib, -leiva, -leiba	*sausage sandwich*
singivõileib, -leiva, -leiba	*ham sandwich*

joogid	**drinks**
jäätisekokteil, -i, -i	*icecream shake*
kohv, -i, -i	*coffee*
kakao, -, -d	*hot chocolate*

koogid	**cakes**
vahukoore/kook, -koogi, -kooki	*whipped cream cake*
õuna/kook, -koogi, -kooki	*apple cake*
kohupiima/kook, -koogi, -kooki	*curd cake*
vaarika/kook, -koogi, -kooki	*raspberry cake*

salatid	**salads**
kartulisalat, -i, -id	*potato salad*
singisalat, -i, -id	*ham salad*
makaronisalat, -i, -id	*macaroni salad*
kurgisalat, -i, -id	*cucumber salad*
tomatisalat, -i, -id	*tomato salad*

NEED ON VÄGA HEAD SEENEPIRUKAD *THESE ARE VERY GOOD MUSHROOM PIES – PLURAL NOMINATIVE CASE*

If you see words like **pirukad** pies, **salatid** salads, **joogid** drinks which all have the ending **-d** note that these words are plural. The ending **-d** is added to the second form of the noun, for instance:

first form	second form	plural
pirukas	piruka	piruka**d**
jook	joogi	joogi**d**
salat	salati	salati**d**

EXERCISE 11

Underline the words that are in the plural.

lihapirukas, baaridaam, ettekandjad, jää, kartulisalat, kliendid, kohupiimapirukad, kohv, konjak, mineraalvesi, sidrunid, tee

In order to practise this grammar topic further do Exercise 17 in the Practice section.

Estonian bars and coffee shops

For drinks and a light snack look for a baar *bar* or kohvik *coffee shop*. The bars and coffee shops usually open between 10–11 am and stay open till 6–7 pm (coffee shops) or 12 pm (bars).

Most bars and coffee shops do not have table service, so you order at the counter and then go and find your table. If there is table service, adding a small tip to the bill is expected (approximately 10% of the bill).

While the menus of bars tend to be international (with some German and Russian influence), the coffee shops can offer more typical Estonian drinks and snacks. Apart from **kohv** *coffee* and **tee** *tea*, some places serve **hõõgvein** *mulled or glowing wine* during the winter season. If you would like to try a typical cold Estonian **alkoholivaba jook** *non-alcoholic drink* ask for a bottle of **kali** *small beer* – an Estonian equivalent of Coca-Cola. Traditional Estonian **limonaad** *lemonade* is called **Kelluke**, a clear fizzy drink resembling Sprite. Estonia has its own **mineraalvesi** *mineral water* springs in Värska, which is also the name of the water brand – **Värska vesi** *Värska mineral water*. It has more minerals in it and has thus a slightly saltier taste than international brands. In addition to juices made of tropical fruits one can also find juices made of wild berries like **pohlamahl** *lingonberry juice*, **jõhvikamahl** *cranberry juice*, **mustikamahl** *blueberry juice*.

Alcoholic drinks

All bars serve **õlu** *beer* and **siider** *cider* as light alcoholic drinks. On festive occasions **šampus** *champagne* is the most common drink.

The biggest Estonian beer brands are **Saku** and **A. Le Coq.** Because of Estonia's geographical position, there is no locally grown grape wine, so all wine is imported. Only **marjavein** *berry wine* is made locally. Traditional Estonian liqueur – **Vana Tallinn-** *Old Tallinn* – is worth a try as it's a combination of tens of different herbs and therefore is definitely good for your health! The best known Estonian **viin** *vodka* is **Viru Valge**.

Lahja alkohol *light drinks* can be asked for as **väike** *small* (0.3 litres) or **suur** *big* (0.5 litres). **Kange alkohol** *hard liquor/spirits* is ordered and poured by the centilitre (cl).

Light snacks at the coffee shop

Most coffee shops have small closed pies or pasties, called **pirukas**, on the menu. They come in a variety of shapes and can be either sweet or savoury, depending on the filling like **lihapirukas** *meat pie*, **kapsapirukas** *cabbage pie*, **seenepirukas** *mushroom pie*, **porgandipirukas** *carrot pie*, **kohupiimapirukas** *curd pie*, **moosipirukas** *jam pie*. Another common dish is **salat** *salad*, which most typically is served in small ready-made portions and consists of either potato or macaroni and other different finely chopped ingredients mixed together with sour cream. Most common salads are **kartulisalat** *potato salad*, **singisalat** *ham salad* and **makaronisalat** *macaroni salad*.

PALUN KAKS SALATIT *TWO SALADS PLEASE – PARTITIVE SINGULAR CASE*

We have already learnt the two basic forms of Estonian nouns. In this unit, we will talk about the third form (called *partitive* as a grammatical term). From this unit on, the third form will be given also in the glossary for all nominal words.

The endings of third form (partitive singular) are:

	first form (nominative)		third form (partitive singular)
-t	salat	*salad*	sala**t**it
i, -e, -a, -u	kohv	*coffee*	kohv**i**
	lill	*flower*	lill**e**
	mahl	*juice*	mahl**a**
	laul	*song*	laul**u**
-d	tee	*tea*	tee**d**

As a very general rule the ending **-t** is used with longer words. The vowel ending (either **-i**, **-e**, **-a**, **-u**) is used with shorter words. The ending **-d** is quite rare and only used with few words, for example tee**d**, või**d**, hea**d**.

To master the formation of partitive singular, you need to know a variety of word groups that we will learn step by step in the following units.

When do we use the third form (partitive singular)?

The third form has many different functions in Estonian. In this unit we will have a look at some of them.

The third form is used with numerals (except one, with which the nominative is used), for instance:

viis pirukat	*five pies*
kaks kohvi	*two coffees*
kolm musta teed	*three black teas*

NB! Note that with numbers we do not use plural nominative as we do in English.

The third form is used with other words to express quantity or measure, for instance

klaas mahla	*a glass of juice*
tass kohvi	*a cup of coffee*
pudel limonaadi	*a bottle of lemonade*
tükk kooki	*a piece of cake*
pakk suitsu	*a box of cigarettes*
pits viina	*a shot of vodka*
purk õlut	*a can of beer*
pits konjakit	*a shot of cognac*

The third form is also used in sentences like **Ma joon mahla** *I drink juice*. **Ma söön salatit** *I eat salad*. **Ma tahan konjakit** *I want cognac*.

The third form is always used in negative sentences, for instance **Meil ei ole mahla** *We don't have juice*. **Meil ei ole konjakit** *We don't have cognac*. **Me ei taha salatit** *We don't have salad*.

EXERCISE 12

Choose the correct form.

1 Palun kaks **musta kohvi/must kohv**.

2 Palun kolm **õunapirukas/õunapirukat**.

3 Palun üks **tee sidruniga/teed sidruniga**.

4 Palun kaks **makaronisalat/makaronisalatit**.

5 Palun pudel **konjak/konjakit**.

6 Palun tass **teed/tee**.

7 Palun klaas **mahla/mahl**.

8 Palun purk **õlu/õlut**.

EXERCISE 13

Use the words given in brackets in the third form.

1 Klient sööb (kartulisalat) _____ ja joob (must kohv) _____

2 Urmas joob (õlu) _____

3 Andres sööb (seenepirukas) _____

4 Andres ei söö (lihapirukas) _____

5 Pille ja Helle joovad (must tee) _____ ja (konjak) _____

6 Helle ja Pille ei söö (salat) _____

In order to practise this grammar topic further do Exercises 18–19 in the Practice section.

MA ARMASTAN SIND *I LOVE YOU* – PARTITIVE CASE OF PERSONAL PRONOUNS

Note that also words like **mina** *I*, **sina** *you* etc. have the third form, for instance:

first form	third form	first form	third form
mina	**mind**	meie	**meid**
sina	**sind**	teie	**teid**
tema	**teda**	nemad	**neid**

Some examples of usage:

Ma armastan **sind**.	*I love you.*
Kas sa armastad **mind**?	*Do you love me?*
Ma armastan **teda**.	*I love her.*
Me ootame **teid**.	*We wait for you.*
Kas te ootate **meid**?	*Are you waiting for us?*
Ma ootan **neid**.	*I am waiting for them.*

EXERCISE 14

Translate the following sentences into English.

1 Kas sa armastad teda?

2 Ta armastab sind.

3 Miks te meid ei armasta?

4 Ta ootab meid.

5 Kas nad ootavad teid?

6 Ta ei oota mind.

In order to practise this grammar topic further do Exercise 20 in the Practice section.

Practice

EXERCISE 15

What does it mean when you are told the following?

1 See salat on lihaga.
  a This salad is with meat.
  b This salad is without meat.

2 See võileib on juustuga.
  a This sandwich is with cheese.
  b This sandwich is without cheese.

3 Vesi on ilma gaasita, aga jääga.
  a The mineral water is with gas and with ice.
  b The mineral water is without gas and without ice.
  c The mineral water is with gas but without ice.
  d The mineral water is without gas but with ice.

EXERCISE 16

Complete the sentences with the words in brackets.

1 Palun anna (mina) *mulle* menüü.

2 Kas ostan (sina) _____ ka kohvi?

3 Palun andke (tema) _____ üks pirukas.

4 Palun tooge (meie) _____ kaks õlut.

5 Mida (teie) _____?

6 Mis ma (sina) _____ toon?

7 Mis ma (nemad) _____ toon?

EXERCISE 17

Write the following words in the plural. If you are not sure about the second form, see Exercise 10.

1 õunamahl *õunamahlad*

2 apelsinimahl _____

3 kirsimahl _____

4 juustuvõileib _____

5 vorstivõileib _____

6 jäätisekokteil _____

7 õunakook _____

8 kartulisalat _____

9 tomatisalat _____

EXERCISE 18

Translate.

1 two teas *kaks teed*

2 three coffees _____

3 one salad _____

4 four salads _____

5 five mushroom pies _____

6 two cakes _____

7 six juices _____

8 three cognacs _____

EXERCISE 19

Think of what you like and don't like to eat and drink. Divide the following words between the sentences. Use the third form.

must kohv, kartulisalat, õlu, kohupiimapirukas, lihapirukas, seenepirukas, tee, konjak, tomatimahl, apelsinimahl, jõhvikamahl, õunakook, pohlakook, makaronisalat

1 Ma söön _____

2 Ma ei söö _____

3 Ma joon _____

4 Ma ei joo _____

5 Ma tahan _____

EXERCISE 20

Fill in the blanks using the words in brackets. Use the third form.

1 Sa armastad (tema) *teda*

2 Ta armastab (meie) _____

3 Me armastame (teie) _____

4 Te armastate (nemad) _____

5 Nad armastavad (mina) _____

6 Ma armastan (sina) _____

Speaking

EXERCISE 21

 04.08

Here are some situations for you to practise. How do you ask for such things? Listen to the correct answers.

1 You would like a glass of orange juice.

2 You would like a can of cider.

3 You would like a box of cigarettes.

4 You would like a shot of cognac.

5 You would like a bottle of mineral water.

6 You would like a cup of tea.

7 You would like a piece of cake.

EXERCISE 22

Complete the dialogue. Listen to the completed dialogue.

 04.09

Ettekandja	Tere. Mida teile?
Sina	Ask for a black coffee.
Ettekandja	Kas koorega või ilma?
Sina	*Say With cream, please.*
Ettekandja	Kas see on kõik?
Sina	Ask for a pie.
Ettekandja	Mis pirukat te soovite?
Sina	Ask what pies they have.
Ettekandja	Meil on liha- ja seenepirukad.
Sina	Ask for a meat pie.
Ettekandja	Kas veel midagi?
Sina	*Say Thank you. Say That is all.*

EXERCISE 23

Do the following.

  a Say *Hello!*

  b Ask for a cup of coffee with cream.

  c Ask what pies they have.

  d Ask if they are with or without meat.

  e Ask for two mushroom pies.

? Test yourself

1 You would like to have a coffee, an orange juice and apple cake. What do you say?
  a Palun üks kohv, õunamahl ja kohupiimakook.
  b Palun üks kohv, apelsinimahl ja õunakook.
  c Palun üks kohv, tomatimahl ja vahukoorekook.

2 You would like to have a large beer. What do you say?
  a Palun üks väike õlu.
  b Palun üks suur õlu.
  c Palun üks suur mineraalvesi.

3 You would like a water without gas. What do you say?
  a Palun üks vesi.
  b Palun üks gaasiga vesi.
  c Palun üks gaasita vesi.

4 The waitress says **Ma toon teie pirukad lauda.** What does it mean?
  a The pies are very good.
  b I will bring the pies to the table.
  c We have no pies.

5 The waitress asks **Kas midagi veel?** What is the correct answer?
  a Ei, see on praegu kõik.
  b Mina maksan.
  c äga tore.

6 How do you say *I love you*?
  a Ma armastan sind.
  b Sa armastad mind.
  c Ta armastab sind.

7 Which one of these words means *cakes*?
  a kook
  b koogi
  c koogid

8 How do you ask *What kind of salads do you have?*
  a Mis salatid teil on?
  b Kas teil on salatit?
  c Mitu salatit teil on?

9 You want to ask what your friend would like to have in the coffee-shop. What do you say?

    a Mis ma sulle võtan?

    b Mis ma neile võtan?

    c Mis ma talle võtan?

10 **Purk õlut** means

    a a glass of beer

    b a bottle of beer

    c a can of beer

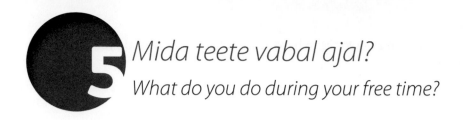

Mida teete vabal ajal?

What do you do during your free time?

In this unit you will learn:
▶ *How to talk about your job and what you do during your free time*
▶ *How to name different nationalities and jobs*

Listening 1

Some amateur painters have gathered at a summer camp. You will hear how the organizer of the camp greets them. Listen to the text and then complete Exercise 1.

 05.01

Mart	Tere tulemast maalilaagrisse! Saame kõigepealt tuttavaks – mina olen laagri korraldaja Mart Päike. Öelge nüüd palun kõik oma nimed ja ametid. Kust te pärit olete? Ja palun öelge ka, mida teile meeldib teha vabal ajal.

Tere tulemast!	*Welcome!*
maali/laager, -laagri, -laagrit	*hobby-painter's camp*
tuttavaks saa/ma, tuttavaks saa/da, saa/n tuttavaks	*to get acquainted*
kõigepealt	*first, to start with*
laager, laagri, laagrit	*camp*
korraldaja, -, -t	*organizer*
nüüd	*now*
kõik	*everybody, all*
oma nimed	*your names*
amet, -i, -it	*profession*
Kust te pärit olete?	*Where are you from?*
mis, mille, mida	*what*
teile meeldib	*you like*
tege/ma, teh/a, tee/n	*to do*
vaba, -, -	*free*
aeg, aja, aega	*time*
vabal ajal	*in your free time*

Note that from this unit on all verbs will also have three forms presented. The explanation is given in 'Mulle meeldib sportida *I like doing sports* – da-infinitive' after Exercise 7, below.

EXERCISE 1

1 Mart says **a** hello, **b** welcome, **c** good morning.

2 Mart Päike is **a** the organizer of the camp, **b** one of the participants, **c** bus driver.

3 The participants have to **a** go to their rooms, **b** go to have a meal, **c** introduce themselves.

Listening 2

You will hear people introducing themselves. Listen to the texts and then complete
Exercises 2–3.

 05.02

a	Joosep	Mina olen Joosep. Ma tulen Pärnust. Ma olen ehitaja. Mulle meeldib sport.
b	Külli	Tere! Minu nimi on Külli, ma tulen Kohtla-Järvelt. Olen ajakirjanik. Vabal ajal meeldib mulle pildistada ja maalida.
c	Kaido	Olen Kaido. Ma tulen Tartust. Mul on oma firma, olen firmajuht. Vabal ajal armastan reisida.
d	Marek	Minu nimi on Marek. Ma olen pärit Hiiumaalt Kärdlast. Mina olen kinnisvaramaakler, aga vabal ajal meeldib mulle hästi süüa.
e	Tanel	Mina olen Tanel. Mina tulen Rakverest. Olen poes müüja. Vabal ajal meeldib mulle jalgpalli mängida.
f	Helen	Tere, mina olen Helen. Ma olen pärit Inglismaalt. Ma olen sekretär. Vabal ajal meeldib mulle ujuda.
g	Lembit	Mina olen Lembit. Mina tulen Võrust. Mina olen raamatupidaja ja vabal ajal meeldib mulle muusikat kuulata.

ma tulen	*I come*
tule/ma, tull/a, tule/n	*to come*
ehitaja, -, -	*construction worker*
mulle meeldib	*I like*
sport, spordi, sporti	*sports*
ajakirjanik, -u, -ku	*journalist*
pildista/ma, -da, -n	*to take photos*
maali/ma, -da, -n	*to paint*
mul on	*I have*
oma, -, -	*one's own*
firma, -, -t	*company, business*
firma/juht, -juhi, -juhti	*director of a business*
armasta/ma, -da, -n	*to love*
reisi/ma, -da, -n	*to travel*
olen pärit	*I come from* (lit. *I am origin of …*)
kinnisvaramaakler, -i, -it	*estate agent*

hästi	*well*
söö/ma, süü/a, söö/n	*to eat*
müüja, -, -t	*shop assistant*
jalgpall, -i, -i	*football, soccer (Am.)*
mängi/ma, -da, -n	*to play*
jalgpalli mängima	*to play football*
sekretär, -i, -i	*secretary*
uju/ma, -da, -n	*to swim*
raamatupidaja, -, -t	*bookkeeper, accountant*
muusika, -, -t	*music*
kuula/ma, -ta, -n	*to listen to*

EXERCISE 2

Listen and draw a line from the name to the right profession, hobby and country/town. The first one is done for you.

name	country/town	who is	who likes
Joosep	Kärdla in Hiiumaa	a shop assistant?	to swim?
Külli	England	an estate agent?	to take photos and paint?
Kaido	Kohtla-Järve	is the owner of his own company?	to eat well?
Marek	Pärnu	a bookkeeper?	to play football?
Tanel	Rakvere	a journalist?	to listen to music?
Helen	Tartu	a secretary?	to travel?
Lembit	Võru	a construction worker?	to do sports?

EXERCISE 3

What do these sentences mean? Choose the correct answer.

1 **Mulle meeldib maalida. a** I like painting. **b** I have a painting.

2 **Mulle meeldib sport. a** I like sports. **b** I do sports.

3 **Mulle meeldib hästi süüa. a** I eat well. **b** I like to eat well.

4 **Kaidole ei meeldi tantsida. a** Kaido likes dancing. **b** Kaido doesn't like dancing.

AMETID *PROFESSIONS*

 05.03

Many names of professions end with **-ja** or **-nik** in Estonian. Listen to the recording and repeat.

näitleja, -, -t	*actor*
lapsehoidja, -, -t	*babysitter*
õpetaja, -, -t	*teacher*

lasteaia kasvataja, -, -t	*kindergarten teacher*
müüja, -, -t	*seller, saleswoman, salesman*
politseinik, -u, -ku	*policeman*
kunstnik, -u, -ku	*artist*
koristaja, -, -t	*janitor*

Listening 3

 05.04

You will hear the organizer of the camp talking about the plan for the day. Listen to the text and then complete Exercise 4.

Nii. Räägin nüüd lühidalt, mida me täna veel teeme. Kõigepealt läheme sööma. Siis on pool tundi vaba aega. Kell viis hakkame töötama. Kell kaheksa on õhtusöök. Pärast seda on vaba aeg, kes soovib, saab tantsida, kes soovib, lihtsalt juttu ajada, kellele meeldib saun, saab saunas käia. Öörahu peab algama kell kaksteist. Mida teeme teisipäeval ja kolmapäeval, seda ütlen teile homme hommikul.

nii	*OK*
rääki/ma, rääki/da, räägi/n	*to tell, speak*
nüüd	*now*
lühidalt	*a little bit* (lit. *shortly*)
täna	*today*
mida veel	*what else*
siis	*then*
pool tundi	*half an hour*
hakka/ma, haka/ta, hakka/n	*to start*
tööta/ma, -da, -n	*to work*
õhtu/söök, -söögi, -sööki	*supper*
pärast seda	*after that*
kes, kelle, keda	*who*
soovi/ma, -da, -n	*to wish*
saa/ma, -da, -n	*can*
tantsi/ma, -da, -n	*to dance*
juttu aja/ma, jutta aja/da, aja/n juttu	*to have a chat*
saun, -a, -a	*sauna*
saunas käi/ma saunas käi/a, käi/n saunas	*to go to the sauna*
öörahu, -, -	*night's rest*
peab	*must*
alga/ma, ala/ta, alga/b	*to start*

EXERCISE 6

Read the examples. Fill in the empty spaces with words in the right form.

Name of the place	Ma lähen, sõidan … kuhu? *I go, I drive …* *where to?*	Ma elan, olen kus? *I live, I am in …* *where?*	Ma olen pärit, tulen kust? *I am from,* *I come from …* *where?*
	-sse	**-s**	**-st**
Tartu *Tartu*	Tartu**sse**	Tartu**s**	Tartu**st**
Tallinn *Tallinn*	Tallinna**sse**	_____	_____
Eesti *Estonia*	Eesti**sse**	_____	_____
Pärnu *Pärnu*	Pärnu**sse**	_____	_____
USA *USA*	USA-**sse**	_____	_____
Jaapan *Japan*	Jaapani**sse**	_____	_____
	Short form	**-s**	**-st**
Soome *Finland*	Soome	Soome**s**	Soome**st**
Rootsi *Sweden*	Rootsi	Rootsi**s**	_____
Läti *Latvia*	Lätti	Läti**s**	_____
Leedu *Lithuania*	Leetu	Leedu**s**	_____
	-le	**-l**	**-lt**
Hiiumaa *island of Hiiumaa*	Hiiumaa**le**	Hiiumaa**l**	Hiiumaa**lt**
Inglismaa *England*	Inglismaa**le**	Inglismaa**l**	Inglismaa**lt**
Kohtla-Järve *Kohtla-Järve*	Kohtla-Järve**le**	Kohtla-Järve**l**	Kohtla-Järve**lt**
Prantsusmaa *France*	Prantsusmaa**le**	_____	_____
Saksamaa *Germany*	Saksamaa**le**	_____	_____
Mustamäe *Mustamäe* *(a district in Tallinn)*	Mustamäe**le**	_____	_____
Saaremaa *island of* *Saaremaa*	Saaremaa**le**	_____	_____

The expression **ma olen pärit** *I come from* is used to express one's origin. The expression **Ma tulen kust?** *I come from where?* is used more to indicate the place you are living in at the moment.

In order to practise this grammar topic further do Exercises 12–15 in the Practice section.

MULLE MEELDIB SPORT *I LIKE SPORTS – ALLATIVE CASE*

The construction *I like* is different in English and Estonian. We use the same case ending **-le** we learnt in the previous unit, which is used with words like **ütlema** *to say*, **andma** *to give*. It is added to the person who 'does the liking', for instance:

Joosepi**le** meeldib sport.   *Joosep likes sports.*

Joosepi**le** ei meeldi see laager.   *Joosep does not like this camp.*

As you can see, the names also take different case endings and like all words the ending is added to the second, not the first form. If the name ends with **a**, **e**, **i**, **o** or **u**, the first and second form are alike. If the name does not end with a vowel, there will be one in the second form, for instance Joosep – Joosepi, Henn – Hennu, Urmas – Urmase etc.

With the words *I*, *you*, *he*, *she*, *we*, *you* and *they*, the construction *I like* … looks like this:

Mulle meeldib sport.	*I like sports.*
Mulle ei meeldi muusika.	*I don't like music.*
Sulle meeldib muusika.	*You like music.*
Sulle ei meeldi sport.	*You don't like sports.*
Talle meeldib Tallinn.	*He/she likes Tallinn.*
Talle ei meeldi see koht.	*He/she doesn't like this place.*
Meile meeldib see koht.	*We like this place.*
Meile ei meeldi Tallinn.	*We don't like Tallinn.*
Teile meeldib Mart.	*You like Mart.*
Teile ei meeldi see laager.	*You don't like this camp.*
Neile meeldib see laager.	*They like this camp.*
Neile ei meeldi Mart.	*They don't like Mart.*

EXERCISE 7

Translate these sentences.

1 Mulle meeldib see maalilaager.

2 Talle ei meeldi see maalilaager.

3 Kas sulle meeldib Tallinn?

4 Kas Joosepile meeldib Tallinn?

5 Joosepile ei meeldi sport.

6 Kas teile meeldib see muusika?

7 Meile ei meeldi Mart.

In order to practise this grammar topic further do Exercise 16 in the Practice section.

MULLE MEELDIB SPORTIDA *I LIKE DOING SPORTS – DA-INFINITIVE*

All verbs (i.e. words like **rääkima** *to speak*, **sööma** *to eat*, etc.) have main forms too: the first form (called **ma**-infinitive as a grammatical term), the second form (called **da**-infinitive as a grammatical term) and the third main form (the I-form). The first form always ends with -ma; the second form can end with either **-ta**, **-da** or **-a**. The I-form always ends with **-n**.

From now on we will present the three forms in the dictionary.

For example the verb **maalima** *to paint* would be presented in the dictionary in the following way **maali/ma**, **-da**, **-n**, i.e maali**ma** (*to paint*) is the first form, maali**da** (*to paint*) is the second form and maali**n** (*I paint*) is the I-form.

When to use the first and when the second form depends on the words the form occurs with in the sentence. The group of words requiring the use of the second form is quite big and for now the rule of thumb is to remember that we use the second form with words expressing feelings and requests (for instance **ma armastan** *I love to*, **mulle meeldib** *I like*, **ma tahan** *I want to*, **ma soovin** *I wish*, etc.).

So we always say **Mulle meeldib maalida** *I like to paint*, (not **Mulle meeldib maalima**).

Note that also modal verbs like **ma saan** *I can, I am able to* and **ma võin** *I am able to, I can* are also used with the second form, so we say: **Me saame õhtul tantsida** *We can dance in the evening* (not **Me saame õhtul tantsima**).

Here are some more examples:

Joosepile **meeldib** sporti**da**.	*Joosep likes to do sports.*
Küllile **meeldib** pildistada ja maali**da**.	*Külli likes to take photos and paint.*
Kaidole **meeldib** reisi**da**.	*Kaido likes to travel.*
Marek **armastab** hästi süü**a**.	*Marek loves to eat well.*
Joosep ei **soovi** tantsi**da**.	*Joosep does not wish to dance.*
Külli ei **taha** puha**ta**.	*Külli does not want to rest.*

See also Appendix 6.

EXERCISE 8

Choose the right form.

1 Küllile meeldib **rääkima/rääkida**.
2 Marekile meeldib autoga **sõitma/sõita**.
3 Joosepile meeldib **pildistama/pildistada**.
4 Talle ei meeldi **tantsima/tantsida**.
5 Kas teile meeldib **reisima/reisida**?
6 Meile meeldib **puhkama/puhata**.

In order to practise this grammar topic further do Exercise 17 in the Practice section.

What do Estonians do in their free time?

Estonians have always been regarded as people who like to read books. The symptom of love for books – bookshelves crammed with all sorts of bindings – can be seen in most Estonian homes. So don't be surprised to find a simple Estonian busdriver who for instance owns a respectable collection of poetry!

Estonians are also famous for their love of music. Festivals like **Jazzkaar, Viljandi Folk** and **Leigo järvemuusika** bring together huge audiences. Every 5 years Estonians gather in Tallinn for the biggest festival of all: **laulupidu** *song festival* where over 30,000 singers dressed in colourful national costumes can be heard singing at the same time. Smaller, local festivals like this take place every summer. With choral music being viewed as one of the symbols of Estonia, you will find many people, children and adults alike, singing actively in choirs.

During the spring and summertime, many Estonians leave the city for a cottage in the countryside to grow their own potatoes and take care of the berry garden and orchard or have barbecue parties and sauna with friends. Home-made apple juice and other preserves fill the shelves in the autumn. During the autumn walking in the forest in search of **seened** *wild mushrooms* and **marjad** *berries* is also a very common pastime.

During the winter an athletic Estonian goes skiing and if not skiing himself at least watches cross-country skiing on the television. Broadcasts of the winter Olympics and other skiing events draw the largest television audiences in Estonia.

HAKKAME MAALIMA! *LET'S START PAINTING! – MA-INFINITIVE*

As we saw earlier **the second form** is used with words like **armastama** *to love*, **meeldima** *to like*, **tahtma** *to want*, **soovima** *to wish*, etc. Now we will learn some words that the first form is always used with.

Among them there are verbs indicating movement like **ma lähen** *I go*, **ma tulen** *I come*, **ma sõidan** *I drive*, etc. and also the verbs **ma hakkan** *I start or will*, and **ma pean** *I have to, I must*. For example:

Kõigepealt **läheme** söö**ma**.	*First, we will go to eat.*
Siis **läheme** sporti**ma**.	*Then we will go to do some sports.*
Kell viis **hakkame** maali**ma**.	*At 5 o'clock we will start painting.*
Kell kümme **hakkame** tantsi**ma**.	*At 10 o'clock we will start dancing.*
Me **peame** lõpeta**ma** kell üksteist.	*We have to finish at 11 o'clock.*
Öörahu **peab** alga**ma** kell kaksteist.	*Night's rest has to start at 12 o'clock.*

Note that if you want to speak about something that takes place in the future (for instance in a sentence like **Ma lähen homme maalilaagrisse** *Tomorrow I will go to the hobby-painters' camp*) Estonian has no specific grammatical indicator, unlike in English. We use the present tense, sometimes in combination with words and expressions indicating the future (like **homme** *tomorrow*, **järgmisel aastal** *next year*, **kell kümme** *at 10 o'clock*, etc.). Also, the verb **hakkama** *to start* can indicate the future tense, for instance **Nüüd hakkame maalima**. *Now we will start painting*. See also Appendix 6.

EXERCISE 9

Choose the right word.

1 Hakkame **süüa/sööma.**
2 Lähen **sportida/sportima**.
3 Ma pean **süüa/sööma**.
4 Nad hakkavad **tantsida/tantsima**.
5 Te peate **maalida/maalima**.
6 Hakkame **lõpetada/lõpetama**.

In order to practise this grammar topic further do Exercise 17 in the Practice section.

Word order

In Estonian, word order is freer than it is in English. For instance, to say *I will go to the hobby-painter's camp tomorrow*, all of these sentences are OK, having just slight differences of meaning:

Ma lähen homme maalilaagrisse.

Ma lähen maalilaagrisse homme.

Homme lähen ma maalilaagrisse.

Maalilaagrisse lähen ma homme.

As a rule of thumb, the verb comes in second place in Estonian sentences.

Practice

EXERCISE 10

Put each line of words in the right order, and then translate them.

1 eile, homme, täna, üleeile, ülehomme

2 laupäev, esmaspäev, reede, kolmapäev, teisipäev, neljapäev, pühapäev

EXERCISE 11

Write the word that follows. Be careful to use the right form. Then translate the phrases. The first one is done for you.

1 esmaspäeval *teisipäeval – on Monday, on Tuesday*

2 kolmapäeval

3 reedel

4 pühapäeval

5 täna

6 üleeile

7 homme

8 kevadel

9 sügisel

10 talvel

EXERCISE 12

Divide the names of places into two groups according to the ending they take for questions **kus?** *where?* and **kust?** *where from?*

-s; -st	*-l; -lt*
Eesti	Hiiumaa

Eesti, Hiiumaa, Inglismaa, Jaapan, Kohtla-Järve, Lasnamäe, Leedu, Läti, Mustamäe, Prantsusmaa, Pärnu, Rootsi, Saaremaa, Saksamaa, Sillamäe, Soome, Taani, Tallinn, Tartu, USA, Õismäe.

EXERCISE 13

Where is he/she from? Join the right name and place. Make a sentence. The first one is done for you. *Pekka on pärit Soomest.*

1	Pekka	**a**	Venemaa
2	Anatoli	**b**	Eesti
3	Michiko	**c**	Hispaania
4	Tiiu	**d**	Soome
5	Michael	**e**	Inglismaa
6	Pierre	**f**	Jaapan
7	Juan	**g**	Prantsusmaa

EXERCISE 14

Choose the correct form.

1 Ma olen pärit **Inglismaale/Inglismaal/Inglismaalt.**

2 Ma olen pärit **Eestisse/Eestis/Eestist**.

3 Ma olen pärit **Hiiumaale/Hiiumaal/Hiiumaalt.**

4 Ma olen pärit **Tartusse/Tartus/Tartust.**

5 Ma elan **Tallinnasse/Tallinnas/Tallinnast.**

6 Ma elan **Lätti/Lätis/Lätist.**

7 Ma elan **Mustamäele/Mustamäel/Mustamäelt.**

8 Ma elan **Jaapanisse/Jaapanis/Jaapanist.**

9 Ma lähen **Soome/Soomes/Soomest.**

10 Ma lähen **USA-sse/USA-s/USA-st.**

11 Ma lähen **Pärnusse/Pärnus/Pärnust.**

12 Ma lähen **Saksamaale/Saksamaal/Saksamaalt.**

EXERCISE 15

Use the words in brackets in the right case.

1 Ma sõidan teisipäeval (Tartu) _____

2 Ma olen (Tartu) _____ kaks päeva.

3 Ma tulen (Tartu) _____ tagasi neljapäeval.

4 Ta sõidab homme (Soome) _____

5 Ta on (Soome) _____ viis päeva.

6 Ta tuleb (Soome) _____ laupäeval.

7 Me läheme ülehomme (Saaremaa) _____

8 Me oleme (Saaremaa) _____ kuus päeva.

9 Me tuleme (Saaremaa) _____ pühapäeval.

EXERCISE 16

Form sentences according to the sample sentence and translate them.

1 Ülo, - / meeldib / Kaie.   *Ülole meeldib Kaie.*

2 Kaie, - / meeldib / Kaido.   _____

3 Kaido, - / meeldib / Piret.   _____

4 Piret, -i / meeldib / Sven.   _____

5 Sven, -i / meeldib / Ruth.   _____

6 Ruth, -i / meeldib / Urmas.   _____

7 Urmas, -e / meeldib / Kärt.   _____

8 Kärt, Kärdi / meeldib / Tiit.   _____

9 Tiit, Tiidu / meeldib / Aet.   _____

10 Aet, Aeda / meeldib / Ülo.   _____

EXERCISE 17

Choose the correct form.

1 Räägin teile, mida me hakkame **tegema/teha.**

2 Kõigepealt läheme **sööma/süüa.**

3 Siis saate natuke **puhkama/puhata**.

4 Kell kaksteist läheme **ujuma/ujuda.**

5 Siis peame natuke **maalima/maalida.**

6 Pärast sõidame **pildistama/pildistada.**

7 Teile kindlasti meeldib autoga **sõitma/sõita.**

8 Õhtul saate saunas käima/käia ja **tantsima/tantsida.**

9 Magama peab **minema/minna** kell kaksteist.

 Speaking

EXERCISE 18

Here are some situations for you to practise. You are walking to the hotel bar to rest.

    a You see a sign at the door which says **Tere tulemast!** What does it mean?

    b There is also the following text on the door: **E–N 12.00–24.00; R–P 12.00–03.00**. What does it mean?

    c Someone says you **Saame tuttavaks!** What does he want?

d Then he says his name and asks **Kust te pärit olete?** How do you answer?

e Then he says **Mina olen firmajuht.** How do you say your profession?

f Then you are asked **Mida teile meeldib teha vabal ajal?** What does it mean?

EXERCISE 19

Complete this dialogue by filling in the missing lines of conversation. You are introducing yourself at a business meeting.

a Say *Hello!*

b Say your name.

c Say you come from America.

d Say you are the director of a business.

EXERCISE 20

Complete this dialogue by filling in the missing lines of conversation. You sit next to a person you don't know in a language class and would like to get to know her a little bit. Everybody is using informal address in the class. After you have completed the dialogue listen and check.

 05.05

Sina	*Say* Let's get acquainted! *Say* I am …
Jane	Väga meeldiv. Mina olen Jane.
Sina	*Ask* Where are you from?
Jane	Mina olen pärit Inglismaalt. Kust sina pärit oled?
Sina	*Say* I am from America.
Jane	Mida sulle meeldib teha vabal ajal?
Sina	*Say* I like to travel and take photos.
Jane	Mulle meeldib ujuda ja saunas käia.

EXERCISE 21

Complete this dialogue by filling in the missing lines of conversation. You are discussing with a new friend what you like to do in your free time. After you have completed the dialogue listen and check.

 05.06

Sõber	Mida sulle meeldib teha vabal ajal?
Sina	*Say you like to swim.*
Sõber	Hmm. Mina ei oska ujuda.
Sina	*Ask your friend what he/she likes to do in his/her free time.*
Sõber	Mulle meeldib muusikat kuulata.
Sina	*Say you like to listen to music too.*

? Test yourself

1 You want to say *Welcome!* What do you say?

   a Tere tulemast!

   b Väga meeldiv!

   c Saame tuttavaks!

2 Which ones are the names of the seasons?

   a kevad, suvi, sügis talv

   b üleeile, eile, täna, homme

   c hommik, päev, õhtu, öö

3 What is the translation of question *When?*

   a Kust?

   b Millal?

   c Kuhu?

4 You want to say you are from England. What do you say?

   a Ma lähen Inglismaale.

   b Ma olen Inglismaal.

   c Ma olen pärit Inglismaalt.

5 You want to ask *Where are you from?* What do you say?

   a Kust sa pärit oled?

   b Mida sulle meeldib teha vabal ajal?

   c Kas sa armastad mind?

6 Which one of the phrases means *during the weekend*?

   a nädalavahetusel

   b laupäev ja pühapäev

   c nädalavahetus

7 How do you say *I like to take photos*?

   a Ma lähen pildistama.

   b Ma hakkan pildistama.

   c Mulle meeldib pildistada.

8 Which one of the sentences means that **Piret likes Marek**?

   a Marekile meeldib Piret.

   b Piretile ei meeldi Marek.

   c Piretile meeldib Marek.

9 How do you say *I don't like to travel*?

  a Mulle meeldib reisida.

  b Mulle ei meeldi reisida.

  c Ma armastan reisida.

10 What does the sentence **Ma lähen Tallinnasse** mean?

  a I am from Tallinn.

  b I live in Tallinn.

  c I will go to Tallinn.

6 Milline on sinu päev?

What's your day like?

In this unit you will learn:
▶ *How to speak about your family and relatives*
▶ *How to talk about daily routines*
▶ *How to say the ordinal numbers*

Listening 1

You will hear how Kaspar and Ave get acquainted. Listen to the dialogues and then complete Exercises 1–2.

 06.01

Kaspar	Tere. Minu nimi on Kaspar. Kas see koht on vaba?
Ave	On küll. Mina olen Ave.
Kaspar	Kellena te töötate, Ave?
Ave	Olen hambaarst. Aga teie?
Kaspar	Mina olen vene keele õpetaja.
Ave	Kas te olete venelane?
Kaspar	Minu vanaisa on venelane, aga minu vanemad on eestlased.
Ave	Väga huvitav! Kui vana teie vanaisa on?
Kaspar	Ta on 92 aastat vana.
Ave	Tõesti?
Kaspar	Jah, ta on väga tubli. Milline on teie pere?
Ave	Mul on mees ja kolm last – kaks tütart ja üks poeg. Ja siis on meil veel suur koer.
Kaspar	Kui vanad teie lapsed on?
Ave	Tütred on juba suured: üks on 20 aastat vana ja teine 22. Nende väike vend on aga kolm aastat vana.
Kaspar	Ja kes on teie abikaasa?
Ave	Minu mees on lendur.
Kaspar	Väga huvitav!

V	
koht, **koha, kohta**	*place*
vaba, -, -	*free*
Kellena te töötate?	*What's your profession? (lit. as who do you work)*
hambaarst, -i, -i	*dentist*
vanaisa, -, -	*grandfather*
venela/ne, -se, -st	*Russian*
vanemad	*parents*
eestla/ne, -se, -st	*Estonian*
väga huvitav	*very interesting*
Kui vana teie vanaisa on?	*How old is your grandfather?*
Ta on 92 aastat vana.	*He is 92 years old.*
Tõesti?	*Really?*
väga tubli	*doing well, good man (lit. untranslatable as one word)*
milli/ne, -se, -st	*what kind of*
pere, -, -t	*family*
mees, mehe, meest	*man, husband*
laps, lapse, last	*child*
tütar, tütre, tütart	*daughter*
poeg, poja, poega	*son*
koer, -a, -a	*dog*
väike(ne), -se, -st	*small*
vend, venna, venda	*brother*
abikaasa, -, -t	*spouse, husband*
lendur, -i, -it	*pilot*

EXERCISE 1

Choose the correct answer according to the dialogue.

1 Ave is **a** teacher, **b** dentist, **c** pilot.

2 Kaspar is **a** teacher of Estonian, **b** teacher of English, **c** teacher of Russian.

3 Kaspar's parents are **a** Estonians, **b** Russians, **c** English.

4 Kaspar's grandfather is **a** 82 years old, **b** 92 years old, **c** 98 years old.

5 Ave has **a** one child, **b** two children, **c** three children.

6 Ave's children are **a** 18, 20 and 4 years old, **b** 2, 13 and 20 years old, **c** 20, 22 and 3 years old.

7 Ave's husband is **a** journalist, **b** construction worker, **c** pilot.

EXERCISE 2

Choose the correct question.

1 You want to know the other person's profession.
   a Kellena te töötate?
   b Kui vana te olete?

2 **You want to ask what the other person likes to do during his/her free time.**

  a Milline on teie pere?

  b Mida teile meeldib teha vabal ajal?

3 **You would like to ask if the other person is Estonian.**

  a Kas te olete eestlane?

  b Kas see koht on vaba?

4 **You would like to ask if the other person has big family.**

  a Kes on teie abikaasa?

  b Kas teil on suur pere?

5 **You would like to ask about the age of other person's children.**

  a Kui vanad teie lapsed on?

  b Kui vana teie vanaisa on?

6 **You would like to ask who is the other person's husband.**

  a Kui vana on teie abikaasa?

  b Kes on teie abikaasa?

Listening 2

 06.02

You will hear Andrus telling about his day. He is 44 years old, married and has two daughters. Listen to the text and then complete Exercises 3–4.

> Mina olen Andrus. Ma ärkan iga päev kell seitse. Siis ma jalutan koeraga väljas. Minu naine teeb samal ajal hommikusöögi. Umbes kell pool kaheksa me sööme hommikust. Siis mina pesen nõusid. Kell kaheksa lähevad lapsed kooli ja mina sõidan jalgrattaga tööle. Tööl ma pean palju suhtlema: helistama, e-maile kirjutama ja inimestega kohtuma. Kell viis ma lähen trenni või sõpradega baari. Pärast trenni ma lähen koju, loen Internetist uudiseid ja vaatan telerit. Lapsed kuulavad muusikat. Mõnikord me mängime naisega malet. Vahel tulevad sõbrad külla. Paar korda kuus käime teatris või ööklubis. Umbes kell üksteist ma lähen magama.

ärka/ma, ärga/ta, ärka/n	*to wake up*
iga päev	*every day*
siis	*then*
jaluta/ma, -da, -n	*to walk*
väljas	*outside*
hommikusööki tege/ma, hommikusööki teh/a tee/n hommikusööki	*to make breakfast*
umbes	*about*

hommikust söö/ma, hommikust süü/a, söö/n hommikust	*to eat breakfast*
nõusid pese/ma, nõusid pest/a, pesen nõusid	*to wash dishes*
jalg/ratas, -ratta, -ratast	*bicycle*
pida/ma, pida/da, pea/n	*to have to, must*
suhtle/ma, suhel/da, suhtle/n	*to communicate*
helista/ma, -da, -n	*to call (on the phone)*
e-mail, -i, -i	*email*
kirjuta/ma, -da, -n	*to write*
e-maile kirjutama	*to write e-mails*
inime/ne, -se, -st	*human, person, man*
kohtu/ma, -da, -n	*to meet*
inimestega kohtuma	*to meet people*
trenn, -i, -i	*training, workout (sport)*
sõber, sõbra, sõpra	*friend*
sõpradega	*with friends*
pärast trenni	*after the workout*
lähen koju	*I go home*
luge/ma, luge/da, loe/n	*to read*
internet, interneti, internetti	*internet*
uudised	*news*
loen internetist uudiseid	*I read news on the internet*
vaata/ma, vaada/ta, vaata/n	*to watch*
teler, -i, -it	*TV (set)*
mõnikord	*sometimes*
malet mängi/ma, malet mängi/da, mängi/n mallet	*to play chess*
vahel	*sometimes*
külla tule/ma, külla tull/a, tule/n külla	*to come to visit*
paar korda kuus	*a couple of times a month*
teatris käi/ma, teatris käi/a, käi/n teatris	*to go to theatre*
ööklubi, -, -	*nightclub*
magama mine/ma, magama minn/a, lähen maga/ma	*to go to sleep*

EXERCISE 3

Listen to what Andrus tells about his day. Put the things he does during the day in the correct order according to the text.

    a Umbes kell üksteist ma lähen magama.

    b Suhtlen, helistan, kirjutan e-maile ja kohtun inimestega.

    c Söidan jalgrattaga tööle.

    d Pesen nõusid.

e Loen internetist uudiseid ja vaatan telerit.

f Lähen koju.

g Kell viis ma lähen trenni.

h Pool kaheksa sööme hommikust.

i Jalutan koeraga.

j Ärkan kell seitse.

EXERCISE 4

Find the sentence for each of the pictures. Do the exercise once more without looking at the text.

a Ma vaatan telerit.

b Ma ei söö hommikust.

c Ma ärkan kell kaheksa.

d Ma sõidan jalgrattaga tööle.

e Ma pesen nõusid.

f Ma helistan inimestele.

g Ma jalutan koeraga.

h Ma loen internetist uudiseid.

i Ma mängin malet.

j Ma lähen magama.

1

2

3

4

5

6

> **INSIGHT**
>
> Find a comfortable time every day to study the language. Spending 30 minutes every day is a much more effective way of learning than three hours once a week.

Language patterns

MUL ON SUUR PERE *I HAVE A BIG FAMILY – ADESSIVE CASE*

Look at the following sentences:

Mul on suur pere.	*I have a big family.*
Sul on suur pere.	*You* (sing.) *have a big family.*
Tal on suur pere.	*He/she has a big family.*
Meil on suur pere.	*We have a big family.*
Teil on suur pere.	*You* (pl.) *have a big family.*
Neil on suur pere.	*They have a big family.*
Avel on oma firma.	*Ave has her own company.*
Kasparil on vanaisa.	*Kaspar has a grandfather.*
Avel on kaks tütart ja poeg.	*Ave has two daughters and a son.*

The construction *I have* is different in English and Estonian. We add the case ending **-l** to the end of the person who is the owner. For instance, **Avel on kolm last** *Ave has three children.* As you can see, for the verb *to have* in Estonian, the word **olema** is used (**olema** is the equivalent of English *to be*).

EXERCISE 5

Translate these sentences.

1 I have a dog.

2 You (sing.) have a daughter.

3 He has a son.

4 We have our own company.

5 You (pl.) have a grandfather.

6 They have children.

In order to practise this grammar topic further do Exercises 10–11 in the Practice section.

Some facts about Estonian population and family

▶ In spite of covering an area of 45,000 sq km Estonia's population ranks among the smallest in Europe: as of January 2000, an estimated 1,361,242 people live in Estonia – a density of only 30.2 people per sq km.

▶ Every third person (approximately 400,000 people) lives in Tallinn and about 70% of the population reside in cities in general.

▶ According to the statistics of 2005 the most typical Estonian family consists of parents with 1 or 2 children.

▶ The average age of marrying is 29 for men and 26 for women; about 50% of the marriages end with a divorce. Cohabitation is quite common in Estonia.

▶ Only every tenth family has more than three children and families with children can be found in the countryside twice as often as in towns.

▶ Fifty per cent of the employed population are women; women's share of employment ranks among the highest in Europe.

But let's leave the statistics for now and learn some useful 'family words'.

 06.03

Listen to the recording and repeat.

ema, -, -	*mother*
isa, -, -	*father*
vanavanemad	*grandparents*
vanemad	*parents*
sugula/ne, -se, -st	*relative*
tädi, -, -	*aunt*
tädi/poeg, -poja, -poega	*cousin* (lit. *son of aunt*)
tädi/tütar, -tütre, -tütart	*cousin* (lit. *daughter of aunt*)
onu, -, -	*uncle*
onu/poeg, -poja, -poega	*cousin* (lit. *son of uncle*)
onu/tütar, -tütre, -tütart	*cousin* (lit. *daughter of uncle*)
õde, õe, õde	*sister*

vend, venna, venda	*brother*
venna/poeg, -poja, -poega	*nephew* (lit. *son of brother*)
venna/tütar, -tütre, -tütart	*niece* (lit. *daughter of brother*)
õe/poeg, -poja, -poega	*nephew* (lit. *son of sister*)
õe/tütar, -tütre, -tütart	*niece* (lit. *daughter of sister*)
ämm, -a, -a	*mother-in-law*
äi, -a, -a	*father-in-law*
minia, -, -t	*daughter-in-law*
väi/mees, -mehe, -meest	*son-in-law*
abielus	*married*
vabaabielus	*cohabiting*
elukaasla/ne, -se, -st	*partner* (someone you live with but are not married to)
lahutatud	*divorced*
lesk	*widow, widower* (both male and female)
vallali/ne, -se, -st	*single*
tüdruk/sõber, -sõbra, -sõpra	*girlfriend*
poiss-sõber, -sõbra, -sõpra	*boyfriend*

MINU VENNA NIMI ON MEELIS *MY BROTHER'S NAME IS MEELIS – GENITIVE CASE*

If you want to tell someone your relative's name, you can say:

Minu onupoja nimi on Siim.	*My cousin's name is Siim.*
Minu ämma nimi on Maret.	*My mother-in-law's name is Maret.*

Note that **minu** *my* is the second form of **mina** *I*. Also, the word for relative has to be in the second form, i.e. **Minu venna** nimi on Meelis.

EXERCISE 6

Translate into Estonian the following:

1 My husband's name is Tõnu.

2 My wife's name is Külli.

3 My child's name is Birgit.

4 My son's name is Kaspar.

5 My daughter's name is Sille.

6 My sister's name is Tiina.

7 My brother's name is Aivar.

RAHVUSED *NATIONALITIES*

 06.04

Most names of nationalities in Estonian end in **-lane.** Listen to the recording and repeat.

eest**lane**	*Estonian*
vene**lane**	*Russian*

ing**lane**	*English*
saks**lane**	*German*
prants**lane**	*French*
itaal**lane**	*Italian*
hispaan**lane**	*Spanish*
jaapan**lane**	*Japanese*

Note that in the dictionary, the words ending in **-lane** or **-ne** will be presented the following way: **eestla/ne, -se, -st**. This means the three forms will read: **eestlane, eestlase, eestlast**.

Although gender is not usually expressed grammatically in Estonian, there are a few cases when it is possible. For instance with nationalities, if you want to stress that the person you are talking about is a woman, you can add the ending **-lanna** i.e. eest**lan**na *Estonian (lady)*, prants**lan**na, *French (lady)* jaapan**lanna** *Japanese (lady)* etc. Remember that in official documents women will still write **eestlane** *Estonian* for their nationality not **eestlanna** *Estonian (lady)*.

Note that the names of nationalities are not written with a capital letter in Estonian.

If you want to say *French restaurant* or *Estonian food*, you can't use the word for nationality but you use the same word we use for languages, e.g. **prantsuse keel** *French (language)* – **prantsuse restoran** *French restaurant*, **eesti keel** *Estonian (language)* – **eesti toit** *Estonian food*.

MA TÖÖTAN ARSTINA *I WORK AS A DOCTOR – ESSIVE CASE*

In answer to the question **Kellena te töötate?** *What's your profession?* (lit. *as who do you work?*) the case ending **-na** is added to the word, for instance **Ma töötan arstina** *I work as a doctor*. You can also say **Ma olen arst** *I am a doctor*. In this case it is not necessary to add any case ending.

Here are some more examples.

Ma töötan ehitaj**ana**.	*I work as a construction worker.*
Peeter töötab ajakirjanik**una**.	*Peeter works as a journalist.*
Kaspar töötab õpetaj**ana**.	*Kaspar works as a teacher.*
Ave töötab hambaarst**ina**.	*Ave works as a dentist.*

EXERCISE 7

Choose the right word.

1 Ma töötan **õpetaja/õpetajana**.

2 Ma olen **õpetaja/õpetajana**.

3 Ma töötan **ehitaja/ehitajana**.

4 Ma olen **ehitaja/ehitajana**

5 Ma töötan **hambaarst/hambaarstina**.

6 Ma olen **ajakirjanik/ajakirjanikuna**.

KUI VANA SA OLED? *HOW OLD ARE YOU?*

The most common question for asking about someone's age is **Kui vana sa oled?** *How old are you?* (sing. informal) or **Kui vana te olete?** *How old are you?* (pl. formal).

The easiest way to answer is by inserting the number in the following sentence:

Ma olen ... aastat vana.   *I am ... years old.*

For instance:

Kui vana sa oled?	*How old are you? (sing. informal)*
Ma olen nelikümmend viis aastat vana.	*I'm 45 years old.*
Kui vana on sinu abikaasa?	*How old is your husband? (sing. informal)*
Minu abikaasa on viiskümmend aastat vana.	*My husband is 50 years old.*
Kui vanad on sinu lapsed?	*How old are your children? (sing. informal)*
Minu poeg on kaheksateist aastat vana ja minu tütar on üheksa aastat vana.	*My son is 18 and my daughter is 9 years old.*

MINU SÜNNIPÄEV ON SEPTEMBRIS *MY BIRTHDAY IS IN SEPTEMBER*

As we have already learnt, in answer to the question **Millal?** *When?* the letter **-l** is usually added to the end of the answer, for instance laupäeva**l** on *Saturday*, hommiku**l** *in the morning* etc. As an exception, when using the name of the month we add **-s** to the answer, for instance septembri**s** *in September*, märtsi**s** *in March* etc.

EXERCISE 8

 06.05

Fill in the blanks, then listen to the correct answers.

mis kuu? *what month?*	millal? mis kuus? *when? in what month?*
jaanuar, -i, -i	jaanuari**s**
veebruar, -i, -i	veebruari**s**
märts, -i, -i	märtsi**s**
aprill, -i, -i	
mai, -, -d	
juuni, -, -t	
juuli, -, -t	
august, -i, -it	
september, septembri, septembrit	
oktoober, oktoobri, oktoobrit	
november, novembri, novembrit	
detsember, detsembri, detsembrit	

In order to further practise this grammar topic do Exercises 12–13 in the Practice section.

MINU SÜNNIPÄEV ON ESIMESEL SEPTEMBRIL *MY BIRTHDAY IS ON THE FIRST OF SEPTEMBER – ORDINAL NUMBERS*

We have already learnt the main numerals (like **üks** *one*, **kaks** *two*, **kolm** *three*). Now we will learn the ordinal numerals (like **esimene** *first*, **teine** *second*, **kolmas** *third* etc). Once you know the main numerals it is very easy to remember the ordinal numerals, as you just have to add **-s** to the second form of the number, i.e.:

first form	second form	ordinal numeral
neli *four*	**nelja** + s =	**neljas** *fourth*
kümme *ten*	**kümne** + s =	**kümnes** *tenth*

Note that **esimene** *first* and **teine** *second* are irregular and that we say kolm**as** *third* (not kolm**es**).

Like most words in Estonian, the ordinal numerals also have three main forms, which are, fortunately, the same (see the following table). If we want to answer the question **millal?** the ending **-l** is added to the second form:

		millal? *when?*
1.	**esime**/ne, -se, -st	esimesel
2.	**tei**/ne, -se, -st	teisel
3.	**kolma**/s, -nda, -ndat	kolmandal
4.	**nelja**/s, -nda, -ndat	neljandal
5.	**viie**/s, -nda, -ndat	viiendal
6.	**kuue**/s, -nda, -ndat	kuuendal
7.	**seitsme**/s, -nda, -ndat	seitsmendal
8.	**kaheksa**/s, -nda, -ndat	kaheksandal
9.	**üheksa**/s, -nda, -ndat	üheksandal
10.	**kümne**/s, -nda, -ndat	kümnendal
11.	**üheteistkümne**/s, -nda, -ndat	üheteistkümnendal
12.	**kaheteistkümne**/s, -nda, -ndat	kaheteistkümnendal
13.	**kolmeteistkümne**/s, -nda, -ndat	kolmeteistkümnendal
14.	**neljateistkümne**/s, -nda, -ndat	neljateistkümnendal
15.	**viieteistkümne**/s, -nda, -ndat	viieteistkümnendal
16.	**kuueteistkümne**/s, -nda, -ndat	kuueteistkümnendal
17.	**seitsmeteistkümne**/s, -nda, -ndat	seitsmeteistkümnendal
18.	**kaheksateistkümne**/s, -nda, -ndat	kaheksateistkümnendal
19.	**üheksateistkümne**/s, -nda, -ndat	üheksateistkümnendal
20.	**kahekümne**/s, -nda, -ndat	kahekümnendal
21.	**kahekümne esime**/ne, -se, -st	kahekümne esimesel
22.	**kahekümne tei**/ne, -se, -st	kahekümne teisel
23.	**kahekümne kolma**/s, -nda, -ndat	kahekümne kolmandal
30.	**kolmekümne**/s, -nda, -ndat	kolmekümnendal

40.	**neljakümne**/s, -nda, -ndat	neljakümnenda**l**
50.	**viiekümne**/s, -nda, -ndat	viiekümnenda**l**
60.	**kuuekümne**/s, -nda, -ndat	kuuekümnenda**l**
70.	**seitsmekümne**/s, -ndat, -dat	seitsmekümnenda**l**
80.	**kaheksakümne**/s, -nda, -ndat	kaheksakümnenda**l**
90.	**üheksakümne**/s, -nda, -ndat	üheksakümnenda**l**
100.	**saja**/s, -nda, -ndat	sajanda**l**
101.	**saja esime**/ne, -se, -st	saja esimese**l**
110.	**saja kümne**/s, -nda, -ndat	saja kümnenda**l**
1000.	**tuhande**/s, -nda, -ndat	tuhandenda**l**
1967.	**tuhande üheksasaja kuuekümne seitsme**/s, -nda, -ndat	tuhande üheksasaja kuuekümne seitsmenda**l**
2000.	**kahe tuhandes**, -nda, -ndat	kahe tuhandenda**l**
2008.	**kahe tuhande kaheksa**/s, -nda –ndat	kahe tuhande kaheksanda**l**

Note that in Estonian there has to be a full stop after an ordinal number i.e.

1. september *1st of September,* **24. juuli** *24th of July.*

Listen to the ordinal numbers 1–20 and repeat.

 06.06

EXERCISE 9

 06.07

Make similar sentences, following the example, then listen and check.

1 Mis kuupäev on täna? *What date is it today?*
   a 4. mai – *Täna on neljas mai.*
   b 10. september – _____
   c 12. oktoober – _____
   d 26. detsember – _____

2 Millal on tema sünnipäev? *When is his birthday?*
   a 2. jaanuar – *Tema sünnipäev on teisel jaanuaril.*
   b 14. veebruar – _____
   c 19. aprill – _____
   d 31. juuli – _____

3 Mis aastal ta on sündinud? *In what year was he/she born?*
   a 1962. a – *Ta on sündinud tuhande üheksasaja kuuekümne teisel aastal.*
   b 1978. a – _____
   c 2007. a – _____

In order to practise this grammar topic further do Exercises 14–16 in the Practice section.

Practice

EXERCISE 10

Make questions using the following example. Translate the questions.

1 They – daughter   Kas neil on tütar?

Do they have a daughter?

2 You (sing.) – car   Kas _____?

3 Maria – husband   Kas _____?

4 He – dog   Kas _____?

5 You (pl.) – family   Kas _____?

EXERCISE 11

Choose the correct form.

1 Joosepile/Joosepil meeldib sportida.

2 Kaidole/Kaidol on oma firma.

3 Avele/Avel on kolm last.

4 Avele/Avel meeldib tantsida.

5 Mulle/Mul on suur koer.

6 Kasparile/Kasparil meeldib juttu ajada.

7 Marekile/Marekil on kaks vanaisa.

8 Lembitule/Lembitul meeldib muusikat kuulata.

EXERCISE 12

Write the months that come before and after in Estonian.

1 _____ märts _____

2 _____ juuli _____

3 _____ november _____

4 _____ veebruar _____

EXERCISE 13

 06.08

Use the words in brackets in the correct form. Listen to the recording for the correct answers. Then read the exercise once more using the real names of the months in the sentences which are relevant to your family.

1 Minu sünnipäev on (jaanuar)

2 Minu ema sünnipäev on (veebruar)

3 Minu isa sünnipäev on (märts)

4 Minu vanaema sünnipäev on (aprill)

5 Minu vanaisa sünnipäev on (mai)

6 Minu venna sünnipäev on (juuni)

7 Minu õe sünnipäev on (juuli)

8 Minu tädi sünnipäev on (august)

9 Minu onu sünnipäev on (september)

10 Minu lapse sünnipäev on (oktoober)

11 Minu sõbra sünnipäev on (november)

12 Minu ülemuse sünnipäev on (detsember)

EXERCISE 14

Find the right match.

1 Kontsert toimub 5. jaanuaril.	**a** Kontsert toimub üheksandal jaanuaril.
2 Kontsert toimub 8. jaanuaril.	**b** Kontsert toimub kolmeteistkümnendal jaanuaril.
3 Kontsert toimub 9. jaanuaril.	**c** Kontsert toimub kaheksateistkümnendal jaanuaril.
4 Kontsert toimub 11. jaanuaril.	**d** Kontsert toimub kahekümne viiendal jaanuaril.
5 Kontsert toimub 13. jaanuaril.	**e** Kontsert toimub viiendal jaanuaril.
6 Kontsert toimub 15. jaanuaril.	**f** Kontsert toimub üheksateistkümnendal jaanuaril.
7 Kontsert toimub 18. jaanuaril.	**g** Kontsert toimub üheteistkümnendal jaanuaril.
8 Kontsert toimub 19. jaanuaril.	**h** Kontsert toimub kolmekümne esimesel jaanuaril.
9 Kontsert toimub 25. jaanuaril.	**i** Kontsert toimub viieteistkümnendal jaanuaril.
10 Kontsert toimub 31. jaanuaril.	**j** Kontsert toimub kaheksandal jaanuaril.

EXERCISE 15

 06.09

Listen to the recording and then fill in the right date.

1 Tema sünnipäev on _____ märtsil.

2 Tema sünnipäev on _____ märtsil.

3 Tema sünnipäev on _____ märtsil.

4 Tema sünnipäev on _____ märtsil.

5 Tema sünnipäev on _____ märtsil.

6 Tema sünnipäev on _____ märtsil.

7 Tema sünnipäev on _____ märtsil.

8 Tema sünnipäev on _____ märtsil.

9 Tema sünnipäev on _____ märtsil.

10 Tema sünnipäev on _____ märtsil.

EXERCISE 16

06.10

Read the following sentences out loud. Listen to the recording to check your answers.

1 Kontsert toimub 5. jaanuaril.

2 Filmifestival algab 28. juunil ja lõpeb 15. augustil.

3 Tema sünnipäev on 30. jaanuaril.

4 Ta on sündinud 1978. aastal.

5 Ma olen sündinud 1982. aastal.

6 Kas sa oled sündinud 1969. aastal?

7 Me oleme sündinud 1954. aastal.

8 Nad on sündinud 2000. aastal.

9 Kas te olete sündinud 1963. aastal?

10 Nad ei ole sündinud 2008. aastal.

 Speaking

EXERCISE 17

Complete this dialogue by filling in the missing lines of conversation. You are looking at the family photos of a friend who has a son and a daughter. After you have completed the dialogue listen and check.

 06.11

Sina	Ask your friend How old is your son?
Sõber	Ta on kümme aastat vana.
Sina	Ask your friend But how old is your daughter?
Sõber	Tütar on viisteist aastat vana.
Sina	Say I also have a daughter.
Sõber	Kui vana sinu tütar on?
Sina	Say She is 17 years old.
Sõber	Millal tema sünnipäev on?
Sina	Say On the 15th of May.

EXERCISE 18

06.12

Complete this dialogue by filling in the missing lines of conversation. You are having a job interview. You have already been asked about your professional skills and now you have to answer some more personal questions. Translate the questions in bold first. After you have completed the dialogue, listen to the recording and check.

   a You are asked **Kui vana te olete?**

   b Say *I am 36 years old.*

   c You are asked **Kas teil on lapsed?**

   d Say you have one daughter.

   e You are asked **Kui vana teie tütar on?**

   f Say *She is 12 years old.*

   g You are asked **Kellena teie abikaasa töötab?**

   h Say *She/he is a journalist.*

   i You are asked **Kas teil on oma auto?**

   j Answer *Yes, I have my own car.*

   k You are asked **Kas te olete eestlane?**

   l Say *I am German, but my father is Swedish.*

EXERCISE 19

06.13

Speak about your day. Listen to the recording to check your answers.

   a Say *I wake up at eight every morning.*

   b Say *Then I walk outside with the dog.*

   c Say *Then I make breakfast.*

   d Say *I drive to work by car.*

   e Say *At work I have to make phone calls, write e-mails and meet people.*

   f Say *At work I also read news from the internet.*

   g Say *At six I go to work out with friends.*

   h Say *After the workout I go home.*

   i Say *Sometimes friends come to visit.*

   j Say *A couple of times a month I go to the theatre.*

   k Say *At twelve o'clock I go to sleep.*

❓ Test yourself

1 You are asked **Kellena te töötate?** What does it mean?
  a How old are you?
  b Is this place free?
  c What is your profession?

2 What is the correct answer to the question **Milline on teie pere?**
  a On küll. Mina olen Kristiina.
  b Mul on abikaasa ja üks poeg.
  c Ta on väga tubli.

3 How do you ask *Do you have a dog?*
  a Ka neil on koer?
  b Kas tal on koer?
  c Kas sul on koer?

4 Who is **vennatütar**?
  a niece (lit. daughter of brother)
  b nephew (lit. son of sister)
  c son in law

5 How is correct to say *My sister's name is Ann*?
  a Minu naise nimi on Ann.
  b Minu õe nimi on Ann.
  c Minu minia nimi on Ann.

6 How do you say *My birthday is on the 12th of December*?
  a Minu sünnipäev on kaheteistkümnendal detsembril.
  b Minu sünnipäev on kaheksateistkümnendal detsembril.
  c Minu sünnipäev on kahekümne teisel detsembril.

7 Ta on sündinud tuhande üheksasaja seitsmekümne üheksandal aastal. What does it mean?
  a He was born in 1971.
  b He was born in 1978.
  c He was born in 1979.

8 What do people usually do in the office?
  a söövad, joovad ja tantsivad
  b helistavad, kirjutavad e-maile ja suhtlevad
  c mängivad malet, vaatavad telerit ja pesevad nõusid

9 How do you ask in Estonian *How old are you?*

   a Kas te olete venelane?

   b Kui vana te olete?

   c Kes on teie abikaasa?

10 What does the sentence **Vahel tulevad sõbrad külla.** mean?

   a Sometimes friends come to visit.

   b Sometimes I go with my friends to the training.

   c Sometimes my friend likes to walk.

Lähme turule!
Let's go to the market!

In this unit you will learn:
▶ *How to buy food at the market*

Listening 1

You will hear people buying food at the market. Listen to the dialogues and complete Exercises 1–2 below.

 07.01

a	**Ostja**	Kui palju see juust maksab?
	Müüja	Seitsekümmend krooni kilo.
	Ostja	Palun siis pool kilo.
	Müüja	Kohe.
b	**Ostja**	Tere. Kui palju need ploomid maksavad?
	Müüja	Kakskümmend krooni kilo.
	Ostja	Palun siis kaks kilo.
	Müüja	Valige ise välja.
c	**Ostja**	Tere. Kui palju see kala maksab?
	Müüja	Kakssada krooni kilo.
	Ostja	Oi, kui kallis!
	Müüja	No aga see on ka väga hea kala.
d	**Ostja**	Tere. Kui palju need sibulad maksavad?
	Müüja	Kümme krooni kilo.
	Ostja	Ohoo, kui odavad!
	Müüja	Jah, see on tõesti väga soodne hind.

 TIP

Please note since 1 January 2011 the Estonian currency has been the Euro.

ostja, -, -t, -id	*buyer*
müüja, -, -t, -id	*seller, salesman/saleswoman*
kui palju	*how much*
juust, -u, -u	*cheese*
maks/ma, -ta, -an	*to cost, to pay*
Kui palju see juust maksab?	*How much does the cheese cost?*
kilo, -, -	*kilo*
siis	*here: in this case*
ploom, -i, -i, -e	*plum*
välja vali/ma, välja vali/da, vali/n välja	*to select*
ise	*yourself*

116

kala, -, -, -sid	*fish*
kallis, kalli, kallist, kalleid	*expensive*
Oi kui kallis!	*Oh, how expensive!*
Väga	*very*
hea, -, -d, häid	*good*
sibul, -a, -at, -aid	*onion*
odav, -a, -at, -aid	*cheap*
Ohhoo kui odavad!	*Oh, how cheap* (pl.)*!*
sood/ne, -sa, -sat, said	*bargain, cheap, good*
hind, hinna, hinda, hindu	*price*

Note that from this unit on, four main forms are given for nouns. See also *'Measures'* after Exercise 9, below.

EXERCISE 1

Listen and decide if the following sentences are **a** true or **b** false.

a 1 The buyer asks about the price of cheese.

   2 Cheese costs 60 crowns a kilo.

   3 He decides to buy one kilo of cheese.

b 1 The buyer asks about the price of pears.

   2 The fruit costs 80 crowns a kilo.

   3 He decides to buy two kilos.

c 1 The buyer asks about the price of fish.

   2 Fish costs 200 crowns a kilo.

   3 He thinks it's a bargain price.

d 1 The buyer asks about the price of onions.

   2 Onions cost 20 crowns a kilo.

   3 He thinks it's not a good price.

EXERCISE 2

What does the seller say? Choose the correct translation.

1 See on väga hea juust.
   a The price of this cheese is very good.
   b This is very good cheese.

2 Valige ploomid ise välja.
   a Select the plums yourself.
   b I will select the plums for you.

3 Kala hind on tõesti väga soodne.
   a The fish costs 100 crowns a kilo.
   b The price of fish is really good.

Listening 2

You will hear some more people buying food at the market. Listen to the dialogues and complete Exercises 3–4 below.

 07.02

a	Ostja	Tervist! Kas teil on taist sinki?
	Müüja	Ikka on. Vaadake, siin.
	Ostja	Aga kas see on äkki väga soolane?
	Müüja	Ei ole soolane, maitske ise!
	Ostja	Mmm. Suurepärane maitse. Ma võtan pool kilo.
b	Ostja	Tere! Palun kaks kilo kollaseid õunu.
	Müüja	Jah, palun. Aga kollaseid õunu on kahte sorti. Kumba te soovite?
	Ostja	Oi, ma ei tea. Ma tahaksin magusaid.
	Müüja	Siis võtke neid. Need on tõesti väga magusad.
	Ostja	Jah, pange siis neid kaks kilo.
c	Müüja	Astuge ligi, proua! Proovige palun neid magusaid maasikaid.
	Ostja	Jah, tõesti väga maitsvad. Aga kas need on eesti omad?
	Müüja	Muidugi! Loomulikult! Need on Lõuna-Eestist.
	Ostja	No siis ma võtan kohe viis kilo.
	Müüja	Jah, palun. Hakkate moosi tegema, jah?
	Ostja	Ei, sööme niisama ära.

 Kas teil on? — *Do you have?*

tai/ne, -se, -st, -seid — *lean*

sink, singi, sinki — *ham*

ikka on — *sure we have*

äkki here: — *maybe*

soola/ne, -se, -st, -seid — *salty*

maits/ma, -ta, -en — *to taste*

maitske — *taste (pl. imperative)*

suurepära/ne, -se, -st, -seid — *excellent*

maitse, -, -t, -id — *taste*

võt/ma, -ta, -an — *to take, to buy*

kolla/ne, -se, -st, -seid — *yellow*

õun, -a, -a, -u — *apple*

sort, sordi, sorti, sorte — *sort, type*

kaks sorti — *two sorts*

kumb, -a, -a, -i — *which one*

tead/ma, -a, tea/n — *to know*

taht/ma, -a, taha/n — *to want*

magus, -a, -at, -aid — *sweet*

pane/ma, pann/a, pane/n — *to put, to give*

pange — *to give (pl. imperative)*

ligi astu/ma, ligi astu/da, astu/n ligi	*to step closer*
proovi/ma, -da, -n	*to try*
maasikas, maasika, maasikat, maasikaid	*strawberry*
maitsev, maitsva, maitsvat, maitsvaid	*tasty*
eesti omad	*Estonian* (pl.)
muidugi	*of course*
loomulikult	*naturally*
Lõuna-Eestist	*from southern Estonia*
moos, -i, -i, -e	*jam*
moosi tege/ma, moosi teh/a, tee/n moosi	*to make jam*
ära söö/ma, ära süü/a, söö/n ära	*to eat up*
niisama	*just so*

EXERCISE 3

Listen and choose the right answer.

a 1 The buyer wants to buy **a** ham, **b** meat, **c** fish.

2 The buyer is worried that maybe the food is **a** very expensive, **b** very salty, **c** very spicy.

3 The buyer says the taste is **a** strange, **b** excellent, **c** bad.

4 The buyer buys **a** one kilo, **b** two kilos, **c** half a kilo.

b 1 The buyer wants to have **a** two kilos of apples, **b** two kilos of oranges, **c** two kilos of pears.

2 There are **a** two sorts of apple, **b** three sorts of apple, **c** four sorts of apple.

3 The buyer would like to have **a** bigger apples, **b** smaller apples, **c** sweeter apples.

4 Eventually she buys **a** one kilo, **b** two kilos, **c** three kilos.

c 1 The saleswoman is selling **a** cranberries, **b** blueberries, **c** strawberries.

2 The berries come from **a** northern Estonia, **b** southern Estonia, **c** western Estonia.

3 The buyer gets **a** three kilos, **b** four kilos, **c** five kilos.

4 She is buying berries for **a** making jam, **b** just eating, **c** reselling.

EXERCISE 4

Choose the correct translation.

1 **Suurepärane maitse! a** Wonderful taste! **b** A lot of taste!

2 **Oi, kui kallis! a** Oh, dear! **b** Oh, how expensive!

3 **See on väga soodne hind. a** The taste is very salty. **b** The price is very cheap.

4 **Kumba te soovite? a** Which one would you like? **b** What would you like?

5 **Astuge ligi! a** Try this! **b** Step closer!

6 **Need on Lõuna-Eestist. a** We are in southern Estonia. **b** These come from southern Estonia.

7 **Proovige palun. a** Please buy. **b** Please try.

Listening 3

You will hear people buying cucumbers (first dialogue) and biscuits (second dialogue). Listen to the dialogues and complete Exercises 5–7 below.

 07.03

a	Ostja	Palun kaks kilo kurke.
	Müüja	Kas panen kotti?
	Ostja	Pange jah.
	Müüja	Nii. Kilo hind on kaheksateist krooni, see teeb kokku kolmkümmend kuus krooni. Ja kott on kroon kakskümmend.
	Ostja	Oi, aga kas teil suuremat kotti ei ole?
	Müüja	On ikka. Palun. Hind on sama.
b	Ostja	Soovin osta pool kilo küpsiseid.
	Müüja	Kas suuremaid või väiksemaid?
	Ostja	Suuremaid.
	Müüja	Kas ma pakin karpi või kotti?
	Ostja	Kas karp on kallim kui kott?
	Müüja	Mõlemad on tasuta.
	Ostja	Pakkige siis palun karpi.
	Müüja	Teeme nii.

V

kurk, kurgi, kurki, kurke	*cucumber, gherkin*
kott, koti, kotti, kotte	*bag*
kotti	*into the bag*
teeb kokku	*makes* (used when calculating numbers)
kroon kakskümmend	*one crown and twenty (cents)*
suurem, -a, -at, -aid	*bigger*
sama, -, -, samu	*same*
soovi/ma, -da, -n	*to wish, want*
ost/ma, -a, -an	*to buy*
küpsis, -e, -t, -eid	*cookie, biscuit*
väike(ne), -se, -st, -si	*small*
väiksem, -a, -at, -aid	*smaller*
pakki/ma, -da, paki/n	*to pack*
karp, karbi, karpi, karpe	*box*
karpi	*into the box*
kallim, -a, -at, -aid	*dearer, more expensive*
mõlemad	*both*
tasuta	*free of charge*
pakkige	*pack* (pl. imperative)
teeme nii	*OK* (lit. *let's do so*)

EXERCISE 5

Listen and choose the right answer.

a **1** Ostja tahab osta **a** kilo kurke, **b** kaks kilo kurke, **c** kolm kilo kurke.

  2 Kilo kurke maksab **a** 16 krooni, **b** 17 krooni, **c** 18 krooni.

  3 Kokku on hind **a** 36 krooni, **b** 35 krooni, **c** 34 krooni.

  4 Kott maksab **a** 1.30, **b** 1.20, **c** 1.40.

  5 Suurem kott maksab **a** 1.30, **b** 1.20, **c** 1.40.

b **1** Ostja tahab osta **a** pool kilo küpsiseid, **b** kilo küpsiseid, **c** kaks kilo küpsiseid.

  2 Ostja soovib **a** suuremaid küpsiseid, **b** väiksemaid küpsiseid, **c** magusamaid küpsiseid.

  3 Müüja ütleb **a** Kas ma pakin karpi või kotti?, **b** Kas ma pakin kotti?, **c** Kas ma pakin karpi?

  4 Karp on **a** kallis, **b** odav, **c** tasuta.

  5 Müüja pakib küpsised **a** karpi, **b** kotti, **c** väikesesse kotti.

EXERCISE 6

Choose the correct translation.

1 **Kas panen kotti? a** Do you have a bag? **b** Shall I put them in a bag?

2 **Kott on kallim kui karp. a** The bag is more expensive than the box. **b** The box is more expensive than the bag.

3 **Sooviksin väiksemaid. a** I would like to have the smaller ones. **b** These are too small.

4 **Hind on sama. a** The price is set. **b** The price is the same.

EXERCISE 7

 07.04

Choose the right response, then listen to check your answers.

1 **Kui palju need sibulad maksavad? a** Viisteist krooni. **b** Ohhoo, kui odavad!

2 **Palun pool kilo kurke. a** Proovige palun. **b** Valige ise välja.

3 **Kas see sink on väga soolane? a** Jah, see on tõesti soodne hind. **b** Ei ole, maitske ise!

4 **Õunu on kahte sorti. Kumba te soovite? a** Ma tahaksin magusaid. **b** Jah, pange siis neid kaks kilo.

5 **Kas need maasikad on Eesti omad? a** Loomulikult! **b** Ei, sööme niisama ära.

6 **Kas panen kotti? a** On ikka. **b** Pange jah.

7 **Kas teil suuremat kotti ei ole? a** Suuremaid. **b** On ikka!

8 **Kas karp on kallim kui kott? a** Pakkige palun karpi. **b** Mõlemad on tasuta.

Listening 4

Janek and Marek are university mates who share the same room in their dormitory. They are discussing what to cook for dinner and who should go and get the necessary ingredients. Listen to the dialogue and then complete Exercise 8.

 07.05

Janek	Kõht on nii tühi! Mida me süüa teeme?
Marek	Oota, ma vaatan, mis meil külmkapis on. Nii – kahjuks on ainult hapukurke ja õlut.
Janek	Kes poodi läheb?
Marek	Sina lähed. Mine ja too palun mune ja sibulaid. Ma teen omletti. Kui neil on, siis osta üks väiksem pudel õli ka.
Janek	Miks mina pean alati poes käima?
Marek	Sest mina teen alati süüa.
Janek	Nojah, eks ma siis lähen. Aga ma ostan siis juba veini, oliive ja juustu ka. Kutsume Annika ja Maarika külla!
Marek	Kutsume jah! Väga hea mõte! Osta siis kindlasti värsket puuvilja ka, kui nad müüvad. Näiteks viinamarju.
Janek	Hea küll. Ma siis lähen. Aga nõusid pesed pärast sina.

kõht, kõhu, kõhtu, kõhte	*stomach*
Kõht on nii tühi.	*I'm so hungry* (lit. *stomach is so empty*)
külm/kapp, -kapi, -kappi, -kappe	*refrigerator*
ainult	*only*
hapu/kurk, -kurgi, -kurki, -kurke	*pickled cucumber*
too/ma, tuu/a, too/n	*to bring*
muna, -, -, mune	*egg*
sibul, -a, -at, -aid	*onion*
tege/ma, teh/a, tee/n	*to make*
omlett, omleti, omletti	*omelette*
ost/ma, -a, -an	*to buy*
väiksem, -a, -at, -aid	*smaller*
õli, -, -	*oil*
miks	*why*
käi/ma, käi/a, käi/n	*to go*
süüa tege/ma, süüa teh/a, tee/n süüa	*to cook food*
juba	*already* (here: in this case)
juust, -u, -u, -e	*cheese*
külla kutsu/ma, külla kutsu/da, kutsu/n külla	*to invite*
mõte, mõtte, mõtet, mõtteid	*idea, thought*
kindlasti	*for sure, certainly*
värske, -, -t, -id	*fresh*
puu/vili, -vilja, -vilja, -vilju	*fruit*

müü/ma, -a, -n	*to sell*
viina/mari, -marja, -marja, -marju	*grape*
nõusid pese/ma, nõusid pes/ta, pese/n nõusid	*to wash the dishes*
pärast	*later, afterwards*

EXERCISE 8

Listen and decide if the following sentences are **a** true or **b** false.

1 Janek is very hungry.

2 There is beer, pickled cucumbers and bread in the refrigerator.

3 Marek suggests making an omelette.

4 Marek asks Janek to bring eggs, onions and a smaller bottle of oil.

5 Marek always goes to the shop.

6 Janek suggests also buying some wine, olives and cheese.

7 Annika and Maarika call to ask if they could come to visit.

8 Marek wants to buy some grapes.

9 Janek will have to wash the dishes later.

> **INSIGHT**
>
> When you want to learn several words at once you can remember them better if you group them thematically. For instance, write the names of different items of food on labels and group them by colour, size, shape, taste etc.

Language patterns

PALUN POOL KILO JUUSTU *HALF A KILO OF CHEESE PLEASE – PARTITIVE SINGULAR CASE*

We have already learnt that words like **pirukas** *pie*, **sink** *ham*, **juust** *cheese* etc. have three main forms:

I	II	III
pirukas	**piruka**	**pirukat**
kohv	**kohvi**	**kohvi**
juust	**juustu**	**juustu**

Now we will continue to study the usage of the third form (we first looked into it in Unit 4).

Here are some constructions when the third form is used:

▶ **kaks pirukat** *two pies*, **kolm kohvi** *three coffees* i.e. with all numbers *two* and upwards
▶ **kilo juustu** *a kilo of cheese*, **tass kohvi** *a cup of coffee* i.e. with other words that express quantity
▶ **Kas teil on juustu?** *Do you have any cheese?* **Meil on juustu** *We have some cheese.* **Osta juustu** *Buy some cheese.* i.e. to express uncertain quantity
▶ **Meil ei ole juustu** *We don't have cheese.* i.e. in negative sentences

In the following table (Exercise 9) we will study how to make the third form of the most common foods. Some useful adjectives are also given.

Note that all the words we will study mark uncountable substances. You will find an explanation about words which are clearly countable by piece, like **muna** *egg*, **õun** *apple*, **kartul** *potato*, etc. in the next grammar section.

EXERCISE 9

 07.06

Study the table. Fill in the missing words as the examples indicate, then listen to check your answers.

Once you have completed the major work, you can always come back to this table if in doubt how to make a certain form.

first form I	second form II	third form III -i
vorst *sausage*	vorst**i**	vorst**i**
vein *wine*	_____	_____
limonaad *lemonade*	_____	_____
šokolaad *chocolate*	_____	_____
sink *ham*	sing**i**	sink**i**
		-u
juust *cheese*	juust**u**	juust**u**
jahu *flour*	jahu	jahu
		-a
piim *milk*	piim**a**	piim**a**
kohupiim *cottage cheese, curd*	_____	_____
sool *salt*	_____	_____
leib *bread (rye bread)*	leiv**a**	leib**a**
sai *white bread*	sai**a**	sai**a**
must *black*		
kala *fish*	kala	kala
kana *chicken*	_____	_____
liha *meat*	_____	_____
hakkliha *minced meat*	_____	_____
värske *fresh*	värske	värske**t**

first form I	second form II	third form III -i
valge *white*	_____	_____
lahja *low fat, light*	_____	_____
keefir *sour milk*	keefir**i**	keefir**t**
jogurt *yoghurt*	_____	_____
ketšup *ketchup*	_____	_____
magus *sweet*	magus**a**	magus**at**
maitsev *tasty*	maitsv**a**	maitsv**at**
suhkur *sugar*	suhkr**u**	_____
roheli/ne *green*	rohelis**e**	rohelis**t**
puna/ne *red*	_____	_____
tai/ne *lean*	_____	_____
väike(ne) *small*	väike**se**	_____
jäätis *icecream*	jäätis**e**	jäätis**t**
tume *dark*	tume**da**	tume**dat**
hele *light (for colour)*	_____	_____
suur *big*	suur**e**	suur**t**
koor *cream*	koore	koort
õlu *beer*	õlle	õlut
vesi *water*	vee	vett
mesi *honey*	mee	mett
		-d
tee *tea*	tee	tee**d**
või *butter*	_____	_____
kakao *cocoa*	_____	_____
hea *good*	_____	_____

Measures

When shopping at the market we often use the third form with the following measures:

sada grammi	*hundred grams of*		**juustu**	*cheese*
pool kilo	*half a kilo of*		**sinki**	*ham*
üks kilo	*one kilo of*		**liha**	*meat*
kaks kilo	*two kilos of*	**+ III form**	**jahu**	*flour*
pakk	*a packet of*		**võid**	*butter*
pudel	*a bottle of*		**veini**	*wine*
karp	*a box of*		**jäätist**	*icecream*
purk	*a jar of*		**moosi**	*jam*
kott	*a bag of*		**suhkrut**	*sugar*

Bear in mind that with numbers bigger than one the third form has to be used, so we say **kaks pudelit limonaadi** *two bottles of lemonade*, **kolm purki moosi** *three jars of jam* etc. With the number one we say **üks pudel limonaadi** *one bottle of lemonade*, **üks purk moosi** *one jar of jam*.

I	II	III
pakk *packet*	**paki**	**pakki**
kott *bag*	**koti**	**kotti**
purk *jar*	**purgi**	**purki**
karp *box*	**karbi**	**karpi**
pudel *bottle*	**pudeli**	**pudelit**
päts *loaf*	**pätsi**	**pätsi**

In order to practise this grammar topic further do Exercises 14–17 in the Practice section.

PALUN KAKS KILO KOLLASEID ÕUNU *TWO KILOS OF YELLOW APPLES PLEASE – PARTITIVE PLURAL*

In the previous grammar section we dealt with words that usually mark uncountable substances (like **tee** *tea*, **või** *butter* etc.). Now we will learn one more grammatical form that is used with countable substances (like **õunad** *apples*, **kurgid** *cucumbers*, **pähklid** *nuts*, **rosinad** *raisins* etc). We will call it the *fourth form*.

The fourth form can have three different types of ending, i.e.:
  -id (usually with longer words)
  -sid (usually with shorter words)
  -e, i, -u (also usually with shorter words)

The endings of the fourth form can be derived from the endings of the third form i.e.:

if the third form ends with: then the fourth form ends with:

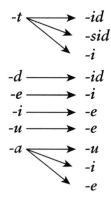

As it is quite complicated to learn all the rules of making the fourth form from this unit on, the fourth form is presented for all new words we learn.

The fourth form is used in the following constructions.

▶ **kilo õunu** *a kilo of apples*, **kott kartuleid** *a bag of potatoes* i.e. with words that express quantity

▶ **Kas teil on kollaseid pirne?** *Do you have any yellow pears?* **Meil on kollaseid pirne.** *We have some yellow pears.* **Osta kollaseid pirne.** *Buy some yellow pears.*, i.e. to express uncertain quantity

▶ **Meil ei ole kollaseid pirne.** *We don't have yellow pears*, i.e. in negative sentences

Note that with numbers we do not use the fourth but the third form (**kolm pirni** *three pears*, **kümme õuna** *ten apples*).

EXERCISE 10

 07.07

In the following table you will find the names of some fruits and vegetables and some common adjectives like **suur** *big*, **punane** *red* etc. Fill in the missing forms. The ending of the fourth form usually depends on the ending of the third form. Listen to the recording to check your answers.

Once you have completed most of the work, you can always look back at this table, if in doubt how to make a certain form!

first form	second form	third form -t	fourth form -id
sibul *onion*	sibula	sibula**t**	sibula**id**
magus *sweet*	_____	_____	_____
valge *white*	_____	_____	_____
maasika/s *strawberry*	maasika	maasika**t**	maasika**id**
jõhvika/s *cranberry*	_____	_____	_____
odav *cheap*	_____	_____	_____
kartul *potato*	kartuli	kartuli**t**	kartul/e/**id**
porgand *carrot*	_____	_____	_____
tomat *tomato*	_____	_____	_____
pähkel *nut*	_____	_____	_____

(Continued)

(Continued)

first form	second form	third form -t	fourth form -id
kallis *expensive*	kalli	kalli**st**	kalle**id**
kolla/ne *yellow*	kolla**se**	kolla**st**	kollase**id**
puna/ne *red*	_____	_____	_____
sini/ne *blue*	_____	_____	_____
rasva/ne *greasy*	_____	_____	_____
väike(ne) *small*	väikse	väike**st**	väikse/**id**
NB! roheli/ne *green*	roheli**se**	roheli**st**	roheli**si**
		-d	**-id**
hea *good*	hea	hea**d**	NB! häid
		-t	**-sid**
hapu *sour*	hapu	hapu**t**	hapusi**d**
roosa *pink*	_____	_____	_____
kirju *colourful,*			
with many colours	_____	_____	_____
		-i	**-e**
pruun *brown*	pruuni	pruun**i**	pruun**e**
ploom *plum*	_____	_____	_____
hall *grey*	_____	_____	_____
komm *candy*	_____	_____	_____
pirn *pear*	_____	_____	_____
kurk *cucumber*	kurgi	kurk**i**	_____
		-a	**-u**
õun *apple*	õuna	õun**a**	õun**u**
mari *berry*	marja	marj**a**	_____
		-a	**-e**
muna *egg*	muna	muna**a**	mun**e**
		-a	**-i**
must *black*	musta	must**a**	must**i**
		-t	**-i**
seen *mushroom*	seene	seen**t**	seen**i**
suur *big*	_____	_____	_____

Here are some examples of usage of the fourth form:

sada grammi	*hundred grams of*		**küpsiseid**	*biscuits*
pool kilo	*half a kilo of*		**õunu**	*apples*
üks kilo	*one kilo of*		**kurke**	*cucumbers*
kaks kilo	*two kilos of*	**+ IV form**	**kartuleid**	*potatoes*

pakk	*a packet of*	**pähkleid**	*nuts*
karp	*a box of*	**komme**	*sweets*
purk	*a jar of*	**seeni**	*mushrooms*
kott	*a bag of*	**maasikaid**	*strawberries*

In order to practise this grammar topic further do Exercises 18–20 in the Practice section.

Estonian markets

Every town in Estonia has a **turg** *market*. In fact, there are usually several: **lihaturg** *meat market*, **kalaturg** *fish market* and **täiturg** or **täika** *flea market* (for selling second-hand items). During the summer **juurviljad** *vegetables* and **puuviljad** *fruits* are sold on **avaturg** *the open air market* by the local farmers. There you can also buy a large variety of **istikud** *young plants* and **lilled** *flowers* for gardens. Compared to more southern countries, an Estonian market is a very quiet place: the sellers do not loudly advertise their goods, the prices are set and no bargaining goes on. The sellers might try to attract your attention by saying things like **Maasikaid läheb?** *Would you like some strawberries?* or **Palun – väga head tomatid!** *Please – the tomatoes are very good!* It is polite to answer **Ei, aitäh, ma praegu ei osta** *No thank you, I'm not buying now* if you do not intend to buy. Still, shopping at the market is recommended as you can get many fresh goods that shops don't sell, like home-grown berries: **punane sõstar** *redcurrant*, **must sõstar** *blackcurrant*, **tikker** *gooseberry*, **vaarikas** *raspberry* and **maasikas** *strawberry*, and **metsamarjad** *wild berries* like **metsmaasikas** *wild strawberry*, **jõhvikas** *cranberry*, **pohl** *lingonberry*, **mustikas** *blueberry*, **murakas** *cloudberry*. In the autumn locally picked wild mushrooms like **kukeseen** *chanterelle* and **puravik** *boletus* can also be found as well as huge piles of **arbuus** *watermelon* and **viinamari** *grapes*, which are brought in from Ukraine and Moldova. If you have a sweet tooth, look for locally produced **mesi** *honey*, which comes in a variety of sorts and colours.

The Estonian meat market is a place to look for tasty cuts of **sealiha** *pork*, **veiseliha** *beef*, **vasikaliha** *veal* or **lambaliha** *mutton*. If you are a sensitive person then you might not enjoy the naturalistic sight of the place but it's well worth a try as you can also buy delicious **suitsuvorst** *smoked sausage* (sometimes even made of **põdraliha** *wild elk*) and **sink** *ham* there. With these sorts of goods you can always ask **Kas maitsta saab?** *Can I have a taste?* and you will be offered a small slice to try.

The most common fish that are caught and sold in Estonia are **räim** *Baltic herring*, **haug** *pike*, **forell** *trout*, **angerjas** *eel*, **lest** *flounder* and **latikas** *bream*.

KELLELT SA ÕUNU OSTAD? *FROM WHOM DO YOU BUY THE APPLES?* – ABLATIVE CASE

We have already learnt how to answer the questions **Kellele?** *Who to?* and **Kellel?** *Who has?* Now we will learn another similar question **Kellelt?** *From whom?*

Look at the examples in the following table – some common words with which the particular endings are used are presented at the top. Fill in the missing forms.

who?	kellele? *who to?* räägid *you tell* kirjutad *you write* helistad *you call* annad *you give*	kellel? *who has?* on *has*	kellelt? *from who?* küsid *you ask* kuuled *you hear* ostad *you buy* saad *you get*
müüja *seller*	müüja**le**	müüja**l**	müüja**lt**
ostja *buyer*	ostja**le**	ostja**l**	ostja**lt**
Janek *Janek*	Janeki**le**	Janeki**l**	Janeki**lt**
sõber *friend*	sõbra**le**	_____	_____
naine *woman*	naise**le**	_____	_____
mees *man*	mehe**le**	_____	_____
laps *child*	lapse**le**	_____	_____
naaber *neighbour*	naabri**le**	_____	_____
abikaasa *husband*	abikaasa**le**	_____	_____
ülemus *boss*	ülemuse**le**	_____	_____

In order to practise this grammar topic further do Exercise 21 in the Practice section.

SUUR, SUUREM, KÕIGE SUUREM *BIG, BIGGER, THE BIGGEST – COMPARATIVE FORMS OF ADJECTIVES*

When comparing things special forms of words like **suur** *big*, **väike** *small*, **ilus** *beautiful*, **kallis** *expensive* are used. In English, we say *big – bigger – biggest*. In Estonian we just add **-m** to the second form i.e. (I) suur (II) suure + **-m** = suure**m**, which means *bigger*. By adding the word **kõige** i.e **kõige suurem** we get the meaning *the biggest*.

The sentences for comparing things would look like this:

Apelsin on **suurem** kui mandariin.	*An orange is bigger than a clementine.*
Mandariin on **magusam** kui apelsin.	*A clementine is sweeter than an orange.*
Greip on **kõige suurem** puuvili.	*Grapefruit is the biggest fruit.*
Maasikamoos on **kõige magusam** moos.	*Strawberry jam is the sweetest jam.*

Note that it is also possible to say Greip on **suurim** puuvili. which means exactly the same as Greip on **kõige suurem** puuvili. This type of construction with the letter **i** cannot be made from all adjectives but it is quite common with words like suur**i**m = kõige suurem – *the biggest*, par**i**m = kõige parem – *the best*, halv**i**m = kõige halvem – *the worst* etc.

EXERCISE 11

Fill in the missing forms. The examples will help you.

suur, -e big	suurem bigger	kõige suurem the biggest
noor, -e *young*	_____	_____
väike(ne), väikse *small*	_____	_____
magus, -a *sweet*	_____	_____

odav, -a *cheap*	_____	_____
kallis, kalli *expensive*	_____	_____
hapu, – *sour*	_____	_____
NB! pikk, pik/a *long, tall*	**pikem**	**kõige pikem**
lai, -a *wide*	_____	_____
vana, – *old*	_____	_____
lahja, – *lean, low-fat*	_____	_____
halb, halva *bad*	_____	_____
NB! hea *good*	**parem**	**kõige parem**

KAS TEIL SUUREMAID EI OLE? *DON'T YOU HAVE BIGGER ONES? – CONJUGATING COMPARATIVES*

As you already know, case endings are added to Estonian words to indicate different meanings. Such endings can also be added to the comparative forms of adjectives we just learnt in the previous grammar part. Fortunately, they all take the same endings, for instance:

first form	second form	third form	fourth form
suurem	suurema	suuremat	suuremaid
ilusam	ilusama	ilusamat	ilusamaid
odavam	odavama	odavamat	odavamaid
väiksem	väiksema	väiksemat	väiksemaid

Forms like this are used for instance in the following types of sentence:

Kas teil on **suuremat** kotti?   *Do you have a bigger bag?*

Kas teil on **odavamat** juustu?   *Do you have any cheaper cheese?*

Palun kaks kilo **väiksemaid** kurke.   *Two kilos of smaller cucumbers please.*

EXERCISE 12

Make sentences following the example of the sample sentence.

1 See on liiga hapu mahl. Kas teil on magusamat?

2 See on liiga magus limonaad. Kas teil on _____?

3 See on liiga kallis sink. Kas teil on _____?

4 See on liiga väike kott. Kas teil on _____?

5 Need on liiga suured kurgid. Kas teil on *väiksemaid*?

6 Need on liiga väiksed õunad. Kas teil on _____?

7 Need on liiga hapud maasikad. Kas teil on _____?

8 Need on liiga odavad kommid. Kas teil on _____?

In order to practise the last two grammar topics further do Exercise 22 in the Practice section.

MA LÄHEN TURULE. MA KÄIN IGA PÄEV TURUL *I GO TO THE MARKET. I GO TO THE MARKET EVERY DAY*

The words **minema**, **minna** *to go*, **lähen** *I go* and **käima**, **käia** *to go*, **käin** *I go* both indicate movement and have the same translation in English. The difference in Estonian is that **minema**, **minna** *to go*, **lähen** *I go* are used when someone goes somewhere just once or just this time, for instance:

Lähen poodi.	*I go to the shop.*
Kas sa lähed koju?	*Are you going home?*
Lähme kohvikusse!	*Let's go to the coffee shop!*
Mine turule.	*Go to the market!*

Käima, käia, käin *I go* is used when talking about someone going somewhere often or regularly, for instance:

Ma käin igal pühapäeval turul.	*I go to the market every Sunday.*
Ta käib tööl.	*He/She goes to work.*
Me käime koolis.	*We go to school.*
Nad käivad kursusel.	*They take courses (lit. go to the courses).*

Note that the words used with **minema** *to go* take the ending **-sse** or **-le** or are in short form (Lähen kohvikusse *I go to the coffee shop*. Anna läheb turule *Anna goes to the market*. Me lähme kinno *We go to the cinema*) but with **käima** they take either the ending **-s** or **-l** (Lähen turule *I go to the market*. Käin turul *I go to the market*).

EXERCISE 13

Insert either **käima** or **minema**.

1 Ta _____ igal esmaspäeval kursusel.

2 Ma _____ täna **kinno**.

3 Kas sa _____ homme hommikul turule?

4 Ma _____ nüüd töö**l**.

5 Me _____ praegu kohvikusse.

6 Ma _____ igal nädalavahetusel kontserdil.

In order to practise this grammar topic further do Exercise 23 in the Practice section.

Practice

EXERCISE 14

Find all the edible things then translate the entire list.

ploom, kott, maasikas, kala, karp, juust, kurk, sink, küpsis, sibul, muna, hind, hapukurk, viinamari, õli, omlett

EXERCISE 15

Choose the correct form.

1 Kahjuks meil ei ole **juust/juustu**.

2 Kahjuks meil ei ole **jogurt/jogurtit**.

3 Kahjuks meil ei ole **limonaad/limonaadi**.

4 Kahjuks meil ei ole **šokolaad/šokolaadi**.

5 Kahjuks meil ei ole **tume õlu/tumedat õlut**.

6 Kahjuks meil ei ole **taine sink/taist sinki**.

7 Kahjuks meil ei ole **punane vein/punast veini**.

8 Kahjuks meil ei ole **must tee/musta teed**.

EXERCISE 16

Use the words in brackets in the correct form then translate the phrases.

1 sada grammi (sink)

2 üks pudel (vein)

3 üks pudel (limonaad)

4 kolmsada grammi (juust)

5 üks kott (jahu)

6 kilo (hakkliha)

7 kaks (kala)

8 pool (kana)

9 kolm (jogurt)

10 kaks (ketšup)

11 kaks (pakk) (roheline tee)

12 kolm (tass) (must kohv)

13 kaks (tume õlu)

14 neli (hele õlu)

15 kaks (pudel) (vesi)

16 kaks (purk) (mesi)

EXERCISE 17

Translate the following:

Do you have …

1 (some) black tea?

2 (any) good ice cream?

3 (any) dark beer?

4 (any) Estonian cheese?

5 (any) lean meat?

6 (any) fresh fish?

7 (any) low-fat yoghurt?

EXERCISE 18

Choose the correct form.

1 Kahjuks meil ei ole **suured jõhvikad/suuri jõhvikaid**.

2 Kahjuks meil ei ole **punaseid õunu/punased õunad**.

3 Kahjuks meil ei ole **pruune seeni/pruunid seened**.

4 Kahjuks meil ei ole **rohelised õunad/rohelisi õunu**.

5 Kahjuks meil ei ole **väikesed kurgid/väikseid kurke**.

6 Kahjuks meil ei ole **odavaid tomateid/odavad tomatid**.

7 Kahjuks meil ei ole **kallid seened/kalleid seeni**.

8 Kahjuks meil ei ole **hapusid marju/hapud marjad**.

EXERCISE 19

Use the words in brackets in correct form then translate the phrases.

1 kolmsada grammi (maasikad)

2 pool kilo (sibulad)

3 viis kilo (kollased kartulid)

4 kolm kilo (sinised ploomid)

5 üks purk (väikesed kurgid)

6 karp (suured munad)

7 natuke (head porgandid)

8 kott (roosad õunad)

9 kaks kilo (magusad pirnid)

10 karp (mustad seened)

EXERCISE 20

Translate the following:

Do you have …

1 (any) white potatoes?

2 (any) cheap tomatoes?

3 (any) sour berries?

4 (any) red plums?

5 (any) big cucumbers?

6 (any) small mushrooms?

7 (any) beautiful cranberries?

8 (any) expensive apples?

9 (any) pink plums?

10 (any) good carrots?

EXERCISE 21

Choose the correct form.

1 Ma helistan **ülemusele/ülemusel/ülemuselt**.

2 Minu **mehele/mehel/mehelt** on suur auto.

3 Ma küsin **ülemusele/ülemusel/ülemuselt** tööd.

4 Ma helistan **lapsele/lapsel/lapselt**.

5 Ma saan **abikaasale/abikaasal/abikaasalt** kirja.

EXERCISE 22

Make similar sentences.

1 õun, kapsas, suur *Kapsas on suurem kui õun.*

2 tort, võileib, magus

3 kohupiim, juust, lahja

4 vein, mahl, kallis

5 jõhvikad, maasikad, hapu
Jõhvikad on hapumad kui maasikad.

6 seened, kommid, magus

7 ploomid, pähklid, väike

8 kartulid, kapsad, suur

EXERCISE 23

Choose the correct form.

1 Ma lähen **diskole/diskol**.

2 Ta läheb **näitusele/näitusel**.

3 Me läheme homme **lillelaadale/ lillelaadal**.

4 Nad lähevad **kohvikus/kohvikusse**.

5 Mine **poodi/poes** ja osta kommi.

6 Mine **turul/turule** ja too liha.

Ma käin igal reedel **diskol/diskole**.

Ta käib tihti **näitusele/näitusel**.

Me käime igal kevadel **lillelaadal/lillelaadale**.

Nad armastavad **kohvikusse/kohvikus käia**.

Ma käin iga päev **poodi/poes** ja ostan kommi.

Käin tavaliselt nädalavahetusel **turule/turul** ja ostan liha.

 Speaking

EXERCISE 24

Fill in the missing lines. Listen to the completed dialogue.

 07.08

Sina	Say *I want to buy a kilo of strawberries.*
Müüja	Kas suuremaid või väiksemaid?
Sina	Say *The smaller ones.*
Müüja	Kas panen kotti või karpi?
Sina	Say *Please pack in the box.*
Müüja	Nii. Kilo hind on nelikümmend krooni.
Sina	Ask how much the cucumbers cost.
Müüja	Kuusteist krooni kilo.
Sina	Ask for half a kilo.
Müüja	Palun. See teeb kokku nelikümmend kaheksa krooni.

EXERCISE 25

Fill in the missing lines. Listen to the completed dialogue.

 07.09

Müüja	Astuge ligi! Proovige palun neid magusaid ploome.
Sina	Say *Yes, they are really sweet.*
Müüja	Proovige pirne ka!
Sina	Say *Excellent taste. Ask are they Estonian?*
Müüja	Ei, need on Ukrainast.
Sina	Ask how much do these pears cost?
Müüja	Kaheksateist krooni kilo.

Sina	Ask *But how much do these plums cost?*
Müüja	Kaksteist krooni kilo.
Sina	Say *Oh, how cheap!*
Müüja	Jah, see on tõesti väga soodne hind.
Sina	Say *I will take half a kilo of them.*

EXERCISE 26

Read the letter. Use a dictionary, if necessary. Write a similar letter of your own using the words and expressions learnt in this unit.

Kallis Mihkel!

Mul ei ole täna aega poodi minna, lähen õhtul veel kursusele. Ole hea, mine ise poodi ja too pakk kohupiima, 10 muna, päts leiba, kaks pakki piima ja üks väiksem arbuus. Kui poes arbuusi ei ole, siis mine palun turule. Tegelikult on vaja osta veel umbes kilo kartuleid ja pool kilo sibulaid, need on ka turul odavamad kui poes. Ja võta siis palun viinamarju ka. Tumedad viinamarjad on paremad kui heledad!

Raha on kapis. Osta endale midagi head ka.

Musi
Ema

⁇ Test yourself

1 You want to know how much the ham costs. What do you say?
   a Kas see on väga soolane sink?
   b Kas teil on taist sinki?
   c Kui palju see sink maksab?

2 You are buying strawberries and the seller asks **Kas pakin karpi või kotti?** What would the correct answer be?
   a Hind on sama.
   b Pakkige palun karpi.
   c Mõlemad on tasuta.

3 Which ones are vegetables?
   a maasikas, jõhvikas, ploom
   b muna, juust, õli
   c sibul, kartul, kapsas

4 You are buying vegetables at the market and the seller says **Maitske palun!** What does it mean?
   a Try please!
   b Wonderful taste!
   c Please buy this!

5 You are buying cucumbers and the seller asks: **Ka soovite suuremaid või väiksemaid?** What does it mean?
   a Would you like a bag or box?
   b Would you like smaller or bigger ones?
   c Would you like a kilo or half a kilo?

6 Which sentence is true?
   a Koor on lahjem kui piim.
   b Suhkur on magusam kui sool.
   c Kapsas on väiksem kui õun.

7 Which ones are packages?
   a purk, pakk, pudel
   b tume, hapu, hele
   c kala, seen, moos

8 You want to buy three big ice creams. How do you end the sentence **Palun kolm…?**
   a suurt jäätist
   b suuri jäätiseid
   c suured jäätised

9 You want to buy three kilos of yellow apples. How do you end the sentence **Palun kolm kilo…?**

   a kollast õuna.

   b kollaseid õunu

   c kollased õunad

10 You want to say you go to the market every day. How do you finish the sentence **Ma käin iga päev…**

   a turg

   b turule

   c turul

Lähme välja!

Let's go out!

In this unit you will learn:

▶ *How to make a phone call*
▶ *How to make an invitation*
▶ *How to understand advertisements and to buy tickets*

Listening 1

You will hear some people making phone calls. Listen to the dialogues and complete the Exercises 1–2.

 08.01

a	**Na ine**	*Hallo!*
	Mees	Tere! Palun Üllet.
	Naine	Jah, ma kohe kutsun.
b	**Naine**	Hallo! Kas Tiina on kodus?
	Mees	Ei ole praegu. Kas ma saan midagi edasi öelda?
	Naine	Las ta helistab Ingridile.
	Mees	Jah, ma ütlen edasi.
c	**Mees**	Tere. Kultuuriministeerium kuuleb.
	Naine	Tervist. Mina olen Tiia Pärnapuu. Kas ma saaksin rääkida proua Lauluga?
	Mees	Kahjuks teda ei ole praegu kohal. Kas ma saan midagi edasi öelda?
	Naine	Ei, ma helistan uuesti.
	Mees	Jah, proovige palun poole tunni pärast uuesti.
d	**Naine**	Hallo! Ma sooviksin rääkida Tiit Talumetsaga.
	Mees	Kellega?
	Naine	Kas see on Talumetsa korter?
	Mees	Ei ole. Teil on vist valeühendus.
	Naine	Vabandust.

Hallo!	*Hello!* (a greeting used on the phone only)
Palun Üllet.	request to talk to someone (lit. **Ülle**, *please*)
kutsu/ma, -da, -n	*to call, invite* (here to ask someone to come to the phone)
kodus	*at home*
praegu	*at the moment*
Kas ma saan midagi edasi öelda?	*Can I take a message?* (lit. *Can I forward something?*)
las ta helistab	*let her call*
edasi ütle/ma, edasi ütel/da, ütle/n edasi	*to forward a message*
Kas ma saaksin rääkida …?	*Could I speak …?*
teda ei ole kohal	*he (she) is not present*
helista/ma, -da, -n	*to call (on the phone), to ring*
uuesti	*again*
proovi/ma, -da, -n	*to try*
poole tunni pärast	*in half an hour's time*
ma sooviksin rääkida	*I would like to speak*
korter, -i, -it, -eid	*apartment, flat*
vist	*probably*
valeühendus, -e, -t, -i	*wrong number*, (lit. *false connection*)

EXERCISE 1

Listen to the dialogues and decide which sentences belong to which dialogue. The first one is done for you.

	a	b	c	d
1 Kas Tiina on kodus?				
2 Palun Üllet.	✓			
3 Teil on vist valeühendus.				
4 Ei, ma helistan uuesti.				
5 Jah, ma ütlen edasi.				
6 Kas ma saan midagi edasi öelda?				
7 Kas see on Talumetsa korter?				

EXERCISE 2

 08.02

Choose the right response. Listen to check your answers.

1 **Palun Üllet. a** Kellega? **b** Jah, ma kohe kutsun.

2 **Kas Tiina on kodus? a** Ei ole praegu. Kas ma saan midagi edasi öelda? **b** Las ta helistab Ingridile.

3 **Teil on vist valeühendus. a** Vabandust. **b** Jah, ma ütlen edasi.

4 **Kas ma saan midagi edasi öelda? a** Ei, ma helistan uuesti. **b** Teil on vist valeühendus.

Listening 2

In these dialogues people are discussing what to do and where to go during the weekend. Listen and then complete the Exercises 3–4 below.

 08.03

---

a Urmas Kas sa teatrisse tahaksid minna?

  Kristin Millal?

  Urmas No näiteks laupäeval.

  Kristin Ja mis etendus seal on?

  Urmas Ballett 'Luikede järv'.

  Kristin Hea meelega!

b Andrus Tere, Annika! Lähme täna õhtul kinno!

  Annika Oh, lahe! Muidugi läheme!

  Andrus Aga mis filmi sa tahaksid vaadata?

  Annika Ma ei tea, mis seal praegu jooksevad.

  Andrus Mingi ameerika märulifilm on ja mingi vene ulmefilm. Ma nimesid ei mäleta.

  Annika Kas midagi muud ei ole?

  Andrus Veel on vist mingi inglise komöödia ja mingi jaapani multikas.

  Annika Aga mida sa ise eelistaks?

  Andrus Mul on ükskõik.

c Lauri Kuule, kas sa sellel nädalavahetusel klubisse tuled?

  Kaupo Ma seekord ei saa. On muud tegemist.

  Lauri No mis siis teha. Eks siis mõni teine kord.

  Kaupo Jah.

---

tahaksid	*would like to*
millal?	*when?*
etendus, -e, -t, -i	*play, show, performance*
ballett, balleti, balletti, ballette	*ballet*
luik, luige, luike, luiki	*swan*
järv, -e, -e, -i	*lake*
lähme = läheme	*we go, here: let's go*
lahe, -da, -dat, -daid	*cool, great (slang)*
film, -i, -i, -e	*film*
jooks/ma, joos/ta, jookse/n	*to run, here: to be on show*
ameerika	*America, here: American*
märulifilm, -i, -i, -e	*action film*
ulmefilm, -i, -i, -e	*science fiction film*
mäleta/ma, -da, -n	*to remember*
midagi mud	*something else*
komöödia, -, -t, -id	*comedy*

multikas, multika, multikat, multikaid	*cartoon*
Mida sa ise eelistaks?	*What would you (yourself) prefer?*
Mul on ükskõik.	*It makes no difference to me.*
muud tegemist	*other things to do*
Mis siis teha!	*Too bad!*
mõni teine kord	*some other time*

EXERCISE 3

Listen and choose the correct answer. For some questions, several answers are correct.

1 Which places are discussed in the dialogues?

- **a** kino
- **b** teater
- **c** kohvik
- **d** klubi
- **e** näitus

2 Which words did you hear in the dialogues?

- **a** esmaspäev
- **b** homme
- **c** täna õhtul
- **d** nädalavahetus
- **e** laupäev

3 Which types of show or performances were discussed?

- **a** ballett
- **b** ulmefilm
- **c** märulifilm
- **d** multikas
- **e** komöödia

4 Which reactions to the invitations did you hear?

- **a** Väga tore!
- **b** Ma seekord ei saa
- **c** Oh, lahe! Muidugi lähme!
- **d** Aitäh, aga ma täna ei tule
- **e** Hea meelega!

EXERCISE 4

 08.04

Choose the right response. Listen to check your answers.

1 Kas sa kinno tahaksid minna? a Oh, lahe! Muidugi lähme! **b** Kas midagi muud ei ole?

2 Lähme täna õhtul teatrisse! a Mul on ükskõik. **b** Ma seekord ei saa. On muud tegemist.

3 Kuule, kas sa laupäeval näitusele tuled? a Hea meelega! **b** No mis siis teha.

4 Kuule, kas sa kohvikusse tahaksid minna? a Aga mida sa ise eelistaks? **b** Muidugi lähme!

Listening 3

In this dialogue someone is buying a ticket at the cinema ticket office. Listen and then complete Exercises 5–6.

 08.05

Ostja	Tere. Öelge palun, mis film see 'Hall planeet' on? Kas see on ulmefilm?
Müüja	Tere! Ei, ei, see ei ole ulmefilm. See on märulifilm, aga üsna lõbus ja vaimukas.
Ostja	Ahah. Nii et see ei ole õudne?
Müüja	Mm-mm. Mitte eriti. Selle filmi režissöör on muide naine, aga tema nimi ei tule mul praegu meelde.
Ostja	Aa, ma tean küll! 'Hall planeet' on ju juba teine osa. Nende filmide režissöör on tõesti väga kuulus.
Müüja	Jah, mängivad ka samad näitlejad.
Ostja	Kui pikk see film on?
Müüja	Poolteist tundi.
Ostja	Olgu. Võtan siis kolm piletit.
Müüja	Seansile, mis kohe algab, jah?
Ostja	Jah.
Müüja	Ja mis ritta?
Ostja	Kas seal on mingi hinnavahe ka?
Müüja	Ei ole. Hind sõltub ainult kellaajast. Kuni kella kuueni maksab pilet kuuskümmend krooni ja alates kella kuuest sada kakskümmend krooni.
Ostja	Siis kuhugi keskele palun.
Müüja	Ma soovitaksin neid kohti siin.
Ostja	Väga hea.
Müüja	Palun. Kolmsada kuuskümmend krooni.

 TIP
Please note since 1 January 2011 the Estonian currency has been the Euro.

mis film?	*what kind of film?*
planeet, planeedi, planeeti, planeete	*planet*
üsna	*quite*
lõbus, -a, -at, -aid	*funny*
vaimukas, vaimuka, vaimukat, vaimukaid	*witty*
õud/ne, -se, -set, -seid	*horrifying*
mitte eriti	*not quite*
muide	*by the way*

selle filmi režissöör	*director of this film (lit. this film's director)*
režissöör, -i, -i, -e	*director*
meelde tule/ma, tull/a, tule/b meelde	*to remember*
teine osa	*second part*
nende filmide režissöör	*director of these films (lit. these films' director)*
kuulus, kuulsa, kuulsat, kuulsaid	*famous*
mängi/ma, -da, -n	*to play, to act*
sama, -, -, samu	*same*
näitleja, -, -t, -id	*actor, actress*
kui pikk	*how long*
poolteist tundi	*an hour and a half*
olgu	*OK*
seanss, seansi, seanssi, seansse	*show (in the cinema)*
Mis ritta?	*To which row?*
rida, rea, rida, ridu	*row*
mingi, -, -t, mingeid	*some kind*
hinnavahe, -, -t, -sid	*price difference*
sõltu/ma, -da, -b	*to depend*
kella/aeg, -aja, -aega	*time, time of the day*
kuni kella kuueni	*until 6 o'clock*
alates kella kuuest	*starting from 6 o'clock*
kuhugi keskele	*somewhere in the middle*
soovita/ma, -da, -n	*to suggest*
koht, koha, kohta, kohti	*place*

EXERCISE 5

Listen and choose the correct answer.

1 The movie 'Grey Planet' is **a** a science fiction film, **b** a comedy, **c** an action film.

2 The ticket salesman describes the film as **a** a horrifying film, **b** a funny and witty film, **c** a very sad film.

3 The director of the film is **a** a man, **b** a woman, **c** an actor in the same film.

4 The film lasts for **a** one hour, **b** an hour and a half, **c** two hours.

5 The buyer buys **a** three tickets, **b** four tickets, **c** five tickets.

6 The price of the ticket depends on **a** the location in the hall, **b** the time of day, **c** the day of the week.

7 The price of the ticket changes at **a** 5 o'clock, **b** 6 o'clock, **c** 7 o'clock.

8 The buyer buys the tickets **a** for the front row, **b** for the back row, **c** somewhere in the middle of the hall.

9 The tickets cost **a** 60 crowns, **b** 120 crowns, **c** 360 crowns altogether.

EXERCISE 6

08.06

Choose the right response. Listen to check your answers.

1 Öelge palun, kas 'Punane öö' on märulifilm?

  a Mitte eriti.

  b Mul on ükskõik.

  c Ei, see ei ole märulifilm.

2 Kui pikk see film on?

  a Umbes kaks tundi.

  b Võtan siis kolm piletit.

  c Aa, ma tean küll!

3 Mis ritta te pileteid soovite?

  a Hind sõltub kellaajast.

  b Kuhugi keskele palun.

  c Väga hea.

4 Kas seal on mingi hinnavahe ka?

  a Hind sõltub ainult kellaajast.

  b Ma soovitaksin neid kohti siin.

  c Olgu.

Listening 4

08.07

You will hear some advertisements about different shows in cinemas and theatres. Listen and then complete Exercise 7.

a

> 3. IX Rahvusooperis Estonia
>
> Kell 19.00 P. Tšaikovski 'Padaemand'
>
> Kassa avatud iga päev 11–19 v.a riiklikel pühadel
>
> Pensionäridele pilet poole hinnaga
>
> Piletite tellimine tööpäeviti tel 681 1260

d

Kinos Ekraan

5.–8. aprillini Eesti filmi päevad

Kavas filmiklassika

Arvo Kruusement 'Kevade' (1969), 'Suvi' (1976) ja
'Sügis' (1990)

c

Ööklubis Parlament

reedel, 24. oktoobril

Klubi missi valimised

Naistele sissepääs tasuta!

Klubi avatakse kell 20.00

d

Emajõe suveteatris

25. 08. lasteetendus 'Seiklus metsas'

Piletite tellimine www.suveteater.ee

Alla 7-aastastele lastele tasuta!

Etenduse algus kell 19.00

rahvusooper, -i, -it, -eid	*national opera*
'Padaemand'	*'Queen of Spades'*
kassa, -, -t, -sid	*ticket office*
avatud	*open*
v.a	*except* (abbreviation of **välja arvatud**)
riiklik, -u, -ku, -ke	*of the state*
püha, -, -, -sid	*holiday*
riiklik püha	*bank holiday*
pensionär, -i, -i, -e	*senior citizen, retired person*
poole hinnaga	*half price*
tellimi/ne, -se, -st, -si	*ordering*

tööpäeviti	*on week days, on working days*
kino, -, -, -sid	*cinema*
aprillini	*until April*
eesti filmi päevad	*Estonian Film Festival* (lit. *days of Estonian film*)
kavas	*on the programme*
filmiklassika, -, -t	*film classics*
ööklubi, -, -, -sid	*night club*
miss, -i, -i, -e	*miss*
valimi/ne, -se, -st, -si	*election, selection*
naistele	*for women*
sissepääs, -u, -u, -e	*entrance*
avatakse	*will be opened*
Emajõe suveteater	*summer theatre of Emajõgi*
toimu/ma, -da, -b	*to take place*
lasteetendus, -e, -t, -i	*play for children*
seiklus, -e, -t, -i	*adventure*
mets, -a, -a, -i	*forest*
alla 7-aastastele lastele	*for kids under the age of 7*
algus, -e, -t, -eid	*beginning, start*

EXERCISE 7

Listen and decide if the following sentences are **a** true or **b** false.

a

1 On the 3rd of October starting at 19.00 Tšaikovski's 'Queen of Spades' is being performed at Estonian National Opera.

2 The ticket office is open from 1 till 7 pm.

3 The ticket office is closed at weekends.

4 You can order tickets over the phone during the weekends.

5 Senior citizens can buy tickets half price.

b

1 The Estonian Film Festival takes place on 5–8 April.

2 Four different films by Arvo Kruusement are being shown – 'Spring', 'Summer', 'Autumn' and 'Winter'.

3 The film 'Kevade' was made in 1969.

4 The film 'Suvi' was made in 1976.

5 The film 'Sügis' was made in 1990.

c

1 On Friday night the nightclub Miss and Mister will be elected.

2 The event takes place on the 24th October.

3 Women have free entrance until 8 o'clock.

4 All drinks are free.

5 The club will be opened at 8 o'clock.

d

1 There is a performance in Emajõe Summer Theatre on the 25th of August.

2 The performance is meant for children.

3 Tickets can be ordered online.

4 Children under 7 years old can enter for half price.

5 The performance starts at 6 o'clock.

> **INSIGHT**
>
> Keep yourself motivated! Once you have completed a unit, why not celebrate? Treat yourself to something nice – a bottle of wine, chocolates or a good movie.

Language patterns

KAS SA TAHAKSID …?   *WOULD YOU LIKE TO …? – CONDITIONAL*

Questions like **Kas sa tahad teatrisse minna?** *Do you want to go to the theatre?* are more polite if you add **-ksi/-ks** to the verb, i.e. Kas sa taha**ksi**d teatrisse minna? The English equivalent for such a type of grammatical construction is *Would you like to go to the theatre?*

The construction has both short and long forms and is quite easy to make. For the short form just replace the ending **-n** in I-form with **-ks**; note that it is the same for all persons, both in singular and plural.

ma tahan *I want to*	**ma tahaks** *I would like to*	**ma ei tahaks** *I would not like to*
sa tahad *you want to*	**sa tahaks** *you would like to*	**sa ei tahaks** *you would not like to*
ta tahab *he/she wants to*	**ta tahaks** *he/she would like to*	**ta ei tahaks** *he/she would not like to*
me tahame *we want to*	**me tahaks** *we would like to*	**me ei tahaks** *we would not like to*
te tahate *you want to*	**te tahaks** *you would like to*	**te ei tahaks** *you would not like to*
nad tahavad *they want to*	**nad tahaks** *they would like to*	**nad ei tahaks** *they would not like to*

For the long form add **-ksi** before the verb ending, i.e. taha**ksi**n, *I would like*; taha**ksi**me *we would like* etc.

ma tahan *I want to*	**ma tahaksin** *I would like to*	**ma ei tahaks** *I would not like to*
sa tahad *you want to*	**sa tahaksid** *you would like to*	**sa ei tahaks** *you would not like to*
ta tahab *he/she wants to*	**ta tahaks** *he/she would like to*	**ta ei tahaks** *he/she would not like to*
me tahame *we want to*	**me tahaksime** *we would like to*	**me ei tahaks** *we would not like to*
te tahate *you want to*	**te tahaksite** *you would like to*	**te ei tahaks** *you would not like to*
nad tahavad *they want to*	**nad tahaksid** *they would like to*	**nad ei tahaks** *they would not like to*

Note that when saying **ta tahaks** *he/she would like to*, the ending **-b** is not used and for **nad tahaksid** *they would like to*, some letters (-va-) have been dropped.

This construction can be used in sentences like the following:

Mis filmi sa tahaksid vaadata? *What film would you like to watch?*
Mida sa ise eelistaksid? *What would you prefer?*
Ma sooviksin kaht piletit. *I would like to have two tickets.*
Mis filmi te soovitaksite vaadata? *What film would you suggest watching?*

EXERCISE 8

Rewrite the sentences using the *would* form.

1 Ma **tahan** täna õhtul kinno minna.
   Ma tahaksin täna õhtul kinno minna.

2 Kas sa **tuled** minuga kinno?
   _____

3 Ma **vaatan** hea meelega komöödiat.
   _____

4 Kas see film **sobib**?
   _____

5 Kas sa **soovid** midagi juua ka?
   _____

In order to practise this grammar topic further do Exercises 15–16 in the Practice section.

KELLA VIIEST KUUENI *FROM 5 TILL 6*

For making sentences like **Kassa on avatud kella viiest kuueni** *The ticket office is open from 5 till 6 o'clock*, we add **-st** to the first (beginning) time and **-ni** to the second time i.e.

13.00–14.00	kella ühe**st** kahe**ni**
16.00–18.00	kella nelja**st** kuue**ni**
11.00–12.00	kella üheteistkümne**st** kaheteistkümne**ni**

Note that in constructions like this, we add endings to the second form. The three forms of numerals are given in the following table.

EXERCISE 9

Fill in the blanks.

	Mis kellast? From when?	Mis kellani? Until when?
üks, ühe, üht	*ühe**st***	*ühe**ni***
kaks, kahe, kaht	_____	_____
kolm, kolme, kolme	_____	_____
neli, nelja, nelja	_____	_____
viis, viie, viit	_____	_____
kuus, kuue, kuut	_____	_____
seitse, seitsme, seitset	_____	_____
kaheksa, kaheksa, kaheksat	_____	_____
üheksa, üheksa, üheksat	_____	_____
kümme, kümne, kümmet	_____	_____
üksteist, üheteistkümne, ühtteist	_____	_____
kaksteist, kaheteistkümne, kahtteist	_____	_____
kakskümmend, kahekümne, kahtkümmend	_____	_____

Note that when the words **veerand** *quarter* and **kolmveerand** *three quarters* are used they do not change, for instance **kella veerand ühest kolmveerand kaheni** *from quarter past twelve till quarter to 2*. When we use the word **pool** *half* it will occur in the form **poole**, for instance **kella poole ühest poole kaheni** *from half past 12 till half past 1*.

In order to practise this grammar topic further do Exercise 17 in the Practice section.

KELL ON VIIS MINUTIT ÜKS LÄBI. KELL ON VIIE MINUTI PÄRAST ÜKS *IT IS FIVE MINUTES PAST ONE. IT IS FIVE MINUTES TO ONE*

We have already learnt how to tell the time (in Unit 1). There we learnt how to say *It's 1 o'clock. It's quarter past 1. It is half past 1. It is a quarter to 2.* Now we will learn how to construct sentences like *It's 5 minutes past 1.* and *It's 5 minutes to 2.*

13.05 Kell on viis minutit üks läbi.	*It's 5 minutes past 1.*
13.10 Kell on kümme minutit üks läbi.	*It's 10 minutes past 1.*
13.12 Kell on kaksteist minutit üks läbi.	*It's 12 minutes past 1.*
13.50 Kell on <u>kümne minuti</u> pärast kaks.	*It's 10 minutes to 2.*
13.55 Kell on <u>viie minuti</u> pärast kaks.	*It's 5 minutes to 2.*
13.58 Kell on <u>kahe minuti</u> pärast kaks.	*It's 2 minutes to 2.*

Note that the underlined words are in the second form.

EXERCISE 10

Put the right pairs together.

1	Kell on kümme minutit kaks läbi.	**a**	18.55
2	Kell on viis minutit seitse läbi.	**b**	14.10
3	Kell on kaks minutit kaksteist läbi.	**c**	11.58
4	Kell on kümne minuti pärast kaks.	**d**	19.05
5	Kell on viie minuti pärast seitse.	**e**	13.50
6	Kell on kahe minuti pärast kaksteist.	**f**	12.02

In order to practise this grammar topic further do Exercise 18 in the Practice section.

TA TULEB KAHE TUNNI PÄRAST TAGASI *HE WILL COME BACK IN 2 HOURS' TIME*

The word **pärast** *after, because of* has several different meanings and ways of usage in Estonian. For instance:

I

Ma tulen **kahe tunni pärast** tagasi.	*I will come back in 2 hours' time.*
Proovige **poole tunni pärast** uuesti.	*Try again in half an hour's time.*
Ta tuleb **viie minuti pärast**.	*He/she will come in 5 minutes.*
Sa tuled **viie päeva pärast** tagasi.	*You will come back in 5 days.*
Ta läheb **kuue kuu pärast** reisile.	*He/she will go on a trip in 6 months' time.*
Ma lõpetan kooli **aasta pärast**.	*I will graduate in a year.*

As you can see in this context, the word **pärast** was used with words indicating an interval of time. Note also that the word pärast is placed after the phrase indicating time (all of which is in the second form).

II

Tulge minu juurde **pärast viit**.	*Come to me after 5.*
Pärast kümmet olen ma majast väljas.	*I will be out of the building after 10 o'clock.*
Pärast tööd lähen trenni.	*After work I will go to do some training.*
Pärast puhkust olen ma palju rõõmsam.	*After the holidays I am much happier.*

As you can see in this context, the word **pärast** is used with words indicating a certain time, occasion or action. In this case, the word **pärast** comes in front of the phrase (all of which is in the third form).

III

Ma teen seda ainult **sinu pärast**.	*I do this because of you.*
Valeühenduse pärast ei saa ma temaga rääkida.	*Because of a wrong connection, I could not talk to him.*

As you can see, the third meaning of **pärast** is *because of something*. In this case, the word **pärast** comes after the main word (which is in the second form).

EXERCISE 11

Find the right match.

1	Ta tuleb kolme tunni pärast.	**a**	Call in 10 minutes' time.
2	Helistage kümne minuti pärast.	**b**	He will come after 3 o'clock.
3	Ta tuleb pärast kolme.	**c**	He will come in 3 hours' time.
4	Pärast viit lähen baari.	**d**	Are you doing this because of me
5	Kas sa teed seda minu pärast?	**e**	I am calling you because of work.
6	Ma helistan teile töö pärast.	**f**	I will go to the bar after 5.

In order to practise this grammar topic further do Exercise 19 in the Practice section.

SELLE FILMI REŽISSÖÖR … *THE DIRECTOR OF THIS FILM … – GENITIVE CASE*

Constructions like **selle filmi** **režissöör** *director of this film* and **selle raamatu** **autor** *author of this book* have a different word order from that in English, i.e. the main word **režissöör** *director*, **autor** *author* is at the end of the phrase. Note also that the underlined part of the phrase is in the second form:

selle režissööri **film**	*this director's film (film of this director)*
selle autori **raamat**	*this author's book (book of this author)*
selle teatri **kava**	*the programme of this theatre*
selle filmi **näitlejad**	*the actors of this film*

The forms of the word **see** *this* are:

I form	**see**
II form	**selle**
III form	**seda**

EXERCISE 12

Translate.

1 selle autori film _____

2 selle teatri näitlejad _____

3 selle filmi näitlejad _____

4 selle raamatu autor _____

In order to practise this grammar topic further do Exercises 20–21 in the Practice section.

KÕIKIDES SUURTES KINODES *IN ALL BIG CINEMAS – PLURAL CASES*

In English, plural forms are usually made by adding **-s** to the end of the word, for instance *cinemas*, *actors*. In Estonian, there are several ways of making the plural forms. Study the following examples:

Need on suure**d** kino**d.**	*These are big cinemas.*
Nende suurte kino**de** kava on sarnane.	*These big cinemas have similar programmes.*
Festival toimub nen**des** suur**tes** kinodes.	*The festival takes place in these big cinemas.*

As you can see, the plural forms in Estonian can be indicated either by **-d**, **-de** or **-te**.

Note that the plural forms of the word **see** *this* is **need** *these* and the three forms are:

I form	**need**
II form	**nende**
III form	**neid**

See also Appendix 3.

EXERCISE 13

Decide in which phrase the plural is used: **a** or **b**. Underline the phrase that contains plural words.

1 **a** see teater, **b** need teatrid

2 **a** huvitavad etendused, **b** huvitav etendus

3 **a** nende filmide režissöör, **b** selle filmi režissöör

4 **a** etenduse algus, **b** etenduste algus

5 **a** selles kinos, **b** nendes kinodes

6 **a** heal näitlejal, **b** headel näitlejatel

7 **a** pensionärile sissepääs odavam, **b** pensionäridele sissepääs odavam

8 **a** lastega peredele sissepääs tasuta, **b** lapsega perele sissepääs tasuta

In order to practise this grammar topic further do Exercise 22 in the Practice section.

PILETITE TELLIMINE *ORDERING TICKETS*

To make constructions like *ordering* and *reading* in Estonian, we just add the ending **-mine** to the stem of the word. Note that this is *not* the same form as *I am reading* – **Ma loen.**

telli/ma	*to order*	**telli**mine	*ordering*
luge/ma	*to read*	**luge**mine	*reading*
suitseta/ma	*to smoke*	**suitseta**mine	*smoking*
vali/ma	*to elect*	**vali**mine	*electing*

The three forms are all similar:

tellimine, tellimise, tellimist

lugemine, lugemise, lugemist

Here are some more examples:

Piletite **tellimine** www.suveteater.ee.	*Ordering tickets www.suveteater.e.*
Suitsetamine keelatud	*Smoking prohibited.*
Festivali **avamine** toimub reedel.	*The opening of the festival will take place on Friday.*
Festivali **lõpetamisele** tuleb palju inimesi.	*For the closing of the festival there will be a large audience (lit. lots of people).*
Täna toimuvad klubi missi **valimised.**	*Today the electing of the club Miss will take place.*

EXERCISE 14

Follow the example and make similar words, then translate them.

1 rääkima   *rääkimine*
2 kuulama   _____
3 vaatama   _____
4 jalutama   _____
5 laulma   _____
6 jooksma   _____
7 istuma   _____

SOME COMMON ABBREVIATIONS

Here are some common abbreviations that are used in advertisements and signs.

v.a	välja arvatud	*except*
s.h.	sealhulgas	*also*
tel	telefon	*telephone*
jne	ja nii edasi	*etc.* (lit. *and so on*)
jmt	ja muu taoline	*etc.* (lit. *and other of the same kind*)
jt	ja teised	*et al.* (lit. *and others*)

TEISIPÄEVITI JA KOLMAPÄEVITI *ON MONDAYS AND TUESDAYS*

In Estonian, we have a special ending to indicate that something takes place on certain days or periods, i.e. **Laupäeviti ma olen tööl** *I work on Saturdays.* **Talviti ma olen linnas** *During the winter I stay in town.*

Here are most common words this construction is used with:

esmaspäev	*Monday*	**esmaspäeviti**	*on Mondays*
teisipäev	*Tuesday*	**teisipäeviti**	*on Tuesdays*
reede	*Friday*	**reedeti**	*on Fridays*
tööpäev	*working day*	**tööpäeviti**	*on working days*
kevad	*spring*	**kevadeti**	*during spring*
suvi	*summer*	**suviti**	*during summer*
sügis	*autumn*	**sügiseti**	*during autumn*
talv	*winter*	**talviti**	*during winter*

BUYING TICKETS FOR THE CINEMA AND THE THEATRE

The major municipal repertory theatres of Estonia are **Eesti Draamateater** *Estonian Drama Theatre* and **Tallinna Linnateater** *Tallinn City Theatre* (both situated in Tallinn), **Vanemuine** in Tartu, **Ugala** in Viljandi, **Endla** in Pärnu and **Rakvere Teater** in Rakvere. As enjoying drama performances is very popular in Estonia, there is a great variety of smaller project theatres and even children have their own **Eesti Noorsoo- ja nukuteater** *Estonian Puppet Theatre* in Tallinn. As there is a professional drama school in Estonia giving higher education to actors, the level of performances is high.

Rahvusooper Estonia *Estonian National Opera* is situated in Tallinn presenting opera, musical and ballet performances. During the summer many musicals are performed in various places in Estonia.

Going to the theatre is an occasion for most people; ladies dress up and men wear suits. It is inappropriate to go to the theatre wearing trainers and casual clothes, but any clean and smart outfit will do. Overcoats are left in the cloakroom; during the winter, you may also leave your winter boots there.

Information about Estonian cinemas and theatres can be found easily on the internet. Often, tickets can also be booked and bought online. If buying tickets at the ticket office you might want to say **Palun kaks piletit ettepoole/tahapoole** *Two tickets closer to the stage please/ away from the stage please* or **Sooviksin piletit kuskile keskele/kuskile ääre peale** *I would like to have a ticket somewhere in the middle/somewhere near the aisle.*

When buying tickets on the internet you might need to know words like **parter** or **põrand** *the ground floor,* **rõdu** *balcony;* **täispilet** *full price ticket;* **sooduspilet** *reduced price ticket.*

Practice

EXERCISE 15

Decide in which sentences the conditional mood is used.

1   **a** Kas sa teatrisse tahad minna? **b** Kas sa teatrisse tahaksid minna?

2   **a** Kas sulle meeldiks balletti vaadata? **b** Kas sulle meeldib balletti vaadata?

3   **a** Kas sa eelistaks märulifilmi või ulmefilmi? **b** Kas sa eelistad märulifilmi või ulmefilmi?

4   **a** Kas sa tuleksid sellel nädalavahetusel minuga klubisse? **b** Kas sa tuled sellel nädalavahetusel minuga klubisse?

5   **a** Mõni teine kord on parem. **b** Mõni teine kord oleks parem.

6   **a** Mis kohti te soovitate? **b** Mis kohti te soovitaksite?

EXERCISE 16

Translate these sentences into Estonian.

1   Would you like to go to the cinema with me?

2   Of course I would like to.

3   What sort of film would you prefer?

4   I would like a science fiction film.

5   In which row would you like the ticket?

6   Somewhere in the middle.

EXERCISE 17

Find the right match.

1   Kassa on avatud 13.00–14.00.   **a**   Kassa on avatud kella kaheksast kaheni.

2   Kassa on avatud 13.00–21.00.   **b**   Kassa on avatud kella kahest kaheksani.

3   Kassa on avatud 8.00–14.00.   **c**   Kassa on avatud kella ühest üheksani.

4   Kassa on avatud 9.00–13.00.   **d**   Kassa on avatud kella üheksast üheni.

5   Kassa on avatud 14.00–20.00.   **e**   Kassa on avatud kella üheksast viieni.

6   Kassa on avatud 9.00–17.00.   **f**   Kassa on avatud kella ühest kaheni.

EXERCISE 18

 08.08

What's the time? Write correct sentences, then listen to check your answers.

1   15.05 _____

2   17.10 _____

3   19.13 _____

4 20.50 _____

5 21.55 _____

6 22.58 _____

EXERCISE 19

Translate the following sentences into Estonian.

1 He will come in half an hour's time.

2 He will come after 4.

3 I am calling you because of the course.

4 He will come in an hour's time.

5 He will come after 6.

6 I am doing this because of him.

EXERCISE 20

Choose the right translation.

1 **selle autori raamat. a** the author of this book **b** the book of this author

2 **selle režissööri film a** the film of this director **b** the director of this film

3 **minu sõbra laps a** the child of my friend **b** the friend of my child

4 **tema abikaasa ülemus a** the boss of his husband **b** the husband of his boss

5 **meie õpetaja koer a** the dog of our teacher **b** the teacher of our dog

EXERCISE 21

Translate the following phrases into Estonian.

1 the book of my child

2 the cost of this ticket

3 the name of this show

4 the address of this cinema

5 the author of this science fiction film

EXERCISE 22

Translate the following sentences. You need to pay attention to the usage of singular and plural.

1 Nende režissööride filmid on väga head.

2 Selles kinos on kallid piletid.

3 Festivali programmis on erinevad filmid.

4 Ööklubides saab tantsida kella kolmeni.

5 Lasteetendustele võivad tulla ka vanemad.

6 Mulle meeldib see näitleja.

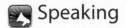 Speaking

EXERCISE 23

Here are some situations for you to practise. You are reading advertisements and discussing with a friend what to do on Saturday night.

1 You suggest going either to the cinema or to the nightclub. Your friend asks **Mida sa ise eelistaks?** What does he mean?

2 You decide to go to the cinema. It seems that only two films are running. How do you ask *Isn't there anything else?*

3 You see an advertisement saying **Esmaspäeviti piletid poole hinnaga.** What does it mean?

4 You see a sign saying **Kassa avatud iga päev v.a. L-P.** What does it mean?

EXERCISE 24

Here are some more situations for you to practise. You are calling the ticket office to ask some questions.

1 You have selected a film and want to ask if it is a comedy. How do you ask that?

2 You want to know how long the film is. How do you ask that?

3 You want to know if there is a price difference between different shows. How do you ask that?

4 Now you are buying tickets. The saleswoman asks you **Mis ritta te soovite?** You would like to have seats somewhere in the middle. How do you say that?

EXERCISE 25

 08.09

You are talking to a friend. Fill in the missing lines and then listen to the completed dialogue.

Sina	Ask *Would you like to go to the cinema?*
Sõber	Millal?
Sina	Say *Tonight*.
Sõber	Oh, lahe! Muidugi lähme!
Sina	Ask *What kind of film would you like to see?*
Sõber	Aga mida sa ise eelistaks?
Sina	Kesklinna kinos jookseb üks komöödia, lähme siis seda vaatama.
Sõber	Väga hea.

EXERCISE 26

 08.10

You are talking to a friend. Fill in the missing lines, and then listen to the completed dialogue.

Sina	Ask *Would you like to go to the theatre this weekend?*
Sõber	Ja mis etendus seal on?
Sina	*Say Some kind of English comedy.*
Sõber	Ma seekord ei saa. On muud tegemist.
Sina	Say *Too bad. Maybe some other time then.*
Sõber	Võib-olla tõesti.

EXERCISE 27

 08.11

You are buying tickets for the evening performance. Fill in the missing lines, and then listen to the completed dialogue.

Müüja	Tere!
Sina	Ask for two tickets.
Müüja	Kas tänasele etendusele?
Sina	Say *Yes, please.*
Müüja	Ja mis ritta?
Sina	Ask *Is there any difference in price?*
Müüja	Ei ole.
Sina	Ask *What places would you suggest?*
Müüja	Ma soovitaksin neid kohti siin.
Sina	Say *OK.* Ask *How long is this performance?*
Müüja	Kaks tundi.
Sina	Say *Very good.*

EXERCISE 28

 08.12

You are calling the ticket office to ask about a movie called 'Helesinine planeet'. Fill in the missing lines. Listen to the completed dialogue.

Müüja	Tere! Kassa kuuleb.
Sina	Say *Hello!* Say *Please tell me what kind of film Blue Planet is.*
Müüja	See on dokumentaalfilm.
Sina	Ask who the director of this film is.
Müüja	Ta on väga kuulus, aga tema nimi ei tule mul praegu meelde.
Sina	Say OK. *Ask how long the film is.*
Müüja	Umbes poolteist tundi.
Sina	Ask how much the tickets cost.
Müüja	Sada kuni kakssada krooni.
Sina	Ask whether the price depends on the time of the day.
Müüja	Ei sõltu.

❓ Test yourself

1 You are calling to find your colleague Marko Rätsep at work. What do you say?
   a Kas see on Marko Rätsepa korter?
   b Las ta helistab Marko Rätsepale.
   c Ma sooviksin rääkida Marko Rätsepaga.

2 A friend invites you to club, but you can't go. How do you answer?
   a Ma seekord ei saa. On muud tegemist.
   b Tulen hea meelega.
   c Mul on ükskõik.

3 Which one is a science fiction film in Estonian?
   a märulifilm
   b ulmefilm
   c multikas

4 You want to buy two tickets for a movie with seats in the middle of the cinema. What do you say?
   a Palun kaks piletit ettepoole.
   b Palun kaks piletit keskele.
   c Palun kaks piletit tahapoole.

5 You see a sign **Pilet poole hinnaga**. What does it mean?
   a the show is sold out
   b free entrance
   c tickets available at half price

6 You see a sign **Kassa töötab iga päev v.a reede.** What does it mean?
   a The ticket office is open every Friday.
   b The ticket office is open every day except Friday.
   c The ticket office is open every day.

7 How to say in Estonian *The ticket office is open from 9 till 14*?
   a Kassa on avatud kella üheksast kaheni.
   b Kassa on avatud kella kaheksast kaheni.
   c Kassa on avatud kella kahest üheksani.

8 **Kell on viie minuti pärast kaksteist.** What's the time?
   a 11.55
   b 12.05
   c 12.15

9 How do you say in Estonian *the programme of this festival*?
  a see festival ja programm
  b selle festivali programm
  c nende festivalide programmid

10 What is the correct translation of *Would you like to go to the theatre?*
  a Kas sa lähed teatrisse?
  b Kas sa tahad teatrisse minna?
  c Kas sa tahaksid teatrisse minna?

9 Ma jäin haigeks
I fell ill

In this unit you will learn:
▶ *How to make an appointment with a doctor*
▶ *How to describe the most common ailments*
▶ *How to understand the doctor's prescriptions and buy medicine at the chemist's*

Listening 1

You will hear a patient talking to the nurse at the hospital's registration desk. Listen to the dialogues and then complete Exercises 1–2.

 09.01

Patsient	Tere, mul oleks vaja kiiresti arsti juurde saada. Mul on hirmus köha.
Õde	Kes on teie perearst?
Patsient	Ma olen välismaalane.
Õde	Kas teil haigekassa kaart on?
Patsient	Jah. Palun.
Õde	Kas teile täna kell üksteist sobiks?
Patsient	Sobib küll.
Õde	Öelge palun veel oma isikukood.
Patsient	See on 47705262199.
Õde	Selge. Minge siis kell üksteist kabinetti number kaheksa. See on teisel korrusel.

V

patsient, patsiendi, patsienti, patsiente	*patient*
õde, õe, õde, õdesid	*nurse*
Mul oleks vaja arsti juurde saada.	*I need to get to the doctor.*
perearst, -i, -i, -e	*general practitioner, GP*
hirmus, hirmsa, hirmsat, hirmsaid	*terrible*
köha, -, -	*cough*
kiiresti	*quickly*
välismaala/ne, -se, -st, -si	*foreigner*
haigekassa kaart, kaardi, kaarti, kaarte	*medical insurance card*
Kas teile sobiks?	*Would … suit you?*

isikukood, -i, -i, -e	identification code
kabinet, -i, -ti, -te	room, surgery
korrus, -e, -t, -eid	floor, storey

EXERCISE 1

Listen and decide if the following sentences are **a** true or **b** false.

1 The patient needs to get to the doctor as soon as possible.

2 His doctor is a foreigner.

3 The patient does not have a medical insurance card.

4 The patient can get to the doctor at 11 o'clock.

5 The nurse asks for the patient's pin code.

6 The nurse asks the patient's name and home address.

7 The patient has to go to room no. 8.

8 The room is situated on the third floor.

EXERCISE 2

Choose the right translation.

1 **Mul oleks vaja arsti juurde saada. a** I am at the doctor. **b** I need to get to the doctor.

2 **Kas teil haigekassa kaart on? a** Do you have a medical insurance card? **b** What is your identification code?

3 **Kas teile kell kolm sobiks? a** Is it possible at 3 o'clock? **b** Would 3 o'clock suit you?

Listening 2

In these dialogues the doctors are questioning the patients about their illnesses. Listen to the dialogues and then complete Exercises 3–4.

 09.02

a Arst	Mis kaebused teil siis on?
Patsient	Mul on palavik ja kurk valutab. Ja mul on hirmus nohu.
Arst	Kui kõrge palavik teil on?
Patsient	Eile õhtul oli kolmkümmend üheksa kraadi ja täna hommikul kolmkümmend seitse viis.
Arst	Kas pea ka õhtul valutas?
Patsient	Valutas küll.
Arst	Teil on ilmselt gripp. Jooge sooja teed ja puhake. Kolme päeva pärast peaksite terve olema.
Patsient	Kas ma siis pean uuesti teie juurde tulema?
Arst	Ei, kui kõik on korras, siis pole vaja tulla.

b **Arst**   Järgmine palun.

Patsient   Tere!

Arst   Tere! Mida te siis kaebate?

Patsient   Mul kõht hirmsasti valutab.

Arst   Mida te hommikul sõite?

Patsient   Ei söönud midagi, jõin ainult kohvi.

Arst   Selge. Ma pean teid läbi vaatama. Heitke palun pikali.

Patsient   Kas siia?

Arst   Jah. Öelge, kui teil valus on.

Patsient   Ai-ai, sealt oli küll väga valus.

Arst   Nii-nii. Ma annan teile saatekirja eriarsti juurde.

arst, -i, -i, -e	*doctor*
kaebus, -e, -t, -i	*complaint*
palavik, -u, -ku	*fever*
kurk, kurgu, kurku	*throat*
valuta/ma, -da, -b	*to ache*
nohu, -, -	*cold, the snuffles*
Kui kõrge?	*How high?*
kraad, -i, -i, -e	*degree*
pea, -, -d, paid	*head*
ilmselt	*probably*
gripp, gripi, grippi	*flu*
puhake	*do rest* (pl. imperative)
kolme päeva pärast	*after 3 days*
peaksite	*you should*
terve, -, -t, -id	*healthy, well*
uuesti	*again*
teie juurde tulema	*come to you*
kui	*if*
kõik on korras	*everything is OK*
pole vaja	*it is not necessary*
järgmi/ne, -se, -st, -si	*next*
kõht, kõhu, kõhtu	*stomach*
hirmsasti	*terribly*
sõite *you* (pl.)	*ate*
ei söönud	*didn't eat*
midagi	*anything*
jõin	*I drank*
ainult	*only*

läbi vaata/ma, läbi vaada/ta, vaata/n läbi	*examine*
pikali heit/ma, pikali hei/ta, heida/n pikali	*to lie down*
sealt oli valus	*it hurt there*
nii-nii	*I see, OK*
saate/kiri, -kirja, -kirja, -kirju	*referal*
eriarst, -i, -i,-e	*specialist doctor*

EXERCISE 3

Listen and choose the correct answer. For some questions several answers are correct.

a

1 The patient has **a** fever, **b** cramps, **c** the snuffles, **d** a sore throat, **e** a headache.
2 In the evening the fever was as high as **a** 37.5 degrees, **b** 39 degrees, **c** 38 degrees.
3 The doctor thinks the patient has **a** flu, **b** pneumonia, **c** a cold, **d** migraine.
4 The doctor suggests the patient should **a** take some medicine, **b** drink warm tea and rest, **c** wait for 2 days and then come back.

b

Listen and choose the correct answer.

1 The patient has **a** a headache, **b** toothache, **c** stomach ache.
2 In the morning the patient **a** drank some coffee, **b** had breakfast, **c** ate and drank nothing.
3 The doctor asks the patient to **a** undress, **b** to lie down, **c** say more about the symptoms.
4 The doctor thinks the patient should **a** consult with a specialist doctor, **b** go home and rest, **c** take some medicine.

EXERCISE 4

Choose the right translation.

1 **Mis kaebused teil on? a** What complaints do you have? **b** How do you feel?
2 **Kui kõrge palavik teil on? a** What is your temperature? **b** Have you measured your temperature?
3 **Kas teil pea valutab? a** Do you have a headache? **b** When does your head ache?
4 **Kas ma pean uuesti teie juurde tulema? a** When do I have to come back? **b** Do I have to come back to you?
5 **Ma pean teid läbi vaatama. a** I need to see what I can do. **b** I need to examine you.
6 **Heitke palun pikali. a** Please lie down. **b** Please stand up.
7 **Öelge, kui teil valus on. a** Please say when it hurts. **b** Please say where it hurts.

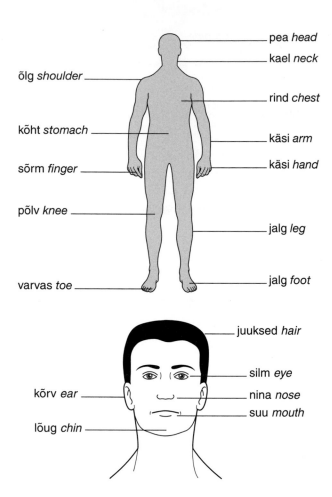

pea *head*
kael *neck*
õlg *shoulder*
rind *chest*
kõht *stomach*
käsi *arm*
käsi *hand*
sõrm *finger*
põlv *knee*
jalg *leg*
jalg *foot*
varvas *toe*

juuksed *hair*
silm *eye*
kõrv *ear*
nina *nose*
suu *mouth*
lõug *chin*

Listening 3

The first dialogue takes place in the dentist's surgery and the second in the casualty department. Listen to the dialogues and then complete Exercises 5–6.

 09.03

a	**Hambaarst**	Nii. Ma kuulan teid.
	Patsient	Mul on kohutav hambavalu.
	Hambaarst	Kas te valuvaigistit juba võtsite?
	Patsient	Jah, aga see ei aidanud.
	Hambaarst	Tehke palun suu lahti. Oi-jah. See hammas tuleb kahjuks välja tõmmata. Ma teen teile valuvaigistava süsti.
	Patsient	Millal see koht ära paraneb?
	Hambaarst	Umbes kolme päeva pärast.
b	**Arst**	Mis siis teiega juhtus?
	Patsient	Ma kukkusin eile ja väänasin jala välja. Õhtul läks jalg paistesse.

V

hambaarst, -i, -i, -e	*dentist*
kuula/ma, -ta, -n	*to listen to*
kohutav, -a, -at, -aid	*terrible, horrible*
valuvaigisti, -, -t, valuvaigisteid	*analgesic, pain killer*
võtsite *took* (pl.)	
ei aidanud	*didn't help*
lahti tege/ma, lahti teh/a, tee/n lahti	*to open*
tehke lahti	*open* (pl imperative)
suu, -, -d	*mouth*
hammas, hamba, hammast, hambaid	*tooth*
tuleb	*has to*
välja tõmb/ama, välja tõmma/ta, tõmba/n välja	*to pull out*
valuvaigistav, -a, -at, -aid	*analgesic*
süst, -i, -i, -e	*injection*
valuvaigistav süst	*analgesic injection*
ära parane/ma, ära parane/da, parane/b ära	*to heal*
juhtu/ma, -da, -b	*to happen*
Mis teiega juhtus?	*What happened to you?*
kukku/ma, -da, kuku/n	*to fall*
kukkusin	*I fell*
välja vääna/ma, välja vääna/ta, vääna/n välja	*to sprain*
väänasin välja	*I sprained*
jalg, jala, jalga, jalgu	*foot* (also *leg*)
paistesse mine/ma, paistesse minn/a, lähe/b paistesse	*to swell up*
läks paistesse	*swelled up*
Kas te röntgenis käisite?	*Did you go to x-ray?*
pilt, pildi, pilti, pilte	*picture*
luu/murd, -murru, -murdu, -murde	*fracture* (of bone)
kipsi pane/ma, kipsi pann/a, pane/n kipsi	*to put into plaster*
ära võt/ma, ära võt/ta, võta/n ära	*to take off*

EXERCISE 5

a

Listen and decide if the following sentences are **a** true or **b** false.

1 The patient has a terrible headache.

2 The patient has already taken some painkillers but they didn't work.

3 The doctor suggests the patient should take stronger painkillers.

4 The doctor suggests she will give the patient an analgesic injection and she will pull the tooth out.

5 The patient should feel better in 3 days' time.

b

Listen and decide if the following sentences are **a** true or **b** false.

1 The patient fell and broke his arm.

2 The patient has already had an x-ray picture taken.

3 The patient bought some painkillers.

4 The doctor suggests putting on a plaster.

5 The plaster has to stay on for three weeks.

EXERCISE 6

Choose the right translation

1 **Kas te juba võtsite valuvaigistit?**
   a Have you already taken the analgesic?
   b Do you want to have an analgesic?

2 **Tehke palun suu lahti.**
   a Please close your mouth.
   b Please open your mouth.

3 **Me teeme teile valuvaigistava süsti.**
   a We will give you some analgesic.
   b I will give you an analgesic injection.

4 **Millal see koht ära paraneb?**
   a When will this place be healed?
   b When will I be well again?

5 **Mis teiega juhtus?**
   a What happened to you?
   b What complaints do you have?

6 **Kas te röntgenis juba käisite?**
   a Have you already had an x-ray done?
   b Do you want to go to x-ray?

7 Selle peab kipsi panema.
   a This needs to be put in plaster.
   b You must keep the plaster on.

8 Kolme nädala pärast võtame kipsi ära.
   a We will take the plaster off in 3 weeks' time.
   b The plaster needs to be on for 3 weeks.

Listening 4

You will hear a dialogue where someone is buying medicine at the chemist's. Listen to the dialogues and complete Exercises 7–8 below.

 09.04

Apteeker	Nii. Mida teile?
Ostja	Palun seda rohtu, mis siin retseptis on.
Apteeker	Jah, palun.
Ostja	Kuidas seda rohtu võtma peab?
Apteeker	Te peate neid võtma kolm korda päevas pärast sööki kaks tabletti korraga.
Ostja	Kas koos veega?
Apteeker	Jah.
Ostja	Mitu tabletti siin pakis on?
Apteeker	Siin on kakskümmend tabletti. See on siin pakendi peal ka kirjas.
Ostja	Kas sellel rohul on mingeid kõrvalmõjusid ka?
Apteeker	Ei tohiks olla. Aga lugege igaks juhuks läbi ka pakendis olev infoleht.
Ostja	Ahah, aitäh.

apteeker, apteekri, apteekrit, apteekreid	*chemist*
ostja, -, -t, -id	*buyer*
rohi, rohu, rohtu, rohtusid	*medicine, drug*
retsept, -i, -i, -e	*prescription*
kolm korda päevas	*three times a day*
pärast sööki	*after a meal*
tablett, tableti, tabletti, tablette	*tablet, pill*
korraga	*at once, at a time*
pakend, -i, -it, -eid	*package, wrapper*
on kirjas	*is written*
mingi, mingi, mingit, mingeid	*some kind of*
kõrvalmõju, -, -, -sid	*side-effect*
ei tohiks olla	*shouldn't have*

igaks juhuks	*just in case*
läbi luge/ma, läbi luge/da, loe/n läbi	*to read through*
pakendis olev infoleht	*information sheet that is in the package*
info/leht, -lehe, -lehte, -lehti	*information sheet*
ahah	*OK*

EXERCISE 7

Listen and choose the correct answer.

1 Ostja soovib **a** retsepti, **b** rohtu, **c** vett.

2 Rohtu tuleb võtta **a** üks kord päevas, **b** kaks korda päevas, **c** kolm korda päevas.

3 Rohtu tuleb võtta **a** enne sööki, **b** pärast sööki, **c** koos söögiga.

4 Rohtu tuleb võtta **a** üks tablett korraga, **b** kaks tabletti korraga, **c** kolm tabletti korraga.

5 Rohtu tuleb võtta **a** koos piimaga, **b** koos veega, **c** koos teega.

6 Pakis on **a** kaksteist tabletti, **b** kaheksateist tabletti, **c** kakskümmend tabletti.

7 Apteeker ütleb: **a** ravimil on kõrvalmõjud, **b** lugege läbi pakendis olev infoleht.

EXERCISE 8

 09.05

Choose the right response. Listen to the correct answers.

1 **Mida teile? a** Palun seda rohtu. **b** Jah, palun.

2 **Kuidas seda rohtu võtma peab? a** Siin on kakskümmend tabletti. **b** Kolm korda päevas kaks tabletti korraga.

3 **Mitu tabletti siin pakendis on? a** Siin on kakskümmend tabletti. **b** See on siin pakendi peal ka kirjas.

4 **Kas sellel rohul mingeid kõrvalmõjusid ka on? a** Ärge võtke koos veega. **b** Ei tohiks olla.

> **INSIGHT**
>
> It is quite normal to get bored studying a language. Take a break and don't push yourself. Instead, revise the units you have already done.

Language patterns

PAST TENSES

When talking about events that took place in the past, we need to use the past tenses. The Estonian language has three past tenses: **lihtminevik** *imperfect*, **täisminevik** *present perfect* and **enneminevik** *past perfect*.

lihtminevik *imperfect*	täisminevik *present perfect*	enneminevik *past perfect*
Ma **käisin** eile arsti juures. *I went to the doctor yesterday.*	Ma **olen** selle arsti juures juba viis korda käinud. *I have gone to this doctor five times already.*	Kui **olin** arsti juures **käinud**, läksin apteeki. *After I had gone to the doctor I went to the chemist's.*
Ma **ei käinud** täna arsti juures. *I didn't go to the doctor today.*	Ma **ei ole** kunagi selle arsti juures käinud. *I have never gone to this doctor.*	Ma **ei olnud** kunagi varem selle arsti juures käinud. *I had never before gone to this doctor.*

In this unit we will have a closer look at how to make and use the forms of the imperfect. The other two past tenses will be studied in future units.

MA KÄISIN ARSTI JUURES *I WENT TO THE DOCTOR – IMPERFECT*

Lihtminevik *imperfect* is used to talk about certain events that happened in the past. Often this tense is used with words and expressions like **natuke aega tagasi** *a while ago*, **kaks tundi tagasi** *2 hours ago*, **eile** *yesterday*, **eelmisel nädalal** *last week*, **möödunud kuul** *last month*, **kaks aastat tagasi** *2 years ago* etc.

Eile ma **käisin** arsti juures.	*I went to the doctor yesterday.*
Eelmisel nädalal me **ostsime** uue korteri.	*We bought a new apartment last week.*
Möödunud kuul ma **puhkasin.**	*Last month I was on holiday.*
Kaks aastat **tagasi elasin** ma teises linnas kui praegu.	*Two years ago I lived in a different town from the one I live in now.*

Now we will study how to make the forms of imperfect. Most words just take **-si** (in third person **-s**), which is placed in front of the personal ending of the present tense and the negative form has the ending **-nud**.

olevik *present*	lihtminevik *imperfect*
Ma **käin** arsti juures. *I go to the doctor.*	Ma **käisin** arsti juures. *I went to the doctor*
Sa **käid** arsti juures. *You go to the doctor.*	Sa **käisid** arsti juures. *You went to the doctor.*
Ta **käib** arsti juures. *He/she goes to the doctor.*	Ta **käis** arsti juures. *He/she went to the doctor.*
Me **käime** arsti juures. *We go to the doctor.*	Me **käisime** arsti juures. *We went to the doctor.*
Te **käite** arst juures. *You go to the doctor.*	Te **käisite** arsti juures. *You went to the doctor.*
Nad **käivad** arsti juures. *They go to the doctor.*	Nad **käisid** arsti juures. *They went to the doctor.*
ma, sa, ta, me, te, nad **ei käi** arsti juures *I, you, he/she, we, you, they don't go to the doctor*	ma, sa, ta, me, te, nad **ei käinud** arsti juures *I, you, he/she, we, you, they didn't go to the doctor*

Note that the he/she form does not end with **-b** as it does in the present tense. Note also that the forms for *you* (sing.) and *they* are exactly the same in the imperfect.

Remember that the affirmative forms of the imperfect (i.e. **ma vaatasin** I *looked*) are based on the first form (i.e. **vaatama** *to look*) and the negative forms (i.e. **ma ei vaadanud** I *didn't look*) on the second form (i.e. **vaadata** *to look*).

vaata/ma *to watch*	**vaada/ta** *to watch*
Ma **vaatasin** seda filmi. *I watched this movie.*	Ma **ei vaadanud** seda filmi. *I didn't watch this movie.*
Sa **vaatasid** seda filmi. *You watched this movie.*	Sa **ei vaadanud** seda filmi. *You didn't watch this movie.*
Ta **vaatas** seda filmi. *He/she watched this movie.*	Ta **ei vaadanud** seda filmi. *He/she didn't watch this movie.*
Me **vaatasime** seda filmi. *We watched this movie.*	Me **ei vaadanud** seda filmi. *We didn't watch this movie.*
Te **vaatasite** seda filmi. *You watched this movie.*	Te **ei vaadanud** seda filmi. *You didn't watch this movie.*
Nad **vaatasid** seda filmi. *They watched this movie.*	Nad **ei vaadanud** seda filmi. *They didn't watch this movie.*

EXERCISE 9

Make the forms of imperfect from the words **puhkama**, **puhata** *to rest*.

IRREGULAR HE/SHE FORM IN THE IMPERFECT

Usually the he/she form has the ending **-s** in the imperfect but there is a group of words that also take **-i** in front of the **--s**. Such words have letter **-t, -d, -s, -l, -r** in front of the ending of the first form.

sõitma *to drive*	*he/she drove* ta sõit**is** (not ta sõits)
leidma *to find*	*he/she found* ta leid**is** (not ta leids)
seisma *to stand*	*he/she stood* ta seis**is** he/she (not ta seiss)
laulma *to sing*	*he/she sang* ta laul**is** he/she (not ta lauls)
naerma *to laugh*	*he/she laughed* ta naer**is** he/she (not ta naers)

In same way **veetma** *to spend (time)*, **tootma** *to produce*, **lootma** *to hope*, **keetma** *to boil*, **kandma** *to carry, to wear*, **tundma** *to feel*, **kuulma** *to hear* etc. also change.

EXERCISE 10

Fill in the missing forms.

saat/ma kirja *to send a letter*	and/ma allkirja *to sign (with signature)*	ost/ma jäätist *to buy icecream*
ma saatsin kirja	ma andsin allkirja	ma _____ jäätist
sa saatsid kirja	sa _____ allkirja	sa ostsid jäätist
ta _____ kirja	ta _____ allkirja	ta _____ jäätist
me _____ kirja	me andsime allkirja	me _____ jäätist
te _____ kirja	te andsite allkirja	te ostsite jäätist
nad _____ kirja	nad andsid allkirja	nad _____ jäätist
ei _____ kirja	ei andnud allkirja	ei _____ jäätist

Note that the words **võtma** *to take*, **jätma** *to leave*, **nutma** *to cry*, **petma** *to cheat* and **katma** *to cover* have two **t**-s in the he/she form, i.e.:

ta võ**tt**is	*he/she took*
ta jä**tt**is	*he/she left*
ta nu**tt**is	*he/she cried*
ta pe**tt**is	*he/she cheated*
ta ka**tt**is	*he/she covered*

EXERCISE 11

Make the forms of imperfect from the word **jätma**.

kaasa võtma *to take along*	jätma *to leave*
ma võtsin passi kaasa	ma _____ passi koju
sa võtsid passi kaasa	sa _____ passi koju
NB! ta võ*tt*is passi kaasa	ta _____ passi koju
me võtsime passi kaasa	me _____ passi koju
te võtsite passi kaasa	te _____ passi koju
nad võtsid passi kaasa	nad _____ passi koju
ei võtnud passi kaasa	ei _____ passi koju

MINEMA *TO GO* – IMPERFECT

The word **minema** *to go* also has irregular forms. As we have already learnt, the forms in the present tense are also irregular (**ma lähen** *I go*, **sa lähed** *you go* etc.) The forms of the imperfect are as follows:

| ma läk**si**n *I went* |
| sa läk**si**d *you went* |
| ta läk**s** *he/she went* |

me läk**si**me *we went*	
te läk**si**te *you went*	
nad läk**si**d *they went*	
ma, sa, ta, me, te, nad **ei läinud**	
I, you, he/she, we, you, they didn't go	

EXERCISE 12

Fill in the blanks with the word **minema** in the imperfect.

1 Eile ma _____ tööle jala.

2 Ma ei _____ autoga, sest tahtsin jalutada.

3 Ka minu abikaasa ei _____ autoga.

4 Ta ei _____ ka jala.

5 Ta _____ rattaga.

6 Minu naabrid ei _____ eile tööle jala.

7 Nad _____ autoga.

8 Millega te eile tööle _____

In order to practise this grammar topic further do Exercise 18 in the Practice section.

MA SAIN TERVEKS *I GOT BETTER* – I-IMPERFECT

In the previous grammar section we learnt that the most common way of making the forms of imperfect is to add **-si** (in third form **-s**) to the word. Yet there are 15 irregular verbs in Estonian where **-i** is used instead of the **-si**. Now we will get acquainted with them in three groups.

I olema *to be,* **tulema** *to come,* **panema** *to put,* **pesema** *to wash,* **pidama** *to have to,* **tegema** *to do,* **nägema** *to see,* **surema** *to die*

The word **olema** *to be* has the following forms in the imperfect:

present tense	imperfect
ma **olen** *I am*	ma **olin** *I was*
sa **oled** *you are*	sa **olid** *you were*
ta **on** *he/she is*	ta **oli** *he/she was*
me **oleme** *we are*	me **olime** *we were*
te **olete** *you are*	te **olite** *you were*
nad **on** *they are*	nad **olid** *they were*
ma, sa, ta, me, te, nad **ei ole**	ma, sa, ta, me, te, nad **ei olnud**

In the same way as **olema** *to be* changes in the imperfect, so do the following words change.

tulema, tulla *to come*

For instance:

Ma **tulin** koju. *I came home.*	Me **tulime** koju. *We came home.*
Sa **tulid** koju. *You came home.*	Te **tulite** koju. *You came home.*
Ta **tuli** koju. *He/she came home.*	Nad **tulid** koju. *They came home.*
ei **tulnud** koju *didn't come home*	

panema, panna *to put*

For instance:

Ma **panin** raha kotti.	Me **panime** raha kotti.
I put money in the bag.	*We put money in the bag.*
Sa **panid** raha kotti.	Te **panite** raha kotti.
You put money in the bag.	*You put money in the bag.*
Ta **pani** raha kotti.	Nad **panid** raha kotti.
He/she put money in the bag.	*They put money in the bag.*
ei **pannud** raha kotti *didn't put money in the bag*	

pidama, pidada *have to, must*

For instance:

Ma **pidin** puhkama.	Me **pidime** puhkama.
I had to rest.	*We had to rest.*
Sa **pidid** puhkama.	Te **pidite** puhkama.
You had to rest.	*You had to rest.*
Ta **pidi** puhkama.	Nad **pidid** puhkama.
He/she had to rest.	*They had to rest.*
ei **pidanud** puhkama *didn't have to rest*	

tegema, teha *to do*

For instance:

Ma **tegin** koogi.	Me **tegime** koogi.
I made a cake.	*We made a cake.*
Sa **tegid** koogi.	Te **tegite** koogi.
You made a cake.	*You made a cake.*
Ta **tegi** koogi.	Nad **tegid** koogi.
He/she made a cake.	*They made a cake.*
ei teinud kooki *didn't make a cake*	

nägema, näha *to see*

For instance:

Ma **nägin** sõpra.	Me **nägime** sõpra.
I saw a friend.	*We saw a friend.*
Sa **nägid** sõpra.	Te **nägite** sõpra.
You saw a friend.	*You saw a friend.*
Ta **nägi** sõpra.	Nad **nägid** sõpra.
He/she saw a friend.	*They saw a friend.*
ei näinud sõpra *didn't see a friend*	

pesema, pesta *to wash*

For instance:

Ma **pesin** pead.	Me **pesime** pead.
I washed (my) head.	*We washed (our) head.*
Sa **pesid** pead.	Te **pesite** pead.
You washed (your) head.	*You washed (your) head.*
Ta **pesi** pead.	Nad **pesid** pead.
He/she washed (his/her) head.	*They washed (their) head.*
ei pesnud pead *didn't wash head*	

Note that the word **pidama** has several different meanings:

Ma pean õppima.	*I have to study.*
Ma pean töötama.	*I must work.*
Ma pean sünnipäeva.	*I celebrate my birthday.*
Ma pean koera.	*I keep a dog.*

Depending on the meaning, the forms of the imperfect can be different. If the meaning is *have to*, *must* (for instance **Ma pean töötama** *I have to work*), we use the *i*-imperfect **Ma pidin töötama** *I had to work*. In all other cases, we use the *si*- imperfect, for instance, **Pidasin sünnipäeva** *I celebrated my birthday*. **Pidasin koera** *I kept a dog*.

EXERCISE 13

First answer the questions affirmatively. Then answer the questions negatively.

1 Kas sa olid eile õhtul kodus? *Jah, olin küll. Ei olnud.*

2 Kas sa tulid täna tööle autoga?

3 Kas sa tegid kohvi?

4 Kas sa nägid meie uut klienti?

5 Kas sa pidid eile palju töötama?

II saama to get, jääma _to stay_

The word **saama** _to get_ has the following forms in the imperfect. Note that in the imperfect there is only one _a_ instead of the two that occur in the present tense.

present tense	imperfect
Ma **saan** palka.	Ma **sain** palka.
I get a salary.	_I got a salary._
Sa **saad** palka.	Sa **said** palka.
You get a salary.	_You got a salary._
Ta **saab** palka.	Ta **sai** palka.
He/she gets a salary.	_He/she got a salary._
Me **saame** palka.	Me **saime** palka.
We get a salary.	_We got a salary._
Te **saate** palka.	Te **saite** palka.
You get a salary.	_You got a salary._
Nad **saavad** palka.	Nad **said** palka.
They get a salary.	_They got a salary._
Ma, sa, ta, me, te, nad **ei saa** palka.	Ma, sa, ta, me, te, nad **ei saanud** palka.
I, you, he/she, we, you, they don't get a salary.	_I, you, he/she, we, you, they didn't get a salary._

EXERCISE 14

Make the forms of the imperfect of the word **jääma** _to stay_ using the word **saama** _to get_ as an analogy.

III jooma _to drink_, **tooma** _to bring_, **looma** _to create_, **sööma** _to eat_, **lööma** _to hit_

The word **jooma** _to drink_ has the following forms in the imperfect. Note that in the imperfect there is õ instead of the two os in the present tense.

present tense	imperfect
Ma **joon** õlut. _I drink beer._	Ma **jõin** õlut. _I drank beer._
Sa **jood** õlut. _You drink beer._	Sa **jõid** õlut. _You drank beer._
Ta **joob** õlut. _He/she drinks beer._	Ta **jõi** õlut. _He/she drank beer._
Me **joome** õlut. _We drink beer._	Me **jõime** õlut. _We drank beer._
Te **joote** õlut. _You drink beer._	Te **jõite** õlut. _You drank beer._
Nad **joovad** õlut. _They drink beer._	Nad **jõid** õlut. _They drank beer._
Ma, sa, ta, me, te, nad **ei joo** õlut.	Ma, sa, ta, me, te, nad **ei joonud** õlut.
I, you, he/she, we, you, they don't drink beer.	_I, you, he/she, we, you, they didn't drink beer._

In the same way as **jooma** *to drink* changes in the imperfect, so do the following words change:

tooma, tuua *to bring*

For instance:

Ma **tõin** süüa. *I brought food.*	Me **tõime** süüa. *We brought food.*
Sa **tõid** süüa. *You brought food.*	Te **tõite** süüa. *You brought food.*
Ta **tõi** süüa. *He/she brought food.*	Nad **tõid** süüa. *They brought food.*
ei toonud süüa *didn't bring food*	

looma, lüüa *to create*

For instance:

Ma **lõin** kunstiteose.	Me **lõime** kunstiteose.
I created a piece of art.	*We created a piece of art.*
Sa **lõid** kunstiteose.	Te **lõite** kunstiteose.
You created a piece of art.	*You created a piece of art.*
Ta **lõi** kunstiteose.	Nad **lõid** kunstiteose.
He/she created a piece of art.	*They created a piece of art.*
ei loonud kunstiteost *didn't create a piece of art*	

sööma, süüa *to eat*

For instance:

Ma **sõin** suppi. *I ate soup.*	Me **sõime** suppi. *We ate soup.*
Sa **sõid** suppi. *You ate soup.*	Te **sõite** suppi. *You ate soup.*
Ta **sõi** suppi. *He/she ate soup.*	Nad **sõid** suppi. *They ate soup.*
ei söönud suppi *didn't eat soup.*	

lööma, lüüa *to hit*

For instance:

Ma **lõin** palli. *I hit the ball.*	Me **lõime** palli. *We hit the ball.*
Sa **lõid** palli. *You hit the ball.*	Te **lõite** palli. *You hit the ball.*
Ta **lõi** palli. *He/she hit the ball.*	Nad **lõid** palli. *They hit the ball.*
ei löönud palli *didn't hit the ball*	

Note that if any of these verbs just mentioned occur as part of a compound verb they also have *i*-imperfect, for instance Ma **jäin** haigeks *I fell ill*. Ma sain terveks *I got better*. etc.

EXERCISE 15

Answer the question **a** affirmatively **b** negatively.

1 Kas sa sõid eile midagi head?

2 Kas sa jõid eile veini?

3 Kas sa said eile palka?

4 Kas sa tõid eile koju lilli?

In order to practise this grammar topic further do Exercises 19–22 in the Practice section.

Where to go for help if you are sick

Solutions for minor health problems can be found at the **apteek** *chemist's*. **Apteeker** *the pharmacist* is a trained specialist who is also able to advise you on doctor's prescribed medicines. Not all towns have **valveapteek** *chemist on duty* which would be open also during the night. Usually the chemist's have normal working hours from 8.00–18.00. Note that the chemists usually have different counters for selling **käsimüügiravimid** *non-prescription drugs* and **retseptiravimid** *prescription drugs* for **antibiootikumid** *antibiotics* and other drugs prescribed by the doctor. If the doctor gives you a **retsept** *prescription* for a medicine, you need to take the prescription to a chemist.

For more serious ailments, you have to see a doctor. The number for the **kiirabi** *ambulance* is 112. In Estonia, ambulance services are free of charge. If your injury is not too severe and you are able to walk you might be asked to go to **traumapunkt** the *trauma department* at any bigger **haigla** *hospital*. **Polikliinik** *outpatients' department* will offer the services of different specialist doctors and it is the first place to go to if you need a doctor's consultation. Most bigger cities also have a **sanatoorium** *sanatorium* and **sünnitusmaja** *special hospital for giving birth*. For dental problems look for **hambaravi** *dental care* or **hambaarst** *dentist*.

Hügieenitarbed *articles of personal hygiene* as well as cosmetic products can also be obtained in most **kaubanduskeskus** *department store* and **supermarket** *supermarkets*.

MU PEA VALUTAB KOHUTAVALT *MY HEAD ACHES TERRIBLY* – ADVERBS

In the sentence Mul on **kohutav** peavalu *I have a terrible headache* the word **kohutav** *terrible* is an adjective.

In the sentence Mu pea valutab **kohutavalt** *My head aches terribly* the word **kohutavalt** *terribly* is an adverb.

It is possible to make an adverb from more or less every adjective. In Estonian, we usually add to the second form of the adjective the ending **-lt**. With some words the ending can be **-sti**. In the following table you will find examples of how the construction is made.

EXERCISE 16

Fill in the missing forms using the sample words for analogy.

first form	second form	adverb (second form + lt)
kohutav _terrible_	kohutava	kohutava**lt** _terribly_
aeglane _slow_	aeglase	_____
tavaline _ordinary_	tavalise	_____
vaikne _quiet_	vaikse	_____
kurb _sad_	kurva	_____
rõõmus _happy_	rõõmsa	_____
		adverb (second form + -sti)
hirmus _terrible_	hirmsa	hirmsa**sti** _horribly_
kiire _fast_	kiire	_____
kõva _hard_	kõva	_____
halb _bad_	halva	_____
hea _good_	hea	**NB!** hä**sti** _well_

EXERCISE 17

Translate into English.

1 Mul on kohutav peavalu.

2 Mu pea valutab kohutavalt.

3 Ta räägib väga aeglaselt.

4 See muusika on väga vaikne.

5 See muusika mängib vaikselt.

6 See on kiire auto.

7 See auto sõidab kiiresti.

8 See on hea arst.

9 See arst ravib hästi.

In order to practise this grammar topic further do Exercises 23–4 in the Practice section.

MA TAHAN TERVEKS SAADA _I WANT TO GET WELL_ – COMPOUND VERBS

In Unit 2 we learnt that the Estonian language has many compound verbs that consist of two words, for instance **aru saama** _to understand_, **haigeks jääma** _to fall ill_ etc. Such verbs are made of the main word, which changes, and an auxiliary, which does not change. For instance in the verb **haigeks jääma**, only the word jääma changes i.e. **ma jään haigeks** _I fall ill_, ta jääb **haigeks** _he/she falls ill_ etc.

One peculiar thing about compound verbs is that in a sentence the main word and auxiliary do not necessarily stand next to one another, often in fact the auxiliary is placed at the end of the sentence. So, in order to understand a sentence you really need to read all of it!

Ta **jääb** väga kergesti **haigeks.**	*He falls ill very easily.*
Ta **jäi** möödunud nädalal **haigeks.**	*He fell ill last week.*
Arst ütles, et ma **saan** varsti **terveks.**	*The doctor said that I will get well soon.*
Ta **ei saanud** kaua aega **terveks.**	*He didn't get well for a long time.*
Ma **loen** retsepti **läbi.**	*I read through the prescription.*
Ma **lugesin** retsepti juba kaks korda **läbi.**	*I read through the prescription twice already.*

In order to practise this grammar topic further do Exercise 25 in the Practice section.

Practice

EXERCISE 18

Change the words in bold into the imperfect. The first one is done for you.

1 Me **töötame** kella viieni. Me *töötasime* kella viieni.

2 Nad **lähevad** parklasse. Nad _____ parklasse.

3 Ta **võtab** oma auto. Ta _____ oma auto.

4 Ta **sõidab** poodi. Ta _____ poodi.

5 Te **ostate** palju süüa. Te _____ palju süüa.

6 Ta **läheb** koju. Ta _____ koju.

7 Me **puhkame**. Me _____

8 Sa **vaatad** telerit. Sa _____ telerit.

9 Te **loete** lehte. Te _____ lehte.

10 Nad **kuulavad** muusikat. Nad _____ muusikat.

11 Me **läheme** magama. Me _____ magama.

EXERCISE 19

Underline the words that have an *i*-imperfect.

andma, haigeks jääma, jooma, kasutama, kuulama, läbi lugema, minema, mõjuma, nägema, olema, otsa saama, panema, pesema, soovima, sööma, tegema, terveks saama, tooma, tulema, võtma, välja tõmbama, välja väänama

EXERCISE 20

Underline the sentence which describes an action or event that took place in the past.

1 **a** Ma külmetun. **b** Ma külmetusin.

2 **a** Minu kurk valutab. **b** Minu kurk valutas.

3 **a** Pea ei valutanud. **b** Pea ei valuta.

4 **a** Ma jäin haigeks. **b** Ma jään haigeks.

5 **a** Ma läksin arsti juurde. **b** Ma lähen arsti juurde.

6 a Arst küsis, mida ma kaeban. **b** Arst küsib, mida ma kaeban.

7 a Arst vaatab mind läbi. **b** Arst vaatas mind läbi.

8 a Arst kirjutas mulle retsepti. **b** Arst kirjutab mulle retsepti.

9 a Ma lähen apteeki. **b** Ma läksin apteeki.

10 a Ma ostan rohtu. **b** Ma ostsin rohtu.

11 a Kodus ma joon sooja teed ja võtan rohtu. **b** Kodus ma jõin sooja teed ja võtsin rohtu.

12 a Ma sain terveks. **b** Ma saan terveks.

EXERCISE 21

First, answer the questions affirmatively. Then answer the questions negatively. After that answer the questions once more according to how it really is.

1 Kas sa olid eile õhtul kodus? *Jah, olin küll. Ei olnud.*

2 Kas sa lugesid eile ajalehte?

3 Kas sa käisid eile kinos?

4 Kas sa vaatasid eile telerit?

5 Kas sa naersid eile?

6 Kas sa ostsid eile midagi?

7 Kas sa jõid eile õlut?

8 Kas sa tegid eile midagi huvitavat?

9 Kas sa nägid eile oma sõpra?

10 Kas sa pesid eile pesu?

EXERCISE 22

Answer the words in brackets, using the right tense.

1 Praegu ma (elama) _____ Tallinnas, aga kümme aastat tagasi ma (elama) _____ Tartus.

2 Praegu ma (töötama) _____ ühes firmas, aga kümme aastat tagasi ma (õppima) _____ ülikoolis.

3 Praegu ma (saama) _____ head palka, aga kümme aastat tagasi ei (saama) _____

4 Praegu ma (olema) _____ abielus, aga kümme aastat tagasi ma ei (olema) _____ abielus.

5 Praegu ma (sõitma) _____ autoga, aga kümme aastat tagasi ma (käima) _____ jala.

6 Praegu ma ei (mängima) _____ kitarri, aga kümme aastat tagasi ma (mängima) _____

7 Praegu ma ei (tegelema) _____ spordiga, aga kümme aastat tagasi (tegelema) _____

EXERCISE 23

Choose the right word.

1 See film on väga **hea/hästi**.

2 Näitlejad mängivad **tavaline/tavaliselt**.

3 Muusika on **vaikne/vaikselt**.

4 Näitlejad räägivad **kõva/kõvasti**.

5 Filmi algus on **kurb/kurvalt**.

6 Filmi lõpp on **rõõmus/rõõmsalt**.

EXERCISE 24

Fill in the blanks according to the example.

1 See on väga aeglane auto. See auto sõidab väga *aeglaselt*.

2 See muusika on liiga vaikne. See muusika mängib liiga.

3 Ta on täna väga rõõmus. Ta naerab

4 See on nii hirmus film. Ma kardan

5 See on väga kiire rong. See rong sõidab väga

6 See õpetaja on hea. See õpetaja õpetab

EXERCISE 25

Underline the compound verbs (i.e. the verbs that consist of two words) then translate the sentences.

1 See hammas tuleb kahjuks <u>välja tõmmata</u>.

2 Ma kukkusin eile ja väänasin jala välja.

3 Lugege läbi ka pakis olev infoleht.

4 Minu mees jäi eile haigeks.

5 Kolme nädala pärast võtame kipsi ära.

6 Me proovisime ka sooja teed juua, aga tee sai otsa.

7 See koht paraneb ära umbes kolme päeva pärast.

Speaking

EXERCISE 26

You are not feeling well and you call the hospital to get an appointment with a doctor. Fill in the missing lines. Listen to the completed dialogue.

09.06

Arst	Tere! Doktor Kivi kuuleb.
Sina	Say *I need to get to the doctor quickly.*
Arst	Mis kaebused teil siis on?
Sina	Say *I have a terrible cough.*
Arst	Kui kõrge palavik teil on?
Sina	Say *Yesterday evening it was 38.5.*
Arst	Kas teile täna kell üks sobiks?
Sina	Say *It's OK.*

EXERCISE 27

You are talking to the doctor. Fill in the missing lines. Listen to the completed dialogue.

 09.07

Arst	Tere! Mida te siis kaebate?
Sina	Say *My head aches terribly.*
Arst	Kas te valuvaigistit juba võtsite?
Sina	Say *Yes, but it didn't help.*
Arst	Mitu tabletti te võtsite?
Sina	Say *I took two tablets in the morning.*
Arst	Võtke seda rohtu veel kolm korda päevas peale sööki üks tablet korraga.
Sina	Ask whether you have to come back again.
Arst	Ei, kui kõik on korras, siis pole vaja tulla.

EXERCISE 28

You are at the chemist's. Fill in the missing lines. Listen to the completed dialogue.

 09.08

Sina	Say *Hello!*
Apteeker	Tere!
Sina	Say *I probably have flu.*
Apteeker	Kas teil kurk ka valutab?
Sina	Say *Yes, it does ache.*
Apteeker	Jooge sooja teed. Ja võtke seda rohtu.
Sina	Ask *How do I have to take this medicine?*
Apteeker	Te peate seda võtma hommikul ja õhtul.
Sina	Ask if this medicine has any side-effects.
Apteeker	Ei tohiks olla.

EXERCISE 29

 09.09

You are calling your friend to say you have fallen ill. Fill in the missing lines then listen to the correct answers.

1 Say you have fallen ill.

2 Say you have a terrible headache.

3 Say you have a sore throat.

4 Say you have a fever of 37.5 degrees.

5 Say you drank some warm tea but it didn't help.

6 Say you probably have flu.

? Test yourself

1 How do you say you have a bad nose and terrible headache?
   a Mul on gripp ja hirmus köha.
   b Mul on nohu ja hirmus peavalu.
   c Mul on hambavalu ja kõrge palavik.

2 You need to get to the doctor as soon as possible. What do you say?
   a Kas ma pean uuesti teie juurde tulema?
   b Ma olen välismaalane.
   c Mul oleks kiiresti vaja arsti juurde saada.

3 The doctor asks *Mida te kaebate?* What does it mean?
   a Do you have a medical insurance card?
   b What complaints do you have?
   c Do you have a headache?

4 Which are the parts of the face?
   a kõht, rind, kael
   b jalg, varvas, põlv
   c silm, suu, lõug

5 You want to know how you should take this medicine. What do you say?
   a Kuidas seda rohtu võtma peab?
   b Mitu tabletti siin pakis on?
   c Kas sellel rohul on mingeid kõrvalmõjusid ka?

6 The doctor says *Te peate võtma valuvaigistit kaks korda päevas enne sööki üks tablett korraga.*
   a You have to take one painkiller twice a day after a meal.
   b You have to take two painkillers once a day before a meal.
   c You have to take one painkiller twice a day before a meal.

7 Which action takes place in the past?
   a Ma võtan rohtu kolm korda päevas.
   b Ma võtsin rohtu kolm korda päevas.
   c Ma ei võta rohtu kolm korda päevas.

8 Which sentence is in the past tense?
   a Ma olen haige.
   b Ma olin haige.
   c Ma ei ole haige.

9 How do you say I ate, and drank coffee, in the morning?

   a Ma söön ja joon kohvi hommikul.

   b Ma sõin ja jõin kohvi hommikul.

   c Ma ei söönud ja joonud kohvi hommikul.

10 How do you say I didn't go to the doctor?

   a Ma ei lähe arsti juurde.

   b Ma läksin arsti juurde.

   c Ma ei läinud arsti juurde.

10 Milline ta välja näeb?

What does she look like?

In this unit you will learn:
▶ *How to describe people's appearance and character*
▶ *How to name items of clothing*

Listening 1

You will listen to two dialogues where people describe other people. Listen to the dialogues and complete Exercise 1 below.

 10.01

a	**Anu**	Tead, mul on uus ülemus.
	Lea	Milline ta siis on?
	Anu	Pikka kasvu lokkis juustega kena mees.
	Lea	Aga iseloom?
	Anu	No seda ei tea ju veel nii ruttu. Aga tundub, et ta on hästi tark ja tõsine inimene.
	Lea	Mmm. Ta vist meeldib sulle.
	Anu	Ah, mine nüüd! Lihtsalt mul on hea meel, et selline asjalik inimene meile tööle tuli.
b	**Ülemus**	Palun minge siis meie külalisele hotelli järele.
	Alluv	Kuidas ma ta ära tunnen?
	Ülemus	Ta on tumeda peaga keskealine sale naine.
	Alluv	Kas ta on pikka kasvu?
	Ülemus	Mitte eriti. Ma helistan talle veel mobiilile, et ta ootaks teid fuajees.

ülemus, -e, -t, -i	*employer, boss*
pikka kasvu	*of tall height*
juuksed, juuste, juukseid	*hair*
lokkis juustega	*with curly hair*
kena, -, -, -sid	*nice, handsome*
iseloom, -u, -u	*character, nature*
tundu/ma, -da, -b	*to seem*
tark, targa, tarka, tarku	*smart, clever*
hästi tark	*very smart, clever*

tõsi/ne, -se, st, -seid	*serious*
inime/ne, -se, -st, -si	*person, man, human being*
Ah, mine nüüd!	*Oh, please!*
lihtsalt	*just*
mul on hea meel	*I am glad*
selli/ne, -se, -st, -seid	*this kind*
asjalik, -u, -ku, -ke	*sensible*
külali/ne, -se, -st, -si	*visitor*
minge meie külalisele	*go and fetch our visitor*
hotelli järele	*from the hotel*
alluv, -a, -at -aid	*employee*
ära tund/ma, ära tund/a, tunne/n ära	*to recognize*
tumeda peaga	*with dark hair* (lit. with dark head)
keskeali/ne, -se, -st, -si	*middle aged*
sale, -da, -dat, -daid	*slim, slender*
kasv, -u, -u	*height*
mitte eriti	*not quite*
helista/ma, -da, -n	*to call*
mobiil, -i, -i, -e	*mobile phone*
oota/ma, ooda/ta, oota/n	*to wait*
fuajee, -, -d, -sid	*(hotel) lobby*

EXERCISE 1

Listen to the dialogue and select the correct answer. For some questions several answers are correct.

a

1 Milline on Anu uus ülemus?
- **a** Ta on lühikest kasvu.
- **b** Ta on lokkis juustega.
- **c** Ta ei ole kena inimene.

2 Milline on Anu ülemuse iseloom?
- **a** Anu ei tea veel, milline iseloom tal on.
- **b** Anu arvab, et ta on tark.
- **c** Anu arvab, et ta on tõsine.

3 Kas Anule meeldib uus ülemus?
- **a** Anu arvab, et ta on asjalik.
- **b** Anul on hea meel, et see inimene neile tööle tuli.
- **c** Anule ei meeldi uus ülemus.

b

1 **Mida ülemus ütleb?**
   a Palun tulge siia!
   b Palun minge meie külalisele järele.
   c Palun helistage mulle mobiilile.

2 **Kus on külaline?**
   a Külaline on lennujaamas.
   b Külaline on hotellis.
   c Külaline on raudteejaamas.

3 **Kuidas külalise ära tunneb?**
   a Ta on tumeda peaga.
   b Ta on umbes kakskümmend aastat vana.
   c Ta on pikka kasvu.

Listening 2

You will hear three dialogues. In the first two, people discuss what clothes are suitable to wear on different occasions. In the third, you will hear people exchanging compliments on clothing. Listen to the dialogues and then complete Exercises 2–3.

 10.02

a	Piret	Tule minuga laupäeval seenele!
	Linda	Olgu. Mis sa mõtlesid selga panna?
	Piret	Ma panen jope ja jalga panen dressipüksid, villased sokid ja kummikud.
	Linda	Ei tea, mis ilm laupäeval on? Kas peab mütsi ka pähe panema ja kindad kätte?
	Piret	Mina ei pane, aga võtan nad igaks juhuks kaasa.
b	Koit	Lähme pühapäeval ooperisse!
	Tiia	Mul pole midagi selga panna.
	Koit	Sa pane pikk pruun seelik ja kõrge kontsaga kingad. Väga ilus!
	Tiia	Kas sina paned siis ka lipsu kaela?
	Koit	Võin panna küll.
c	Anne	Võta mantel ära ja pane siia kappi.
	Mirjam	Oota, kohe.
	Anne	Ja näed, sussid on siin.
	Mirjam	Jah, aitäh. Kohe panen jalga. Nii, olen valmis.
	Anne	Oi, kui kena sa välja näed! See pluus sobib sulle nii hästi.
	Mirjam	Aitäh. Peeter kinkis selle mulle. Aga sul on ka nii kaunis kleit seljas.
	Anne	Ah, mis sa nüüd! Ma ise õmblesin selle.

seen, -e, -t, -i	*mushroom*
tule seenele	*come to pick mushrooms*
mõtle/ma, mõtel/da, mõtle/n	*to think*
selga pane/ma, selga pann/a, pane/n selga	*to wear, to put on*
jope, -, -t, -sid	*jacket*
jalga pane/ma, jalga pann/a, pane/n jalga	*to wear, to put on* (used for footwear and trousers)
dressipüksid	*trousers* (of sports outfit)
villa/ne, -se, -st, -seid	*woollen*
sokk, soki, sokki, sokke	*sock*
kummik, -u, -ut, -uid	*rubber boot*
ilm, -a, -a	*weather*
müts, -i, -i, -e	*hat*
pähe pane/ma, pähe pann/a, pane/n pähe	*to wear, to put on (used for hats)* kindad, kinnaste, kindaid *gloves*
kätte pane/ma, kätte pann/a, pane/n kätte	*to wear, to put on* (used for gloves)
kaasa võt/ma, kaasa võtt/a, võta/n kaasa	*to take along*
mul pole = mul ei ole	*I don't have*
seelik, -u, -ut, -uid	*skirt*
kõrge, -, -t, -id	*high*
konts, -a, -a, -i	*heel*
kingad, kingade, kingi	*shoes*
lips, -u, -u, -e	*tie*
kaela pane/ma, kaela pann/a, pane/n kaela	*to wear, to put on* (used for ties and scarves)
ära võt/ma, ära võtt/a, võta/n ära	*to take off*
mantel, mantli, mantlit, mantleid	*overcoat, coat*
kapp, kapi, kappi, kappe	*wardrobe, closet*
sussid, susside, susse	*slippers*
valmis ole/ma, valmis oll/a, ole/n valmis	*to be ready*
välja näge/ma, välja näh/a, näe/n välja	*to look*
Kui kena sa välja näed!	*How nice you look!*
pluus, -i, -i, -e	*blouse*
sobi/ma, -da, -n	*to suit*
kinki/ma, kinki/da, kingi/n	*to give (as a present)*
kaunis, kauni, kaunist, kauneid	*beautiful*
seljas ole/ma, seljas oll/a, on seljas	*to wear, to have on* (used for shirts, blouses, etc.)
kleit, kleidi, kleiti	*dress*
õmble/ma, õmmel/da, õmble/n	*to sew*
Ah, mis sa nüüd!	*Don't flatter me!*

EXERCISE 2

a

Listen to the dialogue and choose the correct answer. For some questions, several answers are correct.

1 Piret tahab laupäeval minna **a** kontserdile, **b** seenele, **c** turule.

2 Piret paneb jalga **a** dressipüksid, **b** villased sokid, **c** kummikud.

3 Linda tahab panna **a** jope selga, **b** mütsi pähe, **c** kindad kätte.

4 Piret võtab igaks juhuks kaasa **a** mütsi, **b** kindad, **c** koti.

b

Listen to the dialogue and decide if the following sentences are **a** true or **b** false.

1 Koit tahab pühapäeval Tiiaga ooperisse minna.

2 Tiia arvab, et tal pole midagi selga panna.

3 Koit arvab, et lühike kollane seelik ja kõrge kontsaga kingad on väga ilusad.

4 Tiia arvab, et Koit võiks punase lipsu kaela panna.

c

Listen to the dialogue and tick the words you hear in this dialogue.

mantel	☐
sussid	☐
kummikud	☐
pluus	☐
kaunis kleit	☐
pikk pruun seelik	☐
dressipüksid	☐
villased sokid	☐
lips	☐
kõrge kontsaga kingad	☐

EXERCISE 3

Choose the correct translation.

1 **Mis sul seljas on? a** What are you wearing? **b** What are you going to put on?

2 **Mis sa jalga paned? a** What footwear are you wearing? **b** What footwear are you going to put on?

3 **Pane kindad kätte! a** Put the gloves on! **b** Take the gloves off!

Listening 3

Urmas has a new girlfriend. He is describing her to his mother. Listen to the dialogue and then complete Exercises 4–5.

 10.03

Urmas	Kuule, kas ma võiksin ühe tüdruku pühapäeval meile lõunale kutsuda?
Urmase ema	Oi, kas sul on uus pruut?
Urmas	Nojah, võib vist küll niimoodi öelda.
Urmase ema	Oi, kui tore! Mis ta nimi on? Kus te siis kokku saite?
Urmas	Ma kohtusin temaga tegelikult juba eelmisel aastal, me olime koos ühel seminaril. Ja nüüd töötab ta minuga samas majas. Nimi on Maarika.
Urmas ema	Kellena ta siis töötab?
Urmas	Ta töötab sekretärina ja õpib samal ajal veel ülikoolis.
Urmase ema	Siis ta on ju väga tubli inimene! Mida ta õpib?
Urmas:	Ta tahab saada psühholoogiks.
Urmase ema	See kõlab küll huvitavalt!
Urmas	Jah, aga see on natuke ohtlik ka – ta näiteks saab kohe aru, kui ma valetan.
Urmase ema	Aga sa ära siis valeta! Kas sa tead ka, kes ta vanemad on?
Urmas	Nendega ma pole veel kohtunud, aga tundub, et ta on pärit sportlikust perest. Ta käib näiteks lõuna ajal rulluiskudega sõitmas.
Urmase ema	Milline ta siis ka välja näeb?
Urmas	Mulle meeldib see, et ta riietub maitsekalt. Aga see on muidugi naljakas, et ta värvib kogu aeg oma juukseid – heledaks, tumedaks, punaseks, mustaks.
Urmase ema	Oh jah. Mis värvi ta siis praegu on?
Urmas	Ma tegelikult ei tea. Pühapäeval näeme.

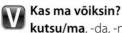

Kas ma võiksin?	*could I?*
kutsu/ma, -da, -n	*to invite*
pruut, pruudi, pruuti, pruute	*girlfriend, fiancée*
niimoodi	*this way*
kokku saa/ma, kokku saa/da, saa/n kokku	*to meet*
kohtu/ma, -da, -n	*to meet*
sama, -, -, -sid	*the same*
samal ajal	*at the same time*
veel	*also*
ülikool, -i, -i, -e	*university*

psühholoog, -i, -i, -e	*psychologist*
ta tahab saada psühholoogiks	*she/he wants to become a psychologist*
kõla/ma, -da, -b	*to sound*
ohtlik, -u, -ku, -ke	*dangerous*
valeta/ma, -da, -n	*to lie*
on pärit	*is from*
sportlik, -u, -ku, -ke	*athletic*
rulluisud	*roller skates*
käib rulluiskudega sõitmas	*goes to roller skate*
riietu/ma, -da, -n	*to dress*
maitsekalt	*tastefully, with taste*
naljakas, naljaka, naljakat, naljakaid	*funny*
värvi/ma, -da, -n	*to colour, to dye*

EXERCISE 4

Listen to the dialogue and decide if the following sentences are **a** true or **b** false.

1 Urmas tahab pühapäeval ühe tüdruku lõunale kutsuda.

2 Ta kohtus selle tüdrukuga juba kaks aastat tagasi.

3 Ta oli koos selle tüdrukuga ühel seminaril.

4 Tüdruk töötab Urmasega samas majas.

5 Tüdruku nimi on Maarika.

6 Maarika töötab psühholoogina.

7 Maarika õpib ülikoolis.

8 Maarika tahab saada sekretäriks.

9 Maarika saab kohe aru, kui Urmas valetab.

10 Maarika vanemad on ka psühholoogid.

11 Maarika käib lõuna ajal rulluiskudega sõitmas.

12 Maarika riietub maitsekalt.

13 Maarikal on mustad juuksed.

EXERCISE 5

Find the correct translation.

1 **Kus te kokku saite? a** Where did you meet? **b** How did you meet?

2 **Kellena ta töötab? a** What's his/her profession? **b** With whom does he/she work?

3 **Kui vana ta on? a** How old is he/she? **b** Who are his/her parents?

4 **Mida ta õpib? a** What does he/she study? **b** Does he/she study?

5 **Kes ta vanemad on? a** How old is he/she? **b** Who are his/her parents?

6 **Milline ta välja näeb? a** Does he/she look good? **b** What does he/she look like?

7 **Mis värvi juuksed tal on? a** What colour is his/her hair? **b** Does he/she colour his/her hair?

> **INSIGHT**
>
> A good way of remembering new words is to find a similar word from your own language. The funnier the association, the better you will remember!

Language patterns

KUIDAS TA VÄLJA NÄEB? *WHAT DOES SHE LOOK LIKE?*

Kasv *Height*

When talking about how tall someone is, we can use the following constructions. Note that all phases in bold are in third form:

Ta on pikka kasvu.	*He/she is (of) tall (height).*
Ta on keskmist kasvu.	*He/she is (of) medium height.*
Ta on lühikest kasvu.	*He/she is (of) short (height).*

If we want to compare two people we can say:

Ta on pikem kui mina or **Ta on minust pikem.**
He/she is taller than me.

Ta on palju pikem kui mina or **Ta on minust palju pikem.**
He/she is much taller than me.

Ta on natuke pikem kui mina or **Ta on natuke minust pikem.**
He/she is a little taller than me.

Ta on lühem kui mina or **Ta on minust lühem.**
He/she is shorter than me.

Ta on palju lühem kui mina or **Ta on minust palju lühem.**
He/she is much shorter than me.

Ta on sama pikk kui mina or **Me oleme ühepikkused.**
He/she is as tall as I am or *We are of the same height.*

Vanus *Age*

Ta on noor.	*He/she is young.*
Ta on vana.	*He/she is old.*
Ta on teismeline.	*He/she is a teenager.*
Ta on keskealine.	*He/she is middle aged.*

Ta on eakas.	*He/she is elderly.*
Ta on vanem kui …	*He/she is older than …*
Ta on noorem kui …	*He/she is younger than …*
Nad on ühevanused.	*They are of the same age.*

More expressions to describe appearance

Ta on sale.	*He/she is slim.*
Ta on kõhn.	*He/she is bony.*
Ta on tüse.	*He/she is corpulent (full figured).*
Ta on paks.	*He/she is fat.*
Ta on tüsedavõitu.	*He/she is on the corpulent side.*

Expressions to describe the colour of one's hair

Tal on heledad juuksed.	*He/she has light hair.*
Ta on heleda peaga.	*He/she has light hair.* (lit. he/she is with light head)
Ta on blond.	*He/she is blonde/blonde.*
Tal on tumedad juuksed.	*He/she has dark hair.*
Ta on tumeda peaga.	*He/she has dark hair.* (lit. he/she is with dark head)
Ta on brünett.	*He/she is brunette.*

For hair you can also say:

Tal on pruunid juuksed.	*He/she has brown hair.*
Tal on punased juuksed.	*He/she has red hair.*
Tal on hallid juuksed.	*He/she has grey hair.*
Tal on lokkis juuksed.	*He/she has curly hair.*
Tal on sirged juuksed.	*He/she has straight hair.*
Tal on pikad juuksed.	*He/she has long hair.*
Tal on lühikesed juuksed.	*He/she has short hair.*
Tal on hobusesaba.	*He/she has a ponytail.*
Ta on kiilaspea.	*He/she is bald.* (lit. he/she is baldheaded)

You may also need to say:

Tal on habe.	*He has a beard.*
Tal on vuntsid.	*He has a moustache.*
Ta näeb väga hea välja	*He/she looks very good.*

In order to practise this grammar topic further do Exercises 8–9 in the Practice section.

MIS TAL SELJAS ON? *WHAT IS SHE WEARING?*

Talking about clothes in Estonian asks for special attention as there are certain constructions that have to be used depending on whether you:

▶ put something on
▶ have something on
▶ or take something off.

In fact, you have to say specifically *where exactly* you put, have or take off the item of clothing, for instance saying *I put the hat on* **Ma panen mütsi pähe** means, literally, *I put the hat on my head.*

Mul on müts peas means *I have the hat on my head* (i.e. *I'm wearing a hat*) and **Ma võtan mütsi peast** means *I take the hat off my head* (i.e. *I take the hat off*).

In fact, there are several parallel constructions having the same meaning for taking an item of clothing off.

Ma **võtan** mütsi **peast.**
Ma **võtan** mütsi **peast ära.**   } *I take the hat off.*
Ma **võtan** mütsi **ära.**

In Estonian, the following body parts are used to specify where the items of clothing are worn: **pea** *head*, **kõrv** *ear*, **kael** *neck*, **selg** *back*, **sõrm** *finger*, **jalg** *leg, foot*.

In the following table, the most common constructions can be found. Note that in the construction **Mul on … seljas** *I have … on* the item of clothing is always in the first form and in the constructions **Ma panen … selga** *I put … on* and **Ma võtan … seljast ära** *I take … off* the items of clothing are in second form in the singular and in first form in the plural.

mul on … seljas	ma panen … selga	ma võtan … seljast (ära)
I have … on (lit. *I have … on the back*)	*I put …. on* (lit. *I put … on the back*)	*I take … off* (lit. *I take … off the back*)
kleit *dress*	kleidi	kleidi
pluus *blouse*	pluusi	pluusi
särk *shirt*	särgi	särgi
nb! seelik *skirt*	seeliku	seeliku
mantel *long overcoat*	mantli	mantli
jope *jacket*	jope	jope
ülikond *suit* (for men)	ülikonna	ülikonna
pintsak *jacket*	pintsaku	pintsaku
vest *waistcoat*	vesti	vesti
kampsun *pullover, sweater*	kampsuni	kampsuni
pesu *underwear*	pesu	pesu
kostüüm *women's two-piece suit*	kostüümi	kostüümi
dress *sweatsuit, sports uniform*	dressi	dressi
mul on … jalas	**Ma panen … jalga**	**Ma võtan … jalast (ära)**
I have … on (lit. *I have … on the leg*)	*I put …. on* (lit. *I put … on the leg*)	*I take … off* (lit. *I take … off the leg*)
püksid *trousers*	püksid	püksid
teksased *jeans*	teksased	teksased
kingad *shoes*	kingad	kingad
saapad *boots*	saapad	saapad
tossud *sport shoes, trainers*	tossud	tossud
sussid *slippers*	sussid	sussid
sokid *socks*	sokid	sokid
sukkpüksid *tights*	sukkpüksid	sukkpüksid
mul on … peas	**ma panen … pähe**	**ma võtan … peast (ära)**
I have … on (lit. *I have … on the head*)	*I put …. on* (lit. *I put … on the head*)	*I take … off* (lit. *I take … off the head*)
müts *hat*	mütsi	mütsi
mul on … käes	**ma panen … kätte**	**ma võtan … käest (ära)**
I have… on (lit. *I have … on the hand*)	*I put …. on* (lit. *I put … on the hand*)	*I take … off* (lit. *I take … off the hand*)
kindad *gloves*	kindad	kindad

mul on ... kaelas	ma panen ... kaela	ma võtan ... kaelast (ära)
I have... on (lit. *I have ... on the neck*)	*I put .... on* (lit. *I put ... on the neck*)	*I take ... off* (lit. *I take ... off the neck*)
sall *scarf*	salli	salli
pärlid *pearls*	pärlid	pärlid
lips *tie*	lipsu	lipsu
mul on ... ees	ma panen ... ette	ma võtan ... eest (ära)
I have ... on (lit. *I have ... on front*)	*I put .... on* (lit. *I put ... on the front*)	*I take ... off* (lit. *I take ... off the front*)
lips *tie*	lipsu	lipsu
prillid *eyeglasses*	prillid	prillid
mul on kõrvas	ma panen kõrva	ma võtan kõrvast (ära)
I have ... on (lit. *I have ... on the ear*)	*I put .... on* (lit. *I put ... on the ear*)	*I take ... off* (lit. *I take ... off the ear*)
kõrvarõngad *earrings*	kõrvarõngad	kõrvarõngad
mul on sõrmes	ma panen sõrme	ma võtan sõrmest (ära)
I have... on (lit. *I have ... on the finger*)	*I put ... on* (lit. *I put ... on the finger*)	*I take ... off* (lit. *I take ... off the finger*)
sõrmus *ring*	sõrmuse	sõrmuse

EXERCISE 6

Group the words according to the parts of body on which you wear them.

tossud, kindad, kingad, kleit, kübar, lips, mantel, müts, pluus, saapad, sall, seelik, sussid, sõrmus, ülikond

mul on seljas	mul on jalas	mul on peas	mul on kaelas	mul on käes	mul on so~rmes
_____	_____	_____	_____	_____	_____
_____	_____	_____	_____	*****	*****
_____	_____	*****	*****	*****	*****
_____	_____	*****	*****	*****	*****
_____	*****	*****	*****	*****	*****

EXERCISE 7

Choose the correct form.

1 Mul on sall **kaela/kaelas/kaelast**.

2 Ma panen salli **kaela/kaelas/kaelast**.

3 Ma võtan salli **kaela/kaelas/kaelast**.

4 Ma võtan pluusi **selga/seljas/seljast**.

5　Ma panen särgi **selga/seljas/seljast**.

6　Mul on särk **selga/seljas/seljast**.

7　Ma panen teksased **jalga/jalas/jalast**.

8　Mul on teksased **jalga/jalas/jalast**.

9　Ma võtan teksased **jalga/jalas/jalast**.

10　Mul on müts **pähe/peas/peast**.

11　Ma võtan mütsi **pähe/peas/peast**.

12　Ma panen kübara **pähe/peas/peast**.

13　Mul on kübar **pähe/peas/peast**.

In order to practise this grammar topic further do Exercises 12 and 13 in the Practice section.

A little more about clothing

As the Estonian climate is quite cold during the winter months (December–February) you will need proper **talveriided** *winter clothing* like **talvejope** *winter jacket*, **talvemantel** *winter coat* or even **kasukas** *fur coat* to be comfortable. If you don't want to have freezing hands and ears also equip yourself with **käpikud** *mittens* or **sõrmikud** *fingered gloves* and a good **talvemüts** *winter hat*. *Another* important item you need to wear on your clothes during the cold and dark seasons is **helkur** *reflector*, which are sold in all kiosks and shops. Helkur should be hung on a piece of string so that it flies about freely at the height of your knees and indicates your presence to vehicle drivers.

Kevad-sügisriided *clothes for the spring and autumn seasons* can be lighter and for the summer **suveriided** *summer clothes* like **lühikesed püksid** *shorts* and **sandaalid** *sandals* are adequate. Estonian dress code is quite casual, except on some occasions. People do dress up for the theatre and opera and enjoy nice outfits on birthdays, graduation and other similar sorts of parties. If you are invited to an Estonian house bear in mind that you are expected to take off your shoes – often you will be offered **sussid** *slippers* to wear instead. When shaking hands you are expected to take off gloves if you happen to wear them. Men should take off their hat when entering a room and it is considered rude to wear a hat while eating, especially by the older generation.

MILLINE ON TEMA ISELOOM? *WHAT'S HIS PERSONALITY LIKE?*

The following list presents some useful words one can use for describing a person's character or personality:

tark, targa, tarka, tarku *smart*

huvitav, -a, -at, -aid *interesting*

töökas, tööka, töökat, töökaid *hard-working*

sõbralik, -u, -ku, -ke *friendly*

lõbus, -a, -at, -aid *merry, cheery*

rumal, -a, -at, -aid *stupid*

igav, -a, -at, -aid *boring*

laisk, laisa, laiska, laisku *lazy*

ebasõbralik, -u, -ku, -ke *unfriendly*

tõsi/ne, -se, -st, -seid *serious*

seltskondlik, -u, -ku, -ke *social*	**tagasihoidlik**, -u, -ku, -ke *shy*
julge, -, -t, -id *brave*	**arg**, ara, arga, argasid *shy, fearful*
rõõmus, rõõmsa, rõõmsat, rõõmsaid *joyful*	**kurb**, kurva, kurba, kurbi *sad*
andekas, andeka, andekat, andekaid *talented, gifted*	**andetu**, -, -t, -id *untalented*
õnnelik, -u, -ku, -ke *happy*	**õnnetu**, -, -t, -id *unhappy*
rahulik, -u, -ku, -ke *peaceful, calm*	**rahutu**, -, -t, -id *restless*
lahke, -, -t, -id *kind*	**kade**, -da, -dat, -daid *envious*
viisakas, viisaka, viisakat, viisakaid *polite*	**eba/viisakas**, -viisaka, -viisakat, -viisakaid *rude*
meeldiv, -a, -at, -aid *pleasant*	**ebameeldiv**, -, -at, -aid *unpleasant*
aus, -a, -at, -aid *honest*	**ebaaus**, -a, -at, -aid *dishonest*
tavali/ne, -se, -st, -si *ordinary*	**ebatavali/ne**, -se, -st, -seid *unique, special*

Opposites can sometimes be made either by: adding the particle **eba-** in front of the word, for instance **viisakas** *polite* **ebaviisakas** *impolite* or adding the particle **-tu** to the end of the word, for instance **andekas** *talented, gifted* andetu *untalented*.

Note that these particles are not used with all words.

TA VÄRVIS JUUKSED PUNASEKS *SHE COLOURED HER HAIR RED* – TRANSLATIVE CASE

If we want to express some kind of change or development, we can do it by adding the ending *-ks* to the word, for instance Ta värvis juuksed punase**ks** *She coloured her hair red*; Ta tahab saada psühholoogi**ks** *She wants to become a psychologist*.

More examples:

Ta värvis maja kollase**ks**.	*He/she painted the house yellow.*
Ta muutus kurva**ks**.	*He/she turned sad.*
Ta muutus rõõmsa**ks**.	*He/she turned happy.*
Ta tegi oma kleidi ümber kostüümi**ks**.	*She turned her dress into a suit.*
Ilm läks külma**ks**.	*The weather turned cold.*
Ilm läks sooja**ks**.	*The weather turned warm.*
Ta tahab saada laulja**ks**.	*He/she wants to become a singer.*
Ta õpib laulja**ks**.	*He/she is studying to become a singer.*
Ta tahab saada parema**ks** inimese**ks**.	*He/she wants to become a better person.*

TA KÄIB RULLUISKUDEGA SÕITMAS *HE GOES ROLLER SKATING* – MAS-FORM

We have already learnt that with verbs indicating movement (like **minema** *to go*, **jooksma** *to run* etc.) we use the *ma-* infinitive, for instance **Ma lähen jalutama** *I go for a walk* (lit. *I go* *to walk).* **Ma jooksen nüüd õppima** *I run now to do some studying* (lit. *I run now to study*). **Ma sõidan ujuma** *I drive to have a swim* (lit. *I drive to swim*).

With the word **käima** to go a special *mas*-construction is used; for instance Ma käin iga päev ujumas *I go swimming* (for a swim) *every day*. This construction is very easy to make as you just add **-s** to the *ma*-infinitive:

uju**ma** *to swim* + s = uju**mas**
jaluta**ma** *to walk* + s = jaluta**mas**
rulluiskudega sõit**ma** *to roller skate* (lit. *to drive with roller skates*) + s = rulluiskudega sõit**mas**

Usually the sentences with **käin + mas-construction** are used to indicate some action that takes place regularly, for instance.

Esmaspäeviti ja kolmapäeviti käin ma **rulluiskudega sõitmas**.
On Mondays and Wednesdays I go roller skating.

Nädalavahetusel käin ma **kala püüdmas**.
During the weekends I go fishing.

Mõnikord käin ööklubis **tantsimas**.
Sometimes I go dancing in the nightclub.

In order to practise this grammar topic further do Exercises 10–11 in the Practice section.

Practice

EXERCISE 8

Find the right match.

1 Ma olen 1.80 pikk. Minu sõber on 2 meetrit pikk.
   a Me oleme ühepikkused.
   b Minu sõber on palju pikem kui mina.
   c Mina olen natuke lühem kui minu sõber.

2 Minu ema on 1.50 pikk.
   a Ta on lühikest kasvu.
   b Ta on keskmist kasvu.
   c Ta on pikka kasvu.

3 Koit on 165 cm pikk. Kristjan on 175 cm pikk.
   a Koit on Kristjanist pikem.
   b Kristjan on Koidust pikem.
   c Kristjan on sama pikk kui Koit.

4 Birgit on 18 aastat vana. Luisa on 28 aastat vana.
   a Birgit ja Luisa on ühevanused.
   b Birgit on vanem kui Luisa.
   c Luisa on vanem kui Birgit.

EXERCISE 9

Translate the following sentences into Estonian.

1 She is slim.

2 She has curly hair.

3 She is middle aged.

4 He is a teenager.

5 She is bony.

6 She has dark hair.

7 She has grey hair.

8 She has short hair.

9 He has a beard and moustache.

10 She looks very good.

EXERCISE 10

Choose the right form.

1 Ta käib lõuna ajal **rulluiskudega sõitma/rulluiskudega sõitmas**.

2 Ta läheb täna jälle **rulluiskudega sõitma/rulluiskudega sõitmas**.

3 Ma lähen homme **juukseid värvima/juukseid värvimas**.

4 Ma käin iga kuu **juukseid värvima/juukseid värvimas**.

5 Me käime nädalavahetusel **tantsima/tantsimas**.

6 Homme me kahjuks ei saa **tantsima/tantsimas** minna.

7 Ma käin **eesti keelt õppima/eesti keelt õppimas**.

8 Tule ka **eesti keelt õppima/eesti keelt õppimas!**

EXERCISE 11

Fill in the blanks with a correct form from the word given in brackets.

1 Lähme (sööma)!

2 Aitäh, aga ma juba käisin (sööma).

3 Tule minuga (ujuma)!

4 Oi, ma ei käi kunagi nii vara (ujuma), vesi on veel külm.

5 Kus sa koeraga (jalutama) _____ käid?

6 Tavaliselt käin kodu juures pargis, aga täna läheme metsa (jalutama)

_____

7 Ma käin tihti sõbra juures (juttu ajama) _____

8 Homme lähen vist jälle tema juurde (juttu ajama) _____

Speaking

EXERCISE 12

Make little drawings of these people. Try describing the pictures without looking at the text.

1 Tal on seljas lühike seelik ja jalas kõrge kontsaga kingad. Tal on pärlid kaelas ja valged kindad käes.

2 Tal on seljas valge T-särk ja jalas dressipüksid ning tossud. Tal on peas must müts.

3 Tal on seljas must ülikond ja mustad kingad. Tal on kaelas ilus lips.

4 Tal on seljas pikk must kleit ja valge vest. Tal on kõrvarõngad kõrvas ja sõrmes ilus sõrmus.

5 Tal on seljas jope ja jalas teksased ja saapad. Tal on kaelas pikk sall. Tal on prillid ees.

EXERCISE 13

10.04

a

It is morning. You are going jogging. Make sentences using the following words. Listen to the correct answers.

1	*dressipüksid*	Ma panen **dressipüksid** *jalga*.
2	sokid	Siis ma panen _____
3	T-särk	Siis ma panen _____
4	jope	Siis ma panen _____
5	sall	Siis ma panen _____
6	müts	Siis ma panen _____
7	kindad	Siis ma panen _____

b

You come back from jogging and want to take a shower. You will have to take all your clothes off. Construct sentences using the same words as in part **a**. Listen to the correct answers.

1	kindad	Ma võtan *kindad käest ära*.
2	müts	Siis ma võtan _____
3	sall	Siis ma võtan _____
4	jope	Siis ma võtan _____
5	T-särk	Siis ma võtan _____
6	sokid	Siis ma võtan _____
7	dressipüksid	Siis ma võtan _____

EXERCISE 14

Your friend invites you on a canoe trip. Fill in the missing lines then listen to the completed dialogue.

 10.05

Sõber	Tule nädalavahetusel kanuuga sõitma!
Sina	Say *OK. Say But I have nothing to wear.*
Sõber	Sa pane teksased ja kampsun.
Sina	Ask whether you should put on a hat and wear gloves too.
Sõber	Mina ei pane.
Sina	Say *I will take them with me just in case.*

EXERCISE 15

You are going to a nightclub with a friend and you're discussing what to wear. Fill in the missing lines then listen to the completed dialogue.

 10.06

Sõber	Mis sa mõtlesid selga panna?
Sina	Say *I will put on a black skirt and wear high-heeled shoes.*
Sõber	Mina panen ka seeliku ja kollase pluusi.
Sina	Say *This blouse suits you very well.*
Sõber	Aitäh. Ema kinkis selle mulle.
Sina	Ask *Will you also put on earrings and pearls?*
Sõber	Võin panna küll.

EXERCISE 16

You have invited an Estonian to your place. Fill in the missing lines then listen to the completed dialogue.

 10.07

Külaline	Tere!
Sina	Say *Please take your coat off and put it in the cupboard.*
Külaline	Oota, kohe!
Sina	Say *Oh, how nice you look!*
Külaline	Ah, mis sa nüüd!
Sina	Say *Please put these slippers on.*
Külaline	Jah, aitäh. Kohe panen jalga.

EXERCISE 17

 10.08

Your sister wants to know about your new boyfriend. Fill in the lines then listen to the completed text.

    a Say *He is a handsome young man.*

    b Say *He is of medium height, taller than you.*

    c Say *He has dark straight hair.*

    d Say *He has a moustache.*

    e Say *He dresses with taste.*

    f Say *He looks very good but he is shy.*

    g Say *It seems that he is very clever.*

    h Say *He wants to become a doctor.*

EXERCISE 18

 10.09

You are a young lady who is describing herself for a lonely hearts chatroom on the internet.

Fill in the lines then listen to the completed text.

    a Say you are 20 years old.

    b Say you have straight red hair.

    c Say you have a ponytail.

    d Say you are tall, but not too tall.

    e Say you are friendly and joyful.

    f Say you want to become a singer.

    g Say that during the weekend you go dancing in the nightclub.

? Test yourself

1 How to say *He is of medium height?*
  a Ta on lühikest kasvu.
  b Ta on keskmist kasvu.
  c Ta on pikka kasvu.

2 *Tal on pikad heledad sirged juuksed.* What does it mean?
  a She has long blonde straight hair.
  b She has long dark straight hair.
  c She has long blonde curly hair.

3 Which are men's clothes and accessories?
  a seelik, sukkpüksid, kostüüm
  b kleit, pärlid, kõrvarõngad
  c lips, ülikond, pintsak

4 How do you say *He is wearing trousers?*
  Tal on püksid …
  a jalas.
  b käes.
  c seljas.

5 Someone says *Võta palun kingad ära.* What does it mean?
  a I am wearing shoes.
  b Please take your shoes off.
  c Please put your shoes on.

6 You would like to pay a compliment to your friend. What should you say?
  a Tule minuga seenele.
  b Mul pole midagi selga panna.
  c Sa näed väga kena välja.

7 Your friend says that he has a new girlfriend. What should you say?
  a Oi kui tore! Kus te kokku saite?
  b Ära valeta! See on ohtlik.
  c Kas ta riietub maitsekalt?

8 Which words are positive in meaning?
  a rumal, igav, laisk
  b õnnetu, ebaviisakas, ebasõbralik
  c tark, lõbus, õnnelik

9 How do you say *We go cycling every evening?* Finish the sentence
Me käime igal õhtul…

   a rattaga sõitma.

   b rattaga sõitmas.

   c rattaga sõitmast.

10 What does the sentence *Ta tahab saada lauljaks* mean?

   a She wants to sing all the time.

   b She wants to become a singer.

   c She wants to listen to music.

11 Kas ühe- või kaheinimesetuba?
Single or double room?

In this unit you will learn:

▶ *How to ask questions about your hotel*

▶ *How to book an appointment at the hairdresser's and a slot at the bowling alley*

▶ *How to report problems with a broken phone*

Listening 1

You will hear a visitor talking to the hotel administrator about having a double room until Friday. He is asking several questions. Listen to the dialogue and then complete Exercises 1–2.

 11.01

Külastaja	Tere. Ma broneerisin kaks nädalat tagasi teie juures ühe toa.
Administraator	Kas ühe- või kaheinimesetoa?
Külastaja	Üheinimesetoa.
Administraator	Kohe vaatame. Kuidas teie nimi on?
Külastaja	Palun. Minu pass on siin.
Administraator	Jah, see broneering on teil täitsa olemas. Kui kauaks te kavatsete jääda?
Külastaja	Kas reedeni saab olla?
Administraator	Saab küll.
Külastaja	Mis kell ma pean reedel toa vabastama?
Administraator	Toa peab vabastama kella kaheteistkümneks. Kui vaja, võite oma kohvri siia minu juurde tuua.
Külastaja	Ahah. Väga tore. Kas tohib veel midagi küsida?
Administraator	Aga palun.
Külastaja	Kas siin hotellis on internetiühendus ka?
Administraator	Jah, kõikides tubades on pistikud ja baaris on traadita Internet ka.
Külastaja	Nii et ma võin oma sülearvuti võrku ühendada? Kui palju see maksab?
Administraator	Interneti kasutamine on toa hinna sees. Nii et see ei maksa midagi.
Külastaja	See on küll tore. Öelge veel palun, kus siin suitsetada tohib?
Administraator	Meie hotellis tohib suitsetada ainult baaris.

Külastaja	Kas seal saab midagi süüa ka?
Administraator	Midagi neil on, aga kui soovite suuremat sööki, siis võite ju alati linna peale minna.
Külastaja	Kus raha vahetada saab?
Administraator	Siin lähedal on pank, seal saate vahetada päris hea kursiga.
Külastaja	Väga tore.
Administraator	Teie toas on ka minibaar ja telefon. Kui neid kasutate, siis nende eest peab eraldi juurde maksma.
Külastaja	Selge see.
Administraator	Siin on teie toa võti. Kui mingeid probleeme või küsimusi on, siis pöörduge minu poole.
Külastaja	Aitäh. Teeme nii.

külastaja, -, -t, -id	*visitor*
broneeri/ma, -da, -n	*to book, to make a reservation*
üheinimese/tuba, -toa, -tuba, -tubasid	*single room*
kaheinimese/tuba, -toa, -tuba, -tubasid	*double room*
broneering, -u, -ut, -uid	*reservation*
broneering on teil täitsa olemas	*you absolutely do have the reservation*
kavatse/ma, -da, -n	*to intend*
vabasta/ma, -da, -n	*to release, to free*
kella kaheteistkümneks	*by 12 o'clock*
kohver, kohvri, kohvrit, kohvreid	*suitcase*
internetiühendus, -e, -t, -i	*internet connection*
pistik, -u, -ut, -uid	*outlet*
traadita internet	*wireless internet*
sülearvuti, -, -t, -arvuteid	*laptop (computer)*
võrk, võrgu, võrku, võrke	*net*
ühenda/ma, -da, -n	*to connect*
kasuta/ma, -da, -n	*to use*
on hinna sees	*is included in the price*
nii et	*so*
see ei maksa midagi	*it doesn't cost anything*
suitseta/ma, -da, -n	*to smoke*
Kas seal saab midagi süüa ka?	*Is it possible to also eat something there?*
kui soovite suuremat sööki	*if you wish something more to eat*
te võite ju	*you can always*
linna peale	*to town*
raha, -, -	*money*
vaheta/ma, -da, -n	*to exchange*
päris hea kursiga	*with quite a good rate*

minibaar, -i, -i, -e	*small bar at the hotel room*
eraldi	*separately*
juurde maks/ma, juurde maks/ta,	*to pay extra*
maksa/n juurde	
selge see	*yes, absolutely; yes I see*
võti, võtme, võtit, võtmeid	*key*
pöördu/ma, -da, -n	*turn to, talk to*
pöörduge minu poole	*turn to me* (plural)

EXERCISE 1

Listen to the dialogue and choose the correct answer.

1 The visitor booked the hotel room **a** one week ago, **b** two weeks ago, **c** three weeks ago.

2 He wants to have a **a** single room, **b** double room, **c** single bed in **a** room for four.

3 He wants to stay until **a** Wednesday, **b** Thursday, **c** Friday

4 He has to release the room at **a** 12 o'clock, **b** 1 o'clock, **c** 2 o'clock.

5 This hotel has internet connections **a** at the lobby, **b** at the restaurant, **c** in all rooms.

6 Connecting to the internet **a** is free of charge, **b** costs 10 kroons per hour, **c** costs 50 kroons per hour.

7 Smoking is allowed **a** in all rooms, **b** at the bar, **c** in the hotel lobby.

8 Meals at this time of day are available **a** at the bar and in town, **b** at the bar only, **c** in town only.

9 It is possible to exchange money **a** in **a** bank in the city centre, **b** in **a** bank nearby, **c** at the hotel.

10 In the room there is also **a** a bathtub, **b a** mini bar and telephone, **c** refrigerator.

EXERCISE 2

 11.02

Read the questions. Choose the correct response. Listen to the recording for the correct answer.

1 **Kas te broneerisite ühe- või kaheinimesetoa? a** Palun. Minu pass on siin. **b** Üheinimesetoa.

2 **Kui kauaks te kavatsete jääda? a** Reedeni. **b** Saab küll.

3 **Mis kell ma pean toa vabastama? a** Ahah. Väga tore. **b** Kella kaheteistkümneks.

4 **Kas tohib veel midagi küsida? a** Aga palun. **b** Kohe vaatame.

5 **Kus siin suitsetada tohib? a** Suitsetada tohib baaris. **b** Siin lähedal on pank, seal saate vahetada päris hea kursiga.

6 **Kus ma saan internetti kasutada? a** Oma toas saate, seal on internetiühendus. **b** Kahjuks ei saa, seal saab ainult juua.

7 **Kus saab raha vahetada? a** Jah, saab ikka. **b** Pangas saate kindlasti.

8 **Kas baaris saab midagi süüa ka? a** Kahjuks ei saa, seal saab ainult juua. **b** Siin saab. Näidake, mis probleem teil on.

Accommodation in Estonia

The **hotell** *hotel* is, of course the first choice and just like everywhere else in the world Estonian hotels are graded by stars. A **motell** *motel* is usually situated on the outskirts of a town and is easily accessible by car. Bed and breakfast-type accommodation is not common in Estonian towns but in the countryside **turismitalu** a *holiday farm* is a nice possibility to consider as most smaller towns do not have a variety of hotels to choose from. **Turismitalu** as a principle is a private enterprise, usually family owned, which offers cosy accommodation (which can be sometimes even be situated in an old barn dwelling), nice traditional meals and sometimes also different cultural and recreational programmes. There are hundreds of **turismitalu** in Estonia and information about them is available on the internet.

Listening 2

Listen to a dialogue that takes place at the bowling alley. Listen and then complete Exercises 3–4.

11.03

Administraator	Tere.
Klient	Tere. Kas ma saaksin laupäeval kaheks tunniks bowlingusaali broneerida?
Administraator	Mis kell te tulla soovite?
Klient	Kas kell kuus on võimalik?
Administraator	Mitmekesi te tulete?
Klient	Me oleme kaheksakesi.
Administraator	Jah, kell kuus on küll mõned vabad rajad. Mitu rada ma teile kinni panen?
Klient	Ma arvan, et kahest rajast piisab.
Administraator	Väga tore. Ma panen siis teie nime ja telefoni kirja.

bowlingusaal, -i, -i, -e	*bowling alley*
kaheks tunniks	*for 2 hours*
broneeri/ma, -da, -n	*to book*
võimalik, -u, -ku, -ke	*possible*
Mitmekesi?	*How many of you together?*
Me oleme kaheksakesi.	*There are eight of us all together.*
vaba, vaba, vaba, vabu	*free*
rada, raja, rada, radu	*track (in a bowling alley)*
kinni pane/ma, pann/a, pane/n kinni	*to book*
piisa/ma, -ta, -b	*to be enough*
kirja pane/ma, pann/a, pane/n kirja	*to write down*

EXERCISE 3

Listen and decide if the following sentences are **a** true or **b** false.

1 Klient tahab bowlingusaali tulla laupäeval.

2 Klient soovib bowlingusaalis olla kolm tundi.

3 Klient soovib bowlingusaali tulla kell viis.

4 Bowlingusaali tuleb üheksa inimest.

5 Klient soovib kinni panna kaks rada.

EXERCISE 4

 11.04

Read the questions. Choose the correct response. Listen to the recording to check your answers.

1 Kas ma saan laupäevaks bowlingusaali broneerida?
  a Kahjuks ei saa, nädalavahetuseks on saal juba broneeritud.
  b Kahjuks ei saa, seal saab ainult juua.

2 Mis kell te bowlingusaali tulla soovite?
  a Me oleme kaheksakesi.
  b Kell kuus.

3 Mitmekesi te tulete?
  a Kaheksakesi.
  b Ma arvan, et kahest rajast piisab.

4 Mitu rada ma teile kinni panen?
  a Ma panen siis teie nime ja telefoni kirja.
  b Ma arvan, et kahest rajast piisab.

Listening 3

You will hear two dialogues that take place at the hairdresser's. Listen to the dialogues and complete Exercises 5–7 below.

 11.05

a	**Klient**	Tere. Kas juuksur Taimi on täna tööl?
	Juuksur	Taimi ei tööta neljapäeviti.
	Klient	Millal ta siis tööl on?
	Juuksur	Ta on siin esmaspäeviti hommikupoole ja reedeti õhtupoole.
	Klient	Tore! Ma sooviksin siis esmaspäevaks aega kinni panna.
	Juuksur	Mis kellaks?
	Klient	Kella kümneks.

	Juuksur	Kell kümme tal juba on üks klient.
	Klient	Äkki te soovitate siis mõnda teist juuksurit, kes oleks esmaspäeva hommikul kell kümme vaba?
	Juuksur	Tulge minu juurde! Mina olen sellel kellaajal vaba küll.
	Klient	Jah, palun pange mulle siis aeg kinni. Ma sooviksin juukseid värvida ja lõigata ka.
	Juuksur	Jah. Te võite isegi tulla natukene varem, kui see teile sobib.
b	**Juuksur**	Mis ma siis teile teen?
	Klient	Ma sooviksin juuksed lühemaks lõigata.
	Juuksur	Kui palju ma lõikan?
	Klient	Võtke kohe kakskümmend sentimeetrit lühemaks.
	Juuksur	Nii palju? Kas teil kahju ei ole?
	Klient	Küll nad kasvavad uuesti.
	Juuksur	Kas te tahtsite värvida ka?
	Klient	Jah, võiks küll.
	Juuksur	Mis värvi me siis teeme?
	Klient	Võiks olla mingi punakas toon, aga mitte liiga tume.
	Juuksur	Ahah. Kas ma pärast teen soengu ka?
	Klient	Jah, föönisoeng palun.
	Juuksur	Tulge palun siia, ma pesen kõigepealt teie pea ära.
	Klient	Ma eile pesin.
	Juuksur	Siis ma teen lihtsalt teil juuksed märjaks, muidu on paha lõigata.
	Klient	Just.

V

juuksur, -i, -it, -eid	*hairdresser*
hommikupoole	*morning, forenoon*
õhtupoole	*evening*
soovita/ma, -da, -n	*to suggest*
mõnda teist	*some other*
lõika/ma, lõiga/ta, lõika/n	*to cut*
Mis ma siis teile teen?	*What can I do for you? (with your hair)?* **Võtke kohe**
kakskümmend sentimeetrit lühemaks.	*Take some 20 cm off (lit. take some 20 cm shorter)*
Kas teil kahju ei ole?	*Aren't you feeling sorry?*
kasva/ma, -da, -n	*to grow*
uuesti	*again*
puna/kas, -ka, -kat, -kaid	*reddish*
toon, -i, -i, -e	*tone (of colour)*
mitte liiga tume	*not too dark*
soeng, -u, -ut, -uid	*hairdo*
föönisoeng, -u, -ut, -uid	*hairdo done with the hair dryer*
märg, märja, märga, märgi	*wet*
muidu	*otherwise*
teen lihtsalt märjaks	*I will make (your hair) just wet*

EXERCISE 5

Listen to dialogue **a** and choose the correct answer.

1 Juuksur Taimi **töötab/ei tööta** neljapäeviti.

2 Juuksur Taimi on tööl esmaspäeviti **hommikupoole/õhtupoole.**

3 Juuksur Taimi on tööl reedeti **hommikupoole/õhtupoole.**

4 Klient soovib aega kinni panna **esmaspäevaks/teisipäevaks.**

5 Klient soovib aega kinni panna kella **üheksaks/kümneks**.

6 Juuksur Taimi **on/ei ole** kell kümme vaba.

7 Klient **saab/ei saa** esmaspäeval kell kümme juuksuri juurde minna.

8 Klient **soovib/ei soovi** juukseid värvida ja lõigata.

9 Klient **võib/ei või** tulla esmaspäeval isegi natuke varem.

EXERCISE 6

Listen to dialogue **b** and answer the questions.

1 What does the client request the hairdresser to do?

2 How much shorter does she want her hair?

3 What does the hairdresser ask?

4 What else does the client request the hairdresser to do?

5 What colour does she want her hair?

6 Does she want some kind of specific hairdo?

7 When did the client wash her hair?

8 Why does the hairdresser want to wet the client's hair?

EXERCISE 7

 11.06

Read the questions. Choose the correct response then listen to the recording to check your answers.

1 **Kas juuksur Ene on kolmapäeval tööl?**
   a Ma olen kolmapäeval vaba küll.
   b Kahjuks Ene ei tööta kolmapäeviti.

2 **Kas ma saaksin esmaspäevaks juuksuri juurde aja kinni panna?**
   a Siin saab. Näidake, mis probleem teil on.
   b Jah, saab ikka.

3 **Mis kellaks te soovite aega kinni panna?**
   a Kell kuus tal on juba üks klient.
   b Kella kuueks.

4 Mis ma siis teile teen?

   a Ma soovin juukseid lõigata ja värvida.

   b Küll nad kasvavad uuesti.

5 Kui palju ma lõikan?

   a Võiks olla mingi punakas toon.

   b Võtke umbes kümme sentimeetrit lühemaks.

6 Mis värvi me teeme?

   a Võiks olla mingi pruun toon, aga mitte liiga hele.

   b Kas teil kahju ei ole?

7 Kas ma pärast teen soengu ka?

   a Jah, palun tehke föönisoeng.

   b Jah, palun lõigake natuke.

8 Kas ma pesen teie pea ära või teen juuksed lihtsalt märjaks?

   a Ma eile pesin pead, juuksed on puhtad.

   b Mul on paha lõigata.

Listening 4

Tuuli's cell phone has broken – the moment she switches it on the battery runs flat. She takes the phone to a shop to find out if the problem can be fixed. Listen to the dialogue and then complete Exercises 8–9.

 11.07

Klienditeenindaja	Mis probleem teil on?
Tuuli	Mu mobiiltelefon läks katki. Kas te oskate selle korda teha?
Klienditeenindaja	Mis tal siis viga on?
Tuuli	Aku saab kohe tühjaks kui telefoni sisse lülitan.
Klienditeenindaja	Jah? Millal te selle telefoni ostsite?
Tuuli	Umbes pool aastat tagasi.
Klienditeenindaja	Kas teil ostutšekk on alles?
Tuuli	Ei ole kahjuks. Ma viskasin selle ära.
Klienditeenindaja	Kahju. Te saate ju aru, et nüüd ma ei saa garantiiremonti teha.
Tuuli	Oeh. Äkki saab ta niisama ära parandada?
Klienditeenindaja	Ma võin aku välja vahetada. See maksab ainult sada krooni.
Tuuli	Üks hetk, ma võtan katte ära ja teen korpuse lahti.
Klienditeenindaja	Oi-oi, ärge nii tehke. Te lõhute selle ära!
Tuuli	Vist on parem, kui te ise selle lahti teete.
Klienditeenindaja	Vaadake, see nupp tuleb alla vajutada. See on juhendis ka kirjas.

TIP

Please note since 1 January 2011 the Estonian currency has been the Euro.

Tuuli		Juhendit mul ei ole, kaotasin ära.
Klienditeenindaja		Ma annan teile uue juhendi. Proovige nüüd ise kinni panna.
Tuuli		Kas nii?
Klienditeenindaja		Just. Te proovige nüüd paar päeva, kas sai korda. Kui ei, siis tulge tagasi.

V

mobiiltelefon, -i, -i, -e	*cell phone*
katki mine/ma, katki minn/a, lähe/b katki	*to break*
korda tege/ma, korda teh/a, tee/n korda	*to fix*
Mis tal siis viga on?	*What's the matter with it then?*
aku, -, -t, -sid	*battery*
tühjaks saa/ma, tühjaks saa/da, saa/b tühjaks	*to empty, to run flat*
sisse lülita/ma, sisse lülita/da, lülita/n sisse	*to switch on*
ostu/tšekk, - tšeki, - tšekki, - tšekke	*receipt*
alles ole/ma, alles oll/a, on alles	*to have (still)*
ära viska/ma, ära visa/ta, viska/n ära	*to throw away*
garantii/remont, -remondi, -remonti	*warranty repairs*
niisama	*just so*
ära paranda/ma, ära paranda/da, paranda/n ära	*to fix*
välja vaheta/ma, välja vaheta/da, vaheta/n välja	*to exchange*
kate, katte, katet, katteid	*cover*
ära võt/ma, ära võtt/a, võta/n ära	*to take off*
korpus, -e, -t, -i	*case, body (of the phone)*
lahti tege/ma, lahti teh/a, tee/n lahti	*to open*
ära lõhku/ma, ära lõhku/da, lõhu/n ära	*to break*
vist on parem	*it's probably better*
nupp, nupu, nuppu, nuppe	*switch, button*
alla vajuta/ma, alla vajuta/da, vajuta/n alla	*to press down*
juhend, -i, -it, -eid	*instruction*
kirjas olema, kirjas oll/a, on kirjas	*to be written*
ära kaota/ma, ära kaota/da, kaota/n ära	*to lose*

proovi/ma, -da, -n	*to try*
kinni pane/ma, kinni pann/a, pane/n kinni	*to close*
korda saa/ma, korda saa/da, saa/n korda	*to be fixed, to be repaired*
tagasi tule/ma, tagasi tull/a, tule/n tagasi	*to return, come back*

EXERCISE 8

Listen to the dialogue and choose the correct answer.

1 Tuuli telefoni aku **saab/ei saa** kohe tühjaks, kui ta telefoni sisse lülitab.

2 Tuuli ostis telefoni umbes **pool aastat tagasi/kolm aastat tagasi**.

3 Tuulil **on/ei ole** ostutšekk alles.

4 Garantiiremonti **saab/ei saa** teha.

5 Tuuli **oskab/ei oska** korpust lahti teha.

6 Nupp **tuleb/ei tule** alla vajutada.

7 Tuulil **on/ei ole** juhend alles.

8 Tuuli **peab/ei pea** paari päeva pärast kindlasti tagasi tulema.

EXERCISE 9

 11.08

Read the questions. Choose the correct response then listen to the recording for the correct answer.

1 **Kus saab mobiiltelefoni parandada?**
   a Oma toas saate, seal on internetiühendus.
   b Siin saab. Näidake, mis probleem teil on.

2 **Mis probleem teil on?**
   a Mu mobiiltelefon läks katki.
   b Ma võin aku välja vahetada.

3 **Mis telefonil viga on?**
   a Ma viskasin selle ära.
   b Aku saab kohe tühjaks, kui telefoni sisse lülitan.

4 **Millal te selle telefoni ostsite?**
   a Umbes pool aastat tagasi.
   b Ma ei saa garantiiremonti teha.

5 **Kas teil ostutšekk on alles?**
   a Kahjuks ei ole.
   b Kahju.

INSIGHT

See how many familiar words you can find on Estonian websites. One of the most popular is www.delfi.ee.

Language patterns

KUS MA SUITSETADA TOHIN? *WHERE MAY I SMOKE?* – MODAL VERBS

In this unit, we will study so called **modal verbs**, which are used to indicate if something is possible or not possible to do; allowed or not allowed to do or if something has to be done or not etc.

saama, saada, saan *to be able to, I can, I could*

For instance, we can use this verb in the following sentences:

Kus ma **saan** internetti kasutada?	*Where can I use the internet?*
Internetti **saate** kasutada oma toas.	*You can use the internet in your room.*
Kes **saab** mulle viis krooni anda?	*Who could give me five crowns?*
Mina **saan**, mul on raha.	*I can, I have money.*
Kas siin **saab** raha vahetada?	*Is it possible to exchange money here?*
Kahjuks ei **saa**.	*Unfortunately, you can't.*

As you can see the word **saama** *to be able to* or *I can, could* is used in situations where we talk or ask about the possibility of doing something (which depends on someone or something else other than the person's own will).

tohtima, tohtida, tohin *I may, to be allowed to*

For instance, we can use this verb in the following sentences:

Kas **tohib** veel midagi küsida?	*May I ask one more thing?*
Jah, ikka **tohib**.	*Yes, of course.* (lit. Yes you may)
Kas toas **tohib** suitsetada?	*Is smoking permitted in the room?*
Ei tohi.	*It is not allowed* (lit. may not)
Meie hotellis **tohib** suitsetada ainult baaris.	*In our hotel, you may only smoke in the bar.*

As these examples show, the word **tohtima** *I may, to be allowed to* is used when we talk about whether something is allowed or not.

võima, võida, võin *I may, I can, to be allowed*

The word **võima** can for instance be used in the following sentences:

Kas toas **võib** suitsetada?	*May one smoke in the room?*
Ei või.	*It is not allowed.* (lit. may not)

Meie hotellis **võib** suitsetada ainult baaris.	In our hotel, one may smoke only in the bar.
Kas ma **võin** oma sülearvuti võrku ühendada?	May I connect my laptop to the internet?
Jah, **võite** küll.	Yes, you may.

Note that the word **võima** in these contexts has the same meaning as **tohtima** in the earlier section.

| Kui soovite süüa, siis **võite** ju alati linna peale minna. | If you wish to eat, you can always go to town. |
| Ma **võin** aku välja vahetada. | I can exchange the battery. |

Here the word **võima** indicates that the possibility of doing something depends on the person's own will.

| Homme **võib** sadama hakata. | It may start raining tomorrow. |
| Ta **võib** jälle hilineda. | He/she might be late again. |

In this context the word **võima** means the probability of the action.

oskama, osata, oskan *to know (how to), to be able to, I can*

The word **oskama** can, for instance, be used in the following sentences:

Kas te **oskate** meie hotelli tulla?	Do you know how to get to our hotel?
Ei oska, mul ei ole linna kaarti.	No, don't, I haven't got the town map.
Kas te **oskate** eesti keelt?	Can you speak Estonian?
Natuke **oskan**.	A little. (lit. little I can)

The word **oskama** indicates that the person has a certain ability to do something.

pidama, pidada, pean *to have to, I must*

The word **pidama** can, for instance, be used in the following sentences:

Minibaari kasutamise eest **peate** eraldi juurde maksma.
You have to pay extra for the usage of the mini-bar.

Kas ma **pean** kella üheks toa vabastama?
Do I have to release the room by 1 o'clock?

Ei pea. Te **peate** toa vabastama kella kaheks.
No you don't. You have to release the room by 2 o'clock.

Te **peate** oma võtmed siia panema.
You must put your keys here.

The word **pidama** indicates that doing something is obligatory.

Note that in impersonal requests, we use the third form in the singular (i.e. **saab**, **võib**, **tohib**, **peab**), for instance

Kus **saab** raha vahetada?	*Where is it possible to exchange money?*
Kas tohib veel midagi küsida?	*Is it possible to ask something more?*
Kas siia **võib** istuda?	*Is it allowed to sit here?*
Toa **peab** vabastama kella kaheteistkümneks.	*The room has to be released by 12 o'clock.*

Bear in mind that with the word **pidama** the first form of the verb is always used. With the words **saama**, **võima**, **tohtima**, **oskama** we always use the second form of the verb.

EXERCISE 10

Choose the word that suits the sentence.

1 Kus **saab/oskab** kohvi juua? Seal on kohvik, seal **saab/oskab**.

2 Kas siia **peab/tohib** auto parkida? **Ei pea/Ei tohi**, siin ei ole parkimiskoht.

3 Kas **tohib/võib** juhtuda, et minu telefon läheb katki? Kõike **tohib/võib** juhtuda.

4 Kas te **peate/oskate** seda telefoni parandada?

5 Kas te **saate/tohite** mulle näidata, kus mu tuba on? **Saan/tohin** muidugi, tulge palun minuga kaasa.

6 Kas siin **tohib/oskab** suitsetada? Jah, **tohib/oskab** küll.

7 Kas ma **tohin/pean** kohe maksma? Ei, **peate/võite** maksta ka hiljem.

8 Kas sa **saad/oskad** minuga basseini tulla? Kahjuks **ei saa/ei oska**, mul ei ole aega.

9 Kas sa **saad/oskad** ujuda? **Saan/oskan** küll, õppisin ujuma juba kümme aastat tagasi.

MITMEKESI TE TULETE? *HOW MANY OF YOU WILL COME?*

The question **mitmekesi**? means *how many of you?* The answer will also end with **-kesi**, which will be added to the second form of the numeral (note that the construction **üksi** *alone* is an exception).

Some examples of usage:

Me töötame **kolmekesi** ühes toas.	*There are three of us working in one room.*
Me läheme täna õhtul **kuuekesi** restorani.	*Tonight the six of us will go to a restaurant.*
Me elame **neljakesi** ühes korteris.	*There are four of us living in an apartment.*
Olen **üksi** kodus.	*I am home alone.*

MU TELEFON LÄKS KATKI *MY TELEPHONE BROKE DOWN* – COMPOUND VERBS

We have already learnt that there are several verbs in Estonian that consist of two words, like **aru saama** *to understand* or **haigeks jääma** *to fall ill*. Such types of verb are called compound verbs.

You already know the meaning of verbs like **minema** *to go*, **saama** *to get*, **tegema** *to do* and **panema** *to put*. Note that if such words occur as part of a compound verb their meaning can be completely different, for instance:

katki minema	*to break down*
otsa saama	*to run out of*
korda tegema	*to fix*
kirja panema	*to write down*
Telefon **läks katki**.	*The phone broke down.*
Mul **sai** raha **otsa**.	*I ran out of money.*
Ta **teeb** telefoni **korda**.	*He fixes the phone.*
Ma **panen** teie nime **kirja**.	*I will write down your name.*

Here are some more examples:

minema	*to go*
katki minema	*to break down*
Mu auto **läks katki**.	My car broke down.
segi minema	*to mix up*
Vabandust, mul **läks** kellaaeg **segi**.	*Sorry, I mixed up the time.*
halvaks minema	*to go stale*
Toit **läks halvaks**.	*The food went stale.*
saama	*to get*
tühjaks saama	*to run flat*
Aku **saab tühjaks**, kui telefoni sisse lülitan.	*The battery runs flat when I switch on the phone.*
otsa saama	*to run out of*
Mul **sai** raha **otsa**.	*I ran out of money.*
tegema	*to do*
lahti tegema	*to open*
Üks hetk, ma **teen** telefoni korpuse **lahti**.	*One moment, I will open the telephone's case.*
katki tegema	*to break*
Oi, te **teete** selle telefoni **katki**!	*Oh, you will break this phone!*

korda tegema	to fix
Kas te oskate selle **korda teha?**	*Do you know how to fix it?*
panema	*to put*
kinni panema	*to book, to reserve; to close*
Mitu rada ma teile **kinni panen?**	*How many tracks shall I book for you?*
Proovige ise telefoni korpus **kinni panna**.	*Try to close the telephone's case yourself.*
kirja panema	*to write down*
Ma **panen** teie nime ja telefoni **kirja**.	*I will write down your name and phone.*
käima panema	*to start, to switch on*
Aidake mul see arvuti **käima panna**.	*Help me to switch on this computer.*

In order to practise this grammar topic further do Exercise 11 in the Practice section.

KAS TE SAAKSITE MU TELEFONI ÄRA PARANDADA? *COULD YOU FIX MY TELEPHONE?* – COMPOUND VERBS

Often one part of the compound verb is the word **ära** for instance **ära minema** *to leave*, **ära kaotama** *to lose*, **ära tegema** *to complete*, **ära sööma** *to eat up*.

ära has two meanings in compound verbs:

▶ It can indicate the complement of an action, for instance Ma **söön** koogi **ära** *I will eat the cake up*; Ma **joon** veini **ära** *I will drink the wine up*; Ma **teen** töö **ära** *I will complete the work*.

▶ It can also indicate withdrawal, leaving or retreat, for instance Ma **lähen** nüüd **ära** *I will leave now*; **Viska** see paber **ära!** *Throw this paper away!*; **Tule** sealt **ära**! *Come away from there!*

Remember that in such constructions the word **ära** does not mean negation as in *don't* sentences. In prohibiting sentences, **ära** is usually at the beginning of the sentence, for instance **Ära joo** seda vett! *Don't drink this water!* **Ära mine** sinna! *Don't go there!* In sentences such as **Joo** see vesi **ära!** *Drink this water up!* and **Mine ära!** *Go away!*, the word order is different and **ära** is positioned at the end of the sentence. It is also possible to construct sentences where the word **ära** is used twice (to indicate negation *and* as a component of the compound verb), for instance **Ära joo** seda vett **ära!** *Don't drink this water up!* **Ära mine ära!** *Don't go away!*

In order to practise this grammar topic further do Exercise 12 in the Practice section.

Practice

EXERCISE 11

Choose the correct expression.

1 Mu telefon **läks katki/läks halvaks/läks segi**.
2 Kas te saate selle **korda teha/lahti teha/katki teha**?

3 Kohe teen korpuse **lahti/teen korpuse korda/teen korpuse katki** ja vaatan, mis juhtus.

4 Teie telefon on korras, ainult aku **saab kohe otsa/saab kohe tühjaks**.

5 Vahetasin aku ära ja **panen korpuse käima/panen korpuse kinni/panen korpuse kirja**.

6 Vabandust, mul **läks kellaaeg katki/läks kellaaeg segi/läks kellaaeg halvaks**.

7 See juhtus sellepärast, et minu kell **läks halvaks/läks katki/läks segi**.

8 Ka raha **sai otsa/sai tühjaks** ja ma ei saanud lasta kella ära parandada.

9 Kas te saate minu nime **kirja panna/kinni panna/käima panna**?

10 Üks hetk. **Panen arvuti käima/Panen arvuti kirja** ja siis kohe teen seda.

11 Kas ma saaksin laua **kirja panna/käima panna/kinni panna**?

12 Jah ikka. Mis kell te soovite tulla? **Teeme restorani korda/Teeme restorani lahti/Teeme restorani katki** kell viis.

EXERCISE 12

Underline the negative sentences.

1 Joo vesi ära. Ära joo vett. Ära joo vett ära.

2 Ära mine. Mine ära. Ära mine ära.

3 Viska see paber ära. Ära viska seda paberit ära.

4 Ära söö seda kooki. Ära söö seda kooki ära. Söö see kook ära.

5 Ära korista seda tuba. Korista see tuba ära. Ära korista seda tuba ära.

 # Speaking

EXERCISE 13

You are booking into a hotel. Fill in the missing lines and then listen to the completed dialogue.

 11.09

Sina	Say *I booked a room 2 weeks ago*.
Administraator	Kas ühe- või kaheinimesetoa?
Sina	Say *A double room*.
Administraator	Kohe vaatame. Kuidas teie nimi on?
Sina	Say *I am [your name]*.
Administraator	Jah, see broneering on olemas. Kui kauaks te kavatsete jääda?
Sina	Say *Until Tuesday*.
Administraator	Väga hea. Siin on teie toa võti.

EXERCISE 14

You are talking to the administrator at the hotel lobby. Fill in the missing lines and then listen to the completed dialogue.

 11.10

Sina	Ask *May I ask something?*
Administraator	Aga palun.
Sina	Ask *Is there an internet connection in this hotel?*
Administraator	Jah. Meil on kõikides tubades ja baaris traadita Internet.
Sina	Ask *How much does it cost?*
Administraator	See ei maksa midagi.
Sina	Say *This is very nice.* Ask *Where can I smoke here?*
Administraator	Meie hotellis ei tohi suitsetada.
Sina	Ask *Where can I exchange money?*
Administraator	Siin lähedal on pank. Seal saate vahetada.
Sina	Say *Thank you. Goodbye.*

EXERCISE 15

Your child has a birthday and you would like to organize a party for him and his friends at the bowling alley. You call the administrator to book the time. Fill in the missing lines and then listen to the completed dialogue.

 11.11

Administraator	Tere. Bowlingusaal kuuleb.
Sina	Say *Can I book the bowling hall for 3 hours on Sunday?*
Administraator	Aga palun. Mis kell te tulla soovite?
Sina	Say *Is it possible to come at 4 o'clock?*
Administraator	Jah. Mitmekesi te tulete?
Sina	Say *There are eight of us.*
Administraator	Väga tore. Mitu rada ma teile kinni panen?
Sina	Say *I think that three tracks will be enough.*
Administraator	Selge. Ma panen siis teie nime ja telefoni kirja.

EXERCISE 16

Here are some situations for you to practise.

1 You would like to go to the hairdresser's on Tuesday morning. You call and you are told **Juuksur töötab esmaspäeviti ja teisipäeviti õhtupoole**. Can you get an appointment for Tuesday morning?

2 You would like to have an appointment at the hairdresser's for Monday. How do you say *I would like to book the time for Monday?*

3 You are asked **Mis kellaks?** How do you say *for 10 o'clock*?

4 You are discussing with the hairdresser what she will do. How do you say you would like to cut and dye your hair? How do you say you would like to cut your hair shorter?

5 You have agreed, that the hairdresser will cut your hair. Now she asks **Kui palju ma lõikan?** What is she asking?

6 You have agreed that the hairdresser will dye your hair. Now she asks: **Mis värvi me siis teeme?** What is she asking?

7 The hairdresser has cut your hair and asks: **Kas ma teen soengu ka?** What is she asking?

8 The hairdresser tells you: **Ma teen teil juuksed märjaks**. What is she going to do?

9 The hairdresser tells you: **Ma pesen teie pea ära**. What is she going to do?

EXERCISE 17

Something is wrong with your watch. You take it to the watch repairer to see if it can be fixed. Fill in the missing lines and then listen to the completed dialogue.

 11.12

Sina	Say *Hello!*
Teenindaja	Mis probleem teil on?
Sina	Say *My watch broke.*
Teenindaja	Kas teil ostutšekk on alles?
Sina	Say *Yes. Please.*
Teenindaja	Väga tore. Me saame kellale garantiiremonti teha.
Sina	Say *Very good. Ask What's wrong with it?*
Teenindaja	Ma teen korpuse lahti ja vaatan. Tulge poole tunni pärast tagasi.
Sina	Say *Let's do so.*

⁇ Test yourself

1 You want to have a double room until Thursday. What do you say?

    a Kas ma saaksin teisipäevani kaheinimesetoa?

    b Kas ma saaksin laupäevani üheinimesetoa?

    c Kas ma saaksin neljapäevani kaheinimesetoa?

2 *Toa peab vabastama üheteistkümneks.* What does it mean?

    a You have to leave the room after eleven o'clock.

    b You have to leave the room before eleven o'clock.

    c You have to leave the room by eleven o'clock.

3 What does *Interneti kasutamine on hinna sees?* mean

    a The price includes use of internet.

    b You can use the internet at the bar.

    c There is internet connection in the hotel.

4 You are booking a hotel room and the assistant asks *Mitmekesi te olete?* What does it mean?

    a How many of you are there?

    b May I ask one more question?

    c How long are you planning to stay?

5 You want an appointment at the hairdresser at eleven o'clock. What do you say?

    a Ma ei ole kell üksteist vaba.

    b Ma sooviksin kella üheteistkümneks aega kinni panna.

    c Võtke üksteist sentimeetrit lühemaks.

6 What words do you use to explain what you need to have done at the hairdresser?

    a piisama, suitsetama, kavatsema

    b lõikama, värvima, pesema

    c sisse lülitama, lahti tegema, ära parandama

7 Your mobile phone is broken. What do you say?

    a Ma ostsin mobiiltelefoni.

    b Ma kaotasin mobiiltelefoni ära.

    c Mu mobiiltelefon läks katki.

8 You take your broken phone to be repaired. The man asks *Mis tal viga on?* What does it mean?

    a When did you buy this phone?

    b Do you have the receipt?

    c What's the matter with it?

9 How do you say *I have to go?*

    a Ma oskan minna.

    b Ma pean minema.

    c Ma saan minna.

10 How do you ask *May I smoke here?*

    a Kas siin tohib suitsetada?

    b Kas sa oskad suitsetada?

    c Kas siin peab suitsetama?

12 Sooviksin korterit üürida
I would like to rent an apartment

In this unit you will learn:
- ▶ *How to read advertisements about apartments for rent*
- ▶ *How to ask questions about an apartment*
- ▶ *How to describe the location of something*

Listening 1

 12.01

You will hear two advertisements about apartments for rent. Listen to the texts **a** and **b** and complete Exercises 1–2 below.

a

> Üürile anda kahetoaline korter kesklinna lähedal puumajas. Ahiküte, WC ja vannituba eraldi. Trepikoda lukus. Maja ees on bussipeatus, lähedal kauplus, kool ja lasteaed. Korter on renoveeritud ja möbleeritud. Hinnas saab tingida!

b

> Üürile anda kolmetoaline korter kesklinna lähedal kivimajas. Keskküte, WC ja vannituba koos. Trepikoda lukus. Maja asub pargi sees, lähedal ostukeskus ja ujula. Korter on renoveeritud. Hind kokkuleppel!

kuulutus, -e, -t, -i	*advertisement, announcement*
üürile and/ma, üürile and/a, anna/n üürile	*to rent*
kahetoali/ne, -se, -st, -si	*two-room(ed) (apartment)*
korter, -i, -it, -eid	*apartment*
lähedal	*nearby, close to*
puumaja, -, -, puumaju	*wooden house, building*
ahi, ahju, ahju, ahjusid	*stove*
küte, kütte, kütet	*heating*
WC	*toilet, WC*
vanni/tuba, -toa, -tuba, -tube	*bathroom*
eraldi	*separately*
trepi/koda, -koja, -koda, -kodasid	*stairwell, entrance hall*
lukus	*locked*

	maja ees	in front of the house
	kauplus, -e, -t, -i	shop
	kool, -i, -i, -e	school
	laste/aed, -aia, -aeda, -aedu	kindergarten
	renoveeritud	renovated, lately decorated
	möbleeritud	furnished
	tingi/ma, -da, -n	to bargain
	hinnas saab tingida	the price can be bargained
	kivimaja, -, -, kivimaju	stone building
	kesk/küte, -kütte, -kütet	central heating
	koos	together, united
	asu/ma, -da, -b	to be located
	pargi sees	inside the park
	ostukeskus, -e, -t, -i	shopping centre, (Am.) mall
	ujula, -, -t, -id	swimming pool
	hind kokkuleppel	the price to be agreed on

EXERCISE 1

Listen to the texts **a** and **b** and tick the appropriate boxes. The first one is done for you.

		the first apartment (text a)	the second apartment (text b)
1	The apartment for rent has two rooms.	☑	☐
2	The apartment for rent has three rooms.	☐	☐
3	The apartment for rent is located in a stone building.	☐	☐
4	The apartment for rent is located in a wooden house.	☐	☐
5	The apartment for rent has stove heating.	☐	☐
6	The apartment for rent has central heating.	☐	☐
7	The apartment for rent has bathroom and toilet in the same room.	☐	☐
8	The apartment for rent has bathroom and toilet in separate rooms.	☐	☐
9	The entrance hall of the apartment is locked.	☐	☐
10	The entrance hall of the apartment is unlocked.	☐	☐
11	The bus stop is behind the house.	☐	☐
12	The bus stop is in front of the house.	☐	☐
13	The apartment needs renovating.	☐	☐
14	The apartment is renovated.	☐	☐
15	The apartment is furnished.	☐	☐
16	The apartment is unfurnished.	☐	☐
17	The price can be bargained.	☐	☐
18	The price cannot be bargained.	☐	☐

EXERCISE 2

Choose the correct translation.

1 **kahetoaline korter kesklinna lähedal a** two roomed apartment near the city centre
b two apartments near the city centre

2 **WC ja vannituba eraldi a** WC and bathroom in the same room **b** WC and bathroom in separate rooms

3 **trepikoda on lukus a** entrance hall is locked **b** entrance hall must be locked

4 **maja ees on bussipeatus a** there is a bus stop in front of the house **b** there is a bus stop behind the house

5 **lähedal kauplus, kool ja lasteaed a** there is **a** shop, school and kindergarten nearby
b I have to go to the shop, school and kindergarten

6 **korter on renoveeritud ja möbleeritud a** the apartment is not renovated and furnished
b the apartment is renovated and furnished

7 **hinnas saab tingida a** the price can be bargained **b** the price can not be bargained

8 **hind kokkuleppel a** the price is agreed upon **b** the price will be agreed upon

Listening 2

 12.02

You will hear two more advertisements about apartments for rent. Listen to the texts **a** and **b** and complete Exercises 3–4.

a

Üheksakorruselises paneelmajas anda üürile kahetaoline (üldpind 54 m2) korter esimesel korrusel. Majas lift, maja ees laste mänguväljak ja parkimiskohad. Asukoht väga hea, ilus vaade järvele. Hinnas saab tingida! Üürile lisanduvad kommunaalkulud pluss elekter.

b

Uues elamurajoonis anda üürile kolmetoaline möbleeritud korter. Maja on kahekorruseline ja asub suure kaubanduskeskuse juures. Majas ainult neli korterit, head naabrid. Roheline ümbrus, maja taga spordiväljak.

üheksakorruseli/ne, -se, -st, -si	*nine storey (house)*
paneel/maja, -, -, -maju	*building of (concrete) elements*
üld/pind, -pinna, pinda	*overall size*
korrus, -e, -t, -eid	*storey*
lift, -i, -i, -e	*elevator, lift*
laste mänguväljak, -u, -ut, -uid	*children's playground*
parkimis/koht, -koha, -kohta, -kohti	*parking spot*
asu/koht, -koha, -kohta, -kohti	*location*
vaade, vaate, vaadet, vaateid	*view*

järv, -e, -e, -i		*lake*	
üür, -i, -l		*rent*	
lisandu/ma, -da, -b		*to be added*	
üürile lisanduvad		*in addition to the rent* (lit. *to the rent will be added*)	
kommunaalkulud		*cost of municipal services* (i.e. electricity, water etc.)	
elekter, elektri, elektrit		*electricity*	
elamurajoon, -i, -i, -e		*dwelling district*	
kaubanduskeskus, -e, -t, -i		*shopping centre*	
ainult		*only*	
naaber, naabri, naabrit, naabreid		*neighbour*	
ümbrus, -e, -t		*surroundings*	
maja taga		*behind the house*	
spordiväljak, -u, -ut, -uid		*sports ground*	

EXERCISE 3

Listen to texts **a** and **b** and put a tick in the appropriate boxes. The first one is done for you.

		Esimene korter (text a)	teine korter (text b)
1	Korter on kahetoaline.	☑	☐
2	Korter on kolmetoaline.	☐	☑
3	Maja on kahekorruseline.	☐	☐
4	Maja on üheksakorruseline.	☐	☐
5	Majas on lift.	☐	☐
6	Maja asub suure kaubanduskeskuse juures.	☐	☐
7	Maja ees on laste mänguväljak.	☐	☐
8	Maja ees on parkimiskohad.	☐	☐
9	Majas on ainult neli korterit.	☐	☐
10	Maja taga on spordiväljak.	☐	☐
11	Korterist on ilus vaade järvele.	☐	☐
12	Korter on möbleeritud.	☐	☐

EXERCISE 4

Choose the correct translation.

1 **asukoht väga hea a** the apartment is very good for living **b** location (of the apartment) is very good

2 **ilus vaade järvele a** beautiful lake nearby **b** nice view of the lake

3 **üürile lisanduvad kommunaalkulud a** in addition to the rent there is also the cost of municipal services **b** the cost of municipal services is included in the rent

4 **roheline ümbrus a** green house **b** green surroundings

Estonian houses

A lot of Estonians live in **korterelamu** *apartment blocks*, although it is becoming increasingly popular to buy or build **eramaja** *your private/own house*. **Ridaelamu** *terraced houses* have also become popular in recent years, especially in **uuselamurajoon** *newly developed neighbourhoods*. Sometimes you can see a sign saying **naabrivalve piirkond** which means that the inhabitants in this area are taking part in the so-called neighbourhood watch scheme in order to diminish crime and possible break-ins.

Korrusmaja is a block of flats; the Soviet-era buildings like that are either five, 9 or 14 storeys high. Depending on the material of construction they are also called **paneelmaja** *concrete element building* or **telliskivimaja** *brick building*. **Korter** *a flat* can also be **üürikorter** *a rented flat*. In advertisements one can often see the expression **kõigi mugavustega korter**, which means that the apartment has central heating and hot water, something that is not self-evident for the older **puumaja** *wooden houses* of Estonia.

Estonian addresses reveal whether it is a single house or a block of flats, for instance *Järve 12* is a single building but *Järve 12–36* is a block of flats (the first number standing for the building and the second for the apartment).

Maamaja or **talu** is a house or farm in the countryside. **Suvila** is a summer house. **Eramaa** means private property. Be aware in the countryside and also in towns that if there is a sign that says **Ettevaatust, kuri koer!** there probably is quite a large and none too friendly dog loose in the yard.

Listening 3

Listen to a dialogue in which the estate agent is talking to a customer about an apartment for rent. Listen to the dialogue and then complete Exercises 5–6.

Maakler	Üks hetk, ma teen ukse lahti ... Nii, tulge palun sisse.
Klient	Jah, aitäh. Mitu tuba siin siis on?
Maakler	Kokku on kolm tuba ja köök. Näete, köögi kõrval on üks tuba, siin keskel on elutuba ja elutoa kõrval on magamistuba.
Klient	Ma näen, et korter on möbleeritud.
Maakler	Jah, siin on kõik olemas, isegi kardinad on akna ees ja vaibad maas.
Klient	Kas ma mööblit võin ümber paigutada? See on natuke imelik, et need riiulid on siin laua ja diivani vahel.
Maakler	Jah, mööblit võib küll ümber paigutada.
Klient	Milline kodutehnika siin korteris on?
Maakler	Köögis on keraamiline pliit, selle kohal on ka mikrolaineahi. Nõudepesumasin on siin valamu ja kapi vahel.
Klient	Aga pesumasin?
Maakler	Pesumasin on ka olemas, see on vannitoa kapi all.
Klient	Kas seda muusikakeskust ka tohib kasutada?
Maakler	Võib küll, aga muusikat ei tohi mängida liiga valjult. See tähendab, naabreid ei tohi segada.
Klient	Kas naabrid on rahulikud?
Maakler	Jah, on küll. Üleval korrusel elab vist üks abielupaar ja all elab üks üksik vanem mees.
Klient	Kus autot parkida saab?
Maakler	Maja ees on tasuline parkimiskoht.
Klient	Kas loomi ka tohib pidada? Mul on kass.
Maakler	Seda peab otse omanikult küsima. Ma usun, et võib küll.
Klient	Kas korteris suitsetada tohib?
Maakler	Suitsetada võite rõdul. Korteris suitsetada ei tohi.
Klient	Kui suur on üür?
Maakler	Neli ja pool tuhat krooni pluss elekter ja kommunaalmaksud.
Klient	Kas lepingu saab sõlmida pooleks aastaks?
Maakler	Jah, miks mitte.
Klient	Millal te paberid valmis saate?
Maakler	Esmaspäeval kindlasti.

> **TIP**
> Please note since 1 January 2011 the Estonian currency has been the Euro.

maakler, -i, -it, -eid	*estate agent*
üks hetk	*one moment*
teen ukse lahti	*I will open the door*
uks, ukse, ust, uksi	*door*
tulge sisse	*come in* (pl. imp.)
tuba, toa, tuba, tube	*room*
köök, köögi, kööki, kööke	*kitchen*
köögi kõrval	*next to the kitchen*

keskel	*in the middle*
elu/tuba, -toa, -tuba, -tube	*living room*
elutoa kõrval	*next to the living room*
magamis/tuba, -toa, -tuba, -tube	*bedroom*
siin on kõik olemas	*this place has everything*
isegi	*even*
kardinad	*curtains*
akna ees	*in front of the window*
vaip, vaiba, vaipa, vaipu	*carpet*
maas	*on the floor (lit. on the ground)*
Kas ma võin …?	*May I …?*
mööbel, mööbli, mööblit	*furniture*
ümber paiguta/ma, ümber paiguta/da, paiguta/n ümber	*to rearrange*
imelik	*strange*
riiul, -i, -it, -eid	*shelf*
laud, laua, lauda, laudu	*table*
diivan, -i, -it, -eid	*sofa*
laua ja diivani vahel	*between the table and sofa*
kodutehnika, -, -t	*home electronics*
keraamili/ne, -se, -st, -si	*ceramic*
pliit, pliidi, pliiti, pliite	*stove, oven*
selle kohal	*above it*
mikrolaine/ahi, -ahju, -ahju, -ahje	*microwave oven*
nõudepesumasin, -a, -at, -aid	*dishwasher*
valamu, -, -t, -id	*sink*
kapp, kapi, kappi, kappe	*cupboard*
valamu ja kapi vahel	*between the sink and cupboard*
pesumasin, -a, -at, -aid	*washing machine*
muusikakeskus, -e, -t, -i	*stereo system*
Kas seda tohib kasutada?	*Is it permissible to use this?*
ei tohi	*you may not*
mängi/ma, -da, -b	*to play (here: music)*
liiga valjult	*too loud*
see tähendab	*this means*
sega/ma, -da, -n	*to disturb*
rahulik, -u, -ku, -ke	*peaceful (here: quiet)*
üleval korrusel	*on the upstairs floor*
abielupaar, -i, -i, -e	*married couple*
üksik, -u, -ut, -uid	*single*
parki/ma, -da, -n	*to park*
tasuli/ne, -se, -st, -si	*paid*
parkimis/koht, -koha, -kohta, -kohti	*parking spot*
loom, -a, -a, -i	*animal*
loomi pida/ma, loomi pida/da, pea/n loomi	*to keep animals*

kass, -i, -i, -e	*cat*
omanik, -u, -ku, -ke	*owner*
seda peab otse omanikult küsima	*you have to ask that directly from the owner*
usku/ma, -da, usu/n	*to believe*
suitseta/ma, -da, -n	*to smoke*
rõdu, -, -, -sid	*balcony*
leping, -u, -ut, -uid	*contract*
sõlmi/ma, -da, -n	*to conclude (a contract)*
pooleks aastaks	*for half a year*
Millal te paberid	*When will you have the*
valmis saate?	*papers ready?*

EXERCISE 5

Listen to the dialogue and decide if the sentences that follow are **a** correct or **b** false.

1 Korteris on kolm tuba ja köök.

2 Magamistuba on elutoa kõrval.

3 Korter on möbleeritud.

4 Akna ees on kardinad ja vaibad on maas.

5 Mööblit ei või ümber paigutada.

6 Köögis on keraamiline pliit ja mikrolaineahi.

7 Nõudepesumasin on valamu all.

8 Pesumasin on valamu ja kapi vahel.

9 Muusikat võib mängida, aga vaikselt.

10 Üleval korrusel elab vist üksik vanem naine.

11 All elab üks vanem abielupaar.

12 Maja taga on tasuline parkimiskoht.

13 Kliendil on koer.

14 Rõdul ei tohi suitsetada.

15 Korteris ei tohi suitsetada.

16 Klient soovib lepingut sõlmida vähemalt aastaks.

17 Paberid saavad valmis teisipäeval.

EXERCISE 6

12.04

Choose the correct response. Listen to the recording to check your answers.

1 **Mitu tuba siin siis on?** **a** Kokku on kolm tuba. **b** Siin keskel on elutuba.

2 **Kas see korter on möbleeritud?** **a** Jah, siin on kõik olemas. **b** See on natuke imelik, et need riiulid on siin laua ja diivani vahel.

3 **Kas ma mööblit võin ümber paigutada?** **a** Jah, võib küll. **b** Jah, siin on kõik olemas.

4 **Milline kodutehnika siin korteris on? a** Siin on keraamiline pliit, nõudepesumasin ja pesumasin. **b** Jah, mööblit võib küll ümber paigutada.

5 **Kas naabrid on rahulikud? a** Jah, on küll. **b** Naabreid ei tohi segada.

6 **Kus autot parkida saab? a** Muusikat ei tohi mängida liiga valjult. **b** Maja ees on tasuline parkimiskoht.

7 **Kas loomi tohib pidada? a** Mul on kass. **b** Ma usun, et võib küll.

8 **Kas korteris suitsetada tohib? a** Ei tohi. **b** Esmaspäevaks kindlasti.

9 **Kas lepingu saab sõlmida pooleks aastaks? a** Esmaspäeval kindlasti. **b** Jah, miks mitte!

10 **Millal te lepingu valmis saate? a** Esmaspäloal kindlasti. **b** Lepingu saab sõlmida pooleks aastaks.

Listening 4

In this dialogue you will hear a husband ringing his wife at home to try to locate the mobile phone he has left behind. Listen to the dialogue and then complete Exercises 7–8.

 12.05

Mees	Armas, ma olen vist oma telefoni koju unustanud. Vaata palun mu laua peale, kas see on seal.
Naine	Oota, kohe. Laua peal on näiteks sinu lips ja mingid CD-plaadid ja ...
Mees	Aga vaata siis palun voodi alla, äkki ma panin ta hommikul sinna.
Naine	Ei ole siin mingit telefoni.
Mees	Äkki ma panin siis telefoni sinna kotti, mis on teleka juures.
Naine	Mis kotti? Siin teleka juures küll mingit kotti ei ole.
Mees	Hmm. Aga äkki ta kukkus kapi taha?
Naine	Oota, ma vaatan. Ei, ei ole siin.
Mees	Ja kapi ette sa juba vaatasid?
Naine	Ja-jaa. Ma võin veel mõnda sahtlisse vaadata. Äkki panid riiulisse raamatute vahele?
Mees	Vaata palun.
Naine	No ei ole siin. Äkki sa võtsid ta töö juurde kaasa? Kas sa oma taskusse vaatasid?
Mees	Mis taskusse?
Naine	No põuetaskusse näiteks?
Mees	Ja ongi siin. Oh mind küll!

armas, armsa, armsat, armsaid	*darling, dear*
unusta/ma, -da, -n	*to forget*
vaata laua peale	*look on the table* (sing. imperative)
CD-plaat, CD-plaadi, CD-plaati, CD-plaate	*CD*

voodi, voodi, voodit, voodeid	*bed*
vaata voodi alla	*look under the* bed *(sing. imp.)*
äkki	*suddenly* (here *may be*)
sinna kotti	*into this bag*
telekas, teleka, telekat, telekaid	*TV set (familiar)*
teleka juures	*by the TV*
kukku/ma, -da, kukun	*to fall*
kukkus kapi taha	*fell behind the cupboard*
Ja kapi ette sa juba vaatasid?	*And you already looked in front of the cupboard?*
mõni, mõne, mõnd, mõnesid	*some*
sahtel, sahtli, sahtlit, sahtleid	*drawer*
mõnda sahtlisse	*into some drawer*
raamatute vahele	*in between the books*
võtsid töö juurde kaasa	*took with you to (the) work(place)*
tasku, -, -t, -id	*pocket*
põue/tasku, -, -t, -id	*breast pocket*
ja ongi siin	*and here it is*
Oh mind küll!	*Oh, silly me!*

EXERCISE 7

Listen to the dialogue and put the following sentences in the right order.

1 Naine lubab vaadata sahtlisse.

2 Mees vaatab oma põuetaskusse, kus on võtmed.

3 Naine otsib kotti, mis peaks olema teleka juures.

4 Naine vaatab kapi ette.

5 Naine vaatab kapi taha.

6 Naine vaatab laua peale, kus on lips ja mingid CD-plaadid.

7 Naine vaatab riiulisse raamatute vahele.

8 Naine vaatab voodi alla.

EXERCISE 8

Find the correct translation.

1	Vaata palun, kas mu telefon on laua peal.	**a**	Maybe I put the phone in the bag?
2	Äkki ma panin telefoni voodi alla?	**b**	Please look, if my phone is on the table.
3	Äkki ma panin telefoni kotti?	**c**	Maybe the phone fell behind the cupboard?
4	Vaata, kas mu telefon on teleka juures.	**d**	Maybe you took the phone with you to work?
5	Äkki telefon kukkus kapi taha?	**e**	Maybe you put the phone between the books?
6	Äkki sa panid telefoni is raamatute vahele?	**f**	Please look if my phone is near the TV.
7	Äkki sa võtsid telefoni töö juurde kaasa?	**g**	Maybe I put the phone under the bed?

More useful words about apartments

Here are some more words you might need when talking about an apartment.

tool, -i, -i, -e	*chair*
tugitool, -i, -i, -e	*armchair*
tekk, teki, tekki, tekke	*blanket*
padi, padja, patja, patju	*pillow*
lina, -, -, linu	*(bed)sheet*
sein, -a, -a, -u	*wall*
lagi, lae, lage, lagesid	*ceiling*
põrand, -a, -at, -aid	*floor*
aken, akna, akent, aknaid	*window*
rõdu, -, -, -sid	*balcony*
kelder, keldri, keldrit, keldreid	*cellar*
saun, -a, -a, -u	*sauna*
tolmuimeja, -, -t, -id	*vacuum cleaner*
arvuti, -, -t, arvuteid	*computer*
toalilled, toalillede, toalilli	*house plants*
nõud, nõude, nõusid	*dishes*
peegel, peegli, peeglit, peegleid	*mirror*
nagi, -, -, -sid	*clothes rack*
garaaž, -i, -i, -e	*garage*

> **INSIGHT**
>
> Do you know that you can involve your subconcious in language learning? If, e.g., you label pieces of furniture, you will find that you remember them with very little effort.

Language patterns

KAHETOALINE KORTER *TWO-ROOM(ED) APARTMENT*

There are several ways to indicate how many rooms an apartment or floors the building has.

The simplest way is to say **Korteris on kolm tuba** *There are three rooms in the apartment.* **Majas on viis korrust** *There are five floors in the house.*

We can also say See on **kolmetoaline** korter *This is a three-room(ed) apartment.* See on **viiekorruseline** maja *This is a five-storey house.*

Forms like **kolmetoaline** *three room(ed)* and **viiekorruseline** *five storey* are constructed in the following way:

kolme (second form of the numeral) + **toa** (second form of the main word) + ending **line** = **kolmetoaline korter** *three-room(ed) apartment.*

viie (second form of the numeral) + **korruse** (second form of the main word) + ending **line** = **viiekorruseline maja** *five-storey house.*

For instance:

üks, ühe *one*	**tuba**, toa *room*	**ühetoaline korter** *one-room apartment*
kaks, kahe *two*	**tuba**, toa *room*	**kahetoaline korter** *two-room apartment*
kolm, kolme *three*	**korrus**, korruse *storey*	**kolmekorruseline maja** *three-storey house*
neli, nelja *four*	**korrus**, korruse *storey*	**neljakorruseline maja** *four-storey house*

We can talk about a person's age in the same way, i.e. we can say **See poiss on kolm aastat vana**. *This boy is 3 years old* but we can also say **See poiss on kolmeaastane** *This boy is 3 years old*. As you can see this form can also be made by adding together the second form of adjective and noun + **-ne**. For instance:

üks, ühe	**nädal**, nädala *week*	**ühenädalane laps** *1-week-old baby*
kümme, kümne	**kuu**, kuu *month*	**kümnekuune laps** *10-month-old baby*
kaksteist, kaheteistkümne	**aasta**, aasta *year*	**kaheteistkümneaastane** or **kaheteistaastane laps** *12-year-old child*
kolmkümmend viis, kolmekümne viie	**aasta**, aasta *year*	**kolmekümne viie aastane mees** *35-year-old man*

Note that almost all words ending in **-ne** have exactly the same endings in the four main forms i.e:

-ne	ühetoali**ne** (first form i.e. nominative)
-se	ühetoali**se** (second form i.e. genitive)
-st	ühetoali**st** (third form i.e. partitive)
-si or **-seid**	ühetoali**si** (fourth form i.e. plural partitive)

Note that if you have more than one long word with similar components in a sentence, the words are often shortened in the following way:

Meie majas on **ühe-**, **kahe-** ja **kolmetoalised** korterid. *In our house there are one-, two- and three-roomed apartments.*

EXERCISE 9

Make similar words using the following example.

1 kolm tuba – *kolmetoaline korter*

2 viis tuba – _____

3 seitse tuba – _____

4 kaks korrust – *kahekorruseline maja*

5 üheksa korrust – _____

6 kuusteist korrust – _____

7 kuusteist aastat – *kuueteistaastane inimene*

8 kaheksateist aastat – _____

9 nelikümmend viis aastat – *neljakümne viie aastane inimene*

10 viiskümmend kolm aastat – _____

TELERI EES *IN FRONT OF THE TV – POSTPOSITIONS*

When we want to indicate the location of something we use words like **taga** *behind*, **ees** *in front* etc. Such words are called postpositions because in Estonian they are placed behind the main word i.e. **laua taga** *behind the table*, **riiuli ees** *in front of the shelf*. Note that the main word is in second form. You will find examples of different postpositions in the following table. Depending on in which direction the objects move, different forms of the postposition are used as postpositions in Estonian have three forms.

kuhu? *where to?*	kus? *where?*	kust? *where from?*
Jänes läheb teleri **ette**. The rabbit goes in front of the TV.	Jänes on teleri **ees**. The rabbit is in front of the TV.	Jänes läheb teleri **eest** ära. lit. The rabbit goes away from in front of the TV.
Jänes läheb teleri **taha**. The rabbit goes behind the TV.	Jänes on teleri **taga**. The rabbit is behind the TV.	Jänes tuleb teleri **tagant** välja. lit. The rabbit comes out from behind of the TV.
Jänes hüppab teleri **peale**. The rabbit jumps on the TV.	Jänes on teleri **peal**. The rabbit is on top of the TV.	Jänes hüppab teleri **pealt** ära. lit. The rabbit jumps away from on top of the TV.
Jänes hüppab teleri **alla**. The rabbit jumps under the TV.	Jänes on teleri **all**. The rabbit is under the TV.	Jänes tuleb teleri **alt** välja. lit. The rabbit comes out from under the TV.
Poiss paneb jänese pildi raamatu **vahele**. The boy puts the rabbit's picture in between the book.	Jänese pilt on raamatu **vahel**. The rabbit's picture is in between the book.	Poiss võtab jänese pildi raamatu **vahelt** ära. lit. The boy takes the rabbit's picture out from in between the book.
Poiss paneb jänese pildi teleri **kohale.** The boy puts the rabbit's picture above the TV.	Jänese pilt on teleri **kohal**. The rabbit's picture is above the TV.	Poiss võtab jänese pildi teleri **kohalt** ära. lit. The boy takes the rabbit's picture away from above the TV.

Juures *near*, ääres *by*, kõrval *next to*

The words **juures** and **ääres** have several different meanings. The word **juures** is usually used in the following contexts:

Ma olen arsti **juures**.	*I am at the doctor's.*
Ta on direktori **juures**.	*He is at the director's.*
Riiul on ukse **juures**.	*The shelf is near the door.*

The word **ääres** is usually used with words like **järv** *lake*, **jõgi** *river*, **meri** *sea*, for instance:

Ma olen mere **ääres.**   *I am at (by) the seaside.*

It is also used with words to indicate objects that stretch out (**tee** *road*, **laud** *table* etc.):

Puud on maantee **ääres.**   *The trees are beside the road.*

Inimesed on laua **ääres.**   *People are beside the table.*

Jänes läheb teleri **juurde.**	Jänes on teleri **juures.**	Jänes tuleb teleri **juurest** ära.
The rabbit goes up to the TV.	*The rabbit is near the TV.*	lit. *The rabbit goes away from the TV.*
Jänes läheb järve **äärde.**	Jänes on järve **ääres.**	Jänes läheb järve **äärest** koju.
The rabbit goes to the lake.	*The rabbit is beside the lake.*	lit. *The rabbit goes home from near the lake.*
Jänes istub poisi **kõrvale.**	Jänes on poisi **kõrval.**	Jänes läheb poisi **kõrvalt** ära.
The rabbit sits next to the boy.	*The rabbit is next to the boy.*	lit. *The rabbit goes away from next to the boy.*

In order to practise this grammar topic further do Exercises 10–14 in the Practice section.

RENOVEERITUD MÖBLEERIMATA KORTER *RENOVATED UNFURNISHED* APARTMENT – *TUD*-FORM, MATA-*FORM*

The ending **-tud** indicates in Estonian that something is done, for instance:

möbleeri**tud** korter	*furnished apartment*
renoveeri**tud** korter	*renovated apartment*
värvi**tud** sein	*painted wall*
lukusta**tud** uks	*locked door*

The ending **-mata** indicates the opposite, i.e. that something is not done or is undone, for instance

möbleeri**mata** korter	*unfurnished apartment*
renoveeri**mata** korter	*undecorated apartment*
värvi**mata** sein	*unpainted wall*
lukusta**mata** uks	*unlocked door*

Practice

EXERCISE 10

Choose the correct translation.

1 **next to the kitchen a** köögi kohal, **b** köögi kõrval
2 **between the table and sofa a** laua ja diivani juures, **b** laua ja diivani vahel

3 **by the sink a** valamu all, **b** valamu juures

4 **inside the microwave oven a** mikrolaineahju sees, **b** mikro-laine ahju peal

5 **behind the stereo system a** muusikakeskuse ees, **b** muusika-keskuse taga

6 **on the balcony a** rõdu peal, **b** rõdu all

7 **by the TV a** teleri juures, **b** teleri taga

8 **under the shelf a** riiuli taga, **b** riiuli all

EXERCISE 11

Look at the picture and decide if the sentences are true or false. Make the false sentences correct.

1   Tool on riiuli ja ukse vahel.   _____

2   Akna ees on kardinad.   _____

3   Lilled on laua peal.   _____

4   Pilt on riiuli kohal.   _____

5   Telefon on laua peal.   _____

6   Muusikakeskus on teleri ees.   _____

7   Kass on tugitooli taga.   _____

8   Raamat on laua all.   _____

9   Tugitool on akna lähedal.   _____

10   Riiul on akna ja ukse vahel.   _____

EXERCISE 12

Look at the picture in Exercise 11 and answer the questions. Use postpositions in your answer.

1 Kus on kass? _____

2 Kus on kruusid? _____

3 Kus on raamatud? _____

4 Kus on padi? _____

5 Kus on lilled? _____

6 Kus on pilt? _____

EXERCISE 13

Choose the correct form.

  1 Mees pani oma telefoni laua **peale/peal/pealt**.

  2 Telefon oli laua **peale/peal/pealt**.

  3 Kass tuli laua **juurde/juures/juurest** ja nägi telefoni.

  4 Ta läks laua **peale/peal/peal**t ja istus telefoni **kõrvale/kõrval/kõrvalt**.

  5 Naine võttis telefoni laua **peale/peal/pealt** ära ja pani teleri **taha/taga/tagant**.

  6 Telefon oli teleri **taha/taga/tagant**.

  7 Mees tuli ja otsis oma telefoni laua **peale/peal/pealt**.

  8 Aga telefon ei olnud enam laua **peale/peal/pealt**.

  9 Mees otsis ka diivani **taha/taga/tagant**, aga ka seal ei olnud telefoni.

10 Siis vaatas mees veel riiuli **alla/all/alt**, aga ka seal ei olnud ka mitte midagi.

11 Mees küsis naiselt, kus telefon on ja naine ütles, et pani telefoni teleri **taha/taga/tagant**.

12 Mees võttis oma telefoni teleri **taha/taga/tagant** ja pani taskusse.

EXERCISE 14

Make similar sentences using the example sentences below.

1	Panen palli laua peale.	*Pall on laua peal.*	*Võtan palli laua pealt.*
2	Panen palli laua alla.		
3	Panen palli teleri taha.		
4	Panen palli riiuli juurde.		
5	Panen palli diivani ette.		
6	Panen palli ukse kõrvale.		
7	Panen palli arvuti ja muusikakeskuse vahele.		

Speaking

EXERCISE 15

 12.06

Find the correct answer to each question. Listen to the recording to check your answers then translate the questions.

1	Mitmetoaline see korter on?		**a**	Viimasel, see tähendab viiendal.
2	Mis korrusel see korter asub?		**b**	Kaks tuba on, üks mitte.
3	Kui suur on korteri üldpind?		**c**	Jah, natuke aega tagasi.
4	Kas korteris on rõdu?		**d**	Maja lähedal on tasuline parkla.
5	Kas korter on möbleeritud?		**e**	75 ruutmeetrit.
6	Kas korter on remonditud?		**f**	Jah, nad on väga toredad inimesed
7	Kas naabrid on rahulikud?		**g**	Umbes 3000 krooni kuus.
8	Kus ma autot saan parkida?		**h**	Siin on kolm tuba ja köök.
9	Kui suur on üür?		**i**	Jah, isegi kaks.

EXERCISE 16

You went to see an apartment for rent and you would like to ask the owner some questions. Fill in the missing lines and then listen to the completed dialogue.

 12.07

Omanik	Tere. Tulge palun sisse.
Sina	Say *Hello. Ask How many rooms are here?*
Omanik	Kaks tuba ja köök. Rõdu on ka. Korter on möbleeritud. Siin on nõudepesumasin ja pesumasin.
Sina	Ask *Is it allowed to use the washing machine?*
Omanik	Võib küll.
Sina	Ask *Are the neighbours quiet?*
Omanik	Ma usun küll. Üleval elab ainult üks üliõpilane.
Sina	Ask *Where can I park the car?*
Omanik	Parkimiskoht on maja taga.
Sina	Ask *How much is the rent?*
Omanik	Kolm tuhat krooni kuus pluss kommunaalkulud.
Sina	Say *Very good. Ask Is it possible to conclude the contract for half a year?*
Omanik	Jah, miks mitte. Ma teen paberid valmis kolmapäeval.
Sina	Say *Thank you.*

EXERCISE 17

 12.08

You are instructing your colleague over the phone to find the wallet you have forgotten at work. Choose the correct sentence. Listen to the recording to check your answers.

1 You think your wallet might be on the table.
2 You think your wallet might be under the table.
3 You think your wallet might be in your drawer.
4 You think the wallet might be under your chair.
5 You think your wallet might be on top of the computer.
6 You think your wallet might be in between the books.
7 You think your wallet might be behind the cupboard.
8 You think your wallet might be in your bag.
9 You think your wallet might be in front of the window.

a Vaata palun laua alla.
b Vaata palun minu tooli alla.
c Vaata palun laua peale.
d Vaata palun raamatute vahele.
e Vaata palun minu kotti.
f Vaata palun minu sahtlisse.
g Vaata palun akna ette.
h Vaata palun kapi taha.
i Vaata palun arvuti peale.

EXERCISE 18

You have lost your watch and you think you left it at your friend's place. You are calling him to ask about the watch. Fill in the missing lines and then listen to the completed dialogue. The first line is done for you.

 12.09

Sina	Tere! Ma olen vist oma kella sinu juurde unustanud.
Sõber	Oota, ma kohe vaatan.
Sina	Say *Look on top of the TV, please.*
Sõber	Ei, ei ole siin.
Sina	Say *Look under the sofa, please.*
Sõber	Jah, ma vaatan. No ei ole siin.
Sina	Say *Maybe it fell behind the cupboard?*
Sõber	Oota, kohe. Ja ongi siin!

❓ Test yourself

1 You see an advertisment that *neljatoaline korter kesklinnas kivimajas* is for rent. What does it mean?
  a a four-room apartment in a wooden house in the city centre
  b a three-room apartment in a stone building in the new residential district
  c a four-room apartment in a stone building in the city centre

2 You would like to rent an apartment. How do you ask if there is a kindergarden, shop and school nearby?
  a Kas maja lähedal on ostukeskus, ujula ja kool?
  b Kas maja lähedal on lasteaed, pood ja kool?
  c Kas maja lähedal on bussipeatus, kesklinn ja kool?

3 How do you say *the apartment is furnished*?
  a korter on möbleeritud
  b korter on möbleerimata
  c korter on renoveeritud

4 Which are electrical devices?
  a kapp, laud, rõdu
  b mikrolaineahi, nõudepesumasin, pliit
  c riiul, vaip, valamu

5 You would like to ask if it is possible to keep animals in the apartment. What do you say?
  a Kas korteris tohib loomi pidada?
  b Kas korteris tohib mööblit ümber paigutada?
  c Kas korteris tohib valjult muusikat kuulata?

6 What does the sentence mean *Raamat on diivani taga?*
  a The book is behind the sofa.
  b The book is on the sofa.
  c The book is under the sofa.

7 How do you say in Estonian *The armchair is next to the shelf*?
  a Tugitool on riiuli taga.
  b Tugitool on riiuli ees.
  c Tugitool on riiuli kõrval.

8 What does the sentence *Maja juures on tasuta parkimiskoht* mean?
  a Parking near the building is not allowed.
  b There is free parking near the building.
  c There is a big shopping centre near the building.

9 You want to know how many rooms are in the apartment. What do you ask?

   a Kas naabrid on rahulikud?

   b Mitu tuba korteris on?

   c Millal te lepingu valmis saate?

10 How do you say *Please put the phone on the shelf?* Palun pane telefon ...

   a riiuli peale

   b riiuli peal

   c riiuli pealt

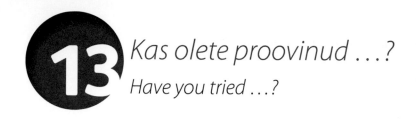

13 Kas olete proovinud …?
Have you tried …?

In this unit you will learn:
- ▶ *How to talk about restaurants and food*
- ▶ *How to buy souvenirs*
- ▶ *How to communicate in a post office*
- ▶ *The names of festival days in Estonia*

Listening 1

Laura is very hungry. She discusses with Janar where to go to eat. Listen to the dialogue and then complete Exercise 1.

 13.01

Laura	Mul on kõht tühi. Lähme kuhugi sööma!
Janar	Jah. Kuskil siin majas oli üks kohvik… Neil on kiire teenindus ja vist ka soodsad hinnad.
Laura	Kiire teenindus? Vastupidi, neil on just väga aeglane teenindus! Ja portsjonid on ka liiga väiksed. Mitte keegi ei käi seal.
Janar	Soovita siis ise midagi.
Laura	Pärnu maanteel on vist mingi uus koht. Ma lehest lugesin, et seal on põnev interjöör ja väga maitsev toit.
Janar	Ega see mingi taimetoitlaste restoran ei ole?
Laura	Ei ole!
Janar	Lähme siis pealegi sinna.

Mul on kõht tühi.	*I am hungry (lit. I have an empty stomach)*
kõht, kõhu, kõhtu	*stomach*
kuhugi	*to somewhere, anywhere*
kuskil	*somewhere, anywhere*
kiire, -, -t, -id	*fast*
teenindus, -e, -t	*service*
vastupidi	*on the contrary*
aegla/ne, -se, -st, -seid	*slow*
Neil on just väga aeglane teenindus.	*They have very slow service.*
portsjon, -i, -it, -eid	*ration*
liiga	*too*
mitte keegi	*nobody*

midagi	something
mingi, mingi, mingit, mingeid	some kind of
põnev, -a, -at, -aid	exciting, interesting
interjöör, -i, -i, -e	interior
maitsev, maitsva, maitsvat, maitsvaid	tasty
taimetoitla/ne, -se, -st, -si	vegetarian
Ega see mingi taimetoitlaste restoran ole?	Isn't it some kind of vegetarian restaurant?
Lähme siis pealegi sinna.	All right, let's go there then.

EXERCISE 1

Listen to the dialogue and answer the questions.

1 What does Laura suggest Janar that they do?

2 What does Janar say about the coffee shop that is located somewhere in the building?

3 What does Laura say about the same coffee shop?

4 What does Janar suggest?

5 What does Laura say about the new place at Pärnu maantee?

6 What does Janar worry about?

7 What does Laura answer?

8 What does Janar reply?

Listening 2

Alo and Sirje are eating out in a restaurant. They are studying the menu and discussing what to eat. Listen to the dialogue and then complete Exercise 2.

 13.02

Alo	Kas sa oled siin kunagi varem käinud?
Sirje	Jah, olen küll. Viimati käisin eelmisel nädalal koos kolleegidega.
Alo	No siis sa kindlasti oskad toitusid soovitada. Kas sa näiteks seda suppi oled proovinud?
Sirje	Jah, see supp on väga hea, aga sa peaksid kindlasti midagi veel tellima, sest see portsjon on üsna väike.
Alo	Ma võtan mingi prae.
Sirje	Küpsetatud kana on neil väga hea.
Alo	Mida sa ise võtad?
Sirje	Mina võtan seekord grillitud kala kastmega. Ja lisandiks mingi salati.
Alo	Kas sa siin sealiha oled söönud?

Sirje	Kunagi ammu sõin. Päris hea oli.
Alo	Ma võtan siis praetud sealiha friikartulitega. Kas joome veini ka? Kas sa majaveini oled maitsnud?
Sirje	Ei, seda ei ole ma kunagi joonud. Ma eelistaksin valget veini, kui sa vastu ei ole.
Alo	Jah, võtame pudeli valget majaveini. Kuidas oleks mingi magustoiduga? Kas tellime kohe või hiljem?
Sirje	Tellime kohe. Mina tahaksin midagi kerget, näiteks jäätist.
Alo	Ma vist praegu ei jaksa magustoitu süüa. Ma võtan lihtsalt ühe kange kohvi.
Sirje	Kas sa nägid, kas kuskil olid tualettruumid ka?
Alo	Need olid vist ukse juures vasakul.
Sirje	Ahah. Ma käin kiiresti ära. Ära sa enne telli!

 kunagi varem   *sometime before*

viimati   *last time*

eelmi/ne, -se, -st, -seid   *previous*

eelmine nädal   *last week*

kolleeg, -i, -i, -e   *colleague*

üsna väike   *quite small*

praad, prae, praadi, parade   *roast meat* (also: *main course*)

küpseta/ma, -da, -n   *to roast (in the oven), also to fry, to bake*

küpsetatud   *roasted (in the oven)*

seekord   *this time*

grilli/ma, -da, -n   *to roast, to broil (over fire or hot coals)*

grillitud   *roasted (over fire or hot coals)*

kaste, kastme, kastet, kastmeid   *sauce*

lisand, -i, -it, -eid   *side dish (i.e. potatoes, rice etc.)*

sealiha, -, -   *pork*

kunagi ammu   *sometime ago*

päris hea   *quite good*

praadi/ma, -da, prae/n   *to fry*

praetud   *fried*

frii/kartulid, -kartulite, -kartuleid   *French fries*

majavein, -i, -i, -e   *house wine*

maits/ma, -ta, -en   *to taste*

kunagi   *ever*

Kuidas oleks   *how about*

magus/toit, -toidu, -toitu, -toite   *dessert*

vastu ole/ma, vastu oll/a,   *to be against (something)*
  ole/n vastu

kohe   *now, immediately*

hiljem   *later*

kerge, -, -t, -id	light
praegu	at the moment
jaksa/ma, -ta, -n	to be able to
kange, -, -t, -id	strong
kuskil	somewhere

EXERCISE 2

Listen to the dialogue once more and decide if the sentences that follow are **a** true or **b** false.

1 Sirje has not been to this restaurant before.

2 Sirje has eaten the soup in this restaurant.

3 Sirje thinks the soup is good but the portion too small to make a meal in itself.

4 Sirje said that the roast chicken in this restaurant is not very good.

5 Sirje will have grilled fish and a salad.

6 Alo will have fried pork with French fries.

7 Sirje has also tried the house wine in this restaurant.

8 Sirje and Alo will have a bottle of white house wine.

9 Sirje wants to have a dessert.

10 Alo will also have icecream for dessert.

11 Alo orders a cup of strong coffee.

12 The toilets are near the door on the left.

RESTAURANT WORDS

Some more words you might need in a restaurant:

lusikas, lusika, lusikat, lusikaid	spoon
kahvel, kahvli, kahvlit, kahvleid	fork
nuga, noa, nuga, nuge	knife
taldrik, -u, -ut, -uid	plate
tass, -i, -i, -e	cup
klaas, -i, -i, -e	glass
kruus, -i, -i, -e	mug
sool, -a, -a	salt
pipar, pipra, pipart	pepper
hamba/ork, -orgi, -orki, -orke	toothpick
tuhatoos, -i, -i, -e	ashtray
välgu/mihkel, -mihkli, -mihklit, -mihkleid	lighter
tikud, tikkude, tikke	matches

Estonian meals

Hommikusöök *breakfast* is usually eaten quite early and at home, around 7 or 8 o'clock before people go to work. Very often the Estonian breakfast consists of **võileivad** *open sandwiches*, which can be made with either **juust** *cheese* or **vorst** *sausage*. **Leib** *bread* means dark rye bread in Estonia, and the white wheat bread is called **sai**. Some people eat **puder** *porridge* or have a **keedetud muna** *boiled egg* to get something more substantial. During breakfast people usually drink **kohv** *coffee*, which, depending on how it is made, is called **masinakohv** (coffee made in coffee machine) or **kannukohv** (coffee made in a pot). **Lahustuv kohv** *instant coffee* is not very popular in Estonia. **Kohvijoomine** *coffee drinking* continues at workplaces as most offices have coffee machines.

Lõuna *lunch* is usually eaten between 12 and 2 o'clock and many restaurants and bars serve a **päevamenüü** *menu of the day* at reduced prices during this time. A proper lunch consists of three courses: **supp** *soup*, **praad** *main course* (either meat, fish or chicken) and **magustoit** *dessert*. Often you see people drinking dairy products with their lunch like **milk** *piim* or **keefir** *a sort of sour milk*.

Õhtusöök *supper* is eaten around 7 o'clock and at home most commonly people will drink tea and eat savoury bits and pieces like **kartulisalat** *potato salad* or **pelmeenid** *dumplings filled with minced meat* with **marineeritud kurgid** *pickled cucumbers* or **seened** *mushrooms*. There are many people who grow or collect their own herbs so when visiting Estonian homes you might be offered **taimetee** *herb tea* made, for instance, from **piparmünt** peppermint or a mixture of herbs.

The restaurants stay open until about midnight and in bigger cities you can find most of the international dishes. Traditional Estonian cuisine is heavily influenced by German cooking and therefore **hapukapsas** *sauerkraut* and **sealiha** *pork* are the most popular national dishes.

Listening 3

Someone is buying presents in a souvenir shop. Listen to the dialogues and then complete Exercises 3–5.

 13.03

a	**Müüja**	Tere!
	Ostja	Tere! Näidake palun mingeid ilusaid mänguasju.
	Müüja	Tüdrukutele on meil väga armsaid käsitsi tehtud nukke ja poistele on igasuguseid puust mänguasju.
	Ostja	Kas need on Eestis tehtud?
	Müüja	On küll. Tulge vaadake neid ise, nii on parem valida.
	Ostja	Väga tore. Ma võtan need kaks. Siis ma sooviksin veel värvilisi küünlaid.
	Müüja	Milliseid te tahate? Punaseid, rohelisi, kollaseid?
	Ostja	Ma võtan eri värve: kaks kollast, kaks punast ja kaks rohelist.
	Müüja	Tore, ma pakin need ära.

Ostja	Äkki teil on ka ingliskeelseid eesti raamatuid?
Müüja	Jah, mõned on. Vaadake neid riiuleid seal.
Ostja	Ma võtan selle.
Müüja	Väga tore. Kas veel midagi?
Ostja	Nüüd on kõik.
Müüja	See teeb kokku kolmsada kaksteist krooni.
Ostja	Palun.
Müüja	Ega teil kaht krooni ei ole? Mul ei ole tagasi anda.
Ostja	Kohe otsin. Palun.
Müüja	Aitäh.
b **Ostja**	Tere, kas teil on müügil eesti komme?
Müüja	Jah, siin letis on kõik eesti kommid.
Ostja	Millised on head?
Müüja	Kõik on head. Eriti head on muidugi šokolaadikommid.
Ostja	Palun siis kilo erinevaid komme.
Müüja	Teeme nii. Ma panen eri sorte, igat sorti sada grammi.
Ostja	Kas te alkohoolseid jooke ka müüte?
Müüja	Jah, veinid on selles riiulis ja kangemad alkohoolsed joogid seal tagapool.
Ostja	Milliseid eesti likööre teil on?
Müüja	Vaadake, kõik eesti liköörid on seal alumisel riiulil.
Ostja	Ma palun selle pudeli, mis maksab kaheksakümmend krooni.
Müüja	Kas see on kõik?
Ostja	Jah. Ühe kilekoti palun ka.
Müüja	Palun. Kas maksate kaardiga või sularahas?
Ostja	Kaardiga.
Müüja	Siia palun siis allkiri ka. See tšekk jääb teile. Aitäh.

TIP

Please note since 1 January 2011 the Estonian currency has been the Euro.

---

mängu/asi, -asja, -asja, -asju	*toy*
armas, armsa, armsat, armsaid	*cute, sweet*
käsitsi tehtud	*handmade*
nukk, nuku, nukku, nuke	*doll*
igasugu/ne, -se, -st, -seid	*any kind of, all kinds of*
vali/ma, -da, -n	*to choose*
värvili/ne, -se, -st, -si	*colourful*
küünal, küünla, küünalt, küünlaid	*candle*
ära pakki/ma, ära pakki/da, paki/n ära	*to wrap up, to pack*
ingliskeel/ne, -se, -set, -seid	*in English (language)*
see teeb kokku	*this will be all together*
tagasi and/ma, tagasi and/a, anna/n tagasi	*to give back*
komm, -i, -i, -e	*candy, sweet*
lett, leti, letti, lette	*counter*
šokolaadikomm, -i, -i, -e	*chocolate candy*

sort, sordi, sorti, sorte	*sort*
alkohool/ne, -se, -set, -seid	*alcoholic*
jook, joogi, jooki, joke	*drink*
liköör, -i, -i -e	*liqueur*
alumi/ne, -se, -st, -si	*lower, bottom*
kaart, kaardi kaarti, kaarte	*here: bank card*
sularaha, -, -	*cash*
all/kiri, -kirja, -kirja, -kirju	*signature*
tšekk, tšeki, tšekki, tšekke	*receipt*

EXERCISE 3

Listen to dialogue **a** and tick items the tourist is looking at and buying.

käsitsi tehtud nukud	☐	kollased küünlad	☐
puust mänguasjad	☐	rohelised küünlad	☐
puust nukud	☐	valged küünlad	☐
punased küünlad	☐	ingliskeelsed eesti raamatud	☐
sinised küünlad	☐	eestikeelsed raamatud	☐

EXERCISE 4

Listen to dialogue **b** and choose the correct answer.

1 Turist soovib osta **a** eesti komme, **b** eesti ploome.

2 Müüja ütleb, et eriti head on **a** eesti kommid, **b** šokolaadikommid.

3 Ostja soovib osta **a** ühesuguseid komme, **b** erinevaid komme.

4 Ostja soovib osta **a** kaks kilo komme, **b** ühe kilo komme.

5 Müüja paneb iga sorti **a** sada grammi, **b** kakssada grammi.

6 Poest saab osta ka **a** veini, **b** piima.

7 Ostja soovib osta **a** likööri, **b** konjakit.

8 Ta ostab pudeli, mis maksab **a** 80 krooni, **b** 90 krooni.

9 Ostja maksab **a** kaardiga, **b** sularahas.

EXERCISE 5

 13.04

Choose the correct response. Listen to the recording to check your answers.

1 **Kas need on Eestis tehtud?**
   a On küll.
   b Väga tore.

2 Milliseid te tahate?

   a Nüüd on kõik.

   b Ma võtan selle.

3 Kas veel midagi?

   a Kohe otsin.

   b Nüüd on kõik.

4 Ega teil kaht krooni ei ole?

   a Mul ei ole tagasi anda.

   b Kohe otsin.

5 Millised kommid on head?

   a Kõik on head.

   b Siin letis on kõik eesti kommid.

6 Äkki teil on ka eesti raamatuid?

   a Jah, mõned on.

   b Tore, ma pakin need ära.

7 Kas maksate kaardiga või sularahas?

   a Kaardiga.

   b Siia palun siis allkiri ka.

Estonian souvenirs

Typical Estonian souvenirs would be **kudumid** *knitwear* including colourful **käpikud** *mittens*, **villased sokid** *wollen socks* and **kampsunid** *sweaters*, which use the traditional Estonian folk patterns and are practical and warm to wear in cold weather. **Käsitöö** *handicraft* made of linen or leather is also popular. Solid clothes racks and other items made by blacksmiths are traditional and typical of Estonia too. In souvenir shops you can find **küünlajalg** *candlesticks* carved out of **paekivi** *limestone*, which is the national rock of *Estonia*. **Merevaik** *amber* is also sold widely, although amber is not found in Estonia. Don't forget to buy either a butter knife or chopping board for your kitchen made of **kadakas** *juniper tree* as it has a nice smell and is very durable.

Listening 4

The following conversation takes place in the post office. Listen to the dialogue and then complete Exercises 6–7.

 13.05

Klient	Tere! Palun üks ilus mark eesti-sisesele kirjale.
Postitöötaja	Millise ma annan?
Klient	Andke palun see õhupallidega mark.
Postitöötaja	See on kallim, see sobib rahvusvahelistele kirjadele.
Klient	Pole hullu, ma võtan ikka selle, mis sellest, et on kallim.
Postitöötaja	Kas veel midagi?
Klient	Kas te võiksite palun selle paki ära kaaluda?
Postitöötaja	Jah, see on üle poole kilo.
Klient	Ma soovin saata selle Inglismaale.
Postitöötaja	Mis siin sees on?
Klient	See on raamat.
Postitöötaja	Ma paneksin ta igaks juhuks turvaümbriku sisse. See maksab kümme krooni.
Klient	Väga tore.
Postitöötaja	Nüüd kirjutage siia nurka saatja aadress ja siia saaja aadress.
Klient	Kas te saaksite mulle palun pastakat laenata?
Postitöötaja	Palun. Kas see läheb lennu- või maapostiga?
Klient	Kumb on kallim?
Postitöötaja	Lennupost on ainult natukene kallim, aga pakk läheb kohale palju kiiremini.
Klient	Siis võiks ikka lennupost olla.
Postitöötaja	Sellisel juhul täitke palun veel see blankett. Ja siia kirjutage tänane kuupäev ja allkiri.
Klient	Kas ma blanketi pean täitma trükitähtedega?
Postitöötaja	Jah, olge nii kena. Nii, siin on tšekk, see eksemplar jääb teile. Hoidke see niikaua alles, kuni pakk on kohale jõudnud.

> **TIP**
>
> Please note since 1 January 2011 the Estonian currency has been the Euro.

mark, margi, marki, marke	stamp
eesti-sise/ne, -se, -st, -seid	domestic (lit. *inside Estonia*)
kiri, kirja, kirja, kirju	letter
õhupall, -i, -i, -e	balloon
sobi/ma, -da, -b	to suit
rahvusvaheli/ne, -se, -st, -si	international
pole hullu	it's OK (slang)
võtan ikka selle	I'll take it anyway
mis sellest	here: in spite, although
ära kaalu/ma, ära kaalu/da, kaalu/n ära	to weigh
üle poole kilo	over half a kilo

saat/ma, saat/a, saad/an	*to send*
sees	*inside*
raamat, -u, -ut, -uid	*book*
igaks juhuks	*just in case*
turvaümbrik, -u, -ut, -uid	*jiffy bag*
turvaümbriku sisse	*into a jiffy bag*
nurk, nurga, nurka, nurki	*corner*
saatja, -, -t, -id	*sender*
saaja, -,-t, -id	*receiver*
pastakas, pastaka, pastakat, pastakaid	*ballpoint pen*
laena/ma, -ta, -n	*to borrow, to lend*
lennupost, -i, -i	*airmail*
maapost, -i, -i	*regular mail*
kumb, kumma, kumba, kumbi	*which one*
täit/ma, täit/a, täida/n	*to fill in*
blankett, blanketi, blanketti, blankette	*form*
täna/ne, -se, -st, -seid	*today's*
trüki/täht, -tähe, -tähte, -tähti	*block letter*
olge nii kena	*be so kind*
eksemplar, -i, -i, -e	*copy, piece*
alles hoid/ma, alles hoid/a, hoia/n alles	*to keep*
niikaua kuni	*as long as*
kohale jõud/ma, kohale jõud/a, jõua/n kohale	*to get to*

EXERCISE 6

Listen to the dialogue and decide if the sentences that follow are true or false.

1 Klient soovib osta ühe postmargi rahvusvahelisele kirjale.

2 Ta ostab õhupallidega margi.

3 Õhupallidega mark on kallim ja sobib rahvusvahelisele kirjale.

4 Kliendi pakk kaalub rohkem kui pool kilo.

5 Klient soovib saata paki Inglismaale.

6 Pakis on kaks raamatut.

7 Turvaümbrik maksab viisteist krooni.

8 Klient peab kirjutama ümbrikule saatja ja saaja aadressi.

9 Lennupost on kiirem ja kallim kui maapost.

10 Klient saadab paki maapostiga.

11 Klient peab täitma blanketi trükitähtedega.

12 Tšeki peab alles hoidma niikaua, kuni pakk on kohale jõudnud.

EXERCISE 7

 13.06

Choose the correct response. Listen to the recording to check your answers.

1 Millise postmargi ma annan?	**a** Jah, see on üle kahe kilo.
2 Kas te võiksite selle paki ära kaaluda?	**b** Jah, palun, pastakas on siin.
3 Mis siin sees on?	**c** Lennupostiga.
4 Kas te saaksite mulle palun pastakat laenata?	**d** Jah, olge nii kena.
5 Kas see läheb lennu- või maapostiga?	**e** See on raamat.
6 Kas ma blanketi pean täitma trükitähtedega?	**f** Andke üks ilus mark eesti-sisesele kirjale.

At the post office

The opening hours of the post offices are the same as that of any official establishment – from 9.00–18.00. The signs for **postkontor** *post office* and the **postkast** *mailbox* in Estonia are bright orange with blue text. Some of the words you might need in a post office are **kiri** *letter*, **postkaart** *postcard*, **ümbrik** *envelope*, **kuller** *courier*.

As **internetikaubandus** *internet shopping* and **postimüük** *catalogue shopping* are popular forms of marketing products in Estonia; parcel machines can be found everywhere in shopping centres.

> **INSIGHT**
>
> You have learned a lot of words and phrases by now. Try making your own texts, just for fun! Compiling short dialogues or keeping a diary in Estonian will greatly improve your language skill. Don't be afraid to make mistakes – that is only normal.

Language patterns

LÄHME KUHUGI SÖÖMA! *LET'S GO SOMEWHERE TO EAT!* – INDEFINITE PRONOUNS AND ADVERBS

When we talk about things that are not concrete we use words like **keegi** *somebody*, **miski** *something*, **kuskil** *somewhere*, **kunagi** *sometime* in the necessary form. Just like other words these words also can take different endings.

Some examples of usage

kes? *who?*	Kas **keegi** tahab süüa? *Does anyone want to eat?*
keda? *whom?*	Kas sa nägid **kedagi**? *Did you see anybody?*
kellele? *to whom?*	Ma andsin oma telefoni **kellelegi**. *I gave my phone to someone.*
kellel? *who has?*	Kas **kellelgi** on aega? *Does anyone have some time?*
kellelt? *from whom?*	Kas sa küsisid **kelleltki**? *Did you ask anyone?* (lit. *from anyone*)
kellega? *with whom?*	Kas sa rääkisid **kellegagi**? *Did you talk to someone?* (lit. *with someone*)
mida? *what?*	Soovitage palun **midagi** head. *Please suggest something good.*

Note that in order to make these forms we add **-gi** or **-ki** (next to **s** and **t**) to the end of the corresponding question i.e.:

kellele? + **gi** = kellele**gi**　　　　　lit. *to someone*

kellelt? + **ki** = kellelt**ki**　　　　　lit. *from anyone*

etc.

Note that the pairs of words like *somebody – anybody, something – anything, somewhere – anywhere, sometime – anytime* are not differentiated in Estonian and we just use one word for each pair of words in English.

kuhu? *where to?*	Lähme **kuhugi** sööma. *Let's go somewhere to eat.*
kus? *where?*	**Kuskil** siin majas peab olema kohvik. *Somewhere in this house should be a coffee-shop.*
kust? *where from?*	Kas sa leidsid **kuskilt** menüü? *Did you find a menu anywhere?*
millal? *when?*	Ma olin siin **kunagi** ammu. *I was here sometime long ago.*

In order to practise this grammar topic do Exercise 15 in the Practice section.

MA EI TAHA MITTE KUHUGI MINNA *I DON'T WANT TO GO ANYWHERE* – NEGATIVE PRONOUNS AND ADVERBS

In the negative sentence we also use the words **keegi**, **miski**, **kuskil**, **kunagi** in the necessary form. We can (but don't have to) add the word **mitte** *no* which will stress the negation.

Note that double negation is permissible in Estonian, but note that it is *not possible* to say **Mitte keegi tahab süüa* as that would be a straight translation from English.

Some examples of usage

(Mitte) keegi ei taha süüa. *No one wants to eat.*
Ma ei näinud **(mitte) kedagi**. *I didn't see anyone.*
Ma ei andnud oma telefoni **(mitte) kellelegi**. *I didn't give my phone to anyone.*
(Mitte) kellelgi ei ole aega. *No one has time.*
Ma ei küsinud **(mitte) kelleltki**. *I didn't ask anyone.*
Ma ei rääkinud **(mitte) kellegagi**. *I didn't talk to anyone.*
Ma ei oska **(mitte) midagi** soovitada. *I can't suggest anything.*
Ma ei taha **(mitte) kuhugi** minna. *I don't want to go anywhere (or I want to go nowhere).*
(Mitte) kuskil siin majas ei ole kohvikut. *There isn't a coffee shop anywhere in this house (or Nowhere in this house is a coffee shop).*
Ma ei leia **(mitte) kuskilt** menüüd. *I don't find a menu anywhere.*
Ma ei ole siin **(mitte) kunagi** olnud. *I have never been here.*

EXERCISE 8

Choose the correct translation.

1	Kas keegi teab, kus on restoran?	**a**	*I went once to a good restaurant.*
2	Ma käisin kunagi ühes heas restoranis.	**b**	*Does anyone have time to come to the coffee shop with me?*
3	Kuskil siin lähedal on üks hea kohvik.	**c**	*I would like to have something good to drink.*
4	Kas kellelgi on aega koos minuga kohvikusse tulla?	**d**	*Does anyone know where the restaurant is?*
5	Ma tahaksin midagi head juua.	**e**	*No one wants to come to the restaurant.*
6	Mitte keegi ei taha restorani tulla.	**f**	*Somewhere near here is a good coffee shop.*
7	Ma ei taha kedagi näha.	**g**	*I have never been to this restaurant.*
8	Ma ei ole selles restoranis kunagi käinud.	**h**	*I don't want to see anyone.*

In order to practise this grammar topic further do Exercise 16 in the Practice section.

KAS SA OLED SEDA VEINI PROOVINUD? *HAVE YOU TRIED THIS WINE?* – PRESENT PERFECT

As we have already discussed in Unit 9, the Estonian language has three past tenses: **lihtminevik** *imperfect*, **täisminevik** *present perfect*, **enneminevik** *past perfect*. In this unit we will discuss the usage of **täisminevik** *the present perfect tense*.

The forms of the present perfect tense are as follows:

Ma **olen** eesti veine **proovinud**.	Ma **ei ole** eesti veine **proovinud**.
I have tried Estonian wines.	*I haven't tried Estonian wines.*
Sa **oled** eesti veine **proovinud**.	Sa **ei ole** eesti veine **proovinud**.
You have tried Estonian wines.	*You haven't tried Estonian wines.*
Ta on eesti veine **proovinud**.	Ta ei ole eesti veine **proovinud**.
He/she has tried Estonian wines.	*He/she hasn't tried Estonian wines.*
Me **oleme** eesti veine **proovinud**.	Me **ei ole** eesti veine **proovinud**.
We have tried Estonian wines.	*We haven't tried Estonian wines.*
Te **olete** seda veine **proovinud**.	Te **ei ole** eesti veine **proovinud**.
You have tried Estonian wines.	*You haven't tried Estonian wines.*
Nad on seda veine **proovinud**.	Nad **ei ole** eesti veine **proovinud**.
They have tried Estonian wines.	*They haven't tried Estonian wines.*

The form of present perfect tense always consists of two words: the verb **olema** *to be* in the present tense + **nud** form (the same as the negative form of imperfect).

Some more examples of the present perfect tense:

Ma **olen** siin üks kord varem ka **käinud**. *I have been here once before also.*

Ma **olen** kunagi seda veini **proovinud**. *I have tried this wine sometime before.*

Ma **ei ole** siin mitte kunagi varem **olnud**. *I have never been here before.*

Ma **ei ole** varem seda magustoitu **söönud**. *I have not eaten this dessert before.*

Note that in Estonian we may also use **täisminevik** in cases when in English the continuous tense is used i.e.:

Ma **olen** sind kolm tundi **oodanud**. *I have been waiting for you for 3 hours.*

Ma **olen** siin juba terve päeva **istunud**. *I have been sitting here for the whole day.*

Ma **olen** Eestis **elanud** ainult mõned kuud. *I have been living in Estonia for some months only.*

The simplest way to answer questions, which are in the present perfect tense, is just to say **jah**, **olen küll** *yes, I have* or **ei ole** *no, I haven't*.

For instance:

Kas sa oled sellist kooki varem söönud? *Have you eaten this kind of cake before?*

Jah, olen küll. *Yes, I have*

or

Ei ole. *No, I haven't.*

EXERCISE 9

Make similar sentences.

1 Ma olen eesti keelt õppinud neli kuud.   Me _____

   Sa _____   Te _____

   Ta _____   Nad _____

2 Ma ei ole kunagi läti keelt õppinud.   Me _____

   Sa _____   Te _____

   Ta _____   Nad _____

In order to practise this grammar topic further do Exercise 17 in the Practice section.

Estonian holidays

Vana-aastaõhtu *New Year's Eve*

The New Year's Eve is a big time for celebrations in Estonia. People gather at homes, restaurants or nightclubs to hold parties which culminate in **ilutulestik** *fireworks* at midnight. Local municipalities have fireworks in most city centres and often different towns compete to see who will have the most expensive one. People open bottles of champagne and wish **Head uut aastat!** *Happy New Year!* to each other at midnight. A few minutes past midnight the Estonian President will give an annual speech broadcast on national television.

Vastlapäev *Shrove Tuesday*

In February bars and restaurants will all of a sudden start serving **vastlakuklid** *sweet buns* filled with whipped cream and sprinkled with sugar powder. Another ancient Shrove Tuesday tradition, which is still very much alive in Estonia, is to go sledging.

Vabariigi aastapäev (Eesti Vabariigi aastapäev (iseseisvuspäev)) *Independence Day*

The Estonian Independence Day is on 24 February and it marks the day in 1918 when Estonia declared independence. The blue, black and white national tricolors decorate houses and many people go to light candles in graveyards to commemorate those who passed away in wars of the last century. On the evening of the 24th, the President will hold a reception for significant Estonian persons, politicians and diplomats.

Lihavõttepühad *Easter*

In Estonia only **Suur reede** *Good Friday* is a bank holiday. Colouring yellow eggs with onion skins and eating them on Easter Sunday is a tradition in Estonia. To get an even brownish colour onion skins are just sprinkled in the water where the eggs are boiled. For a more artistic result people wrap onion skins around the eggs with some cloth and string to keep them in place. This method results in very bright and mottled patterns. At the Easter table people knock the eggs with the aim of breaking the other person's eggshell and wish each other **Häid lihavõttepühi!** *Happy Easter!*

Emadepäev *Mother's day* Isadepäev *Father's day*

Emadepäev is celebrated on the second Sunday of May and **Isadepäev** on the second Sunday of November. No specific traditions can be associated with these days – **emme** *mom* and **issi** *dad* are just given small presents and flowers. But there is another day when some shops can run out of flowers: **naistepäev** *the women's day* on 8 March is when men buy flowers to show their respect to women. At some workplaces small parties are held.

Jaanipäev *Midsummer's day*

Jaanilaupäev *Midsummer's eve* on the 23rd of June is a bank holiday to mark the victory of Võnnu battle in the war of independence in 1919. It is also the second most important celebration besides Christmas, when all Estonians who can leave the city and gather in the countryside to light the **jaanituli** *midsummer bonfire* and dance and sing around it until the early morning hours. The sun only sets for a very short while and it is the only night when **sõnajalg** *the fern* is said to blossom, the finder of which could expect great wealth and happiness.

Eesti taasiseseisvumispäev *Restoration day of independence*

There is one more bank holiday during the summer on the 20th of August. It's called **taasiseseisvumispäev** *the new Independence Day* to mark the restoration of the independent Republic of Estonia in 1991. Sometimes open-air rock concerts are held with the repertoire consisting of national songs.

Esimene koolipäev *The first day of school*

September 1 is the day when all schools officially start. All the towns are milling with schoolchildren either in festive school uniforms that some schools have adapted or in white shirts and dark skirts and trousers carrying flowers to their teachers. Festive ceremonies are held in all schools to welcome the pupils back to school.

Mardipäev *St Martin's day*; Kadripäev *St Catherine's day*

On 9 and 24 November children in funny costumes go from house to house expecting candy or biscuits in exchange for singing, dancing or reciting poems. This is to celebrate **Mardipäev** (10 November) and **Kadripäev** (25 November) that traditionally were ancient peasant holidays. So if you hear outside your door some children reciting, singing and shouting do let them in and treat them to chocolate or candy.

Jõulud *Christmas*

Christmas in Estonia is primarily a family-centred holiday, when the old and young gather to have a festive Christmas dinner beside the candle-lit and decorated **jõulukuusk** *Christmas tree*. The dinner takes place on **jõululaupäev** *the day before Christmas*, on 24 December. This is also the evening when **jõuluvana** *Santa Claus* may pay a visit to houses where children and, in this case, also adults are expected to recite a poem or sing a song in order to receive a present. Christmas dinner traditionally consists of **seapraad** *roast pork* or **verivorstid** *black pudding* accompanied with **hapukapsad** *sauerkraut* and **pohlamoos** *lingonberry jam*. Another Christmas treat is **piparkoogid** *gingerbread*, which can be sugar-frosted for decoration. Weeks before **jõulukaardid** *Christmas cards* will have been mailed to friends and relatives with wishes like **Rahulikke jõule ja head uut aastat!** *Peaceful Christmas and a Happy New Year!*

On Christmas Eve Estonian graveyards will be lit up with candles to remember those who have passed away.

Sünnipäev *Birthday*

Sünnipäev *birthday* is an important day for Estonians, even for adults. Estonians do not celebrate **nimepäev** *name day* but friends, family and sometimes even colleagues do expect that the **sünnipäevalaps** *birthday boy/girl* will throw a birthday party. Often such parties are held at home where people gather to eat nice food including **tort** *fancy cake* and savoury dishes like **kartulisalat** *potato salad* etc. It is very common to give flowers to the **sünnipäevalaps**, and often also a small **kingitus** *present* which can be almost anything (starting from a book and ending with a bottle of alcohol for a man, for instance). To congratulate someone on their birthday you say **Palju õnne sünnipäevaks! Juubel** *jubilees* are often celebrated in a bigger fashion, where especially the older generation will sing traditional songs at a long table and maybe even dance. People will dress up for such an occasion and buy more expensive presents for the jubilarian.

SUPP, SUPI, SUPPI – TYPES OF NOUNS

In Unit 3 we breifly discussed typical sound changes in Estonian. Now we will have a closer look at some typical changes once more. Note that the sound changes do not occur in all Estonian words, yet in words where they do take place, usually the first, third and fourth form are similar and the second form differs.

EXERCISE 10

Study the words and fill in the missing forms.

first form (nominative)	second form (genitive)	third form (partitive)	fourth form (plural partitive)
I			
kk, pp, tt	**k, p, t**	**kk, pp, tt**	**kk, pp, tt**
nu**kk** *doll*	nu**k**u	nu**kk**u	nu**kk**e
pa**kk** *parcel*	pa**k**i	pa**kk**i	pa**kk**e
tše**kk** *receipt*	tše**k**i	_____	_____
su**pp** *soup*	su**p**i	su**pp**i	su**pp**e
tre**pp** *stairs*	_____	_____	_____
ko**tt** *bag*	ko**t**i	ko**tt**i	ko**tt**e
blanke**tt** *form*	blanke**t**i	_____	_____
II			
k, p, t	**g, b, d**	**k, p, t**	**k, p, t**
joo**k** *drink*	joo**g**i	joo**k**i	joo**k**e
mär**k** *badge, sign*	mär**g**i	_____	_____
see**p** *soap*	see**b**i	see**p**i	see**p**e
kar**p** *box*	kar**b**i	_____	_____
toi**t** *food*	toi**d**u	toi**t**u	toi**t**e
tor**t** *cake*	tor**d**i	_____	_____
III			
k, t	**—**	**k, t**	**k, t**
kas**k** *birchtree*	kase	kas**k**e	kas**k**i
kuus**k** *sprucetree*	_____	_____	_____
leh**t** *leaf, sheet*	lehe	leh**t**e	leh**t**i
vah**t** *foam*	vahu	_____	_____

IV

g, b, d	—	g, b, d	g, b, d
si**g**a *pig*	sea	si**g**a	si**g**u
lu**g**u *story*	loo	_____	lu**g**usid
tu**b**a *room*	toa	tu**b**a	tu**b**e
lu**b**a *permission*	_____	_____	_____
praa**d** *roast meat*	prae	praa**d**i	praa**d**e
poo**d** *shop*	poe	_____	_____

Note that in the fourth group the whole word changes. Fortunately, there aren't many words like this.

MA SÖÖN KOOKI. MA SÖÖN KOOGI ÄRA *I AM EATING THE CAKE. I WILL EAT THE CAKE UP* – OBJECT

Naine sööb kooki. A woman is eating cake.

Naine sõi koogi ära. A woman ate the cake up.

Note that when we talk about an (continuous) action that is taking place or that took place, the third form in the singular is used. When we talk about the result of an action, the second form is used.

SINGULAR

I am doing something.	*I have done something. I have finished something.*
third form (partitive singular)	**second form** (genitive singular)
Sa *__sööd__* **suppi.** *You are eating soup.*	Sa *__sõid__* **supi** *__ära__*. *You ate the soup up.*
Ma *__joon__* **õlut.** *I am drinking beer.*	Ma *__jõin__* **õlle** *__ära__*. *I drank the beer up.*
Ta *__loeb__* **raamatut**. *He/she is reading a book.*	Ta *__luges__* **raamatu** *__läbi__*. *He/she read the book through.*

Note that when we indicate that something has been done (the result is achieved) or is finished, we often add words like **ära**, **läbi**, i.e. Ma **sõin** supi **ära** *I ate the soup up* etc.

EXERCISE 11

Choose the correct translation.

1 I am eating soup. **a** Ma söön suppi. **b** Ma sõin supi ära.

2 I eat the soup up. **a** Ma söön suppi. **b** Ma sõin supi ära.

3 He drank the tea up. **a** Ta joob teed. **b** Ta jõi tee ära.

4 We eat the bread up. **a** Me sööme leiva ära. **b** Me sõime leiva ära.

5 Did you eat ice cream? **a** Kas sa sõid jäätist? **b** Kas sa sõid jäätise ära?

In order to practise this grammar topic further do Exercise 18 in the Practice section.

PLURAL

Unfortunately, words in singular and plural behave differently, so when we talk about an (continuous) action that is taking place or took place we use the fourth form with words in the plural.

I am doing something.	*I have done something/I have finished something.*
partitive singular	**plural nominative**
Ma _**söön**_ **küpsiseid**.	Ma _**sõin**_ **küpsised** _**ära**_.
I am eating cookies.	*I ate the biscuits up.*
Me _**joome**_ erinevaid **veine**.	Me _**jõime**_ kõik **veinid** _**ära**_.
We are drinking different wines.	*We drank all the wines up.*
Sa _**loed**_ neid **raamatuid**.	Sa _**lugesid**_ kõik **raamatud** _**läbi**_.
You are reading these books.	*You read all the books through.*

When we talk about the result of an action we use plural nominative (the second form + d).

Note that the same applies to sentences which indicate future, i.e. in Estonian the verb is in the present tense:

Ma **joon** õlle **ära**.	*I will drink the beer up.*
Ma **söön** supi **ära**.	*I will eat the soup up.*
Ma **loen** raamatu **läbi**.	*I will read the book through.*

EXERCISE 12

Underline the sentences in which the activity is finished.

1 a Ta sööb salatit. **b** Ta sõi salati ära. **2 a** Nad jõid konjaki ära. **b** Nad joovad konjakit. **3 a** Ta luges raamatud läbi. **b** Ta loeb raamatuid. **4 a** Ta kirjutab tšekki. **b** Ta kirjutas tšeki. **5 a** Ta koristas korteri ära. **b** Ta koristab korterit. **6 a** Ta luges ajalehed läbi. **b** Ta loeb ajalehti. **7 a** Ta koristab tube. **b** Ta koristas toad ära.

PRONUNCIATION

Words like **mahl** *juice*, **vein** *wine*, **tool** *chair* etc. have similar second and third forms i.e. their spelling is exactly the same. In spoken language, the second and third form are pronounced slightly differently, i.e. some sounds in the third form are more stressed. It will take some time before you will be able to differentiate and pronounce the forms like Estonians do. Still, don't worry – most of the time the context will help others to understand you anyway, even if your pronunciation isn't perfect.

EXERCISE 13

13.07

Listen to the sentences and repeat. The sounds to stress more are given in bold.

kolmas vorm	teine vorm
third form, pronounced longer with more stress	Second form, pronounced shorter with less stress
Joon ma**h**la. I am drinking juice.	Joon mahla ära. I drink the juice up.
Joon p**ii**ma. I am drinking milk.	Joon piima ära. I drink the milk up.
Joon ve**i**ni. I am drinking wine.	Joon veini ära. I drink the wine up.
Joon ko**h**vi. I am drinking coffee.	Joon kohvi ära. I drink the coffee up.
Söön ko**mm**i. I am eating candy.	Söön kommi ära. I eat the candy up.
Söön **õ**una. I am eating apple.	Söön õuna ära. I eat the apple up.
Söön ban**aa**ni. I am eating banana.	Söön banaani ära. I eat the banana up.

EXERCISE 14

13.08

Underline the words that need to be pronounced longer and with more stress. Listen and check.

1 a Ma joon mahla. **b** Ma joon mahla ära. **2 a** Ma söön kommi ära. **b** Ma söön kommi. **3 a** Ma valin palli välja. **b** Ma valin palli. **4 a** Ma joon veini ära. **b** Ma joon veini. **5 a** Ma joon piima. **b** Ma joon piima ära. **6 a** Ma söön õuna ära. **b** Ma söön õuna.

In order to practise this grammar topic further do Exercises 19–20 in the Practice section.

Practice

EXERCISE 15

Choose the correct form.

1 Lähme **kuskil/kuskile** sööma.

2 **Kuskil/kuskilt** siin on üks hea kohvik.

3 Ma ei leia seda kohvikut **kuskile/kuskilt**.

4 Mitte **keegi/kedagi** ei joo õlut.

5 Kas sa rääkisid **kellelgi/kellegagi**?

6 Kas sa oled siin **kunagi/keegi** varem käinud?

EXERCISE 16

 13.09

Give a negative answer, then listen to check. The first one is done for you.

1 Kuhu sa tahad sööma minna? – *Mitte kuhugi*

2 Kus siin lähedal on restoran? – _____

3 Kes tellis õlut? – _____

4 Mida sa süüa soovid? – _____

5 Kellega sa rääkisid? – _____

6 Kellel on raha? – _____

7 Millal sa raha tagasi soovid saada? – _____

8 Kellele sa helistasid? – _____

EXERCISE 17

Answer the questions positively and then negatively. Then do the exercise once more and answer the questions truthfully!

1 Kas te olete Tartus käinud? _____

2 Kas te olete eesti õlut joonud? _____

3 Kas te olete eesti toite proovinud? _____

4 Kas te olete eesti keele kursusel käinud? _____

5 Kas te olete eesti muusikat kuulanud? _____

6 Kas te olete näinud eesti filme? _____

7 Kas te olete rääkinud eesti keeles? _____

8 Kas te olete kirjutanud eesti keeles? _____

9 Kas te olete lugenud eesti ajalehti? _____

10 Kas te olete eesti keelt õppinud? _____

EXERCISE 18

Choose the correct form.

1 Ma joon **õlle/õlut**.

2 Ma joon **õlle/õlut** ära.

3 Sa jood **konjaki/konjakit**.

4 Sa jood **konjaki/konjakit** ära.

5 Ta sööb **supi/suppi**.

6 Ta sööb **supi/suppi** ära.

7 Me sööme **prae/praadi**.

8 Me sööme **prae/praadi** ära.

9 Te loete **menüü/menüüd**.

10 Te loete **menüü/menüüd** läbi.

11 Nad loevad **lehe/lehte**.

12 Nad loevad **lehe/lehte** läbi.

EXERCISE 19

Choose the correct form.

1 Ma kirjutan **meile/meilid**.

2 Ma kirjutan **meile/meilid** valmis.

3 Sa koristad **tube/toad**.

4 Sa koristad **tube/toad** ära.

5 Ta loeb **ajalehti/ajalehed**.

6 Ta luges **ajalehti/ajalehed** läbi.

7 Me joome **huvitavaid jooke/huvitavad** joogid.

8 Me joome **huvitavaid jooke/huvitavad joogid** ära.

9 Me sööme **häid pirukaid/head pirukad**.

10 Me sööme **häid pirukaid/head pirukad** ära.

EXERCISE 20

Use the words in brackets in the correct form. Use the third form. Then write the sentences in plural (use the fourth form).

1 Näidake palun (see mänguasi) _____

2 Näidake palun (see punane küünal) _____

3 Näidake palun (see ingliskeelne raamat) _____

4 Näidake palun (see eestikeelne raamat) _____

5 Näidake palun (see suur nukk) _____

6 Näidake palun (see ilus mänguasi) _____

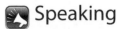 Speaking

EXERCISE 21

You meet an Estonian friend in town who has invited you out for a meal. Now you are studying the menu and discussing what to have. Complete this dialogue by filling in the missing lines of conversation. After you have completed the dialogue, listen and check.

13.10

Sina	Ask *Have you been in this restaurant sometime before too?*
Sõber	Jah, viimati käisin kaks nädalat tagasi koos abikaasaga. Ma oskan toitusid soovitada!
Sina	Ask *Have you tried this soup?*
Sõber	Jah, see supp on hea, aga portsjon on väga suur.
Sina	Say *Then I will have some kind of roast.* Ask *What will you have?*
Sõber	Ma võtan grillitud kana friikartulitega.
Sina	Say *I will also take grilled chicken and French fries.*
Sõber	Kas joome veini ka?
Sina	Say *I would prefer beer.*
Sõber	Kas sa eesti õlut oled maitsnud?
Sina	Say *No I have never drunk Estonian beer before.*
Sõber	Võtame siis kaks pudelit eesti õlut. Kuidas oleks mingi magustoiduga?
Sina	Say *I'm probably not able to eat dessert now.*
Sõber	Võib-olla tellime siis magustoitu ja kohvi hiljem.
Sina	Say *Yes, let's do so.*

EXERCISE 22

Complete this dialogue by filling in the missing lines of conversation. You are in a souvenir shop looking for something to take back home. After you have completed the dialogue, listen to the recording and check.

 13.11

Müüja	Tere!
Sina	Say *Hello!* Ask *Do you have on sale some kind of hand-made toys?*
Müüja	Jah, meil on väga ilusaid käsitsi tehtud nukke.
Sina	Ask *Are these made in Estonia?*
Müüja	On küll.
Sina	Say *I will take these two.*
Müüja	Tore, ma pakin need ära. Kas see on kõik?
Sina	Say *Yes; one plastic bag also please.*
Müüja	See teeb kokku sada kaheksakümmend krooni. Kas maksate sularahas või kaardiga?
Sina	Say *In cash, please.*
Müüja	Ega teil üht krooni ei ole?
Sina	Say *Let me see now.* Say *Please.*
Müüja	Aitäh.

EXERCISE 23

Complete this dialogue by filling in the missing lines of conversation. You are at the post office trying to send a CD (**CD-plaat**) to England. After you have completed the dialogue listen to the recording and check.

 13.12

Postitöötaja	Tere! Mida teile?
Sina	Ask *Could you please weigh this parcel?*
Postitöötaja	Jah, kohe. See on sada viiskümmend grammi.
Sina	Say *I wish to send it to England.*
Postitöötaja	Mis siin sees on?
Sina	Say *It is a CD.*
Postitöötaja	Ma panen ta igaks juhuks turvaümbriku sisse.
Sina	Ask how much it costs.
Postitöötaja	Viis krooni. Kas see läheb lennu- või maapostiga?
Sina	Ask *Which one is more expensive?*
Postitöötaja	Lennupost on umbes kümme krooni kallim.
Sina	Say *Then it could be the regular mail.*
Postitöötaja	Kirjutage palun siia nurka saatja aadress ja siia saaja andmed.
Sina	Ask *With block letters?*
Postitöötaja	Jah, olge nii kena. Kas maksate kaardiga või sularahas?
Sina	Say *With card.*
Postitöötaja	Siia palun allkiri. Hoidke tšekk niikaua alles, kuni pakk on kohale jõudnud.

？ Test yourself

1 Which expressions are correct to say that you are hungry?
  a Mul on kõht tühi.
  b Soovita siis midagi.
  c Lähme siis pealegi sinna.

2 What are the courses of a meal?
  a pipar, sool, suhkur.
  b lusikas, nuga, kahvel.
  c supp, praad, magustoit.

3 The waiter asks *Kas tellite kohe või hiljem?* What does it mean?
  a Are you paying with cash or card?
  b Are you ordering now or later?
  c Are you paying together or separately?

4 What do you say to indicate that you are a vegetarian?
  a Ma käin kiiresti ära.
  b Ma võtan mingi prae.
  c Ma olen taimetoitlane.

5 You want to have a bottle of white wine. What do you say?
  a Ma võtan midagi kerget.
  b Ma võtan mingi salati.
  c Ma võtan pudeli valget veini.

6 How do you ask *Have you tried this before?*
  a Kas sa oled siin varem käinud?
  b Kas sa oled seda varem proovinud?
  c Kas sa oled siin varem olnud?

7 You would like to see some Estonian books. What do you say?
  a Näidake palun mingeid eesti komme.
  b Näidake palun mingeid eesti raamatuid.
  c Näidake palun mingeid eesti mänguasju.

8 The seller asks *Milliseid te tahate?* What does it mean?
  a Would you like anything else?
  b What kind would you like?
  c Would you like to have a closer look?

9 How do you ask *Which one is more expensive?*

   a Mis siin sees on?

   b Kas veel midagi?

   c Kumb on kallim?

10 *Mitte keegi ei taha süüa.* What does it mean?

   a Someone wants to eat.

   b Everybody wants to eat.

   c Nobody wants to eat.

14 Sõidame!

Let's go!

In this unit you will learn:
- ▶ *How to ask for and give directions*
- ▶ *How to hire a car*
- ▶ *How to get around Estonia*

Listening 1

A tourist is asking for directions. Listen to the dialogue and then complete Exercises 1–2 below.

 14.01

Turist	Vabandage, kas te teate, kus siin on lähim raamatukauplus?
Võõras	Las ma mõtlen. Siin lähedal ei olegi vist raamatukauplust. Te peate kesklinna sõitma.
Turist	Millega?
Võõras	Kõige kiiremini saate trolliga. Trollipeatus on kohe siin lähedal.
Turist	Kas lähen otse edasi?
Võõras	Jah, minge otse mööda seda tänavat kuni järgmise ristmikuni. Seal pöörake paremale.
Turist	Nii.
Võõras	Sealt paistavad mõned suured telliskivimajad, minge nendest mööda. Siis juba näete isegi, et kus see peatus on.
Turist	Mis number trolliga ma minema pean?
Võõras	Vist enamik trolle läheb kesklinna, aga mina ise sõidan tavaliselt ühega või kahega.
Turist	Kas see peatus on samal teepoolel või pean minema üle tee?
Võõras	Peatus on ikka samal teepoolel.
Turist	Kui kaua see troll siis kesklinna sõidab?
Võõras	Umbes pool tundi. Kui te juba ühest suurest kahe torniga kirikust mööda sõidate, siis oletegi kesklinnas. Üks raamatupood on sealsamas nurga peal, peaaegu trollipeatuse juures.
Turist	Aitäh! Ma püüan üles leida.

lähim, -a, -at, -aid	*the closest*
raamatukauplus, -e, -t, -i	*bookstore*
Siin lähedal ei olegi vist raamatukauplust.	*There isn't a bookstore near here.*
kõige kiiremini	*the fastest*
lähedal	*close*

otse edasi	*straightforward*
mööda	*along, by, also: past something*
mööda seda tänavat	*along this street*
kuni	*up to, until*
järgmi/ne, -se, -st, -seid	*next*
ristmik, -u, -ku, -ke	*crossing*
minge kuni järgmise ristmikuni	*go up to the next crossing*
pööra/ma, -ta, -n	*to turn*
paremale	*to the right*
paist/ma, -a, -ab	*to be seen, to be visible*
mõni, mõne, mõnd, mõnesid	*some*
minge nendest mööda	*go past these*
näge/ma, näh/a, näe/n	*to see*
Siis juba näete isegi, et kus see peatus on.	*Then you will see yourself where the stop is.*
enamik, -u, -ku, -ke	*most*
sama, sama, sama, samu	*same*
samal teepoolel	*at the same side of the road*
üle	*across, over*
üle tee	*across the road*
kui kaua?	*how long?*
umbes	*about*
torn, -i, -i, -e	*tower*
kirik, -u, -ut, -uid	*church*
Siis oletegi kesklinnas.	*Then you will already be in the town centre.*
sealsamas	*at the very same place, here: just there*
nurga peal	*on the corner*
peaaegu	*almost*
püüd/ma, püüd/a, püüa/n	*to try*
üles leid/ma, üles leid/a, leia/n üles	*to find*

EXERCISE 1

Listen to the dialogue and decide if the sentences that follow are **a** true or **b** false.

1 Turist tahab minna turule.

2 Turist peab sõitma kesklinna.

3 Turist peab sõitma trolliga.

4 Trollipeatus on lähedal.

5 Turist peab minema otse kuni järgmise ristmikuni ja pöörama seal paremale.

6 Kindlasti saab kesklinna trolliga number üks ja kolm.

7 Peatus on samal teepoolel.

8 Troll sõidab kesklinna umbes tund aega.

9 Kesklinnas on suur kahe torniga kirik.

10 Raamatupood on trollipeatuse juures.

EXERCISE 2

Choose the correct translation.

1 **lähim raamatukauplus a** the closest bookstore **b** the boosktore is close

2 **kohe siin lähedal a** close by **b** I will go at once

3 **otse edasi a** straightforward **b** next to

4 **mööda seda tänavat a** pass this road **b** along this road

5 **kuni järgmise ristmikuni a** at the next crossing **b** until the next crossing

6 **pöörake paremale a** turn right **b** turn left

7 **minge nendest majadest mööda a** go past these houses **b** go up to these houses

8 **samal teepoolel a** the same side of the road **b** the opposite side of the road

9 **üle tee a** accross the road **b** along the road

10 **nurga peal a** behind the corner **b** on the corner

Listening 2

Tuuli has asked Ivar to come over but Ivar is unable to find Tuuli's house. He makes a phone call to ask for directions. Listen to the dialogue and the complete Exercises 3–4 below.

 14.02

Ivar	Tere, Tuuli. Hakkasin sinu juurde tulema, aga ma ei leia kuidagi sinu maja üles.
Tuuli	Kus sa oled?
Ivar	Ostukeskuse juures.
Tuuli	Ahah. Siis tule kõigepealt üle tänava ja pööra vasakule. Kas sa paremat kätt väikest parki näed?
Ivar	Jah. Kas lähen läbi pargi?
Tuuli	Ei, tule mööda seda tänavat otse edasi.
Ivar	Jah, nüüd paistab ees mingi mänguväljak. Kas lähen selleni välja?
Tuuli	Mänguväljak? Kuule, sa tulid vist valele poole. Pööra palun ümber ja mine tuldud teed tagasi.
Ivar	Oeh. Ma võtan parem takso. Sa tead ju, et ma vihkan jalgsi käimist!
Tuuli	Ära muretse, ma hakkasin sulle juba vastu tulema. Ma muide juba näen sind!
Ivar	Ah seal sa oledki! Tere!

V	**ostukeskus**, -e, -t, -i	*shopping centre*
	vasakule	*to the left*
	paremat kätt	*on the right hand*
	park, pargi, parki, parke	*park*
	läbi	*through*
	läbi pargi	*through the park*
	mänguväljak, -u, -ut, -uid	*playground*
	Kas lähen selleni välja?	*Shall I go up to it?*
	vale, -, -t, -sid	*wrong*
	pool, -e, -t, -i	*side*
	ümber pööra/ma, ümber pööra/ta, pööra/n umber	*to turn around*
	tagasi mine/ma, tagasi minn/a, lähe/n tagasi	*to go back*
	mine tuldud teed tagasi	*go back the way you came*
	vihka/ma, viha/ta, vihka/n	*to hate*
	muretse/ma, -da, -n	*to worry*
	vastu tule/ma, vastu tull/a, tule/n vastu	*to come to meet*
	muide	*by the way*
	Ah seal sa oledki!	*Ah, there you are!*

EXERCISE 3

Tuuli is instructing Ivar how to find her home. In the dialogue you hear some landmarks they discuss. Read the following list and tick the landmarks you hear.

kahe torniga kirik	☐
mänguväljak	☐
ostukeskus	☐
raamatupood	☐
suured telliskivimajad	☐
taksopeatus	☐
trollipeatus	☐
väike park	☐

EXERCISE 4

Listen to the dialogue and choose the correct answer.

1 Ivar on ostukeskuse **juures/taga**.

2 Tuuli ütleb: Tule kõigepealt üle tänava ja pööra **vasakule/paremale**.

3 Ivar küsib: Kas lähen **läbi pargi/pargist mööda**?

4 Tuuli ütleb: **Mine tagasi./Tule otse edasi**.

5 Ivar küsib: **Kas lähen mänguväljakuni?/Kas lähen mänguväljakust mööda**?

6 Tuuli ütleb: **Sa tulid valele poole./Sa tulid õigele poole**.

7 Tuuli ütleb: **Pööra palun ümber./Mine otse edasi**.

8 Ivar ütleb: **Ma tulen parem bussiga./Ma võtan parem takso**.

9 Ivar ütleb: Ma **armastan/vihkan** jalgsi käimist!

10 Tuuli ütleb: **Ära muretse!/Pole viga**!

11 Tuuli ütleb: Ma hakkasin sulle **vastu tulema/vastu sõitma**.

12 Tuuli ütleb: **Tule siia!/Ma juba näen sind**!

13 Ivar ütleb: **Ah sina see oledki!/Ah seal sa oledki!**

Listening 3

A client is talking to an attendant in a car rental bureau. Listen to the dialogue and then complete Exercises 5–6.

 14.03

Klient	Tere! Ma sooviksin autot rentida. On see võimalik?
Teenindaja	Jah, muidugi. Teil peab ainult olema kehtiv juhiluba ja pass. Rendihind tuleb krediitkaardiga ette maksta.
Klient	Mul on juhistaaži täpselt kaks aastat. Kas sellest piisab?
Teenindaja	Piisab küll. Me sõlmime teiega muidugi ka lepingu, seal on kõik tingimused kirjas.
Klient	Ja mis hinnaga te rendite?
Teenindaja	See sõltub sellest, millist autot te soovite ja kui kauaks.
Klient	Mul oleks nädalavahetuseks vaja niisugust suuremat pereautot.
Teenindaja	Kas te soovite automaatkäigukastiga masinat või tavalist?
Klient	Tegelikult on mul ükskõik.
Teenindaja	Siis ma soovitaksin teile näiteks seda viie uksega džiipi. Sellel on automaatkäigukast ja konditsioneer ka.
Klient	Ahah. Aga meil on peres ka väike laps. Kas ma saan ka turvaistme rentida?
Teenindaja	Jah, seda saab küll väikese lisatasu eest.
Klient	Väga tore. Kas ma pean auto siia tagasi tooma või oleks võimalik see ka mõnes teises linnas tagastada?
Teenindaja	Meil on kontorid kõikides suuremates linnades.
Klient	Väga tore.
Teenindaja	Olge nii kena täitke palun see ankeet ära ja siis vaatame auto üle.

V	**võimalik**, -u, -ku, -ke	*possible*
	renti/ma, renti/da, rendi/n	*to rent, hire*
	teenindaja, -, -t, -id	*tender, attendant*
	kehtiv, -a, -at, -aid	*valid*
	juhi/luba, -loa, -luba, -lube	*driving licence*
	pass, -i, -i, -e	*passport*
	rendi/hind, -hinna, -hinda, -hindu	*rental price*
	krediit/kaart, -kaardi, -kaarti, -kaarte	*credit card*
	ette maks/ma, ette maks/ta, maksa/n ette	*to pay in advance*
	tuleb ette maksta	*has to be paid in advance*
	juhistaaž, -i, -**i**	*driving experience*
	täpselt	*exactly*
	piisa/ma, -ta, -b	*to be enough*
	kas sellest piisab?	*is that enough?*
	sõlmi/ma, -da, -n	*to conclude (a contract)*
	leping, -u, -ut, -uid	*contract*
	tingimus, -e, -t, -**i**	*condition*
	on kirjas here:	*are written*
	kui kauaks?	*for how long?*
	vaja ole/ma, vaja oll/a, on vaja	*to be needed*
	niisugu/ne, -se, -st, -seid	*this kind*
	pereauto, -, -t, -sid	*family car*
	automaatkäigukast, -i, -i, -e	*automatic gearbox*
	masin, -a, -at, -aid here:	*car*
	ükskõik	*all the same*
	džiip, džiibi, džiipi, džiipe	*jeep*
	konditsioneer, -i, -i, -e	*air conditioner*
	turva/iste, -istme, -istet, -istmeid	*safety seat (for baby)*
	lisatasu, -, -, -sid	*extra cost*
	lisatasu eest	*for extra cost*
	tagasi too/ma, tagasi tuu/a, too/n tagasi	*to bring back*
	mõni, mõne, mõnd, mõnesid	*some*
	tagasta/ma, -da, -n	*to return, to bring back*
	kontor, -i, -it, -eid	*office*
	täit/ma, täit/a, täida/n	*to fill in*
	ankeet, ankeedi, ankeeti, ankeete	*form*
	üle vaata/ma, üle vaada/ta, vaata/n üle here:	*to have a look*

EXERCISE 5

Listen to the dialogue and decide if the following sentences are **a** true or **b** false.

   1 Klient soovib bussi rentida.

   2 Kliendil peab olema kehtiv juhiluba.

   3 Rendihind tuleb krediitkaardiga ette maksta.

   4 Piisab, kui on üks aasta juhistaaži.

   5 Kõik tingimused on kirjas rendilepingus.

   6 Rendihind sõltub sellest, millist autot klient soovib ja kui kauaks.

   7 Klient soovib rentida autot nädalavahetuseks.

   8 Klient soovib kindlasti autot, millel on automaatkäigukast.

   9 Klient soovib väiksemat pereautot.

  10 Teenindaja soovitab kliendile viie uksega džiipi.

  11 Sellel džiibil on tavaline käigukast ja ka konditsioneer.

  12 Kliendi peres on väike laps.

  13 Klient soovib rentida turvaistet.

  14 Auto saab tagastada ka mõnes teises linnas.

EXERCISE 6

Choose the correct translation.

1 **I would like to hire a car.**
   a Ma sooviksin autot rentida.
   b On see võimalik?

2 **You have to have a valid driving licence.**
   a Teil peab olema kehtiv pass.
   b Teil peab olema kehtiv juhiluba.

3 **The cost of rental has to be paid in advance with a credit card.**
   a Mul on juhistaaži täpselt kaks aastat.
   b Rendihind tuleb krediitkaardiga ette maksta.

4 **Is this enough?**
   a Kas sellest piisab?
   b Mis hinnaga te rendite?

5 **It depends on which kind of car you would like.**
   a See sõltub sellest, millist autot te soovite.
   b Mul oleks vaja niisugust suuremat pereautot.

6 **Would you like to have a car with automatic gearbox?**
   a Kas te soovite automaatkäigukastiga masinat?
   b Kas sellel on automaatkäigukast ka?

7 In fact, it is all the same for me.
   a Olge nii kena.
   b Tegelikult on mul ükskõik.

8 You can have it for little extra cost.
   a Ma tahaksin rentida turvaistme.
   b Seda saate väikese lisatasu eest.

9 Please fill in this form.
   a Palun vaatame nüüd auto üle.
   b Palun täitke see ankeet ära.

At the petrol station

The **bensiinijaam** or **tankla** *petrol station* can be either self-service operated by **pangakaart** *bank card* and **paberraha** *bank notes* or a manned station where one can also find a shop and sometimes even a bar or coffee shop.

Some words you might need in a petrol station are **bensiin** *petrol* or *fuel*, **diisel** *diesel*. **(Mootori)õli** is *oil*, **aku** is *battery*, **pidurid** is *brakes*.

If you need a car wash, look for **autopesula.** If you need to pump your tyres, look for **õhk** *air*.

Some of the most common problems that might occur on your car are:

tuli ei põle	*the light is not working*
auto ei käivitu	*the car won't start*
aku on tühi	*the battery is flat*
kumm on katki	*the tyre is flat*
lüliti ei tööta	*the switch does not work*

Turvavööd *seatbelts* are obligatory in Estonia both in front and back seats, also babies and small children have to have **turvaiste** *safety seats* of their own. Be aware that during dusk and dawn animals like roe deer and elk can cross roads and also smaller animals like foxes and hedgehogs cause hazards on the road. In the spring, signs are put up to warn drivers of migrating frogs.

> **INSIGHT**
>
> If you haven't been able to use the language yet, how about going to Estonia to practise speaking or find someone to chat with over the internet. Good luck with your efforts!

Language patterns

MINGE ÜLE TEE JA LÄBI PARGI GO ACROSS THE ROAD AND THROUGH THE PARK

The most common expressions for asking and giving directions are as follows:

Vabandage, kuidas ma saan … *Excuse me, how can I go to …*

1 … Viru tänava**le** *to Viru street*/Raekoja platsi**le** to Raekoja *square*/turule *to the market/* Õismäele *to Õismäe (a district in Tallinn)/*Vabaduse väljakule *to Vabaduse square?*

2 … Viru keskuse**sse** *to Viru centre*/ujulasse *to a swimming pool/*kunstimuuseumi**sse** *to an art museum?*

3 … kesklinna *to the city centre*/ülikooli *to the university*/Kosmose kinno *to the cinema 'Kosmos'*/Kadriorgu to Kadriorg *(a park in Tallinn)*/bussijaama *to the bus station?*

4 … mere **äärde** *to the seaside/*Estonia teatri **juurde** *to the Estonia theatre?*

As you can see the names of the locations can have three different endings: **-le** (the first group), **-sse** (the second group), no endings, i.e. the short form (third group). Also the postpositions can be used (the fourth group).

In order to give and understand directions you need to know some important words.

Üle *Across*

Minge … **go üle** tee *across the road/***üle** väljaku *across the square/***üle** platsi *across the square/***üle** tänava *across the road/***üle** raudtee *across the railway/***üle** silla *across the bridge.*

Note that with the word **üle** *across* we use the second form.

Läbi *Through*

Minge … *go* **läbi** pargi *through the park/***läbi** värava *through the gate/***läbi** tunneli *through the tunnel/***läbi** metsa *through the forest.*

Note that with the word **läbi** *through* we use the second form.

Mööda (I) *By, along*

Minge … *go* **mööda** seda tänavat *by (along) this street/***mööda** Viru tänavat *by (along) Viru street.*

Note that with the word **mööda** *by, along* we use the third form.

Mööda (II) *Past*

Minge suurest kirikust **mööda** *past the big church.* Minge väikese**st** poe**st mööda** *past the small shop.*

With the word **mööda** we use the ending -st.

Note that the word **mööda** has two different meanings!

Kuni *Up to, as far as*

Minge … go **kuni** järgmise ristmikuni *up to the next crossing/***kuni** kollase majani *up to the yellow house.*

Note that with the word **kuni** *up to, as far as* we use the ending **-ni**.

You may also need the following expressions:

Pöörake (keerake) paremale.	*Turn right.*
Pöörake (keerake) vasakule.	*Turn left.*
Minge otse.	*Go straight.*

Minge edasi.	*Go onwards.*
Minge tagasi.	*Go backwards.*
See on nurga peal.	*It is on the corner.*
See on kohe trollipeatuse juures.	*It is by the trolleybus stop.*
Paremat kätt on väike park.	*On the right hand there is a small park.*
Vasakut kätt on mets.	*On the left hand there is a forest.*
Siis oletegi kohal.	*Then you will be there.*
See on üsna kaugel.	*It is quite far.*
Sinna on umbes viis kilomeetrit.	*It is about five kilometres away. (lit. to there it is about five kilometres).*
See on lähedal.	*It is close.*
Sinna on paarsada meetrit.	*It is couple of hundred metres away.*

In order to practise this grammar topic further do Exercise 10 in the Practice section.

MA SÕIDAN KOLLASE AUTOGA *I DRIVE A YELLOW CAR*

We have already learnt that a pronoun, adjective and noun belonging together in a sentence have the same endings, for instance:

Ma istun selles kollases autos.　　*I am sitting in this yellow car.*

Yet you need to remember four endings to which this rule does not apply:

-ni, minge selle kaupluse**ni** (not: *selleni kaupluseni).
Go up to this shop.

-na, ta on tuntud hea ajakirjaniku**na** (not: *heana ajakirjanikuna).
He is known as a good journalist.

-ta, lähen reisile ilma suure koti**ta** (not: *ilma suureta kotita)
I will go on a trip without a big bag.

-ga, sõidan selle kollase auto**ga** (not: *sellega kollasega autoga)
I drive this yellow car.

As you can see, these endings are added to the noun only and all the other words are just in the second form.

More examples of usage:

	singular	*plural*
-ni	Sõitke suure_ kollase_ maja**ni**.	Sõitke suurte_ kollaste_ majade**ni**.
milleni?	*Drive up to a big yellow house.*	*Drive up to big yellow houses.*
up to what?		
-na	Ta on tuntud hea_ autojuhi**na**.	Nad on tuntud heade_
kellena?	*He/She is known as a*	*autojuhtidena.*

as whom?	good driver.	They are known as good drivers.
-ta	Ilma täpse_ kaardita sa seda	Ilma täpsete_ kaartide**ta** te neid
kelleta?	kohta ei leia.	kohti ei leia.
milleta?	*Without a precise map you*	*Without precise maps you will*
without whom?	*will not find this place.*	*not find these places.*
without what?		
-ga	Ma räägin kalli_ sõbra**ga**.	Ma räägin kallite_ sõprade**ga**.
kellega?	*I talk with a dear friend.*	*I talk with dear friends.*
millega?	Ma töötan hea_ arvuti**ga**.	Ma töötan heade_ arvutite**ga**.
with whom?	*I work on a good computer.*	*I work on good computers.*
with what?		

EXERCISE 7

Add the correct endings, as necessary.

1 Selle_ tänaval on palju kauplusi.

2 Minge kuni selle_ suure_ ristmikuni.

3 Selle_ uue_ kaupluses on hea valik.

4 Ta räägib oma uu-e_ naabriga.

5 Me tuleme sinu juurde ilma väiksema_ lapseta.

6 Kas te tulete koos oma väikese_ koeraga?

7 Meie väikese_ koerale ei meeldi autoga sõita.

In order to practise this grammar topic further do Exercises 11–12 in the Practice section.

Getting around Estonia

Estonia stretches about 240 km from north to south and 350 km from east to west. The total area is about 45 000 square kilometers. People from larger countries find it very strange that there are in fact no distant places in Estonia – you can travel everywhere within a day, in fact four or five hours is enough to get comfortably from one end of Estonia to the other.

The northernmost point is the island of Vaindloo in the Baltic Sea and on the mainland the Purekkari peninsula. The most southern point is the village of Naha. In the west the farthest island is Nootamaa, the most north-eastern point the town of Narva.

Administratively Estonia is divided into 15 **maakond** *counties*. All counties are divided into smaller **vald** *municipalities*.

You need to take **praam** *the ferry* to get to the Estonian islands like Saaremaa, Hiiumaa, Vormsi etc. Everything on the mainland is accessible by car; **asfalttee** *asphalt roads* connect all cities and bigger villages and are reasonably well signposted. Still, it is very useful to purchase a **teedeatlas** *road atlas* when travelling in Estonia by car as sometimes it can be difficult to find the right road out of town. An updated road atlas is published almost every year and can be bought at a bigger **bensiinijaam** *petrol station* or bookshop.

There is an extensive network of **kruusatee** *gravel roads* connecting the more remote villages. During the winter some of them can be difficult to access. If you are in Estonia during the winter and feel really adventurous, check if some of the **jäätee** *ice roads* are open. During cold winters some of the Estonian islands (like Saaremaa, Vormsi, Kihnu etc.) can be driven to by car over the frozen sea. The ice roads can be used only during daytime and you have to follow strict rules concerning the weight of your car, driving speed etc.

Rong *train* can be used to travel between the bigger cities like Tallinn, Tartu and Narva, but the most common way to travel is by **buss** *bus*. **Ekspressbuss** *express buses* are faster, but if you have plenty of time you can also use the ordinary buses. The tickets are either sold at the bus station or bought straight from the driver. Nowadays some of the buses and trains running between the two biggest cities, Tallinn and Tartu, also provide Wifi connection.

The internal flights in Estonia are almost nonexistent as there are just some small lines operating which take people to the islands of Estonia.

SÕITMA, SÕITA, SÕIDAN – *TYPES OF VERBS*

We have already studied the sound changes that take place in nouns and adjectives. Similar changes also take place in verbs.

The sound changes that take place in verbs are of two types:

▶ either the first and second form are similar and the third form differs, for instance **lugema**, **lugeda**, loen

▶ the first and third form are similar and the second form differs, for instance **ootama**, oodata, **ootan**.

We will have a closer look at some most typical groups of verbs. Fill in the blanks.

I kk – k, pp – p, tt – t

first form	second form	third form
ku**kk**uma *to fall*	ku**kk**uda	ku**k**un
le**pp**ima *to agree*	_____	_____
ha**kk**ama *to start*	ha**k**ata	ha**kk**an
ru**tt**ama *to hurry*	_____	_____
võ**t**ma *to take*	võ**tta**	võ**t**an
ka**t**ma *to cover*	_____	_____

II k – g, p – b, t – d

first form	second form	third form
sõi**t**ma *to drive*	sõi**t**a	sõi**d**an
või**t**ma *to win*	_____	_____
vaa**t**ama *to look*	vaa**d**ata	vaa**t**an
oo**t**ama *to wait*	_____	_____
näi**t**ama *to show*	_____	_____

III k disappears, t disappears

first form	second form	third form
püh**k**ima *to wipe*	püh**k**ida	pühin
mah**t**uma *to fit*	_____	_____
os**k**ama *to know how to, can*	osata	os**k**an
koh**t**ama *to meet*	_____	_____

IV g disappears, b disappears, d disappears

first form	second form	third form
lu**g**ema *to read*	lu**g**eda	loen
pi**d**ama *to keep*	pi**d**ada	pean
püü**d**ma *to try*	püü**d**a	püüan
lei**d**ma *to find*	lei**d**a	leian
jõu**d**ma *to reach, to be able to*	jõu**d**a	jõuan

The weather

The temperature in Estonia varies widely, being typically 15–18 C during the summer months and −4–6 C in the winter. The fluctuations of the temperature in the winter can be quite drastic, literally: −22 C in the morning can rise to +10 C by the evening. **Valge aeg** *daylight time* in the summer is about 20 hours, the shortest day in the winter **pime aeg** *time without daylight* lasting only for 6 hours.

The easiest way to describe the weather is to say **Ilm on ilus** *The weather is beautiful* or **Ilm on halb** *The weather is bad.* You can also say **Täna on ilus ilm** *The weather is beautiful today* or **Täna on kole ilm** *The weather is horrible today.* Some more expressions to describe the good weather are: **päike paistab** *the sun is shining*, **taevas on selge** *the sky is clear*, **täna on soe ilm** *the weather is warm today*, **sooja on kakskümmend viis kraadi** or **täna on kakskümmend viis kraadi sooja** *the temperature is 25 degrees (above zero)*, **täna on kuum ilm** *the weather is hot today.*

Some expressions to describe the weather that's not so good are: **taevas on pilves** *the sky is clouded over*, **väljas on tugev tuul** *it is very windy outside.* (lit. *there is strong wind outside.*). We can also say **Puhub tugev/keskmine/nõrk tuul.** *Strong/moderate/weak wind is blowing*, **külma on kümme kraadi** or **täna on kümme kraadi külma** *the temperature is 10 degrees (below zero).*

Sajab vihma *it is raining* (lit. *it is raining rain*), **sajab lund** *it is snowing* (lit. *it is raining snow*), **sajab lörtsi** *it is raining sleet*, **sajab rahet** *it is hailing.* (lit. *it is raining hail).* Note that the third form is used with the word **sajab.** When it is raining we can just say **Sajab.** *It is raining.* without adding the word **vihm** *rain.* The really bad weather is called **koerailm** lit. *dog's weather.* The word for *icicle* is **jääpurikas**, sometimes in the winter you can see warning signs indicating that icicles are being cleared from buildings.

MINGE OTSE EDASI *GO STRAIGHT FORWARD – PLURAL IMPERATIVE*

We have learnt in Unit 3 how to express a request or wish. This grammatical form is called the imperative. In this unit we will have a closer look on how to form the plural forms of the imperative.

EXERCISE 8

Study the forms and fill in the blanks.

I

second form, ending -da	plural imperative, ending -ge	plural imperative, negative form
luge**da** *to read*	Luge**ge**! *Read!*	Ärge luge**ge**! *Don't read!*
helista**da** *to call*	_____	_____
jaluta**da** *to walk*	_____	_____
mängi**da** *to play*	_____	_____

Usually the forms of imperative are created from the second form, in this case the second infinitive ends with **-da**, the plural form of the imperative has the ending **-ge**. In negative sentences, we add the word **ärge**.

II

second form, ending -ta	plural imperative, ending -ke	plural imperative, negative form
pööra**ta** *to turn*	Pööra**ke**! *Turn!*	Ärge pööra**ke**! *Don't turn!*
ooda**ta** *to wait*	_____	_____
vaada**ta** *to look*	_____	_____
näida**ta** *to show*	_____	_____
NB! sõi**ta** *to drive*	Sõit**ke**! *drive!*	Ärge sõit**ke**! *don't drive!*
NB! võt**ta** *to take*	Võt**ke**! *take!*	Ärge võt**ke**! *don't take!*

If the second form ends with **-ta**, the plural form of the imperative has the ending **-ke**. In negative sentences we add the word ärge.

NB!

second infinitive, ending -da	plural imperative, ending -ke	plural imperative, negative form
NB! an**da** *to give*	And**ke**! *Give!*	Ärge and**ke**! *Don't give!*
kan**da** *to carry*	_____	_____

NB! There are a few words that have the second form ending in **-da**, but the plural imperative still ends with **-ke**.

Second infinitive, ending -a	Plural imperative, ending -ge	Plural imperative, negative form
minn**a** *to go*	Min**ge**! *Go!*	Ärge min**ge**! *Don't go!*
tull**a** *to come*	_____	_____
oll**a** *to be*	_____	_____
NB! süü**a** *to eat*	Söö**ge**! *Eat!*	Ärge söö**ge**! *Don't eat!*
NB! juu**a** *to drink*	_____	_____
NB! tuu**a**	_____	_____
NB! teh**a** *to do*	Teh**ke**! *Do!*	Ärge teh**ke**! *Don't do!*

The plural imperative ending is usually **-ge** of the words whose second form ends with **-a-.**

In order to practise this grammar topic further do Exercise 13 in the Practice section.

KIIRESTI, KIIREMINI, KÕIGE KIIREMINI *FAST, FASTER, FASTEST* – COMPARATIVE FORMS OF ADVERBS

We have already learnt that actions can be described by adverbs, for instance in a sentence **Auto sõidab kiiresti, aga buss sõidab aeglaselt** *The car drives fast but the bus slowly*, the words **kiiresti** *fast* and **aeglaselt** *slowly* are adverbs. If we want to compare some actions, specific forms of adverbs have to be used. Depending on the ending such words can be divided into two groups:

I

ending -sti	ending -mini	kõige + ending -mini
Laev sõidab **kiiresti**.	Rong sõidab **kiiremini** kui laev.	Lennuk sõidab kõige **kiiremini**.
The boat runs fast.	*The train runs faster than the boat.*	*The plane runs the fastest.*
NB! Klient räägib	Sekretär räägib	Mehaanik räägib kõige
kõvasti.	**kõvemini** kui klient.	**kõvemini**.
The client talks loudly.	*The secretary talks more loudly than the client.*	*The mechanic speaks the loudest.*
NB! Peeter laulab **hästi**.	Paul laulab **paremini** kui Peeter.	Piia laulab **kõige paremini**.
Peeter sings well.	*Paul sings better than Peter.*	*Piia sings the best.*

As you can see when the adverb ends with **-sti**, then it changes to **-mini** in a comparative sentence, for instance kiire**sti** *fast* – kiire**mini** *faster*. If we add the word **kõige** *most*, we get the construction **kõige kiiremini** *the fastest*.

Note that for some words the vowel of the first form changes into **-e**, for instance kõv**a**sti *loud* – kõv**e**mini *louder*, halv**a**sti *bad* – halv**e**mini *worse*.

NB! The word **hästi** *well* is also an exception in English: **hästi** *well*, **paremini** *better*, **kõige paremini** *the best*.

II

ending -lt	ending -malt	ko~ige + ending -malt
Klient räägib **aeglaselt**.	Teenindaja räägib **aeglasemalt** kui klient.	Juhataja räägib **kõige aeglasemalt**.
The client speaks slowly.	*The attendant speaks more slowly than the client.*	*The boss speaks the slowest.*
Reet räägib vaikselt.	Maarika räägib	Peeter räägib kõige
Reet speaks quietly.	**vaiksemalt** kui Reet.	**vaiksemalt**.
	Maarika speaks more quietly than Reet.	*Peeter speaks the quietest of all.*

If the adverb ends with **-lt**, then it changes to **-malt** in comparative sentence, for instance aeglase**lt** *slowly* – aeglasema**lt** *slower*. If we add the word **kõige** *most*, we get the construction **kõige aeglasemalt** *the slowest*.

EXERCISE 9

Fill in the blanks.

-sti

kiiresti *fast*	kiiremini	kõige kiiremini
ilusasti *beautifully*	_____	_____
NB! kõv**a**sti *loud*	kõvemini	kõige kõvemini

halvasti *badly*	_____	_____
NB! hästi *well*	paremini	_____
-lt		
vaikselt *quietly*	vaiksemalt	kõige vaiksemalt
huvitavalt *interestingly*	_____	_____
NB! targalt *cleverly*	targemalt	kõige targemalt
soojalt *warmly*	_____	_____

In order to practise this grammar topic further do Exercise 14 in the Practice section.

Practice

EXERCISE 10

Choose the right sentence for each picture. Use the expressions for giving directions (see also 'Language patterns' section, above).

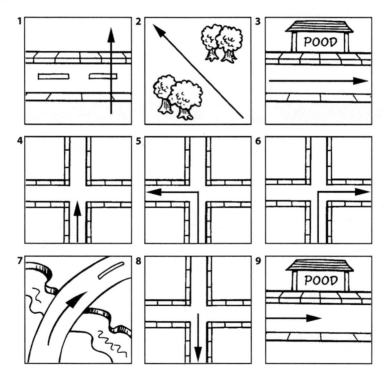

Mine tagasi.
Mine poest mööda.
Mine poeni.
Mine kuni ristmikuni.
Mine läbi pargi.

Pööra vasakule.
Mine üle tänava.
Pööra paremale.
Mine üle silla.

EXERCISE 11

Choose the correct form.

Ilma milleta sa ei saa elada? *Without what can't you live?*

1 Ilma **kiire autota/kiireta autota**.

2 Ilma **heata toiduta/hea toiduta**.

3 Ilma **huvitavata tööta/huvitava tööta**.

4 Ilma **heade sõpradeta/headeta sõpradeta**.

5 Ilma **toredateta reisideta/toredate reisideta**.

EXERCISE 12

Choose the correct form.

1 Ma sõidan **punasega autoga/punase autoga**.

2 Sa sõidad **suure bussiga/suurega bussiga**.

3 Ta sõidab **vanaga rongiga/vana rongiga**.

4 Me sõidame **kiire lennukiga/kiirega lennukiga**.

5 Te sõidate **uuega laevaga/uue laevaga**.

6 Nad sõidavad **kalli rattaga/kalliga rattaga**.

EXERCISE 13

Write the words in bold in plural. The first one has been done for you.

1 **Loe** seda raamatut. *Lugege seda raamatut!*

2 **Helista** mulle!

3 **Pööra** paremale!

4 **Vaata** siia!

5 **Sõida** linna!

6 **Võta** see kaart!

7 **Anna** mulle kaart!

8 **Mine** otse edasi!

9 **Ole** hea!

10 **Tule** kohe siia!

11 **Tee** kiiresti!

12 **Ära söö** seda jäätist!

13 **Ära joo** nii palju õlut!

14 **Ära oota** mind!

EXERCISE 14

Make comparative sentences using the example.

1 kiiresti/aeglaselt

Lennuk sõidab kiiremini kui *auto. Auto sõidab* aeglasemalt *kui lennuk.*

2 kõvasti/vaikselt

Mina räägin _____ kui minu sõber. Minu sõber räägib _____ kui mina.

3 halvasti/hästi

Ma räägin eesti keelt _____ kui inglise keelt. Ma räägin inglise keelt _____ kui eesti keelt.

4 huvitavalt/igavalt

Minu sõber jutustab _____. kui mina. Ma jutustan _____ kui minu sõber.

 # Speaking

EXERCISE 15

You are waiting for an Estonian friend to come and visit you. She calls you to tell you she can't find your house. Fill in the missing lines. Listen to the completed dialogue.

 **14.04**

Sõber	Tere! Ma ei leia kuidagi sinu maja üles.
Sina	Ask *Where are you?*
Sõber	Mingi mänguväljaku juures.
Sina	Say *Come across the street.*
Sõber	Jah. Kas ma nüüd pööran paremale?
Sina	Say *No, turn left.*
Sõber	Ees paistab üks kaubanduskeskus. Kas lähen selleni välja?
Sina	Say *Yes.* Say *My house is on the corner.*
Sõber	Aitäh! Ma muide juba näen sinu maja!

EXERCISE 16

You are giving directions to a friend you are meeting at the new bowling alley. Fill in the lines. Listen to the completed text.

    a Say *The bowling alley is in the city centre.*
    b Tell your friend he has to drive to the city centre.
    c Say the fastest way he will get there is by bus.
    d Say *The bowling alley is right there on the corner almost next to the bus stop.*

EXERCISE 17

Which questions might you want to ask when renting a car? Tick the appropriate questions.

1 Kas on võimalik autot rentida? ☐
2 Kas peatus on samal teepoolel? ☐
3 Mis hinnaga te rendite? ☐
4 Kas ma saan ka džiipi rentida? ☐
5 Kas ma pean auto siia tagasi tooma? ☐
6 Kas on võimalik auto ka mõnes teises linnas tagastada? ☐
7 Kui kaua see buss kesklinna sõidab? ☐
8 Mis number bussiga ma minema pean? ☐
9 Kas teil on automaatkäigukastiga autot? ☐
10 Kas teil on viie uksega masinat? ☐
11 Kas rendihind tuleb ette maksta? ☐
12 Kas sularahas saab maksta? ☐
13 Kas ma saan ka turvaistme rentida? ☐
14 Kas ma saan auto rentida viieks päevaks? ☐

EXERCISE 18

You would like to rent a bigger car for 3 days. Fill in the missing lines then listen to the completed dialogue.

 14.05

Teenindaja	Tere!
Sina	Say *Hello!* Say *I would like to rent a car.*
Teenindaja	Millist autot te soovite ja kui kauaks?
Sina	Say *I need a bigger car for a weekend.*
Teenindaja	Kas te soovite džiipi või tavalist masinat?
Sina	Say *In fact it is all the same to me.*
Teenindaja	Siis ma soovitaksin teile seda viie uksega džiipi.
Sina	Ask *Does it have an automatic gearbox?*
Teenindaja	Jah, sellel on küll automaatkäigukast.
Sina	Ask *Does the rental price have to be paid in advance?*
Teenindaja	Jah, rendihind tuleb krediitkaardiga ette maksta. Palun täitke see ankeet ära ja siis vaatame auto üle.
Sina	Say *Thank you.*

? Test yourself

1 You are looking for a bookshop. What do you say?

   a Vabandage, kus siin on lähim bussipeatus?

   b Vabandage, kus siin on lähim telliskivimaja?

   c Vabandage, kus siin on lähim raamatukauplus?

2 You are told *Minge otse*. What are you supposed to do?

   a Go straight.

   b Turn left.

   c Turn right.

3 Someone asks for directions. You want to say *Go across the road and turn left*. What do you say?

   a Minge üle tee ja pöörake vasakule.

   b Minge läbi pargi ja pöörake paremale.

   c Minge üle tee ja pöörake paremale.

4 You want to tell your friend you can't find his house. What do you say?

   a Ma hakkasin sulle vastu tulema.

   b Ma vihkan jalgsi käimist.

   c Ma ei leia su maja üles.

5 What is the opposite of *kiiresti*?

   a kõvasti

   b vaikselt

   c aeglaselt

6 Someone is speaking very quietly. How do you say *Please speak louder?*

   a Palun rääkige aeglasemalt.

   b Palun rääkige paremini.

   c Palun rääkige kõvemini.

7 You want to tell your friends *Please wait for me!* What do you say?

   a Oota mind!

   b Oodake mind!

   c Ärge oodake mind!

8 You want to rent a car. What do you say?

   a Soovitan teile seda autot.

   b Soovin auto tagastada.

   c Soovin autot rentida.

9 You are renting a car and the attendant tells you *Teil peab olema kehtiv juhiluba*. What does it mean?

    a You have to have extensive driving experience.

    b You have to have a valid driving licence.

    c You have to conclude a contract.

10 You are renting a car and the attendant tells you *Me sõlmime teiega lepingu*. What does it mean?

    a The company will conclude a contract with you.

    b You have to pay in advance with a credit card.

    c We have offices in all larger cities.

Key to the exercises

Note that for exercises in which you have to choose between two answers (answer 1/answer 2), the correct answer in the key will be given correspondingly as either **a** or **b**.

UNIT 1

Ex1 1 d **2** b **3** c **4** a, c **Ex2 1** f **2** d e **3** c **4** a, b **5** – **6** b **7** d **8** e **Ex3 1** Tere hommikust! (Tere!) **2** Tere päevast! (Tere!) **3** Tere õhtust! (Tere!) **Ex5 a** 1 **b** 3 c **6** d **4** e **7** f **5** g **2 Ex6 1** b **2** e **3** g **4** a **5** f **6** c **7** h **8** d **Ex7 1** c **2** a **3** b **Ex8 1** b **2** c **3** c **4** a, b **5** a **Ex9 1** b **2** b **3** a **4** b **Ex10 1** b, c **2** a, b **3** a, b **4** b, c **5** a, c **6** a, c **7** a, b **Ex11 1** f **2** b **3** e **4** a **5** c **6** d **Ex13** 1, 6, 3, 4, 7, 10, 8, 5, 9, 11, 2, 12 **Ex14 a 6 b** 3 c **7 d** 5 e **8** f **1 g** 4 h 2 **Ex15 1** kaheksa **2** üksteist **3** viis **4** neli **5** üheksa **6** üks **7** seitse **8** kuus **9** kümme **10** kolm **11** kaksteist **12** kaks **Ex16** kolm, kuus, üheksa **Ex17** üks, kaks, kolm, neli, viis, kuus, seitse, kaheksa, üheksa, kümme, üksteist, kaksteist **Ex18 1** a **2** b **3** a **4** b **5** b **6** a **7** b **8** a **Ex19 1** Kell on üksteist hommikul. **2** Kell on veerand viis. **3** Kell on pool seitse õhtul. **4** Kell on kolmveerand kolm. **5** Kell on viis. **6** Kell on veerand kümme hommikul. **7** Kell on pool kaks. **8** Kell on veerand üks. **Ex20 1** Aitäh!; Head isu! **2** Palun. **3** Both are correct. **4** Vabandust!; Palun vabandust! **5** Terviseks! **6** Head ööd! **Ex21 a** Tere hommikust! **b** Mis kell on? **c** Kell on kaheksa. **d** Aitäh. **Ex22** Tere! / Kell on pool neli.

Test yourself

1 a, **2** c, **3** c, **4** b, **5** a, **6** b, **7** b, **8** a, **9** c, **10** b.

UNIT 2

Ex1 1 c **2** a **3** – **4** – **5** b **6** c **7** a **8** b **Ex4 1** – **2** a **3** b **4** a **5** b **6** c **Ex5 1** b **2** b **3** a **Ex6 1** d **2** a **3** c **4** b **Ex8 1** c **2** b **3** d **4** – **5** a, d **6** b **7** b **8** d **9** c **10** a **Ex9 1** a **2** a **3** b **4** a **5** b **6** a **Ex11 1** c **2** e **3** f **4** a **5** b **6** d **7** a **Ex12 1** Kas te (teie) olete Jaan Mägi? **2** Kas te (teie) olete õpetaja? **3** Kas te (teie) olete kohalik? **4** Jah, ma (mina) olen Jaan Mägi. **5** Ei, ma (mina) ei ole Kristjan Saar. Ma (Mina) olen Jüri Kask. **Ex13 1** c **2** d **3** e **4** a **5** b **6** a **Ex14 1** Ma saan Kauriga tuttavaks. **2** Sa saad Kauriga tuttavaks. **3** Ta saab Kauriga tuttavaks. **4** Me saame Kauriga tuttavaks. **5** Te saate Kauriga tuttavaks. **6** Nad saavad Kauriga tuttavaks. **Ex15 1** olen **2** olete **3** ole **4** oleme **5** oled **6** ole **7** on **8** on **Ex16 1** Ma (Mina) **2** Sa (Sina) **3** Ta (Tema) **4** Me (Meie) **5** Te (Teie) **6** Nad (Nemad) **Ex17 1** a **2** a **3** b **4** a **5** a **6** b **7** a **Ex18 1** Jah, räägin küll. Ei räägi. **2** Jah, räägime küll. Ei räägi. **3** Jah, räägivad küll. Ei räägi. **4** Jah, räägib küll. Ei räägi. **Ex19 1** Kas te räägite eesti keelt? Ei räägi. **2** Kas ta räägib prantsuse keelt? Jah, räägib küll. **3** Kas nad räägivad hispaania keelt? Jah, räägivad küll. **4** Kas nad räägivad inglise keelt? Ei räägi. **5** Kas sa räägid saksa keelt? Ei räägi. **Ex20 1** b **2** a **3** b **4** a **5** b **6** b **Ex21** Formal: **1** Kas te olete Peeter Pääsuke? **2** Kas te räägite inglise keelt? **3** Mis on teie nimi? **4** Mis on teie perekonnanimi? Informal: **1** Kas sa oled Peeter Pääsuke? **2** Kas sa räägid inglise keelt? **3** Mis on sinu nimi? **4** Mis on sinu perekonnanimi? **Ex22 1** Vabandust, ma ei saa aru. **2** Ei ole. **3** You say your surname. **4** You say if you can or can't speak Estonian. **5** You say how you are. **6** You say Väga meeldiv and say your name. **Ex23 1** Jah, räägin küll. **2** Kahjuks ei räägi. **3** Vabandust. Ma ei saa aru. **4** Natuke. **5** Kuidas palun? **Ex24** Tere hommikust! / Minu nimi on (Anne). / Väga meeldiv. Kas te räägite inglise keelt? / Kas te räägite saksa keelt? **Ex25 1** Tere! **2** Mina olen Anna / Peter. **3** Kuidas on teie nimi? **4** Kuidas palun? **5** Väga meeldiv. **Ex26 1** Tere! **2** Kuidas läheb? **3** Hästi. Aga sul? **4** Tänan küsimast. Normaalselt.

Test yourself

1 c, **2** a, **3** c, **4** b, **5** b, **6** a, **7** c, **8** b, **9** b, **10** a.

UNIT 3

Ex1 bussipeatus, infopunkt, kohvik, suur saal, taksopeatus, tualett, väljapääs **Ex2** 1 a **2** a **3** b **4** b **Ex3** 1 a
2 b **3** a, c **Ex4** 1 a **2** a **3** a **Ex5** 1 b, c, d **2** a, b, d **3** a, c, d **Ex6** 1 To the city centre. **2** To Pärnu maantee. 9.
3 To the hotel Viru; 100 crowns. **4** To the Kumu art museum; about 80 crowns. **Ex7** 1 a, b **2** b, c **3** a, c
Ex8 1 b **2** b **3** a **4** – **5** a **6** – **7** c **8** – **Ex9** 1 a, c, d **2** a, b, d **3** b, c, d **Ex10** 1 trammis **2** muuseumis **3** sadamas
4 kesklinnas **5** suures hotellis **6** tualetis **7** väljakul **8** tänaval **9** seinal **10** teel **Ex11** 1 Pärnu maanteele
2 võistlusele **3** Vabaduse väljakule **4** sadamasse **5** kaubanduskeskusesse (kaubanduskeskusse) **6** taksosse
7 muuseumisse **8** kauplusesse (kauplusse) **9** kesklinna **10** infopunkti **11** kohviku juurde **12** kaupluse
juurde **Ex12** 1 Tee! Ära tee! **2** Sõida! Ära sõida! **3** Vaata! Ära vaata! **4** Räägi! Ära räägi! **Ex13** 1 laevaga
2 lennukiga **3** jalgrattaga **4** autoga **5** metrooga **6** rongiga **7** marsruuttaksoga **Ex14 Part 2 a** kaksteist
b kuusteist **c** kakskümmend **d** kakskümmend kaheksa **e** kolmkümmend seitse **f** seitsekümmend
g sada **h** kolm tuhat **Ex15** The ending -s: kesklinnas, sadamas, trammis, tualetis, teatris, lennujaamas. The
ending -l: näitusel, turul, väljakul, maanteel, laual, trepil **Ex16** 1 a **2** b **3** b **4** a **5** b **6** a **Ex17** 1 a **2** b **3** b **4** b
5 b **6** b **7** b **Ex18** 1 kohvikusse **2** apteeki **3** lennujaama **4** infopunkti **5** turule **6** teatrisse **7** bussipeatusse
8 tööle **Ex19** 1 b **2** a **3** a **4** b **5** b **6** a **Ex20** 1 Sõitke palun hotelli juurde. **2** Vaadake, seal on loomaaed!
3 Minge apteeki! **4** Öelge, kus on bussipeatus! **Ex21** infopunkt, kaubanduskeskus, kohvik, loomaaed,
sadam, turg **Ex22** 1 Teatrisse sõidame laevaga. **2** Turule sõidame rongiga. **3** Tööle sõidame lennukiga.
4 Apteeki sõidame autoga. **5** Infopunkti sõidame jalgrattaga. **Ex23** 1 d **2** a **3** f **4** h **5** k **6** j **7** g **8** i **9** c **10** e
11 l **12** b **Ex24** 60, 100, 12, 5000, 41, 72, 300, 18, 90 **Ex25** 1 See on siin. **2** See on seal. **3** Vist sealpool.
4 Ma tõesti ei tea. **Ex26** Tere! / Vabandage, kas see buss läheb lennujaama? / Mis bussid lennujaama
lähevad? / Aitäh. **Ex27 a** Tere. **b** Vabandage, kus on bussipeatus? **c** Aitäh. **d** Kas see buss läheb kesklinna?
e Kui palju see maksab? **f** Aitäh. **Ex28 a** Tere. Mis bussid lähevad kunstimuuseumi juurde? **b** Kuidas
palun? Kaheksateist ja kuuskümmend üks, jah? **c** Kas see on kunstimuuseum? **d** Ahah. Aitäh.

Test yourself

1 b, **2** b, **3** a, **4** a, **5** c, **6** a, **7** a, **8** b, **9** b, **10** c.

UNIT 4

Ex1 1 c **2** a **3** b **4** c **Ex2** 1 b **2** a **3** c **4** b **Ex3** 1 a **2** b **3** a **Ex4** 1 false, the client wants to buy one pie
(eventually buys 2 pies) **2** true **3** false, the client wants mushroom pies **4** true **Ex5** 1 true **2** false, she
wants to have water without gas **3** true **Ex6** 1 false, Helle would like to have a cup of black tea **2** true
3 true **4** true **5** false, Pille orders two cognacs **Ex7** 1 b **2** a **3** a **4** a **5** b **Ex8** 1 coffee with cream **2** coffee
without cream **3** coffee with sugar **4** coffee without sugar **5** water with gas **6** water without gas
7 juice with ice **8** juice without ice **9** tea without lemon **10** coffee with cognac **Ex9** 1 Please buy me a
coffee. **2** What will you have? **3** What shall I get for him (her)? **4** Please give us a beer. **5** Please give me
the menu. **6** One tea with lemon for me please. **7** Please bring us two meat pies. **Ex11** ettekandjad,
kliendid, kohupiimapirukad, sidrunid **Ex12** 1 a **2** b **3** a **4** b **5** b **6** a **7** a **8** b **Ex13** 1 kartulisalatit, musta
kohvi **2** õlut **3** seenepirukat **4** lihapirukat **5** musta teed, konjakit **6** salatit **Ex14** 1 Do you love him
(her)? **2** He (She) loves you. **3** Why don't you love us? **4** He (She) is waiting for us. **5** Are they waiting
for you? **6** He (She) isn't waiting for me. **Ex15** 1 a **2** a **3** d **Ex16** 1 mulle (minule) **2** sulle (sinule)
3 talle (temale) **4** meile **5** teile **6** sulle (sinule) **7** neile (nendele) **Ex17** 1 õunamahlad **2** apelsinimahlad
3 kirsimahlad **4** juustuvõileivad **5** vorstivõileivad **6** jäätisekokteilid **7** õunakoogid **8** kartulisalatid
9 tomatisalatid **Ex18 a** kaks teed **b** kolm kohvi **c** üks salat **d** neli salatit **e** viis seenepirukat **f** kaks kooki
g kuus mahla **h** kolm konjakit **Ex19 Third forms:** musta kohvi, kartulisalatit, õlut, kohupiimapirukat,
lihapirukat, seenepirukat, teed, konjakit, tomatimahla, apelsinimahla, jõhvikamahla, õunakooki,
pohlakooki, makaronisalatit **Ex20** 1 teda **2** meid **3** teid **4** neid **5** mind **6** sind **Ex21** 1 Palun üks
apelsinimahl. **2** Palun üks purk siidrit. **3** Palun üks pakk suitsu. **4** Palun üks pits konjakit. **5** Palun
üks pudel mineraalvett. **6** Palun üks tass teed. **7** Palun üks tükk kooki. **Ex22** Palun üks must kohv. /
Koorega palun. / Palun (veel) üks pirukas. / Mis pirukad teil on? / Palun üks lihapirukas. / Aitäh. See

on kõik. **Ex23 a** Tere! **b** Palun üks kohv koorega. **c** Mis pirukad teil on? **d** Kas need on lihaga või (ilma) lihata? **e** Palun kaks seenepirukat.

Test yourself

1 b, **2** b, **3** c, **4** b, **5** a, **6** a, **7** c, **8** a, **9** a, **10** c.

UNIT 5

Ex1 1 b **2** a **3** c **Ex2** Joosep – Pärnu, construction worker, likes to do sports / Külli – Kohtla-Järve, journalist, likes to take photos and paint / Kaido – Tartu, owner of his own company, likes to travel / Marek – Kärdla in Hiiumaa, estate agent, likes to eat well / Tanel, Rakvere, shop assistant, likes to play football / Helen – England, secretary, likes to swim / Lembit – Võru, bookkeeper, likes to listen to music **Ex3 1** a **2** a **3** b **4** b **Ex4 1** a **2** b **3** b **4** c **5** b **Ex5** esmaspäeval, teisipäeval, kolmapäeval, neljapäeval, reedel, laupäeval, pühapäeval **Ex6** Tallinnas, Tallinnast; Eestis, Eestist; Pärnus, Pärnust; USA-s, USA-st; Jaapanis, Jaapanist; Rootsist; Lätist; Leedust; Prantsusmaal, Prantsusmaalt; Saksamaal, Saksamaalt; Mustamäel, Mustamäelt; Saaremaal, Saaremaalt. **Ex7 1** I like this hobby painter's camp. **2** He (She) doesn't like this hobby painter's camp. **3** Do you like Tallinn? **4** Does Joosep like Tallinn? **5** Joosep doesn't like sports. **6** Do you like this music? **7** We don't like Mart. **Ex8 1** b **2** b **3** b **4** b **5** b **6** b **Ex9 1** b **2** b **3** b **4** b **5** b **6** b **Ex10 1** üleeile *the day before yesterday*, eile *yesterday*, täna *today*, homme *tomorrow*, ülehomme *the day after tomorrow* **2** esmaspäev *Monday*, teisipäev *Tuesday*, kolmapäev *Wednesday*, neljapäev *Thursday*, reede *Friday*, laupäev *Saturday*, pühapäev *Sunday* **Ex11 1** esmaspäeval *on Monday* teisipäeval *on Tuesday* **2** kolmapäeval *on Wednesday* neljapäeval *on Thursday* **3** reedel *on Friday* laupäeval *on Saturday* **4** pühapäeval *on Sunday* esmaspäeval *on Monday* **5** täna *today* homme *tomorrow* **6** üleeile *the day before yesterday* eile *yesterday* **7** homme *tomorrow* ülehomme *the day after tomorrow* **8** kevadel *in the spring* suvel *in the summer* **9** sügisel *in the autumn* talvel *in the winter* **10** talvel *in the winter* kevadel *in the spring* **Ex12** -s, -st: Eesti, Jaapan, Leedu, Läti, Pärnu, Rootsi, Soome, Taani, Tallinn, Tartu, USA -lt: Hiiumaa, Inglismaa, Kohtla-Järve, Lasnamäe, Mustamäe, Prantsusmaa, Saaremaa, Saksamaa, Sillamäe, Õismäe **Ex13 1** Pekka on pärit Soomest. **2** Anatoli on pärit Venemaalt. **3** Michiko on pärit Jaapanist. **4** Tiiu on pärit Eestist. **5** Michael on pärit Inglismaalt. **6** Pierre on pärit Prantsusmaalt. **7** Juan on pärit Hispaaniast. **Ex14 1** c **2** c **3** c **4** c **5** b **6** b **7** b **8** b **9** a **10** a **11** a **12** a **Ex15 1** Tartusse **2** Tartus **3** Tartust **4** Soome **5** Soomes **6** Soomest **7** Saaremaale **8** Saaremaal **9** Saaremaalt **Ex16 1** Ülole meeldib Kaie. *Ülo likes Kaie.* **2** Kaiele meeldib Kaido. *Kaie likes Kaido.* **3** Kaidole meeldib Piret. *Kaido likes Piret.* **4** Piretile meeldib Sven. *Piret likes Sven.* **5** Svenile meeldib Ruth. *Sven likes Ruth.* **6** Ruthile meeldib Urmas. *Ruth likes Urmas.* **7** Urmasele meeldib Kärt. *Urmas likes Kärt.* **8** Kärdile meeldib Tiit. *Kärt likes Tiit.* **9** Tiidule meeldib Aet. *Tiit likes Aet.* **10** Aedale meeldib Ülo. *Aet likes Ülo.* **Ex17 1** a **2** a **3** b **4** a **5** a **6** a **7** b **8** b, b **9** a **Ex18 a** Welcome! **b** The place is open from Monday till Thursday from 12.00 till 24.00 and from Friday till Sunday from 12.00 till 3.00. **c** Let's get acquainted. **d** Ma olen pärit (the country you come from). **e** Ma olen (your profession). **f** What do you like to do during your free time? **Ex19 a** Tere! **b** Minu nimi on (your name). **c** Ma olen pärit Ameerikast. **d** Ma olen firmajuht. **Ex20** Saame tuttavaks! Mina olen (Michael). / Kust sa pärit oled? / Mina olen pärit Ameerikast. / Mulle meeldib reisida ja pildistada. **Ex21** Mulle meeldib ujuda. / Mida sulle meeldib vabal ajal teha? / Mulle meeldib ka muusikat kuulata.

Test yourself

1 a, **2** a, **3** b, **4** c, **5** a, **6** a, **7** c, **8** c, **9** b, **10** c.

UNIT 6

Ex1 1 b **2** c **3** a **4** b **5** c **6** c **7** c **Ex2 1** a **2** b **3** a **4** b **5** a **6** b **Ex3** j, i, h, d, c, b, g, f, e, a **Ex4 1** c **2** b **3** d **4** e **5** f **6** a **7** h **8** i **9** j **10** g **Ex5 1** Mul (Minul) on koer. **2** Sul (Sinul) on tütar. **3** Tal (Temal) on poeg. **4** Meil on oma firma. **5** Teil on vanaisa. **6** Neil (Nendel) on lapsed. **Ex6 1** Minu mehe (abikaasa) nimi on Tõnu. **2** Minu naise (abikaasa) nimi on Külli. **3** Minu lapse nimi on Birgit. **4** Minu poja nimi on Kaspar. **5** Minu tütre nimi on Sille. **6** Minu õe nimi on Tiina. **7** Minu venna nimi on Aivar. **Ex7 1** b **2** a **3** b **4** a **5** b **6** a **Ex8** jaanuaris, veebruaris, märtsis, aprillis, mais, juunis, juulis, augustis, septembris, oktoobris, novembris, detsembris **Ex9 1 a** Täna on neljas mai. **b** Täna on kümnes september. **c** Täna on kaheteistkümnes oktoober. **d** Täna on kahekümne kuues detsember. **2 a** Tema sünnipäev on teisel jaanuaril. **b** Tema sünnipäev on neljateistkümnendal veebruaril. **c** Tema sünnipäev on üheksateistkümnendal aprillil. **d** Tema sünnipäev on kolmekümne esimesel juulil. **3 a** Ta on sündinud tuhande üheksasaja kuuekümne teisel aastal. **b** Ta on sündinud tuhande üheksasaja seitsmekümne kaheksandal aastal. **c** Ta on sündinud kahe tuhande seitsmendal aastal. **Ex10 1** Kas neil on tütar? *Do they have a daughter?* **2** Kas sul on auto? *Do you have a car?* **3** Kas Marial on mees (abikaasa)? *Does Maria have a husband?* **4** Kas tal on koer? *Does he/she have a dog?* **5** Kas teil on pere? *Do you have family?* **Ex11 1** a **2** b **3** b **4** a **5** b **6** a **7** b **8** a **Ex12 1** veebruar, aprill **2** juuni, august **3** oktoober, detsember **4** jaanuar, märts **Ex13 1** jaanuaris **2** veebruaris **3** märtsis **4** aprillis **5** mais **6** juunis **7** juulis **8** augustis **9** septembris **10** oktoobris **11** novembris **12** detsembris **Ex14 1** e **2** j **3** a **4** g **5** b **6** i **7** c **8** f **9** d **10** h **Ex15 1** teisel (2.) **2** viieteistkümnendal (15.) **3** kaheteistkümnendal (12). **4** kaheksateistkümnendal (18.) **5** kahekümnendal (20). **6** kaheksandal (8.) **7** üheksandal (9.) **8** kahekümne esimesel (21.) **9** esimesel (1.) **10** kahekümne kaheksandal (28.) **Ex16 1** Kontsert toimub viiendal jaanuaril. **2** Filmifestival algab kahekümne kaheksandal juunil ja lõpeb viieteistkümnendal augustil. **3** Tema sünnipäev on kolmekümnendal jaanuaril. **4** Ta on sündinud tuhande üheksasaja seitsmekümne kaheksandal aastal. **5** Ma olen sündinud tuhande üheksasaja kaheksakümne teisel aastal. **6** Kas sa oled sündinud tuhande üheksasaja kuuekümne üheksandal aastal? **7** Me oleme sündinud tuhande üheksasaja viiekümne neljandal aastal. **8** Nad on sündinud kahe tuhandendal aastal. **9** Kas te olete sündinud tuhande üheksasaja kuuekümne kolmandal aastal? **10** Nad ei ole sündinud kahe tuhande kaheksandal aastal. **Ex17** Kui vana on sinu poeg? / Aga kui vana on sinu tütar? / Mul on ka tütar. / Ta on seitseteist aastat vana. / Viieteistkümnendal mail. **Ex18 a** How old you are? **b** Ma olen kolmkümmend kuus aastat vana. **c** Do you have children? **d** Mul on üks tütar. **e** How old is your daughter? **f** Ta on kaksteist aastat vana. **g** Who is your husband / wife? **h** Ta on ajakirjanik. **i** Do you have your own car? **j** Jah, mul on oma auto. **k** Are you Estonian? **l** Ma olen sakslane, aga mu isa on rootslane. **Ex19** Possible answers. **a** Ma tõusen iga päev kell kaheksa. **b** Siis ma jalutan väljas koeraga. **c** Siis ma teen hommikusööki. **d** Ma sõidan tööle autoga. **e** Tööl ma pean helistama, kirjutama meile ja kohtuma inimestega. **f** Tööl ma loen veel uudiseid Internetist. **g** Kell kuus ma lähen (koos) sõpradega trenni. **h** Pärast trenni ma lähen koju. **i** Mõnikord (Vahel) tulevad sõbrad külla. **j** Paar korda kuus ma käin teatris. **k** Kell kaksteist ma lähen magama.

Test yourself

1 c, **2** b, **3** c, **4** a, **5** b, **6** a, **7** c, **8** b, **9** b, **10** a.

UNIT 7

Ex1a 1 true **2** false, the cheese costs 70 crowns a kilo **3** false, he decides to buy half a kilo of cheese **b 1** false, the buyer asks about the price of plums **2** false, the fruit costs 20 crowns a kilo **3** true **c 1** true **2** true **3** false, he thinks it is very high price **d 1** true **2** false, onions cost 10 crowns a kilo **3** false, he thinks it is a bargain price **Ex2 1** b **2** a **3** b **Ex3 a 1** a **2** b **3** b **4** c **b 1** a **2** a **3** c **4** b **c 1** c **2** b **3** c **4** b **Ex4 1** a **2** b **3** b **4** a **5** b **6** b **7** b **Ex5 a 1** b **2** c **3** a **4** b **5** b **b 1** a **2** a **3** a **4** c **5** a **Ex6 1** b **2** a **3** a **4** b **Ex7 1** a **2** b **3** b **4** a **5** a **6** b **7** b **8** b **Ex8 1** true **2** false, there is beer and pickled cucumbers in the refrigerator but no bread **3** true **4** true **5** false, it is Janek who always goes to the shop **6** true **7** false, Janek suggests to invite Annika and Maarika to come and visit **8** true **9** false, it is Marek who will have to do the dishes later **Ex9** veini, veini; limonaadi, limonaadi; šokolaadi, šokolaadi; kohupiima, kohupiima; soola, soola; musta, musta; kana, kana; liha, liha; hakkliha, hakkliha; valge, valget; lahja, lahjat; jogurti, jogurtit; ketšupi, ketšupit; maitsvat; suhkrut; punase, punast; taise, taist; väikest; heleda, heledat; koore, koort; või, võid; kakao, kakaod; hea, head **Ex10** magusa, magusat, magusaid; valge, valget, valgeid; jõhvika, jõhvikat, jõhvikaid; odava, odavat, odavaid; porgandi, porgandit, porgandeid;

tomati, tomatit, tomateid; pähkli, pähklit, pähkleid; punase, punast, punaseid; sinise, sinist, siniseid; rasvase, rasvast, rasvaseid; roosa, roosat, roosasid; kirju, kirjut, kirjusid; ploomi, ploomi, ploome; halli, halli, halle; kommi, kommi, komme; pirni, pirni, pirne; kurke; marju; suure, suurt, suuri **Kellelt sa õunu ostad? Ablative case** sõbral, sõbralt; naisel, naiselt; mehel, mehelt; lapsel, lapselt; naabril, naabrilt; abikaasal, abikaasalt; ülemusel, ülemuselt **Ex11** noorem, kõige noorem; väiksem, kõige väiksem; magusam, kõige magusam; odavam, kõige odavam; kallim, kõige kallim; hapum, kõige hapum; laiem, kõige laiem; vanem, kõige vanem; lahjem, kõige lahjem; halvem, kõige halvem **Ex12 1** magusamat **2** hapumat **3** odavamat **4** suuremat **5** väiksemaid **6** suuremaid **7** magusamaid **8** kallimaid **Ex13 1** käib **2** lähen **3** lähed **4** käin **5** läheme **6** käin **Ex14** ploom, maasikas, kala, juust, kurk, sink, küpsis, sibul, muna, hapukurk, viinamari, õli, omlett; *plum, bag, strawberry, fish, box, cheese, cucumber, ham, biscuit, onion, egg, price, pickled cucumber, grape, oil, omelette* **Ex15 1** b **2** b **3** b **4** b **5** b **6** b **7** b **8** b **Ex16 1** sinki *hundred grams of ham* **2** veini *one bottle of wine* **3** limonaadi *one bottle of lemonade* **4** juustu *three hundred grams of cheese* **5** jahu *one bag of flour* **6** hakkliha *kilo of minced meat* **7** kala *two fishes* **8** kana *half a chicken* **9** jogurtit *three yoghurts* **10** ketšupit *two ketchups* **11** pakki rohelist teed *two packets of green tea* **12** tassi musta kohvi *three cups of black coffee* **13** tumedat õlut *two dark beers* **14** heledat õlut *four light beers* **15** pudelit vett *two bottles of water* **16** purki mett *two jars of honey* **Ex17** Kas teil on … **1** musta teed **2** head jäätist **3** tumedat õlut **4** eesti juustu **5** taist liha **6** värsket kala **7** lahjat jogurtit **Ex18 1** b **2** a **3** a **4** b **5** b **6** a **7** b **8** a **Ex19 1** maasikaid *three hundred grams of strawberries* **2** sibulaid *half a kilo of onions* **3** kollaseid kartuleid *five kilos of yellow potatoes* **4** siniseid ploome *three kilos of blue plums* **5** väikseid kurke *one jar of small cucumbers* **6** suuri mune *box of big eggs* **7** häid porgandeid *a little bit of good carrots* **8** roosasid õunu *bag of pink apples* **9** magusaid pirne *two kilos of sweet pears* **10** musti seeni *box of black mushrooms* **Ex20** Kas teil on … **1** valgeid kartuleid **2** odavaid tomateid **3** hapusid marju **4** punaseid ploome **5** suuri kurke **6** väikseid seeni **7** ilusaid jõhvikaid **8** kalleid õunu **9** roosasid ploome **10** häid porgandeid **Ex21 1** a **2** b **3** c **4** a **5** c **Ex22** Possible answers. **1** Kapsas on suurem kui õun. **2** Tort on magusam kui võileib. **3** Kohupiim on lahjem kui juust. **4** Vein on kallim kui mahl. **5** Jõhvikad on hapumad kui maasikad. **6** Kommid on magusamad kui seened. **7** Pähklid on väiksemad kui ploomid **8** Kapsad on suuremad kui kartulid. **Ex23 1** a, a **2** a, b **3** a, a **4** b, b **5** a, b **6** b, b **Ex24** Ma soovin osta kilo maasikaid. / Väiksemaid. / Palun pange karpi. / Kui palju kurgid maksavad? / Palun pool kilo. **Ex25** Jah, need on tõesti magusad. / Suurepärane maitse. Kas need on eesti omad? / Kui palju need pirnid maksavad? / Aga kui palju need ploomid maksavad? / Oi, kui odavad! / Ma võtan neid pool kilo.

Test yourself

1 c, **2** b, **3** c, **4** a, **5** b, **6** b, **7** a, **8** a, **9** b, **10** c.

UNIT 8

Ex1 1 b **2** a **3** d **4** c **5** b **6** b, c **7** d **Ex2 1** b **2** a **3** a **4** a **Ex3 1** a, b, d **2** c, d, e **3** a, b, c, d, e **4** b, c, e **Ex4 1** a **2** b **3** a **4** b **Ex5 1** c **2** b **3** b **4** b **5** a **6** b **7** b **8** c **9** c **Ex6 1** c **2** a **3** b **4** a **Ex7 a 1** false, the performance takes place in September, not October **2** false, the ticket office is open from eleven, not one o'clock **3** false, the ticket office is open all days except national holidays **4** false, the tickets can be ordered online on working days only **5** true **b 1** true **2** false, the film 'Winter' is not shown **3** true **4** true **5** true **c 1** false, only the nightclub miss, not mister will be elected **2** true **3** false, women have free entrance regardless of the time **4** false, nothing is said about free drinks **5** true **d 1** true **2** true **3** true **4** false, children under 7 years have free entrance **5** false, the performance starts at seven o'clock **Ex8 1** Ma tahaks(in) täna õhtul kinno minna. **2** Kas sa tuleks(id) minuga kinno? **3** Ma vaataks(in) hea meelega komöödiat. **4** Kas see film sobiks? **5** Kas sa sooviks(id) midagi juua ka? **Ex9** ühest üheni, kahest kaheni, kolmest kolmeni, neljast neljani, viiest viieni, kuuest kuueni, seitsmest seitsmeni, kaheksast kaheksani, üheksast üheksani, kümnest kümneni, üheteistkümnest üheteistkümneni, kaheteistkümnest kaheteistkümneni, kahekümnest kahekümneni **Ex10 1** b **2** d **3** f **4** e **5** a **6** c **Ex11 1** c **2** a **3** b **4** f **5** d **6** e **Ex12 1** this author's film/film of this author **2** this theatre's actors / the actors of this theatre **3** this film's actors / the actors of this film **4** this book's author / the author of this book **Ex13 1** b **2** a **3** a **4** b **5** b **6** b **7** b **8** a **Ex14** rääkimine *speaking* **2** kuulamine *listening* **3** vaatamine *watching* **4** jalutamine *walking* **5** laulmine *singing* **6** jooksmine *running* **7** istumine *sitting* **Ex15 1** b **2** a **3** a **4** a **5** b **6** b **Ex16 1** Kas sa tahaks(id) minuga kinno tulla? **2** Muidugi tahaks(in). **3** Mis filmi sa eelistaks(id)? **4** Mulle meeldiks ulmefilm. **5** Mis ritta sa pileti sooviks(id)? **6** Kuhugi keskele. **Ex17 1** f **2** c **3** a **4** d **5** b **6** e **Ex18 1** Kell on viis minutit kolm läbi. **2** Kell on kümme minutit viis läbi. **3** Kell on kolmteist minutit seitse läbi. **4** Kell on kümne minuti pärast üheksa. **5** Kell on viie minuti pärast kümme. **6** Kell on kahe minuti pärast üksteist. **Ex19 1** Ta tuleb poole tunni pärast. **2** Ta tuleb pärast nelja. **3** Ma helistan teile / sulle kursuse pärast. **4** Ta tuleb tunni pärast. **5** Ta tuleb pärast kuut. **6** Ma teen seda tema pärast. **Ex20 1** b **2** a **3** a **4** a **5** a **Ex21 1** minu lapse raamat **2** selle pileti hind **3** selle etenduse nimi **4** selle kino aadress **5** selle ulmefilmi autor **Ex22 1** The films of these directors are very good. **2** In this cinema the tickets are expensive. **3** There are different films in the programme of the festival. **4** It is possible to dance in the nightclubs until three o'clock. **5** The parents can also come to the children's perfomances. **6** I like this actor. **Ex23 1** What would you prefer? **2** Kas midagi muud ei ole? **3** On Mondays the tickets are half price. **4** The ticket office is open every day except Saturday to Sunday. **Ex24 1** Kas see on komöödia? **2** Kui pikk see film on? **3** Kas seal on mingi hinnavahe ka? **4** Palun kuhugi keskele. **Ex25** Kas sa tahaksid kinno minna? / Täna õhtul. / Mis filmi sa tahaksid vaadata? **Ex26** Kas sa tahaksid nädalavahetusel teatrisse minna? / Mingi inglise komöödia. / Kahju. Võib-olla mõni teine kord. **Ex27** Palun kaks piletit. / Jah, palun. / Kas seal on hinnavahe? / Mis kohti te soovitaksite? / Olgu. Kui pikk see etendus on? / Väga hea. **Ex28** Tere! Öelge palun, mis film on Helesinine planeet. / Kes on selle filmi režissöör? / Olgu. Kui pikk see film on? / Kui palju piletid maksavad? / Kas hind sõltub kellaajast?

Test yourself

1 c, **2** a, **3** b, **4** b, **5** c, **6** b, **7** a, **8** a, **9** b, **10** c.

UNIT 9

Ex1 1 true **2** false, no the patient himself is a foreigner **3** false, he has a medical insurance card **4** true **5** false, the nurse asks for the patient's identification code **6** false, nobody asks about the patient's home address and name **7** true **8** false, the room is on the second floor **Ex2 1** b **2** a **3** b **Ex3 a 1** a, c, d **2** b **3** a **4** b **b 1** c **2** a **3** b **4** a **Ex4 1** a **2** a **3** a **4** b **5** b **6** a **7** a **Ex5 a 1** false, the patient has a terrible toothache **2** true **3** false, the doctor suggests the tooth should be pulled out **4** true **5** true **b 1** false, the patient fell and sprained his leg **2** true **3** false, no he did not buy any painkillers **4** true **5** true **Ex6 1** a **2** b **3** b **4** a **5** a **6** a **7** a **8** a **Ex7 1** b **2** c **3** b **4** b **5** b **6** c **7** b **Ex8 1** a **2** b **3** a **4** b **Ex9** ma puhkasin, sa puhkasid, ta puhkas, me puhkasime, te puhkasite, nad puhkasid; ma ei puhanud, sa ei puhanud, ta ei puhanud, me ei puhanud, te ei puhanud, nad ei puhanud. **Ex10** saatis, saatsime, saatsite, saatsid, saatnud; andsid, andis; ostsin, ostis, ostsime, ostsid, ostnud **Ex11** jätsin, jätsid, jättis, jätsime, jätsite, jätsid, jätnud **Ex12 1** läksin **2** läinud **3** läinud **4** läinud **5** läks **6** läinud **7** läksid **8** läksite **Ex13 1** Jah, olin küll. Ei olnud. **2** Jah, tulin küll. Ei tulnud. **3** Jah, tegin küll. Ei teinud. **4** Jah, nägin küll. Ei näinud. **5** Jah, pidin küll. Ei pidanud. **Ex14** ma jäin, sa jäid, ta jäi, me jäime, te jäite, nad jäid; ma ei jäänud, sa ei jäänud, ta ei jäänud, me ei jäänud, te ei jäänud, nad ei jäänud **Ex15 1** Jah, sõin küll. Ei söönud. **2** Jah, jõin küll. Ei joonud. **3** Jah, sain küll. Ei saanud. **4** Jah, tõin küll. Ei toonud. **Ex16** aeglaselt, tavaliselt, vaikselt, kurvalt, rõõmsalt, kiiresti, kõvasti, halvasti **Ex17 1** I have a terrible headache. **2** My head aches terribly. **3** He/She speaks very slowly. **4** This music is very quiet. **5** This music plays very quietly. **6** This is a fast car. **7** This car drives fast. **8** This is a good doctor. **9** This doctor treats well. **Ex18 1** töötasime **2** läksid **3** võttis **4** sõitis **5** ostsite **6** läks **7** puhkasime **8** vaatasid **9** lugesite **10** kuulasid **11** läksime **Ex19** haigeks jääma, jooma, nägema, olema, otsa saama, panema, pesema, sööma, tegema, terveks saama, tooma, tulema **Ex20 1** b **2** b **3** a **4** a **5** a **6** a **7** b **8** a **9** b **10** b **11** b **12** a **Ex21 1** Jah, olin küll. Ei olnud. **2** Jah, lugesin küll.

Ei lugenud. **3** Jah, käisin küll. Ei käinud. **4** Jah, vaatasin küll. Ei vaadanud. **5** Jah, naersin küll. Ei naernud.
6 Jah, ostsin küll. Ei ostnud. **7** Jah, jõin küll. Ei joonud. **8** Jah, tegin küll. Ei teinud. **9** Jah, nägin küll. Ei
näinud. **10** Jah, pesin küll. Ei pesnud. **Ex22 1** elan, elasin **2** töötan, õppisin **3** saan, saanud **4** olen, olnud
5 sõidan, käisin **6** mängi, mängisin **7** tegele, tegelesin **Ex23 1** a **2** b **3** a **4** b **5** a **6** a **Ex24 1** aeglaselt
2 vaikselt **3** rõõmsalt **4** hirmsasti **5** kiiresti **6** hästi **Ex25 1** välja tõmmata *Unfortunately this tooth needs
to be pulled out.* **2** väänasin välja *I fell yesterday and sprained my leg.* **3** lugege läbi *Read through the
information sheet that is in the package.* **4** jäi haigeks *My husband fell ill yesterday.* **5** võtame ära *We will
take off the plaster in three weeks' time.* **6** sai otsa *We also tried to drink hot tea, but we ran out of tea.*
7 paraneb ära *This place will heal in about three days.* **Ex26** Mul oleks vaja kiiresti arsti juurde saada. / Mul
on hirmus köha. / Eile õhtul oli 38,5 / Sobib küll. **Ex27** Mu pea valutab hirmsasti (kohutavalt). / Jah, aga
see ei aidanud. / Ma võtsin hommikul kaks tabletti. / Kas ma pean uuesti teie juurde tulema?
Ex28 Tere! / Mul on vist gripp. / Jah, valutab küll. / Kuidas ma seda rohtu võtma pean? / Kas sellel rohul
on ka mingeid kõrvalmõjusid? **Ex29 1** Ma jäin haigeks. **2** Mul on hirmus peavalu. **3** Mu kurk valutab.
4 Mul on palavik 37,5. **5** Ma jõin kuuma teed, aga see ei aidanud. **6** Mul on vist gripp.

Test yourself

1 b, **2** c, **3** b, **4** c, **5** a, **6** c, **7** b, **8** b, **9** b, **10** c.

UNIT 10
Ex1 a 1 b **2** a, b, c **3** a, b **b 1** b **2** b **3** a **Ex2 a 1** b **2** a, b, c **3** b, c **4** a, b **b 1** true **2** true **3** false, Koit thinks
long brown skirt and high heels are very beautiful **4** false, Tiia does not say anything about the colour
of the tie **c** mantel, sussid, pluus, kaunis kleit **Ex3 1** a **2** b **3** a **Ex4 1** true **2** false, Urmas met the girl last
year **3** true **4** true **5** true **6** false, Maarika works as a secretary **7** true **8** false, Maarika wants to become a
psychologist **9** true **10** false, the profession of Maarika's parents is not mentioned in the dialogue
11 true **12** true **13** It is not clear what colour her hair is at the moment. **Ex5 1** a **2** a **3** a **4** a **5** b **6** b **7** a
Ex6 Mul on seljas kleit, mantel, pluus, seelik, ülikond. Mul on jalas tossud, kingad, saapad, sussid. Mul on
peas kübar, müts. Mul on kaelas lips, sall. Mul on käes kindad. Mul on sõrmes sõrmus. **Ex7 1** kaelas
2 kaela **3** kaelast **4** seljast **5** selga **6** seljas **7** jalga **8** jalas **9** jalast **10** peas **11** peast **12** pähe **13** peas
Ex8 1 b **2** a **3** b **4** c **Ex9 1** Ta on sale. **2** Tal on lokkis juuksed. **3** Ta on keskealine. **4** Ta on teismeline. **5** Ta
on kõhn. **6** Tal on tumedad juuksed. **7** Tal on hallid juuksed. **8** Tal on lühikesed juuksed. **9** Tal on habe ja
vuntsid. **10** Ta näeb väga hea välja. **Ex10 1** b **2** a **3** a **4** b **5** b **6** a **7** b **8** a **Ex11 1** sööma **2** söömas
3 ujuma **4** ujumas **5** jalutamas **6** jalutama **7** juttu ajamas **8** juttu ajama **Ex13 a 1** dressipüksid jalga
2 sokid jalga **3** T-särgi selga **4** jope selga **5** salli kaela **6** mütsi pähe **7** kindad kätte **b 1** kindad käest ära
2 mütsi peast ära **3** salli kaelast ära **4** jope seljast ära **5** T-särgi seljast ära **6** sokid jalast ära **7** dressipüksid
jalast ära **Ex14** Olgu. Aga mul ei ole midagi selga panna. / Kas ma pean mütsi ka pähe panema ja
kindad kätte? / Ma võtan need igaks juhuks kaasa. **Ex15** Ma panen musta seeliku selga ja kõrge
kontsaga kingad jalga. / See pluus sobib sulle väga hästi. / Kas sa paned kõrvarõngad ja pärlid ka?
Ex16 Võta palun mantel ära ja pane kappi. / Oi, kui kena sa välja näed! / Pane palun sussid jalga.
Ex17 a Ta on kena noormees. **b** Ta on keskmist kasvu, pikem kui sina. **c** Tal on tumedad sirged juuksed.
d Tal on vuntsid. **e** Ta riietub maitsekalt. **f** Ta näeb väga hea välja, aga ta on arg. **g** Tundub, et ta on väga
tark. **h** Ta tahab saada arstiks. **Ex18 a** Ma olen kakskümmend aastat vana. **b** Mul on sirged punased
juuksed. **c** Mul on hobusesaba. **d** Ma olen pikka kasvu, aga mitte liiga pikk. **e** Ma olen sõbralik ja
rõõmus. **f** Ma tahan saada lauljaks. **g** Nädalavahetusel ma käin ööklubis tantsimas.

Test yourself

1 b, **2** a, **3** c, **4** a, **5** b, **6** c, **7** a, **8** c, **9** b, **10** b.

UNIT 11

Ex1 1 b **2** a **3** c **4** a **5** c **6** a **7** b **8** a **9** b **10** b **Ex2 1** b **2** a **3** b **4** a **5** a **6** a **7** b **8** a **Ex3 1** true **2** false, the client wants the bowling alley for two hours **3** false, the client wants to come at six o'clock **4** false, eight people will come **5** true **Ex4 1** a **2** b **3** a **4** b **Ex5 1** b **2** a **3** b **4** a **5** b **6** b **7** a **8** a **9** a **Ex6 1** The client wants to cut her hair. **2** Twenty centimetres. **3** So much? Aren't you feeling sorry? **4** The client wants to dye her hair. **5** Reddish, but not too dark. **6** Yes, she wants a hairdo done with the hair dryer. **7** Yesterday. **8** Then it is better to cut the hair. **Ex7 1** b **2** b **3** b **4** a **5** b **6** a **7** a **8** a **Ex8 1** a **2** a **3** b **4** b **5** b **6** a **7** b **8** b **Ex9 1** b **2** a **3** b **4** a **5** a **Ex10 1** a, a **2** b, **3** b, b **4** b **5** a, a **6** a, a **7** b, b **8** a, a **9** b, b **Ex11 1** läks katki **2** korda teha **3** teen korpuse lahti **4** saab kohe tühjaks **5** panen korpuse kinni **6** läks kellaaeg segi **7** läks katki **8** sai otsa **9** kirja panna **10** Panen arvuti käima **11** kinni panna **12** Teeme restorani lahti **Ex12 1** Ära joo vett. Ära joo vett ära. **2** Ära mine. Ära mine ära. **3** Ära viska seda paberit ära. **4** Ära söö seda kooki. Ära söö seda kooki ära. **5** Ära korista seda tuba. Ära korista seda tuba ära. **Ex13** Ma panin toa kinni (broneerisin toa) kaks nädalat tagasi. / Kaheinimesetoa. / Ma olen (Karl Kask). / Teisipäevani. **Ex14** Kas ma võin midagi küsida? / Kas siin hotellis on internetiühendus? / Kui palju see maksab? / See on väga tore. Kus ma siin suitsetada tohin? / Kus ma saan raha vahetada? / Aitäh. Head aega. **Ex15** Kas ma saan pühapäeval kolmeks tunniks bowlingusaali kinni panna? / Kas saab tulla kell neli? / Kaheksakesi. / Ma arvan, et kolmest rajast piisab. **Ex16 1** No you can't because the hairdresser works in the evening on Tuesdays. **2** Ma sooviksin esmaspäevaks aega kinni panna. **3** Kella kümneks. **4** Ma sooviksin juukseid lõigata ja värvida. Ma sooviksin juuksed lühemaks lõigata. **5** She asks, how much shall I cut? **6** She asks, what colour shall we make (your hair)? **7** She asks, shall I also make a hair do? **8** She will make your hair wet. **9** She is going to wash your hair. **Ex17** Tere! / Mu kell läks katki. / Jah. Palun. / Väga hea. Mis tal viga on? / Teeme nii.

Test yourself

1 c, **2** c, **3** a, **4** a, **5** b, **6** b, **7** c, **8** c, **9** b, **10** a.

UNIT 12

Ex1 1 text a **2** text b **3** text b **4** text a **5** text a **6** text b **7** text b **8** text a **9** text a, text b **10** – **11** – **12** text a **13** – **14** text a, text b **15** text a **16** It is not clear in text *b* if the apartment is furnished or unfurnished **17** text a, text b **18** – **Ex2 1** a **2** b **3** a **4** a **5** a **6** b **7** a **8** b **Ex3 1** text a **2** text b **3** text b **4** text a **5** text a **6** text b **7** text a **8** text a **9** text b **10** text b **11** text a **12** text b **Ex4 1** b **2** b **3** a **4** b **Ex5 1** true **2** true **3** true **4** true **5** false, it is allowed to move the furniture around **6** true **7** false, the dishwasher is between the sink and cupboard **8** false, the washing machine is under the bathroom cupboard **9** true **10** false, a married couple lives upstairs **11** false, a single old man lives downstairs **12** false, the parking spot is in front of the house **13** false, the client has a cat **14** false, it is allowed to smoke on the balcony **15** true **16** the client wants to conclude the contract for half a year **17** false, the documents will be ready on Monday **Ex6 1** a **2** a **3** a **4** a **5** a **6** b **7** b **8** a **9** b **10** a **Ex7** 6, 8, 3, 5, 4, 1, 7, 2 **Ex8 1** b **2** g **3** a **4** f **5** c **6** e **7** d **Ex9 1** kolmetoaline korter **2** viietoaline korter **3** seitsmetoaline korter **4** kahekorruseline maja **5** üheksakorruseline maja **6** kuueteist(kümne) korruseline maja **7** kuueteistaastane inimene **8** kaheksateist(kümne) aastane inimene **9** neljakümne viie aastane inimene **10** viiekümne kolme aastane inimene **Ex10 1** b **2** b **3** b **4** a **5** b **6** a **7** a **8** b **Ex11 1** true **2** true **3** true **4** false, pilt on riiuli kõrval. **5** true **6** false, muusikakeskus on riiuli peal **7** false, kass on diivani peal **8** false, raamat on laua peal **9** false, tugitool on ukse lähedal **10** true **Ex12** Possible answers: **1** Kass on diivani peal. **2** Kruusid on laua peal. **3** Raamatud on riiuli peal. **4** Padi on diivani peal. **5** Lilled on laua peal. **6** Pilt on riiuli kõrval. **Ex13 1** peale **2** peal **3** juurde **4** peale, kõrvale **5** pealt, taha **6** taga **7** pealt **8** peal **9** tagant **10** alla **11** taha **12** tagant **Ex14 1** Pall on laua peal. Võtan palli laua pealt. **2** Pall on laua all. Võtan palli laua alt. **3** Pall on teleri taga. Võtan palli teleri tagant. **4** Pall on riiuli juures. Võtan palli riiuli juurest. **5** Pall on diivani ees. Võtan palli diivani eest. **6** Pall on ukse kõrval. Võtan palli ukse kõrvalt. **7** Pall on arvuti ja muusikakeskuse vahel. Võtan palli arvuti ja muusikakeskuse vahelt. **Ex15 1** h *How many rooms are there* *in this apartment?* **2** a *On which floor is the apartment?* **3** e *What is the overall size of the apartment?* **4** i *Does the apartment have a balcony?* **5** b *Is the apartment furnished?* **6** c *Is the apartment renovated?* **7** f *Are the neighbours quiet?* **8** d *Where can I park the car?* 9 g *How big is the rent?* **Ex16** Tere. Mitu tuba siin on? / Kas pesumasinat tohib kasutada? / Kas naabrid on rahulikud? / Kus ma saan autot parkida? / Kui suur on üür? / Väga tore. Kas saab lepingu sõlmida pooleks aastaks? / Aitäh. **Ex17 1** c **2** a **3** f **4** b **5** i **6** d **7** h **8** e **9** g **Ex18** Vaata palun teleri peale. / Vaata palun diivani alla. / Võib-olla ta kukkus kapi taha?

Test yourself

1 c, **2** b, **3** a, **4** b, **5** a, **6** a, **7** c, **8** b, **9** b, **10** a.

UNIT 13

Ex1 1 Laura suggests to go somewhere to eat. **2** Janar says that the coffee shop has fast service and good prices. **3** Laura says this coffee shop, on the contrary, has very slow service, too small portions and nobody goes there. **4** Janar says that Laura should suggest a place. **5** Laura says that this place has an interesting interior and very tasty food. **6** Janar is worried that this is some kind of vegetarian restaurant. **7** Laura answers that this is not (a vegetarian restaurant). **8** Janar says that they should go there then. **Ex2 1** false, Sirje has been to this restaurant, last time she was here last week with her colleagues **2** true **3** true **4** false, Sirje says the roast chicken is very good **5** true **6** true **7** false, Sirje has not drunk the house wine in this restaurant **8** true **9** true **10** false, he will only have a cup of strong coffee **11** true **12** true **Ex3** käsitsi tehtud nukud, puust mänguasjad, punased küünlad, kollased küünlad, rohelised küünlad, ingliskeelsed eesti raamatud **Ex4 1** a **2** b **3** b **4** b **5** a **6** a **7** a **8** a **9** a **Ex5 1** a **2** b **3** b **4** b **5** a **6** a **7** a **Ex6 1** false, the client wants a stamp for regular mail (within Estonia) **2** true **3** true **4** true **5** true **6** false, there is one book in the parcel **7** false, the jiffy bag costs 10 crowns **8** true **9** true **10** false, the client sends the parcel by air mail **11** true **12** true **Ex7 1** f **2** a **3** e **4** b **5** c **6** d **Ex8 1** d **2** a **3** f **4** b **5** c **6** e **7** h **8** g **Ex9 1** Ma olen eesti keelt õppinud neli kuud. Sa oled eesti keelt õppinud neli kuud. Ta on eesti keelt õppinud neli kuud. Me oleme eesti keelt õppinud neli kuud. Te olete eesti keelt õppinud neli kuud. Nad on eesti keelt õppinud neli kuud. **2** Ma ei ole kunagi läti keelt õppinud. Sa ei ole kunagi läti keelt õppinud. Ta ei ole kunagi läti keelt õppinud. Me ei ole kunagi läti keelt õppinud. Te ei ole kunagi läti keelt õppinud. Nad ei ole kunagi läti keelt õppinud. **Ex10 I** tšekki, tšekke; trepi, treppi, treppe; blanketti, blankette **II** märki, märke; karpi, karpe; torti, torte **III** kuuse, kuuske, kuuski; vahtu, vahte **IV** lugu; loa, luba, lube; poodi, poode **Ex11 1** a **2** b **3** b **4** a **5** a **Ex12 1** b **2** a **3** a **4** b **5** a **6** a **7** b **Ex14 1** a **2** b **3** b **4** b **5** a **6** b **Ex15 1** b **2** a **3** b **4** a **5** b **6** a **Ex16 1** Mitte kuhugi **2** Mitte kuskil **3** Mitte keegi **4** Mitte midagi **5** Mitte kellegagi **6** Mitte kellelgi **7** Mitte kunagi **8** Mitte kellelegi **Ex17 1–10** Olen küll. Ei ole. **Ex18 1** b **2** a **3** b **4** a **5** b **6** a **7** b **8** a **9** b **10** a **11** b **12** a **Ex19 1** a **2** b **3** a **4** b **5** a **6** b **7** a **8** b **9** a **10** b **Ex20 1** seda mänguasja **2** seda punast küünalt **3** seda ingliskeelset raamatut **4** seda eestikeelset raamatut **5** seda suurt nukku **6** seda ilusat mänguasja; **1** neid mänguasju **2** neid punaseid küünlaid **3** neid ingliskeelseid raamatuid **4** neid eestikeelseid raamatuid **5** neid suuri nukke **6** neid ilusaid mänguasju **Ex21** Kas sa oled siin restoranis varem käinud? / Kas sa oled seda suppi proovinud? / Siis ma võtan mingi prae. Mida sina võtad? / Ma võtan ka grillitud kana ja friikartulid. / Ma eelistaksin õlut. / Ma ei ole kunagi varem eesti õlut joonud. / Ma vist praegu ei jaksa magustoitu süüa. / Jah, teeme nii. **Ex22** Tere! Kas teil on müügil mingeid käsitsi tehtud nukke? / Kas need on Eestis tehtud? / Ma võtan need kaks. / Jah. Ühe kilekoti palun ka. / Sularahas. Palun. / Kohe otsin. Palun. **Ex23** Kas te võiksite palun selle paki ära kaaluda? / Ma soovin saata selle Inglismaale. / See on CD. / Kui palju see maksab? / Kumb on kallim? / Siis võiks olla maapost. / Kas trükitähtedega? / Kaardiga.

Test yourself

1 a, **2** c, **3** b, **4** c, **5** c, **6** b, **7** b, **8** b, **9** c, **10** c.

UNIT 14

Ex1 1 false, the tourist wants to go to a bookshop **2** true **3** true **4** true **5** true **6** false, the stranger goes to town centre by trolleybuses one or two **7** true **8** false, the trolleybus goes to the city centre about half an hour **9** true **10** true **Ex2 1** a **2** a **3** a **4** b **5** b **6** a **7** a **8** a **9** a **10** b **Ex3** mänguväljak, ostukeskus, väike park **Ex4 1** a **2** a **3** a **4** b **5** a **6** a **7** a **8** b **9** b **10** a **11** a **12** b **13** b **Ex5 1** false, she wants to rent a car **2** true **3** true **4** false, it is not said in the dialogue that one year of driving experience is OK **5** true **6** true **7** true **8** false, it doesn't matter to the client what kind of gear box the car has **9** false, the client wants a bigger family car **10** true **11** false, the jeep has automatic gearbox **12** true **13** true **14** true **Ex6 1** a **2** b **3** b **4** a **5** a **6** a **7** b **8** b **9** b **Ex7 1** Sellel **2** selle suure **3** selles uues **4** uue **5** väiksema **6** väikese **7** väikesele **Sõitma, sõita, sõidan. Types of verbs I** leppida, lepin; rutata, ruttan; katta, katan **II** võita, võidan; oodata, ootan; näidata, näitan **III** mahtuda, mahun; kohata, kohtan **Ex8 I** Helistage! Ärge helistage!; Jalutage! Ärge jalutage! Mängige! Ärge mängige! **II** Oodake! Ärge oodake!; Vaadake! Ärge vaadake! Näidake! Ärge näidake! **NB!** Kandke! Ärge kandke! Tulge! Ärge tulge! Olge! Ärge olge! Jooge! Ärge jooge! Tooge! Ärge tooge! **Ex9** ilusamini, kõige ilusamini; halvemini, kõige halvemini; kõige paremini; huvitavamalt, kõige huvitavamalt; soojemalt, kõige soojemalt **Ex10 1** Mine üle tänava. **2** Mine läbi pargi. **3** Mine poest mööda. **4** Mine kuni ristmikuni. **5** Pööra vasakule. **6** Pööra paremale. **7** Mine üle silla. **8** Mine tagasi. **9** Mine poeni. **Ex11 1** a **2** b **3** b **4** a **5** b **Ex12 1** b **2** a **3** b **4** a **5** b **6** a **Ex13 1** Lugege seda raamatut! **2** Helistage mulle! **3** Pöörake paremale! **4** Vaadake siia! **5** Sõitke linna! **6** Võtke see kaart! **7** Andke mulle kaart! **8** Minge otse edasi! **9** Olge hea! **10** Tulge kohe siia! **11** Tehke kiiresti! **12** Ärge sööge seda jäätist! **13** Ärge jooge nii palju õlut! **14** Ärge oodake mind! **Ex14** Possible answers: **1** kiiremini, aeglasemalt **2** kõvemini, / vaiksemalt **3** halvemini, paremini **4** huvitavamalt, igavamalt **Ex15** Kus sa oled? / Tule üle tänava. / Ei, pööra vasakule. / Jah. Minu maja on nurga peal. **Ex16 a** Bowlingusaal on kesklinnas. **b** Sa pead sõitma kesklinna. **c** Kõige kiiremini saad (sa) bussiga. **d** Bowlingusaal on sealsamas nurga peal peaaegu bussipeatuse juures. **Ex17** 1, 3, 4, 5, 6, 9, 10, 11, 12, 13, 14 **Ex18** Tere! Ma sooviksin autot rentida. / Mul on vaja suuremat autot nädalavahetuseks. / Tegelikult on mul ükskõik. / Kas sellel on automaatkäigukast? / Kas rendihind tuleb ette maksta? / Aitäh.

Test yourself

1 c, **2** a, **3** a, **4** c, **5** c, **6** c, **7** b, **8** c, **9** b, **10** a.

Estonian–English vocabulary

aasta, -, -t, -id *year*

abielupaar, -i, -i, -e *married couple*

abikaasa, -, -t, -sid *spouse, husband*

aeg, aja, aega *time*

aeg-ajalt *now and again*

aegla/ne, -se, -st, -seid *slow*

aga *but*

ahi, ahju, ahju, ahje *stove, oven*

ainult *only*

aita/ma, aida/ta, aita/n *keda? kellel mida teha? to help*

aitäh *thank you, thanks*

ajakirjanik, -u, -ku, -ke *journalist*

aken, akna, akent, aknaid *window*

aku, -, -t, -sid *battery*

alates *starting from*

alga/ma, ala/ta, alga/b *to start*

algus, -e, -t, -i *beginning, start*

alkohool/ne, -se, -set, -seid *alcoholic*

alla vajuta/ma, alla vajuta/da, vajuta/n alla *to press down*

alles hoid/ma, alles hoid/a, hoian alles *to keep*

alles ole/ma, alles oll/a, on alles *to have (still)*

all/kiri, -kirja, -kirja, -kirju *signature*

alluv, -a, -at, -aid *employee*

alumi/ne, -se, -st, -si *lower, bottom*

amet, -i, -it, -eid *profession*

ammu *long ago*

ankeet, ankeedi, ankeeti, ankeete *form, (Am.) blank*

apteek, apteegi, apteeki, apteeke *chemists*

apteeker, apteekri, apteekrit, apteekreid *chemist*

arbuus, -i, -i, -e *watermelon*

armas, armsa, armsat, armsaid *darling, dear, cute, sweet*

armasta/ma, -da, -n *keda? mida? to love*

arst, -i, -i, -e *doctor*

aru saa/ma, aru saa/da, saa/n aru *kellest? millest? to understand*

arva/ma, -ta, -n *to guess, to think*

asjalik, -u, -ku, -ke *sensible*

asu/koht, -koha, -kohta, -kohti *location*

asu/ma, -da, -b *to be located, to be situated*

automaatkäigukast, -i, -i, -e *automatic gear box*

ava/ma, -da, -n *to open*

baaridaam, -i, -i, -e *bartender (female)*

baarman, -i, -i, -e *bartender (male), barman*

ballett, balleti, balletti, ballette *ballet*

blankett, blanketi, blanketti, blankette *form, (Am.) blank*

bowlingusaal, -i, -i, -e *bowling hall*

broneeri/ma, -da, -n *to book, to make a reservation*

broneering, -u, -ut, -uid *reservation*

buss, -i, -i, -e *bus*

bussi/juht, -juhi, -juhti, -juhte *bus driver*

bussipeatus, -e, -t, -i *bus stop*

CD-plaat, CD-plaadi, CD-plaati, CD-plaate *CD*

diivan, -i, -it, -eid *sofa*

dressi/püksid, -pükste, -pükse *trousers of sports uniform*

džiip, džiibi, džiipi, džiipe *jeep*

edasi *forward, ahead, further*

edasi ütle/ma, edasi ütel/da, ütle/n edasi *to forward a message*

eelista/ma, -da, -n *keda? mida? to prefer*

eelmi/ne, -se, -st, -seid *previous*

ees *in front of*

ees/nimi -nime, -nime, -nimesid *first name*

eesti *Estonian*

Eesti-sise/ne, -se, -st, -seid *domestic (lit. inside Estonia)*

eestla/ne, -se, -st, -si *Estonian*

ehitaja, -, -t, -id *construction worker*

ei *no, not*

eksemplar, -i, -i, -e *copy, piece*

ela/ma, -da -n *to live*

elamurajoon, -i, -i, -e *dwelling district*

elekter, elektri, elektrit *electricity*

elu/tuba, -toa, -tuba, -tube *living room*

e-mail, -i, -i, -e *e-mail*

enamik, -u, -ku, -ke *most*

eraldi *separately*

eriarst, -i, -i, -e *specialist doctor*

etendus, -e, -t, -i *play, show, performance*

ette maks/ma, ette maks/ta, maksa/n ette *to pay in advance*

ettekandja, -, -t, -id *waitress*

film, -i, -i, -e *film*

filmiklassika, -, -t *film classics*

firma, -, -t, -sid *company, business*

firma/juht, -juhi, -juhti, -juhte *director of a business*

frii/kartulid, -kartulite, -kartuleid *french fries*

fuajee, -, -d, -sid *(hotel) lobby*

föönisoeng, -u, -ut, -uid *hairdo done with the hot air blower*

gaas, -i, -i, -e *gas*

garantii/remont, -remondi, -remonti *warranty repairs*

grilli/ma, -da, -n *to roast, to broil (over fire or hot coals)*

gripp, gripi, grippi *flu*

haigekassa -, -t, -sid *(workmen's) sick-fund*

hakka/ma, haka/ta, hakka/n mida tegema? *to start*

hakkama saa/ma, hakkama saa/da, saa/n hakkama kellega? millega? *to manage*

hambaarst, -i, -i, -e *dentist*

hammas, hamba, hammast, hambaid *tooth*

hapukoor, -e, -t *sour cream, smetana*

hapu/kurk, -kurgi, -kurki, -kurke *pickled cucumber*

haridus, -e, -t *education*

harjunud ole/ma, harjunud oll/a, ole/n harjunud kellega? millega? mida tegema? *to be used to*

hea, -, -d, häid *good*

helista/ma, -da, -n kellele? *to call (on the phone), to ring*

hetk, hetke, hetke, hetki *moment*

hiljem *later*

hind, hinna, hinda, hindu *price*

hinnavahe, -, -t, -sid *price difference*

hirmsasti *terribly*

hirmus, hirmsa, hirmsat, hirmsaid *terrible, terribly*

homme *tomorrow*

hommik, -u, -ut, -uid *morning*

hommikupoole *in the morning, forenoon*

hommikust söö/ma, hommikust süü/a, söö/n hommikust *to eat breakfast*

hommiku/söök, -söögi, -sööki, -sööke *breakfast*

hotell, -i, -i, -e *hotel*

huvitav, -a, -at, -aid *interesting*

hästi *nicely, well*

iga *every*

igaks juhuks *just in case*

igasugu/ne, -se, -st, -seid *any kind of, all kind of*

ilm, -a, -a *weather*

ilma *without*

ilmselt *probably*

ilus, -a, -at, -aid *beautiful*

imelik, -u, -ku, -ke *strange*

info/leht, -lehe, -lehte, -lehti *information sheet*

infopunkt, -i, -i, -e *information desk, information office*

inglise *English*

ingliskeel/ne, -se, -set, -seid *in English (language)*

inime/ne, -se, -st, -si *person, man, human being*

interjöör, -i, -i, -e *interior*

internet, interneti, internetti *internet*

internetiühendus, -e, -t, -i *internet connection*

ise, enda, ennast *yourself*

isegi *even*

iseloom, -u, -u, -e *character, nature*

isikukood, -i, -i, -e *personal code, identification code*

istu/ma, -da, -n *to sit*

isu, -, -, -sid *appetite*

ja *and*

jaga/ma, -da, -n *to divide*

jah *yes*

jahu, -, - *flour*

jaksa/ma, -ta, -n *mida teha? to be able to*

jalg, jala, jalga, jalgu *foot, also leg*

jalga pane/ma, jalga pann/a, pane/n jalga *to wear, to put on (used for footwear and trousers)*

jalgpall, -i, -i, -e *football, (Am.) soccer*

jalg/ratas, -ratta, -ratast, -rattaid *bicycle*

jaluta/ma, -da, -n *to walk*

jook, joogi, jooki, jooke *drink, beverage*

jooks/ma, joos/ta, jookse/n *to run, to be on show*

joo/ma, juu/a, joo/n *to drink*

jope, -, -t, -sid *jacket*

juba *already, in this case*

juhend, -i, -it, -eid *instruction*

juhiluba/-load, -lubade, -lube *driving licence*

juhistaaž, -i, -i *driving experience*

juhtu/ma, -da, -b *to happen*

just *just, exactly, precisely*

juttu aja/ma, juttu aja/da, aja/n juttu *kellega? to have a chat, to talk*

juuksed, juuste, juukseid *hair*

juuksur, -i, -it, -eid *hairdresser*

juurde maks/ma, juurde maks/ta, maksa/n juurde *to pay extra*

juures *at, near*

juust, -u, -u *cheese*

järele mine/ma, järele minn/a, lähe/n järele *kellele? millele? kuhu? to fetch, to get*

järgmi/ne, -se, -st, -si *next*

järv, -e, -e, -i *lake*

jää, -, -d *ice*

ka *also, too*

kaart, kaardi, kaarti, kaarte *card, bank card*

kaasa tule/ma, kaasa tull/a, tule/n kaasa kellega? *to come along, to come with*

kaasa võt/ma, kaasa võtt/a, võta/n kaasa *to take along, to take with you*

kabinet, -i, -ti, -te *room, surgery*

kaebus, -e, -t, -i *complaint*

kaela pane/ma, kaela pann/a, pane/n kaela *to wear, to put on (used with ties and scarves)*

kaheinimese/tuba, -toa, -tuba, -tubasid *double room*

kahetoali/ne, -se, -st, -si *two room(ed) (apartment)*

kahju ole/ma, kahju oll/a, on kahju *to feel sorry*

kahjuks *unfortunately*

kaks, kahe, kaht *two*

kala, -, -, -kalu *fish*

kallis, kalli, kallist, kalleid *expensive*

kange, -, -t, -id *strong*

kapp, kapi, kappi, kappe *wardrobe, closet, cupboard*

kardinad, kardinate, kardinaid *curtains*

karp, karbi, karpi, karpe *box*

kartulisalat, -i, -it, -eid *potato salad*

kas *interrogative particle used in questions*

kass, -i, -i, -e *cat*

kassa, -, -t, -sid *ticket office*

kaste, kastme, kastet, kastmeid *sauce*

kasuta/ma, -da, -n mida? *to use*

kasv, -u, -u *height*

kasva/ma, -da, -n *to grow*

kate, katte, katet, katteid *cover*

katki mine/ma, katki minn/a, lähe/b katki *to break*

kaubanduskeskus, -e, -t, -i *department store, (Am.) mall shopping centre*

kaunis, kauni, kaunist, kauneid *beautiful*

kauplus, -e, -t, -i *shop*

kava, -, -, -sid *programme*

kavatse/ma, -da, -n mida teha? *to intend*

keel, -e, -t, -i *language*

kehtiv, -a, -at, -aid *valid*

kell, -a, -a, -i *clock*

kella/aeg, -aja, -aega, -aegu *time, time of the day*

kellena? *As who?*

kelner, -i, -it, -eid *waiter*

kena, -, -, -sid *nice, handsome*

keraamili/ne, -se, -st, -si *ceramic*

kerge, -, -t, -id *light*

kes, kelle keda *who*

keskeali/ne, -se, -st, -si *middle aged*

keskel *in the middle*

kesk/küte, -kütte, -kütet *central heating*

kesklinn, -a, -a, -u *city center*

kiire, -, -t, -id *fast*

kiiresti *quickly*

kilo, -, -, -sid *kilo*

kindad, kinnaste, kindaid *gloves*

kindlasti *for sure, certainly*

kingad, kingade, kingi *shoes*

kinki/ma, -da, kingi/n *to give (as a present)*

kinni *closed*

kinni pane/ma, kinni pann/a, pane/n kinni *to book, to close*

kinnisvaramaakler, -i, -it, -eid *real estate broker*

kino, -, -, -sid *cinema*

kipsi pane/ma, kipsi pann/a, pane/n kipsi *to put into plaster*

kiri, kirja, kirja, kirju *letter*

kirik, -u, -ut, -uid *church*

kirja pane/ma, kirja pann/a, pane/n kirja *to write down*

kirjas ole/ma, kirjas oll/a, on kirjas *to be written*

kirjuta/ma, -da, -n *to write*

kivi/maja, -maja, -maja, -maju *stone building*

klient, kliendi, klienti, kliente *client*

koer, -a, -a, -i *dog*

kogemus, -e, -t, -i *experience*

kohal ole/ma, kohal oll/a, ole/n kohal *to be present*

kohal *above*

kohale jõud/ma, kohale jõud/a, jõua/n *kohale to get to*

kohalik, -u, -ku, -ke *local (person)*

kohe *at once, immediately, now, right away*

koht, koha, kohta, kohti *place*

kohtu/ma, -da, -n *to meet*

kohupiima/pirukas, -piruka, -pirukat, -pirukaid *curd pie*

kohutav, -a, -at, -aid *terrible, horrible*

kohv, -i, -i, -e *coffee*

kohver, kohvri, kohvrit, kohvreid *suitcase*

kohvik, -u, -ut, -uid *cafe, coffee-shop*

kokku saa/ma, kokku saa/da, saa/n kokku *to meet*

kokku tegema, kokku teh/a, tee/b kokku *to make up (used when calculating numbers)*

kokku/lepe, -leppe, -lepet, -leppeid *agreement*

koli/ma, -da, -n *to move*

kolla/ne, -se, -st, -seid *yellow*

kolleeg, -i, -i, -e *colleague*

kolm, kolme kolme *three*

kolmapäev, -a, -a, -i *Wednesday*

kolmveerand, -i, -it *three quarters*

komm, -i, -i, -e *candy, sweet*

kommunaal/kulud, -kulude, -kulusid *cost of municipal services*

komöödia, -, -t, -id *comedy*

konditsioneer, -i, -i, -e *air conditioner*

konjak, -i, -it, -eid *cognac*

kontor, -i, -it, -eid *office*

konts, -a, -a, -i *heel*

kool, -i, -i, -e *school*

koos *together, united*

kord, korra, korda, kordi *order, procedure, principle, time*

korda saa/ma, korda saa/da, saa/n korda *to get fixed, to be repaired*

korda tege/ma, korda teh/a, teen/korda *to fix*

korpus, -e, -t, -i *case, body*

korraldaja, -, -t, -id *organiser*

korras *alright, OK*

korrus, -e, -t, -eid *floor, storey*

korter, -i, -it, -eid *apartment, flat*

kott, koti, kotti, kotte *bag*

kraad, -i, -i, -e *degree*

krediit/kaart, -kaardi, -kaarti, -kaarte *credit card*

kroon, -i, -i, -e *crown*

kui *if*

kui kaua? *How long?*

kui kauaks? *For how long?*

kui kõrge? *How high?*

kui palju? *How much?*

kui vana? *How old?*

kuidas? *How?*

kuigi *although*

kukku/ma, -da, kuku/n *to fall*

kumb, kumma, kumba, kumbi *which one*

kummik, -u, -ut, -uid *rubber boot*

kunagi *sometime, ever*

kuni *up to, until*

kunstimuuseum, -i, -i, -e *art museum*

kurk, kurgi, kurki, kurke *cucumber, gherkin*

kurk, kurgu, kurku, kurke *throat*

kurss, kursi, kurssi, kursse *rate*

kus? *Where?*

kuskil *somewhere, anywhere*

kutsu/ma, -da, -n *to call, to ask someone to come to the phone), to invite*

kuu, -, -d, kuid *month*

kuula/ma, -ta, -n keda? mida? *to listen to*

kuulus, kuulsa, kuulsat, kuulsaid *famous*

kuulutus, -e, -t, -i *advertisement, announcement*

kuum, -, a, -a, -i *hot*

kõht, kõhu, kõhtu *stomach*

kõigepealt *first, to start with*

kõik *all, everything, everybody*

kõla/ma, -da, -b *to sound*

kõrge, -, -t, -id *high*

kõrval *next to*

kõrvalmõju, -, -, -sid *side effect*

käi/ma, -a, -n kus? *to go to*

käsitsi *by hand*

kätte pane/ma, kätte pann/a, pane/n kätte *to wear, to put on (used for gloves)*

kätte saa/ma, kätte saa/da, saa/n kätte *to receive*

köha, -, - *cough*

köök, köögi, kööki, kööke *kitchen*

külali/ne, -se, -st, -si *visitor, guest*

külastaja, -, -t, -id *visitor*

küll *certainly, indeed, surely, well*

külla kutsu/ma, külla kutsu/da, kutsu/n külla *to invite*

külla tule/ma, külla tull/a, tule/n külla *to come to visit*

külm/kapp, -kapi, -kappi, -kappe *refrigerator*

küpseta/ma, -da, -n *to roast (in the oven), also to fry, to bake*

küpsis, -e, -t, -eid *cookie, biscuit*

küsi/ma, -da, -n *to ask*

küte, kütte, kütet *heating*

küünal, küünla, küünalt, küünlaid *candle*

laager, laagri, laagrit, laagreid *camp*

laena/ma, -ta, -n *to borrow, to lend*

lahe, -da, -dat, -daid *cool, great (slang)*

lahti tege/ma, lahti teh/a, tee/n lahti *to open*

laps, lapse, last, lapsi *child*

lapsehoidja, -, -t, -id *babysitter*

lask/ma, las/ta, lase/n *to let*

laste/aed, -aia, -aeda, -aedu *kindergarten*

lasteetendus, -e, -t, -i *children play*

laud, laua, lauda, laudu *table*

laul/ma, -da, -an *to sing*

lendur, -i, -it, -eid *pilot*

lennujaam, -a, -a, -u *airport*

lennupost, -i, -i *air mail*

leping, -u, -ut, -uid *contract*

lett, leti, letti, lette *counter*

lift, -i, -i, -e *elevator*

ligi astu/ma, ligi astu/da, astu/n ligi *to step closer*

liha/pirukas, -piruka, -pirukat, -pirukaid *meat pie*

lihtsalt *just*

liiga *too*

liiter, liitri, liitrit, liitreid *litre*

liköör, -i, -i -e *liqueur*

lips, -u, -u, -e *tie*

lisa/ma, -da, -n *to add*

lisand, -i, -it, -eid *side dish*

lisandu/ma, -da, -b *to be added*

lisatasu, -, -, -sid *extra cost*

lokkis *curly*

loom, -a, -a, -i *animal*

looma/aed, -aia, -aeda, -aedu *zoo*

loomi pida/ma, loomi pida/da, pea/n loomi *to keep animals*

loomulikult *naturally*

luge/ma, -da, loen *to read*

luik, luige, luike, luiki *swan*

lukus *locked*

luu/murd, -murru, -murdu, -murde *fracture (of bone)*

lõbus, -, -at, -aid *funny*

lõika/ma, lõiga/ta, lõika/n *to cut*

läbi *through*

läbi luge/ma, läbi luge/da, loe/n läbi *to read through*

läbi vaata/ma, läbi vaada/ta, vaata/n läbi *to examine*

lähedal *nearby, close to*

lähim, -a, -at, -aid *the closest*

lühidalt *a little bit (lit. shortly)*

ma (mina), mu (minu), mind *I*

maakler, -i, -it, -eid *(real estate) broker*

maali/laager, -laagri, -laagrit, -laagreid *hobby-painter's camp*

maali/ma, -da, -n *to paint*

maan/tee, -tee, -teed, -teid *road, highway*

maapost, -i, -i *regular mail*

maas *on the floor (lit. on the ground)*

maasikas, maasika, maasikat, maasikaid *strawberry*

magama mine/ma, magama minn/a, lähe/n magama *to go to sleep*

magamis/tuba, -toa, -tuba, -tube *bedroom*

magus, -a, -at, -aid *sweet*

magus/toit, -toidu, -toitu, -toite *dessert*

maitse, -, -t, -id *taste*

maitsekalt *tastefully, with taste*

maitsev, maitsva, maitsvat, maitsvaid *tasty*

maits/ma, -ta, -en *to taste*

maja, -, -, -maju *house, building*

majavein, -i, -i, -e *house wine*

maks/ma, -ta, -an *to cost, to pay*

male, -, -t *chess*

mantel, mantli, mantlit, mantleid *overcoat, coat*

mari, marja, marja, marju *berry*

mark, margi, marki, marke *stamp*

masin, -a, -at, -aid *machine, car*

me (meie), me (meie), meid *we*

meelde tule/ma, meelde tull/a, tule/b meelde *to remember*

meeldiv, -a, -at, -aid *pleasant*

mees, mehe, meest, mehi *man, husband*

meie (me), meie, meid *we*

mets, -a, -a, -i *forest*

mida? *What?*

midagi *something, anything*

mikrolaine/ahi, -ahju, -ahju, -ahje *microwave oven*

miks? *Why?*

millal? *When?*

milli/ne, -se, -st, -seid *what kind of*

mina (ma), minu, mind *I*

mine/ma, minn/a, lähe/n kuhu? kust? *to go*

mineraal/vesi, -vee, -vett *mineral water*

mingi, mingi, mingit, mingeid *some kind of*

minibaar, -i, -i, -e *small bar at the hotel room*

minu jaoks *for me*

mis, mille, mida *what*

miss, -i, -i, -e *miss*

mitmekesi? *How many of you together?*

mitte keegi, mitte kellegi, mitte kedagi *nobody*

mobiil, -i, -i, -e *mobile phone*

mobiiltelefon, -i, -i, -e *cell phone*

moos, -i, -i, -e *jam*

muide *by the way*

muidu *otherwise*

muidugi *of course*

multikas, multika, multikat, multikaid *cartoon*

muna, -, -, mune *egg*

muretse/ma, -da, -n kelle pärast? mille pärast? *to worry*

musi, -, -, -sid *kiss, peck*

must, -a, -a, -i *black, also dirty*

muu, muu, muud, muid *else, other*

muusik, -u, -ut, -uid *musician*

muusika, -, -t *music*

muusikakeskus, -e, -t, -i *stereo system*

mõlemad, mõlemate, mõlemaid *both*

mõni, mõne, mõnd, mõnesid *some*

mõnikord *sometimes*

mõte, mõtte, mõtet, mõtteid *idea, thought*

mõtle/ma, mõtel/da (mõel/da), mõtle/n *to think*

mäleta/ma, -da, -n *to remember*

mängi/ma, -da, -n mida? *to play, to act*

mängu/asi, -asja, -asja, -asju *toy*

mänguväljak, -u, -ut, -uid *playground*

märg, märja, märga, märgi *wet*

märjaks tege/ma, märjaks teh/a, tee/n märjaks *to make wet*

märulifilm, -i, -i, -e *action film*

mööbel, mööbli, mööblit *furniture*

mööda *along, by, also: past*

müts, -i, -i, -e *hat*

müüja, -, -t, -id *shop assistant, seller, salesman/ saleswoman*

müü/ma, -a, -n *to sell*

naaber, naabri, naabrit, naabreid *neighbour*

nad (nemad), nende, neid *they*

nai/ne, -se, -st, -si *woman*

naljakas, naljaka, naljakat, naljakaid *funny*

natuke(ne) *a little*

need, nende, neid *these*

neiu, -, -t, -sid *young lady, girl*

nemad (nad), nende, neid *they*

nii *so, OK*

niimoodi *this way, so*

niisama *just so*

niisugu/ne, -se, -st, -seid *this kind*

nimi, nime, nime, nimesid *name*

nohu, -, - *cold, the snuffles*

noor/mees -mehe, -meest, -mehi *young man*

normaalselt *OK (lit. normally)*

nukk, nuku, nukku, nukke *doll*

number, numbri, numbrit, numbreid *number*

nupp, nupu, nuppu, nuppe *switch, button*

nurk, nurga, nurka, nurki *corner*

nõrk, nõrga, nõrka, nõrku *weak*

nõud, nõude, nõusid *dishes*

nõudepesumasin, -a, -at, -aid *dishwasher*

nädal, -a, -at, -aid *last week*

nädalavahetus, -e, -t, -i *weekend*

näge/ma, näh/a, näe/n *to see*

näita/ma, näida/ta, näita/n keda? mida? *to show*

näitleja, -, -t, -id *actor, actress*

nüüd *now*

odav, -a, -at, -aid *cheap*

ohtlik, -u, -ku, -ke *dangerous*

ole/ma, oll/a, ole/n *to be*

oma, -, - *one's own*

omanik, -u, -ku, -ke *owner*

omlett, omleti, omletti, omlette *omelette*

oota/ma, ooda/ta, oota/n *to wait*

osa, , -, -, osi *part*

oska/ma, osa/ta, oska/n mida teha? *to know, can*

ostja, -, -t, -id *buyer*

ost/ma, -a, -an *to buy*

ostukeskus, -e, -t, -i *shopping centre, (Am.) mall*

ostu/tšekk, -tšeki, -tšekki, -tšekke *receipt*

otse *straight*

otsusta/ma, -da, -n *to decide*

paber, -i, -it, -eid *paper, document*

paha, -, -, -sid *bad, uncomfortable*

paistesse mine/ma, paistesse minn/a, lähe/b paistesse *to swell up*

paist/ma, paist/a, paista/b *to be seen, to be visible*

pakend, -i, -it, -eid *package, wrapper*

pakki/ma, -da, paki/n *to pack*

palavik, -u, -ku *fever*

palun *please*

paneel/maja, -maja, -maja, -maju *building of (concrete) elements*

pane/ma, pann/a, pane/n *to give, to put, to pour*

paremale *to the right*

paremat kätt *on the right hand*

park, pargi, parki, parke *park*

parki/ma, -da, pargin *to park*

parkimis/koht, -koha, -kohta, -kohti *parking spot*

pass, -i, -i, -e *passport*

pastakas, pastaka, pastakat, pastakaid *ballpoint pen*

pats, -i, -i, -e *braid*

patsient, patsiendi, patsienti, patsiente *patient*

pea, -, -d, päid *head*

peaaegu *almost*

peatus, -e, -t, -i *stop*

pehme, -, -t, -id *soft*

pensionär, -i, -i, -e *senior citizen, retired person*

pere, -, -t, -sid *family*

perearst, -l, -l, -e *general practitioner, GP*

pereauto, -, -t, -sid *family car*

perekonna/nimi, -nime, -nime, nimesid *surname*

pese/ma, pes/ta, pese/n *wash*

pesumasin, -a, -at, -aid *washing machine*

pida/ma, -da, pea/n *must, have to, should*

piisa/ma, -ta, -b *to be enough*

pikali heit/ma, pikali heit/a, heida/n pikali *to lay down*

pikk, pika, pikka, pikki *long*

pildista/ma, -da, -n keda? mida? *to take photos*

pilt, pildi, pilti, pilte *picture*

pingeli/ne, -se, -st, -si *intense*

pipar, pipra, pipart *pepper*

pirukas, piruka, pirukat, pirukaid *small pie, pasty*

pistik, -u, -ut, -uid *outlet*

planeet, planeedi, planeeti, planeete *planet*

pliit, pliidi, pliiti, pliite *stove, oven*

ploom, -i, -i, -e *plum*

pluus, -i, -i, -e *blouse*

poeg, poja, poega, poegi *son*

pole = ei ole *negative of the word olema*

pool, -e, -t, -i *side; half*

poolteist *one and a half*

portsjon, -i, -it, -eid *ration*

praad, prae, praadi, praade *roast meat, also: main course*

praadi/ma, -da, prae/n *to fry*

praegu *at the moment*

prantsuse *French*

probleem, -i, -i, -e *problem*

proovi/ma, -da, -n mida? mida teha? *to try*

pruut, pruudi, pruuti, pruute *girlfriend, fiancée*

psühholoog, -i, -i, -e *psychologist*

puhka/ma, puha/ta, puhka/n *to rest*

puhul *in the case of*

punakas, punaka, punakat, punakaid *reddish*

puu/maja, -maja, -maja, -maju *wooden house, building*

puu/vili, -vilja, -vilja, -vilju *fruit*

põhimõtteliselt *in principle*

põnev, -a, -at, -aid *exiting, interesting*

põuetasku, -, -t, -id *breast pocket*

päev, -a, -a, -i *day*

pähe pane/ma, pähe pann/a, pane/n pähe *to wear, to put on (used for hats)*

pärast *after, later, afterwards; because*

pärit ole/ma, pärit oll/a, ole/n pärit kust? *to be from somewhere*

pööra/ma, -ta, -n *to turn*

pöördu/ma, -da, -n kelle poole? *to turn to, talk to*

püha, -, -, -sid *holiday*

püüd/ma, püüd/a, püüa/n mida teha? *to try to*

raamat, -u, -ut, -uid *book*

raamatukauplus, -e, -t, -i *bookstore*

raamatupidaja, -, -t, -id *bookkeeper, accountant*

rada, raja, rada, radu *track (in a bowling hall)*

raha, -, - *money*

rahulik, -u, -ku, -ke *peaceful, quiet*

rahvusvaheli/ne, -se, -st, -si *international*

reede, -, -t, -id *Friday*

reisi/ma, -da, -n *to travel*

rendi/hind, -hinna, -hinda, -hindu *renting price*

renti/ma, -da, -n *to rent*

režissöör, -i, -i, -e *director (of a film)*

retsept, -i, -i, -e *prescription*

rida, rea, rida, ridu *row*

riietu/ma, -da, -n *to dress*

riiklik, -u, -ku, -ke *of the state*

riiul, -i, -it, -eid *shelf*

ristmik, -u, -ku, -ke *crossing*

rohi, rohu, rohtu, rohtusid *medicine, drug*

rosinad, rosinate, rosinaid *raisin*

rull/uisud, -uiskude, -uiske *roller skates*

rõdu, -, -, -sid *balcony*

rõõsk koor, rõõsa koore, rõõska koort *cream*

rääki/ma, -da, räägi/n kellega? millest? kellest? *to tell, speak*

röntgen, -i, -it, -eid *x-ray*

sa (sina), su (sinu), sind *you (singular)*

saaja, -, -t, -id *receiver*

saal, -i, -i, -e *hall*

saa/ma, -da, -n *can; to get, to get to*

saate/kiri, -kirja, -kirja, -kirju *referral*

saatja, -, -t, -id *sender*

saat/ma, saat/a, saad/an *to send*

sada, saja, sada, sadu *hundred*

sadam, -a, -at, -aid *harbor*

sahtel, sahtli, sahtlit, sahtleid *draw*

saksa *German*

sale, -da, -dat, -daid *slim, slender*

sama, -, -, samu *same*

saun, -a, -a, -u *sauna*

seal *there*

sealiha, -, - *pork*

sealpool *in that direction*

sealsamas *at the very same place, just there*

seanss, seansi, seanssi, seansse *show (in the cinema)*

see, selle, seda *it, this*

seejärel *after that*

seekord *this time*

seelik, -u, -ut, -uid *skirt*

seen, -e, -t, -i *mushroom*

seene/pirukas, -piruka, -pirukat, -pirukaid
mushroom pie

sees *inside*

sega/ma, -da, -n keda? mida? *to disturb, to mix*

seiklus, -e, -t, -i *adventure*

seis/ma, seis/ta, seis/an *to stand, to wait*

sekretär, -i, -i, -e *secretary*

selga pane/ma, selga pann/a, pane/n selga *to
wear, to put on*

selge *OK, clear*

seljas ole/ma, seljas oll/a, on seljas *to wear,
to have on (used for shirts, blouses, coats,
jackets etc.)*

selli/ne, -se, -st, -seid *this kind*

sibul, -a, -at, -aid *onion*

sidrun, -i, -it, -eid *lemon*

siin *here*

siis *then, in this case*

sina (sa), sinu (su), sind *you (singular)*

sink, singi, sinki *ham*

sisse lülita/ma, sisse lülita/da, lülita/n sisse *to
switch on*

sisse tule/ma, sisse tull/a, tule/n sisse *to come in*

sissepääs, -u, -u, -e *entrance*

sobi/ma, -da, -b kellele? millega? millega? *to suit*

soeng, -u, -ut, -uid *hairdo*

sokk, soki, sokki, sokke *sock*

sood/ne, -sa, -sat, said *bargain, cheap, good*

soola/ne, -se, -st, -seid *salty*

soovi/ma, -da, -n mida? mida teha? *to wish*

soovita/ma, -da, -n mida? kellel mida teha? *to
suggest*

sort, sordi, sorti, sorte *sort, type*

spordiväljak, -u, -ut, -uid *sports ground*

sport, spordi, sporti *sports*

sportla/ne, -se, -st, -si *sportsman*

sportlik, -u, -ku, -ke *athletic*

suhtle/ma, suhel/da, suhtle/n kellega? *to
communicate*

suitseta/ma, -da, -n *to smoke*

sularaha, -, - *cash*

sussid, susside, susse *slippers*

suu, -, -d, suid *mouth*

suur, -e, -t, -i *big*

suurepära/ne, -se, -st, -seid *excellent*

sõber, sõbra, sõpra, sõpru *friend*

sõit/ma, sõit/a, sõid/an *to drive, to go*

sõlmi/ma, -da, -n *to conclude (a contract)*

sõltu/ma, -da, -b kellest? millest? *to depend*

sõstar, sõstra, sõstart, sõstraid *currant*

söök, söögi, sööki, sööke *meal*

söö/ma, süü/a, söö/n *to eat*

süle/arvuti, -arvuti, -arvutit, -arvuteid *laptop
(computer)*

süst, -i, -i, -e *injection*

süüa tege/ma, süüa teh/a, tee/n süüa *to cook
(food)*

šokolaadikomm, -i, -i, -e *chocolate candy*

ta (tema), ta (tema), teda *he, she*

tablett, tableti, tabletti, tabette *tablet, pill*

taga *behind*

tagasi and/ma, tagasi and/a, anna/n tagasi *to
give back*

tagasi mine/ma, tagasi minn/a, lähe/n tagasi *to
go back*

tagasi too/ma, tagasi tuu/a, too/n tagasi *to
bring back*

tagasi tule/ma, tagasi tull/a, tule/n tagasi *to come back*

tagasta/ma, -da, -n *to return, to bring back*

taht/ma, taht/a, taha/n keda? mida? *to want, to wish*

taimetoitla/ne, -se, -st, -si *vegetarian*

tai/ne, -se, -st, -seid *lean*

takso, -, -t, -sid *taxi*

takso/juht, -juhi, -juhti, -juhte *taxi driver*

taksopeatus, -e, -t, -i *taxi stop*

tantsi/ma, -da, -n *to dance*

tark, targa, tarka, tarku *smart, clever*

tasku, -, -t, -id *pocket*

tasuli/ne, -se, -st, -si *paid*

tasuta *free of charge*

te (teie), te (teie), teid *you (plural)*

tead/ma, tead/a, tea/n *to know*

tee, -, -d, -sid *tea, road*

teenindaja, -, -t, -id *tender, attendant*

teenindus, -e, -t *service*

teepool, -e, -t, -i *side of the road*

tegele/ma, -da, -n kellega? millega? *to practise*

tege/ma, teh/a, tee/n *to do; to make*

teie (te), teie (te), teid *you (plural)*

tei/ne, -se, -st, -si *other, second*

teisipäev, -a, -a, -i *Tuesday*

telekas, teleka, telekat, telekaid *TV (slang)*

teler, -i, -it, -eid *TV (set)*

tellimi/ne, -se, -st, -si *ordering*

tema (ta), tema (ta), teda *he, she*

tere *hello*

tere tulemast *welcome*

terve, -, -t, -id *healthy, well*

tervis, -e, -t *health*

tingi/ma, -da, -n *to bargain*

tingimus, -e, -t, -i *condition*

tohti/ma, tohti/da, tohi/n *to be allowed to*

toimu/ma, -da, -b *to take place*

too/ma, tuu/a, too/n *to bring*

toon, -i, -i, -e *tone*

tore, -da, -dat, -daid *pleasant, nice*

torn, -i, -i, -e *tower*

traadita *wireless*

tramm, -i, -i, -e *tram*

trenn, -i, -i, -e *training, workout (for sports)*

trepi/koda, -koja, -koda, -kodasid *stair well, entrance hall*

trepp, trepi, treppi, treppe *stairs*

troll, -i, -i, -e *trolleybus*

trüki/täht, -tähe, -tähte, -tähti *block letter*

tšekk, tšeki, tšekki, tšekke *receipt*

tualett, tualeti, tualeti, tualette *toilet, WC*

tuba, toa, tuba, tube *room*

tubli, -, -t, -sid *doing well, good man (lit. untranslatable as one word)*

tugev, -a, -at, -aid *strong*

tule/ma, tull/a, tule/n kust? kuhu? *to come*

tume, -da, -dat, -daid *dark*

tund, tunni, tundi, tunde *hour*

tundu/ma, -da, -b *to seem*

turist, -i, -i, -e *tourist*

turva/iste, -istme, -istet, -istmeid *safety seat (for babies)*

turvaümbrik, -u, -ut, -uid *jiffy bag*

tuttavaks saa/ma, tuttavaks saa/da, saa/n tuttavaks *to get acquainted*

tõesti *really*

tõsi/ne, -se, -st, -seid *serious*

tõttu *because of*

tähenda/ma, -da, -b mida? *to mean*

täit/ma, täit/a, täid/an *to fill in*

täna *today*

täna/ne, -se, -st, -seid *today's*

tänav, -a, -at, -aid *street*

täpselt *exactly*

tööle asu/ma, tööle asu/da, asu/n tööle *to start work*

tööta/ma, tööta/da, tööta/n *to work*

tühi, tühja, tühja, tühje *empty*

tühjaks saa/ma, tühjaks saa/da, saa/b tühjaks *to empty, to run flat*

tütar, tütre, tütart, tütreid *daughter*

u (umbes) *about*

ujula, -, -t, -id *swimming pool*

uju/ma, -da, -n *to swim*

uks, ukse, ust, uksi *door*
ulmefilm, -i, -i, -e *science fiction film*
umbes *about*
unusta/ma, -da, -n *to forget*
usku/ma, -da, usu/n keda? mida? *to believe*
uudised, uudiste, uudiseid *news*
uuesti *again*

v.a (välja arvatud) *except*
vaade, vaate, vaadet, vaateid *view*
vaarikas, vaarika, vaarikat, vaarikaid *raspberry*
vaata/ma, vaada/ta, vaata/n *to watch*
vaba, vaba, vaba, vabu *free*
vabanda/ma, -da, -n *to apologize*
vabandust *sorry*
vabasta/ma, -da, -n *to release, to free*
vahel *sometimes; between*
vaheta/ma, -da, -n *to exchange*
vaimukas, vaimuka, vaimukat, vaimukaid *witty*
vaip, vaiba, vaipa, vaipu *carpet*
vaja ole/ma, vaja oll/a, on vaja *to be needed*
vala/ma, -da, -n *to pour*
valamu, -, -t, -id *sink*
vale, -, -t, -sid *wrong*
valeta/ma, -da, -n *to lie*
valeühendus, -e, -t, -i *wrong number, (lit. false connection)*
vali/ma, -da, -n *to choose*
valimi/ne, -se, -st, -si *election, selection*
valjult *loud*
valmis *ready*
valmis olema, valmis oll/a, ole/n valmis *to be ready*
valmis saa/ma, valmis saa/da, saa/n valmis *to get ready*
valmista/ma, -da, -n *to prepare*
valus, -s, -at, -aid *painful*
valuta/ma, -da, -b *to ache*
valuvaigistav, -a, -at, -aid *analgesic*
valu/vaigisti, -vaigisti, -vaigistit, -vaigisteid *analgesic, painkiller*
vanaisa, -, -, -sid *grandfather*
vanemad, vanemate, vanemaid *parents*

vanni/tuba, -toa, -tuba, -tube *bathroom*
vara/ne, -se, -st, -seid *earlier*
varem *before, earlier*
vasakul *on the left*
vastu ole/ma, vastu oll/a, ole/n vastu *to be against (something)*
vastu tule/ma, vastu tull/a, tule/n vastu *to come to meet*
vastupidi *on the contrary*
veel *also*
veerand, -i, -it *quarter*
vend, venna, venda, vendi *brother*
venela/ne, -se, -st, -si *Russian*
viga ole/ma, viga oll/a, on viga *to be wrong*
vihka/ma, viha/ta, vihka/n keda? mida? *to hate*
viimati *last time*
viina/mari, -marja, -marja, -marju *grape*
villa/ne, -se, -st, -seid *woollen*
vist *probably, perhaps*
voodi, voodi, voodit, voodeid *bed*
või *or, also butter*
võib-olla *maybe*
või/ma, -da, -n mida teha ? *can, to be allowed to*
võimalik, -u, -ku, -ke *possible*
võrk, võrgu, võrku, võrke *net*
võti, võtme, võtit, võtmeid *key*
võt/ma, võtt/a, võta/n *to take, get, to buy*
võõras, võõra, võõrast, võõraid *stranger*
väga *very*
väike(ne), väikese, väikest, väikseid *small*
välismaala/ne, -se, -st, -si *foreigner*
välja näge/ma, välja näh/a, näe/n välja *to look*
välja tõmb/ama, välja tõmma/ta, tõmba/n välja *to pull out*
välja vaheta/ma, välja vaheta/da, vaheta/n välja *to exchange*
välja vali/ma, välja vali/da, vali/n välja *to select*
välja vääna/ma, välja vääna/ta, vääna/n välja *to sprain*
väljapääs, -u, -u, -e *exit*
väljas *outside*
värske, -, -t, -id *fresh*

värvili/ne, -se, -st, -si colourful
värvi/ma, -da, -n to colour

WC, -, -d, -sid toilet, WC

õde, õe, õde, õdesid nurse
õhtu, -, -t, -id evening
õhtupoole in the evening
õhtu/söök, -söögi, -sööki, -sööke supper, dinner
õhupall, -i, -i, -e balloon
õli, -, - oil
õlu, õlle, õlut beer
õmble/ma, õmmel/da, õmble/n to sew
õpetaja, -, -t, -id teacher
õpila/ne, -se, -st, -si student
õud/ne, -se, -set, -seid horrifying
õun, -a, -a, -u apple

äkki suddenly, also maybe
ära jää/ma, ära jää/da, jää/b ära to be cancelled
ära kaalu/ma, ära kaalu/da, kaalu/n ära to weigh
ära kaota/ma, ära kaota/da, kaota/n ära to lose
ära lõhku/ma, ära lõhku/da, lõhu/n ära to break
ära pakki/ma, ära pakki/da, paki/n ära to wrap up, to pack
ära paranda/ma, ära paranda/da, paranda/n ära to fix
ära parane/ma, ära parane/da, parane/b ära to heal
ära söö/ma, ära süü/a, söö/n ära to eat up
ära tund/ma, ära tund/a, tunne/n ära to recognize
ära viska/ma, ära visa/ta, viska/n ära to throw away

ära võt/ma, ära võt/ta, võta/n ära to take off
äri/mees, -mehe, -meest, -mehi businessman
ärka/ma, ärga/ta, ärka/n to wake up

öö, -, -d, öid night
ööklubi, -, -, -sid night club
öörahu, -, - night's rest

üheinimese/tuba, -toa, -tuba, -tubasid single room
üheksakorruseli/ne, -se, -st, -si nine storey (house)
ühenda/ma, -da, -n to connect
üks, ühe, üht one
üksik, -u, -ut, -uid single
ükskõik all the same
üld/pind, -pinna, pinda overall size
üle across, over
üle vaata/ma, üle vaada/ta, vaata/n üle to have a look, to inspect
ülemus, -e, -t, -i employer, boss
üles leid/ma, üles leid/a, leia/n üles to find
ülikool, -i, -i, -e university
ümber paiguta/ma, ümber paiguta/da, paiguta/n ümber to rearrange
ümber pööra/ma, ümber pööra/ta, pööra/n ümber to turn around
ümbrus, -e, -t surroundings
üsna quite
ütle/ma, ütel/da (öel/da), ütle/n to say, tell
üür, -i, -i rent
üürile and/ma, üürile and/a, anna/n üürile to rent

English–Estonian vocabulary

[interrogative particle used in questions] **kas**

a little **natuke(ne)**

a little bit (lit. shortly) **lühidalt**

about **u (umbes)**

about **umbes**

above **kohal**

academy of music **muusikaakadeemia, -, -t, -id**

ache (verb) **valuta/ma, -da, -b**

across, over **üle**

action film **märulifilm, -i, -i, -e**

actor, actress **näitleja, -, -t, -id**

add **lisa/ma, -da, -n**

adventure **seiklus, -e, -t, -i**

advertisement, announcement **kuulutus, -e, -t, -i**

after that **seejärel**

after, later, afterwards; because **pärast**

again **uuesti**

agency **agentuur, -i, -i, -e**

agreement **kokku/lepe, -leppe, -lepet, -leppeid**

air conditioner **konditsioneer, -i, -i, -e**

airmail **lennupost, -i, -i**

airport **lennu/jaam, -a, -a, -u**

alcoholic **alkohool/ne, -se, -set, -seid**

all the same **ükskõik**

all, everything, everybody **kõik**

almost **peaaegu**

along, by (also past) **mööda**

already, in this case **juba**

all right, OK **korras**

also **veel**

also, too **ka**

although **kuigi**

although **olgugi et**

although **ehkki**

analgesic **valuvaigistav, -a, -at, -aid**

analgesic, painkiller **valu/vaigisti, -, -t, -vaigisteid**

and **ja**

animal **loom, -a, -a, -i**

anniversary **aastapäev, -a, -a, -i**

anthem **hümn, -i, -i, -e**

any kind of, all kinds of **igasugu/ne, -se, -st, -seid**

apartment, flat **korter, -i, -it, -eid**

apologize **vabanda/ma, -da, -n**

appetite **isu, -, -, -sid**

apple **õun, -a, -a, -u**

army parade **sõjaväeparaad, -i, -i, -e**

art museum **kunsti/muuseum, -i, -i, -e**

as who? **kellena?**

ask **küsi/ma, -da, -n**

at first, provisionally **esialgu**

at once, immediately, now, **kohe**

right away at the moment **praegu**

at the place **kohapeal**

at the very same place, just there **sealsamas**

at, near **juures**

athletic **sportlik, -u, -ku, -ke**

automatic gearbox **automaatkäigukast, -i, -i, -e**

babysitter **lapsehoidja, -, -t, -id**

babysitting **lapsehoidmi/ne, -se, st**

bad, uncomfortable **paha, -, -, -sid**

bag **kott, koti, kotti, kotte**

balcony **rõdu, -, -, -sid**

ballet **ballett, balleti, balletti, ballette**

balloon **õhupall, -i, -i, -e**

ball-point pen **pastakas, pastaka, pastakat, pastakaid**

band **bänd, -i, -i, -e**

bartender (female) **baaridaam, -i, -i, -e**

bartender (male), barman **baarman, -i, -i, -e**

bargain (verb) **tingi/ma, -da, -n**

bargain, cheap, good **sood/ne, -sa, -sat, said**

bathroom **vanni/tuba, -toa, -tuba, -tube**

battery **aku, -, -t, -sid**

be **ole/ma, oll/a, ole/n**

be able to **jaksa/ma, -ta, -n mida teha?**

be added **lisandu/ma, -da, -b**

be against (something) **vastu ole/ma, vastu oll/a, ole/n vastu**

be allowed to **tohti/ma, tohti/da, tohi/n**

be cancelled **ära jää/ma, ära jää/da, jää/b ära**

be enough **piisa/ma, -ta, -b**

be from somewhere **pärit ole/ma, olla pärit, ole/n pärit kust?**

be located, be situated **asu/ma, -da, -b**

be needed **vaja ole/ma, vaja oll/a, on vaja**

be present **kohal ole/ma, kohal oll/a, ole/n kohal**

be ready **valmis olema, valmis oll/a, ole/n valmis**

be seen, be visible **paist/ma, paist/a, paista/b**

be used to **harjunud ole/ma, harjunud oll/a,**

be written **kirjas ole/ma, kirjas oll/a, on kirjas**

be wrong **viga ole/ma, viga oll/a, on viga**

beautiful **ilus, -a, -at, -aid**

beautiful **kaunis, kauni, kaunist, kauneid**

because **of tõttu**

bed **voodi, voodi, voodit, voodeid**

bedroom **magamis/tuba, -toa, -tuba, -tube**

beer **õlu, õlle, õlut**

before, earlier **varem**

beginning, start **algus, -e, -t, -eid**

behind **taga**

believe **usku/ma, usku/da, usu/n keda? mida?**

berry **mari, marja, marja, marju**

bicycle **jalg/ratas, -ratta, -ratast, -rattaid**

big **suur, -e, -t, -i**

big festive pastry **kringel, kringli, kringlit, kringleid**

black (also dirty) **must, -a, -a, -i**

block letter **trüki/täht, -tähe, -tähte, -tähti**

blouse **pluus, -i, -i, -e**

boil (verb) **keetma, keeta, keedan**

book **raamat, -u, -ut, -uid**

book, close **kinni pane/ma, pann/a, pane/n kinni**

book, make a reservation **broneeri/ma, -da, -n**

bookkeeper, accountant **raamatupidaja, -, -t, -id**

bookstore **raamatukauplus, -e, -t, -i**

borrow, lend **laena/ma, -ta, -n**

both **mõlemad, mõlemate, mõlemaid**

bowl **kauss, kausi, kaussi, kausse**

bowling hall **bowlingu/saal, -i, -i, -e**

box **karp, karbi, karpi, karpe**

braid **pats, -i, -i, -e**

brass band (orchestra) **puhkpilli/orkester, -orkestri, -orkestrit, -orkestreid**

break (verb) **ära lõhku/ma, ära lõhku/da, lõhu/n ära**

break (verb) **katki minema, katki minn/a, lähe/b katki**

breakfast **hommiku/söök, -söögi, -sööki, -sööke**

breast pocket **põue/tasku, -, -t, -id**

bring **too/ma, tuu/a, too/n**

bring back **tagasi too/ma, tuu/a, too/n tagasi**

broadcast **üle/kanne, -kande, -kannet, -kandeid**

brother **vend, venna, venda, vendi**

building of (concrete) **elements paneel/maja, -maja, -maja, -maju**

bus **buss, -i, -i, -e**

busdriver **bussi/juht, -juhi, -juhti, -juhte**

bus stop **bussipeatus, -e, -t, -i**

businessman **äri/mees, -mehe, -meest, -mehi**

but **aga**

buy **ost/ma, -a, -an**

buyer **ostja, -, -t, -id**

by hand **käsitsi**

by hand **kättpidi**

by the way **muide**

café, coffee shop **kohvik, -u, -ut, -uid**

call (on the phone), ring **helista/ma, helista/da, helista/n kellele?**

call, ask someone (to come **kutsu/ma, kutsu/da, kutsu/n** *to the phone), invite*

camp **laager, laagri, laagrit, laagreid**

can, be allowed to **või/ma, -da, -n mida teha?**

can; get, get to **saa/ma, -da, -n**

candle **küünal, küünla, küünalt, küünlaid**

candy, sweet **komm, -i, -i, -e**

card, bank card **kaart, kaardi, kaarti, kaarte**

cardamom **kardemon, -i, -i**

carpet **vaip, vaiba, vaipa, vaipu**

cartoon **multikas, mutika, multikat, multikaid**

case, body **korpus, -e, -t, -i**

cash **sularaha, -, -**

cat kass, -i, -i, -e

CD CD-plaat, CD-plaadi, CD-plaati, CD-plaate

celebrate tähista/ma, -da, -n mida?

cell phone mobiiltelefon, -i, -i, -e

central heating kesk/küte, -kütte, -kütet

ceramic keraamili/ne, -se, -st, -si

certainly, indeed, surely, well küll

certificate tunnistus, -e, -t, -i

character, nature iseloom, -u, -u, -e

cheap odav, -a, -at, -aid

cheese juust, -u, -u

chemist apteeker, apteekri, apteekrit,
    apteekreid

chemist's apteek, apteegi, apteeki, apteeke

chess male, -, -t

child laps, lapse, last, lapsi

children play lasteetendus, -e, -t, -i

chocolate candy šokolaadikomm, -i, -i, -e

choose vali/ma, -da, -n

chop (verb) hakki/ma, hakki/da, haki/n

church kirik, -u, -ut, -uid

cinema kino, -, -, -sid

cinnamon kaneel, -i, -i

city centre kesk/linn, -a, -a, -u

client klient, kliendi, klienti, kliente

clock kell, -, -, -i

closed kinni

closest (the) lähim, -a, -at, -aid

cocoa powder kakao/pulber, -pulbri, -pulbrit

coffee kohv, -i, -i, -e

cognac konjak, -i, -it, -eid

cold, the snuffles nohu, -, -

colleague kolleeg, -i, -i, -e

colour (verb) värvi/ma, -da, -n

colourful värvili/ne, -se, -st, -si

come tule/ma, tull/a, tule/n kust? kuhu?

come along, come with kaasa tule/ma, kaasa
    tull/a, tule/n kaasa kellega?

come back tagasi tule/ma, tull/a, tule/n tagasi

come in sisse tule/ma, sisse tull/a, tule/n sisse

come to meet vastu tule/ma, vastu tull/a, tule/n
    vastu

come to visit külla tule/ma, külla tull/a, tule/n
    külla

comedy komöödia, -, -t, -id

communicate suhtle/ma, suhel/da, suhtle/n
    kellega?

company, business firma, -, -t, -sid

complaint kaebus, -e, -t, -i

conclude (a contract) sõlmi/ma, -da, -n

condition tingimus, -e, -t, -i

connect ühenda/ma, -da, -n

construction worker ehitaja, -, -t, -id

contract leping, -u, -ut, -uid

cook (food) süüa tege/ma, süüa teh/a, tee/n süüa

cookie, biscuit küpsis, -e, -t, -eid

cool (verb) jahtu/ma, -da, -b

cool, great (slang) lahe, -da, -dat, -daid

copy, piece eksemplar, -i, -i, -e

corner nurk, nurga, nurka, nurki

cost of municipal services kommunaal/kulud,
    kulude, kulusid

cost, pay maks/ma, -ta, -an

cough köha, -, -

counter lett, leti, letti, lette

cover kate, katte, katet, katteid

cream rõõsk koor, rõõsa koore, rõõska koort

cream filling kreem, -i, -i, -e

credit card krediit/kaart, -kaardi, -kaarti, -kaarte

crossing ristmik, -u, -ku, -ke

crown kroon, -i, -i, -e

crush purusta/ma, -da, -n

cube kuubik, -u, -ut, -uid

cucumber, gherkin kurk, kurgi, kurki, kurke

curd pie kohupiima/pirukas, -piruka, -pirukat,
    -pirukaid

curly lokkis

currant sõstar, sõstra, sõstart, sõstraid

curriculum vitae elu/lugu, -loo, -lugu, -lugusid

curtains kardinad, kardinate, kardinaid

customer klient, kliendi, klienti, kliente

cut (verb) lõika/ma, lõiga/ta, lõika/n

dance (verb) tantsi/ma, -da, -n

dangerous ohtlik, -u, -ku, -ke

dark tume, -da, -dat, -daid

darling, dear, cute, sweet armas, armsa, armsat, armsaid

daughter tütar, tütre, tütart, tütreid

day päev, -a, -a, -i

decide otsusta/ma, -da, -n

degree kraad, -i, -i, -e

dentist hambaarst, -i, -i, -e

department store, kaubanduskeskus, -e, -t, -i (Am.) mall shopping centre depend sõltu/ma, -da, -b kellest? millest?

dessert magus/toit, -toidu, -toitu, -toite

dill till, -i, -i

diploma diplom, -i, -it, -eid

diplomat diplomaat, diplomaadi, diplomaati, diplomaate

director (of a film) režissöör, -i, -i, -e

director of a business firma/juht, -juhi, -juhti, -juhte

dishes nõud, nõude, nõusid

dishwasher nõudepesumasin, -a, -at, -aid

disturb, mix sega/ma, -da, -n keda? mida?

divide jaga/ma, -da, -n

do; make tege/ma, teha, teen

doctor arst, -i, -i, -e

dog koer, -a, -a, -i

doing well, good man (lit. tubli, -, -t, -sid untranslatable as one word)

doll nukk, nuku, nukku, nukke

domestic (lit. inside Estonia) Eesti-sise/ne, -se, -st, -seid

door uks, ukse, ust, uksi

double room kaheinimese/tuba, -toa, -tuba, -tubasid

drain kurna/ma, -ta, -n

drawer sahtel, sahtli, sahtlit, sahtleid

dress (verb) riietu/ma, -da, -n

drink (verb) joo/ma, juu/a, joo/n

drink, beverage jook, joogi, jooki, jooke

drive, go sõit/ma, -a, sõid/an

driving experience juhistaaž, -i, -i

driving licence juhi/load, -lubade, -lube

driving school autokool, -i, -i, -e

earlier vara/ne, -se, -st, -seid

eat söö/ma, süü/a, söö/n

eat breakfast hommikust söö/ma, hommikust süü/a,

eat up ära söö/ma, ära süü/a, söö/n ära

education haridus, -e, -t

egg muna, -, -, -e

election, selection valimi/ne, -se, -st, -si

electricity elekter, elektri, elektrit

elevator lift, -i, -i, -e

else, other muu, muu, muud, muid

email e-mail, -i, -i, -e

employee alluv, -a, -at –aid

employer, boss ülemus, -e, -t, -i

empty tühi, tühja, tühja, tühje

empty, run flat tühjaks saa/ma, tühjaks saa/da, saa/b tühjaks

English inglise

entrance sissepääs, -u, -u, -e

estate agent kinnisvaramaakler, -i, -it, -eid

estate agent maakler, -i, -it, -eid

Estonian eesti

Estonian eestla/ne, -se, -st, -si

even isegi

evening õhtu, -u, -ut, -uid

every iga

exactly täpselt

examine läbi vaata/ma, läbi vaada/ta, vaata/n läbi

excellent suurepära/ne, -se, -st, -seid

except v.a (välja arvatud)

exchange (verb) vaheta/ma, -da, -n

exchange (verb) välja vaheta/ma, välja vaheta/da, vaheta/n välja

exciting, interesting põnev, -a, -at, -aid

exit väljapääs, -u, -u, -e

expensive kallis, kalli, kallist, kalleid

experience kogemus, -e, -t, -i

extra cost lisatasu, -, -, -sid

fall (verb) kukku/ma, -da, kuku/n

family pere, -, -t, -sid

family car **pereauto, -, -t, -sid**

famous **kuulus, kuulsa, kuulsat, kuulsaid**

fast **kiire, -, -t, -id**

feel sorry **kahju ole/ma, kahju oll/a, on kahju**

fetch, get **järele mine/ma, järele minn/a,**

fever **palavik, -u, -ku**

fill in **täit/ma, täit/a, täid/an**

film **film, -i, -i, -e**

film classics **filmiklassika, -, -t**

find **üles leid/ma, üles leid/a, leia/n üles**

first aid **training esmaabi/kursused, -kursuste, -kursusi**

first name **ees/nimi -nime, -nime, -nimesid**

first, start with **kõigepealt**

fish **kala, -, -, -sid**

fix **ära paranda/ma, ära paranda/da, paranda/n ära**

fix **korda tege/ma, korda teh/a, teen/korda**

flag **lipp, lipu, lippu, lippe**

floor, storey **korrus, -e, -t, -eid**

flour **jahu, -, -**

flu **gripp, gripi, grippi**

foot (also leg) **jalg, jala, jalga, jalgu**

football, (Am.) soccer **jalgpall, -i, -i, -e**

for how long? **kui kauaks?**

for me **minu jaoks**

for sure, certainly **kindlasti**

foreigner **välismaala/ne, -se, -st, -si**

forest **mets, -a, -a, -i**

forget **unusta/ma, -da, -n**

form, (Am.) blank **ankeet, ankeedi, ankeeti, ankeete**

form, (Am.) blank **blankett, blanketi, blanketti, blankette**

forward a message **edasi ütle/ma, edasi ütelda, ütle/n edasi**

forward, ahead, further **edasi**

fracture (of bone) **luu/murd, -murru, -murdu, -murde**

free **vaba, vaba, vaba, vabu**

free of charge **tasuta**

French **prantsuse**

French fries **frii/kartulid, -kartulite, -kartuleid**

fresh **värske, -, -t, -id**

Friday **reede, -, -t, -id**

friend **sõber, sõbra, sõpra, sõpru**

fruit **puu/vili, -vilja, -vilja, -vilju**

fry **praadi/ma, -da, prae/n**

full-time (job) **täis/koht, -koha, -kohta, -kohti**

funny **lõbus, -, -at, -aid**

funny **naljakas, naljaka, naljakat, naljakaid**

furniture **mööbel, mööbli, mööblit**

gas **gaas, -i, -i, -e**

general practitioner, GP **perearst, -i, -i, -e**

German **saksa**

get acquainted **tuttavaks saa/ma, tuttavaks saa/da, saa/n tuttavaks**

get fixed, be repaired **korda saa/ma, saa/da, saa/n korda**

get ready **valmis saa/ma, valmis saa/da, saa/n valmis**

get to **kohale jõud/ma, jõud/a, jõua/n kohale**

girlfriend, fiancée **pruut, pruudi, pruuti, pruute**

give (as a present) **kinki/ma, kinkida, kingin**

give back **tagasi and/ma, tagasi anda, annan tagasi**

give up **loobu/ma, -da, -n millest?**

give, put, pour **pane/ma, pann/a, pane/n**

gloves **kindad, kinnaste, kindaid**

go **mine/ma, minn/a, lähe/n kuhu? kust?**

go back **tagasi mine/ma, minn/a, lähe/n tagasi**

go to **käi/ma, -a, -n kus?**

go to sleep **magama mine/ma, magama minn/a,**

good **hea, -, -d, häid**

grandfather **vanaisa, -, -, -sid**

grape **viina/mari, -marja, -marja, -marju**

greet **tervita/ma, -da, -n keda?**

grow **kasva/ma, -da, -n**

guess, think **arva/ma, -ta, -n**

guitar **kitarr, -i, -i, -e**

hair **juuksed, juuste, juukseid**

hairdo **soeng, -u, -ut, -uid**

hairdo done with the hair drier **fööni/soeng, -u, -ut, -uid**

hairdresser **juuksur, -i, -it, -eid**

hall **saal, -i, -i, -e**

ham **sink, singi, sinki**

happen **juhtu/ma, -da, -b**

harbour **sadam, -a, -at, -aid**

hat **müts, -i, -i, -e**

hate (verb) **vihka/ma, viha/ta, vihka/n keda? mida?**

have (still) **alles ole/ma, alles oll/a, on alles**

have a chat, talk **juttu aja/ma, juttu ajada, ajan juttu kellega?**

have a look at, inspect **üle vaata/ma, vaada/ta, vaata/n üle**

he, she **ta (tema), ta (tema), teda**

he, she **tema (ta), tema (ta), teda**

head **pea, -, -d, päid**

heal **ära parane/ma, parane/da, parane/b ära**

health **tervis, -e, -t**

healthy, well **terve, -, -t, -id**

heat **kuumus, -e, -t**

heat (verb) **kuumuta/ma, -da, -n**

heating **küte, kütte, kütet**

heel **konts, -a, -a, -i**

height **kasv, -u, -u**

hello **tere**

help **aita/ma, aida/ta, aita/n keda? kellel mida teha?**

here **siin**

high **kõrge, -, -t, -id**

hobby-painter's camp **maali/laager, -laagri, -laagrit**

hoist (verb) **heiska/ma, heisa/ta, heiska/n**

holiday **püha, -, -, -sid**

home-made berry liqueur **marjanaps, -i, -i, -e**

horrifying **õud/ne, -se, -set, -seid**

hotel **hotell, -i, -i, -e**

hour **tund, tunni, tundi, tunde**

house wine **majavein, -i, -i, -e**

house, building **maja, -, -, sid**

how high? **kui kõrge?**

how long? **kui kaua?**

how many of you altogether? **mitmekesi?**

how much? **kui palju?**

how old? **kui vana?**

how? **kuidas?**

hundred **sada, saja, sada, sadu**

I **ma (mina), mu (minu), mind**

I **mina (ma), minu, mind**

ice **jää, -, -d**

icing **glasuur, -i, -i, -e**

idea, thought **mõte, mõtte, mõtet, mõtteid**

if **kui**

in English (language) **ingliskeel/ne, -se, -set, -seid**

in front of **ees**

in principle **põhimõtteliselt**

in that direction **sealpool**

in the case of **puhul**

in the evening **õhtu/poole**

in the middle **keskel**

in the morning, forenoon **hommikupoole**

inconvenient **tüli/kas, -ka, -kat, -kaid**

information desk, information office **infopunkt, -i, -i, -e**

information sheet **info/leht, -lehe, -lehte, -lehti**

injection **süst, -i, -i, -e**

inside **sees**

instruction **juhend, -i, -it, -eid**

intend **kavatse/ma, -da, -n mida teha?**

intense **pingeli/ne, -se, -st, -si**

interesting **huvitav, -a, -at, -aid**

interior **interjöör, -i, -i, -e**

international **rahvusvaheli/ne, -se, -st, -si**

internet **internet, interneti, internetti**

internet connection **interneti/ühendus, -e, -t, -i**

invite **külla kutsu/ma, kutsu/da, kutsu/n külla**

it, this **see, selle, seda**

jacket **jope, -, -t, -sid**

jam **moos, -i, -i, -e**

jeep **dšiip, dšiibi, dšiipi, dšiipe**

jiffy bag **turvaümbrik, -u, -ut, -uid**

job interview **tööintervjuu, -, -d, -sid**

journalist **ajakirjanik, -u, -ku, -ke**

just **lihtsalt**

just in case **igaks juhuks**

just so **niisama**

just, exactly, precisely **just**

keep **alles hoid/ma, alles hoid/a, hoi/an alles**

keep animals **loomi pida/ma, loomi pida/da, pea/n loomi**

key **võti, võtme, võtit, võtmeid**

kilo **kilo, -, -, -sid**

kindergarten **laste/aed, -aia, -aeda, -aedu**

kitchen **köök, köögi, kööki, kööke**

kitchen towel **rätik, -u, -ut, -uid**

know **tead/ma, -a, tea/n**

know, can **oska/ma, osa/ta, -n mida teha?**

lake **järv, -e, -e, -i**

language **keel, -e, -t, -i**

laptop (computer) **süle/arvuti, -arvuti, -arvutit, -arvuteid**

last time **viimati**

last week **nädal, -, -at, -aid**

later **hiljem**

lay down **pikali heit/ma, pikali hei/ta, heida/n pikali**

lean **tai/ne, -se, -st, -seid**

lemon **sidrun, -i, -it, -eid**

let **lask/ma, las/ta, lase/n**

letter **kiri, kirja, kirja, kirju**

lie **valeta/ma, -da, -n**

light **kerge, -, -t, -id**

liqueur **liköör, -i, -i -e**

listen to **kuula/ma, -ta, -n keda?mida?**

litre **liiter, liitri, liitrit, liitreid**

live **ela/ma, -da -n**

living room **elu/tuba, -toa, -tuba, -tube**

lobby (of hotel) **fuajee, -, -d, -sid**

local (person) **kohalik, -u, -ku, -ke**

location **asu/koht, -koha, -kohta, -kohti**

locked **lukus**

long **pikk, pika, pikka, pikki**

long ago **ammu**

look **välja näge/ma, välja näh/a, näe/n välja**

lose **ära kaota/ma, ära kaota/da, kaota/n ära**

loud **valjult**

love (verb) **armasta/ma, -da, -n keda? mida?**

lower, bottom **alumi/ne, -se, -st, -si**

machine, car **masin, -a, -at, -aid**

mainly **põhiliselt**

make up (used when calculating numbers) **kokku tegema, kokku teh/a, tee/b kokku**

make wet **märjaks tege/ma, märjaks teh/a, teen märjaks**

man, husband **mees, mehe, meest, mehi**

manage **hakkama saa/ma, hakkama saa/da, saa/n hakkama kellega? millega?**

march (verb) **marssi/ma, -da, marsin**

marinate **marineeri/ma, -da, -n**

married couple **abielu/paar, -i, -i, -e**

maybe **võib-olla**

mayonnaise **majonees, -i, -i**

meal **söök, söögi, sööki, sööke**

mean **tähenda/ma, -da, -b mida?**

meat pie **liha/pirukas, -piruka, -pirukat, -pirukaid**

medicine, drug **rohi, rohu, rohtu, rohtusid**

meet **kohtu/ma, -da, -n**

meet **kokku saa/ma, kokku saa/da, saa/n kokku**

melt, dissolve **ära sula/ma, ära sula/da, sulab ära**

member **liige, liikme, liiget, liikmeid**

microwave oven **mikrolaine/ahi, -ahju, -ahju, -ahje**

mida **tegema?**

middle aged **keskeali/ne, -se, -st, -si millest?**

mineral water **mineraal/vesi, -vee, -vett**

mini-bar (in the hotel room) **mini/baar, -i, -i, -e**

miss **miss, -i, -i, -e**

mobile phone **mobiil, -i, -i, -e**

moment **hetk, hetke, hetke, hetki**

money **raha, -, -**

month **kuu, -, -d, kuid**

morning **hommik, -u, -ut, -uid**

most **enamik, -u, -ku, -ke**

mouth **suu, -, -d, suid**

move **koli/ma, -da, -n**

mushroom **seen, -e, -t, -i**

mushroom pie **seenepiru/kas, -ka, -kat, -kaid**

music **muusika, -, -t**

musician **muusik, -u, -ut, -uid**

must, have to, should **pida/ma, -da, pea/n**

name **nimi, nime, nime, nimesid**

naturally **loomulikult**

nearby, close to **lähedal**

negative of the word **olema pole = ei ole**

neighbour **naaber, naabri, naabrit, naabreid**

net **võrk, võrgu, võrku, võrke**

news **uudised, uudiste, uudiseid**

newspaper office **toimetus, -e, -t, -i**

next **järgmi/ne, -se, -st, -si**

next to **kõrval**

nice, handsome **kena, -, -, -sid**

nicely, well **hästi**

night **öö, -, -d, öid**

night's rest **öö/rahu, -, -, -sid**

nightclub **ööklubi, -, -, -sid**

nine-storey (house) **üheksakorruseli/ne, -se, -st, -seid**

no, not **ei**

nobody **mitte keegi, mitte kellegi, mitte kedagi**

now **nüüd**

now and again **aeg-ajalt**

number **number, numbri, numbrit, numbreid**

nurse **õde, õe, õde, õdesid**

of course **muidugi**

of the size of **suuru/ne, -se, -st, -seid**

of the state **riiklik, -u, -ku, -ke**

office **kontor, -i, -it, -eid**

oil **õli, -, -**

OK (lit. normally) **normaalselt**

OK, clear **selge**

omelette **omlett, omleti, omletti, omlette**

on the contrary **vastupidi**

on the floor (lit. on the ground) **maas**

on the left **vasakul**

on the right hand **paremat kätt**

one **üks, ühe, üht**

one and a half **poolteist**

one by one **ükshaaval**

one's own **oma, -, -**

onion **sibul, -a, -at, -aid**

only **ainult**

open (verb) **ava/ma, -da, -n**

open (verb) **lahti tege/ma, lahti teh/a, tee/n lahti**

or (also butter) **või**

order, procedure, principle, time **kord, korra, korda, kordi**

ordering **tellimi/ne, -se, -st, -si**

organizer **korraldaja, -, -t, -id**

other, second **tei/ne, -se, -st, -si**

otherwise **muidu**

outlet **pistik, -u, -ut, -uid**

outside **väljas**

overall size **üld/pind, -pinna, pinda**

overcoat, coat **mantel, mantli, mantlit, mantleid**

owner **omanik, -u, -ku, -ke**

pack (verb) **pakki/ma, -da, paki/n**

package, wrapper **pakend, -i, -it, -eid**

paid **tasuli/ne, -se, -st, -si**

painful **valus, -s, -at, -aid**

paint (verb) **maali/ma, -da, -n**

paper, document **paber, -i, -it, -eid**

parents **vanemad, vanemate, vanemaid**

park **park, pargi, parki, parke**

park (verb) **parki/ma, parki/da, pargi/n**

parking spot **parkimis/koht, -koha, -kohta, -kohti**

parliament **riigikogu, -, -**

parsley **petersell, -i, -i**

part **osa, , -, -, osi**

passport **pass, -i, -i, -e**

pastry (before cooking) **tainas, taina, tainast**

patient **patsient, patsiendi, patsienti, patsiente**

pay extra **juurde maks/ma, maks/ta, maksa/n juurde**

pay in advance **ette maks/ma, ette maks/ta, maksa/n ette**

pay per hour **tunni/tasu, -, -**

peaceful, quiet **rahulik, -u, -ku, -ke**

peel (verb) **ära koori/ma, ära koori/da, koori/n ära**

pepper **pipar, pipra, pipart**

person of cultural importance **kultuuritegela/ne, -se, -st, -si**

person, man, human being **inime/ne, -se, -st, -seid**

pickled cucumber **hapu/kurk, -kurgi, -kurki, -kurke**

picture **pilt, pildi, pilti, pilte**

pilot **lendur, -i, -it, -eid**

pin code, identification code **isikukood, -i, -i, -e**

place **koht, koha, kohta, kohti**

planet **planeet, planeedi, planeeti, planeete**

play, act **mängi/ma, -da, -n mida?**

play, show, performance **etendus, -e, -t, -i**

playground **mänguväljak, -u, -ut, -uid**

pleasant **meeldiv, -a, -at, -aid**

pleasant, nice **tore, -da, -dat, -daid**

please **palun**

plum **ploom, -i, -i, -e**

pocket **tasku, -, -t, -id**

poem **luuletus, -e, -t, -i**

pork **sea/liha, -, -**

possible **võimalik, -u, -ku, -ke**

pot, pan **pott, poti, potti, potte**

potato salad **kartulisalat, -i, -it, -eid**

pour **vala/ma, -da, -n**

powder sugar **tuhk/suhkur, -suhkru, -suhkrut**

practise **tegele/ma, -da, -n kellega? millega?**

prefer **eelista/ma, -da, -n keda? mida?**

prepare **valmista/ma, -da, -n**

prescription **retsept, -i, -i, -e**

president **president, presidendi, presidenti, presidente**

press down **alla vajuta/ma, vajuta/da, vajuta/n alla**

previous **eelmi/ne, -se, -st, -seid**

price **hind, hinna, hinda, hindu**

price difference **hinnavahe, -, -t, -sid**

probably **ilmselt**

probably, perhaps **vist**

probation time **katse/aeg, -aja, -aega**

problem **probleem, -i, -i, -e**

profession **amet, -i, -it, -eid**

programme **kava, -,-, -sid**

psychologist **psühholoog, -i, -i, -e**

pull out **välja tõmb/ama, välja tõmma/ta, tõmba/n välja**

put into plaster **kipsi pane/ma, kipsi pann/a, pane/n kipsi**

quarter **veerand, veerandi, veerandit**

quickly **kiiresti**

quite **üsna**

raise **kerki/ma, -da, -b**

raisin **rosinad, rosinate, rosinaid**

raspberry **vaarikas, -ka, -kat, -kaid**

rate **kurss, kursi, kurssi, kursse**

ration **portsjon, -i, -it, -eid**

read **luge/ma, luge/da, loe/n**

read through **läbi luge/ma, läbi luge/da, loe/n läbi**

ready **valmis**

really **tõesti**

rearrange **ümber paiguta/ma, ümber paiguta/da, paiguta/n ümber**

receipt **ostu/tšekk, -tšeki, -tšekki, -tšekke**

receipt **tšekk, tšeki, tšekki, tšekke**

receive **kätte saa/ma, kätte saa/da, saa/n kätte**

receiver **saaja, -,-t, -id**

reception **vastu/võtt, -võtu, -võttu, -võtte**

recognize **ära tund/ma, ära tund/a, tunne/n ära**

reddish **puna/kas, -ka, -kat, -kaid**

referral **saate/kiri, -kirja, -kirja, -kirju**

refrigerator **külm/kapp, -kapi, -kappi, -kappe**

regular mail **maapost, -i, -i**

release, free **vabasta/ma, -da, -n**

remember **mäleta/ma, -da, -n**

remember **meelde tule/ma, tull/a, tule/b meelde**

rent (verb) **renti/ma, renti/da, rendi/n**

rent **üür, -i, -i**

rent (verb) **üürile and/ma, üürile and/a, anna/n üürile**

renting price **rendi/hind, -hinna, -hinda, -hindu**

republic **vaba/riik, -riigi, -riiki, -riike**

reservation **broneering, -u, -ut, -uid**

residential district **elamurajoon, -i, -i, -e**

rest (verb) **puhka/ma, puha/ta, puhka/n**

return, bring back **tagasta/ma, -da, -n**

right (i.e. side) **paremale**

road, highway **maan/tee, -, -d, -teid**

roast (in the oven), fry, bake **küpseta/ma, -da, -n**

roast meat (also main course) **praad, prae, praadi, praade**

roast, broil (over fire/hot coals) **grilli/ma, -da, -n**

roll **rull, -i, -i, -e**

roll (verb) **rulli/ma, -da, -n**

roller skates **rull/uisud, -uiskude, -uiske**

room **tuba, toa, tuba, tube**

room, surgery **kabinet, -i, -ti, -te**

row (verb) **rida, rea, rida, ridu**

rubber boot **kummik, -u, -ut, -ud**

run, be on show **jooks/ma, joos/ta, jookse/n**

Russian **venela/ne, -se, -st, -si**

safety seat (for babies) **turva/iste, -istme, -istet, -istmeid**

salty **soola/ne, -se, -st, -seid**

same **sama, -, -, samu**

sauce **kaste, kastme, kastet, kastmeid**

sauna **saun, -a, -a, -u**

say, tell **ütle/ma, ütel/da (öel/da), ütle/n**

school **kool, -i, -i, -e**

science fiction film **ulmefilm, -i, -i, -e**

season (verb) **maitsesta/ma, -da, -n**

seasonings **maitse/ained, -ainete, -aineid**

secondary school, gymnasium **keskkool, -i, -i, -e**

secretary **sekretär, -i, -i, -e**

see **näge/ma, näh/a, näe/n**

seem **tundu/ma, -da, -b**

select (verb) **välja vali/ma, välja valida, valin välja**

sell **müü/ma, -a, -n**

send **saat/ma, saat/a, saad/an**

sender **saatja, -, -t, -id**

senior citizen, retired person **pensionär, -i, -i, -e**

sensible **asjalik, -u, -ku, -ke**

separately **eraldi**

serious **tõsi/ne, -se, st, -seid**

service **teenindus, -e, -t**

sew **õmble/ma, õmmel/da, õmble/n**

shelf **riiul, -i, -it, -eid**

shoes **kingad, kingade, kingi**

shop **kauplus, -e, -t, -i**

shop assistant, seller, salesman/saleswoman **müüja, -, -t, -id**

shopping centre, (Am.) mall **ostukeskus, -e, -t, -i**

show (verb) **näita/ma, näida/ta, näita/n keda? mida?**

show (in the cinema) **seanss, seansi, seanssi, seansse**

side **külg, külje, külge, külgi**

side dish **lisand, -i, -it, -eid**

side of the road **teepool, -e, -t, -i**

side; half **pool, -e, -t, -i**

side-effect **kõrvalmõju, -, -, -sid**

signature **all/kiri, -kirja, -kirja, -kirju**

significant **silma/paistev, -paistva, -paistvat, -paistvaid**

sing **laul/ma, laul/da, laula/n**

single **üksik, -u, -ut, -uid**

single room **üheinimese/tuba, -toa, -tuba, -tubasid**

sink **valamu, -, -t, -id**

sit **istu/ma, -da, -n**

skirt **seelik, -u, -ut, -uid**

slim, slender **sale, -da, -dat, -daid**

slippers **sussid, susside, susse**

slow **aegla/ne, -se, -st, -seid**

small **väike(ne), väikese, väikest, väikseid**

small pie, pasty **pirukas, piruka, pirukat, pirukaid**

smart, clever **tark, targa, tarka, tarku**

smoke (verb) **suitseta/ma, -da, -n**

so, OK **nii**

sock **sokk, soki, sokki, sokke**

sofa **diivan, -i, -it, -eid**

soft **pehme, -, -t, -id**

soldier **sõdur, -i, -it, -eid**

solution **lahendus, -e, -t, -i**

some **mõni, mõne, mõnd, mõnesid**

some kind of **mingi, mingi, mingit, mingeid**

something, anything **midagi**

sometime, ever **kunagi**

sometimes **mõnikord**

sometimes; between **vahel**

somewhere, anywhere **kuskil**

son **poeg, poja, poega, poegi**

sorry **vabandust**

sort, type **sort, sordi, sorti, sorte**

sound (verb) **kõla/ma, -da, -b**

sour cream, smetana **hapukoor, -e, -t**

specialist doctor **eriarst, -i, -i**

speech **kõne, -, -t, -sid**

sports **sport, spordi, sporti**

sportsground **spordiväljak, -u, -ut, -uid**

sportsman **sportla/ne, -se, -st, -si**

spouse, husband **abikaasa, -, -t, -sid**

sprain (verb) **välja vääna/ma, välja vääna/ta, vääna/n välja**

spread (verb) **määri/ma, -da, -n**

sprinkle, shake **raputa/ma, -da, -n mida?**

stairs **trepp, trepi, treppi, treppe**

stairwell, entrance hall **trepi/koda, -koja, -koda, -kodasid**

stamp **mark, margi, marki, marke**

stand, wait **seis/ma, seis/ta, seis/an**

start (verb) **alga/ma, ala/ta, alga/b**

start (verb) **hakka/ma, haka/ta, hakka/n**

start work **tööle asu/ma, tööle asuda, asu/n tööle**

starting from **alates**

step closer **ligi astu/ma, ligi astu/da, astu/n ligi**

stereo system **muusikakeskus, -e, -t, -i**

stomach **kõht, kõhu, kõhtu**

stone building **kivi/maja, -, -, -maju**

stop **peatus, -e, -t, -i**

stove, oven **pliit, pliidi, pliiti, pliite**

stove, oven **ahi, ahju, ahju, ahje**

straight **otse**

strange **imelik, -u, -ku, -ke**

stranger **võõras, võõra, võõrast**

strawberry **maasi/kas, -ka, -kat, -kaid**

street **tänav, -a, -at, -aid**

strong **kange, -, -t, -id**

strong **tugev, -a, -at, -aid**

student **õpila/ne, -se, -st, -si**

suddenly (also maybe) **äkki**

suggest **soovita/ma, -da, -n mida? kellel mida teha?**

suit (verb) **sobi/ma, -da, -b kellele? millega?**

suitcase **kohver, kohvri, kohvrit, kohvreid**

supper, dinner **õhtu/söök, -söögi, -sööki, -sööke**

surname **perekonna/nimi, -nime, nime, nimesid**

surroundings **ümbrus, -e, -t**

swan **luik, luige, luike, luiki**

sweet **magus, -a, -at, -aid**

swell up **paistesse mine/ma, paistesse minn/a**

swim (verb) **uju/ma, -da, -n**

swimming pool **ujula, -, -t, -id**

switch on **sisse lülita/ma, sisse lülita/da, lülita/n sisse**

switch, button **nupp, nupu, nuppu, nuppe**

table **laud, laua, lauda, laudu**

tablet, pill **tablett, tableti, tabletti, tabette**

take along, take with you **kaasa võt/ma, kaasa võtt/a, võta/n kaasa**

take off **ära võt/ma, ära võt/ta, võta/n ära**

take photos **pildista/ma, -da, -n keda? mida?**

take place **toimu/ma, -da, -b**

take, get, buy **võt/ma, võtt/a, võta/n**

taste **maitse, -, -t**

taste (verb) **maits/ma, -ta, -en**

tastefully, with taste **maitsekalt**

tasty **maitsev, maitsva, maitsvat, maitsvaid**

taxi **takso, -, -t, -sid**

taxi stop **taksopeatus, -e, -t, -eid**

taxi driver **takso/juht, -juhi, -juhti, -juhte**

tea, road **tee, -, -d, -sid**

teacher **õpetaja, -, -t, -id**

tell, speak **rääki/ma, rääki/da, räägi/n kellega? millest? kellest?**

tender, attendant **teenindaja, -, -t, -id**

terrible, horrible **kohutav, -a, -at, -aid**

terrible, terribly **hirmus, hirmsa, hirmsat, hirmsaid**

terribly **hirmsasti**

thank you, thanks **aitäh**

then, in this case **siis**

there **seal**

these **need, nende, neid**

they **nad (nemad), nende, neid**

they **nemad (nad), nende, neid**

think **mõtle/ma, mõtel/da (mõel/da), mõtle/n**

this kind **niisugu/ne, -se, -st, -seid**

this kind **selli/ne, -se, -st, -seid**

this time **seekord**

this way, so **niimoodi**

three **kolm, kolme kolme**

three-quarters **kolmveerand, kolmveerandi, kolmveerandit**

throat **kurk, kurgu, kurku, kurke**

through **läbi**

throw away **ära viska/ma, ära visa/ta, viska/n ära**

ticket office **kassa, -, -t, -sid**

tie **lips, -u, -u, -e**

time **aeg, aja, aega**

time, time of the day **kella/aeg, -aja, -aega, -aegu**

today **täna**

today's **täna/ne, -se, -st, -seid**

together, united **koos**

toilet, WC **tualett, tualeti, tualeti, tualette**

toilet, WC **WC, -, -d, -sid**

tomorrow **homme**

tone **toon, -i, -i, -e**

too **liiga**

tooth **hammas, hamba, hammast, hambaid**

tourist **turist, -i, -i, -e**

tower **torn, -i, -i, -e**

toy **mängu/asi, -asja, -asja, -asju**

track (in a bowling hall) **rada, raja, rada, radu**

training **koolitus, -e, -t, -i**

training, workout (for sports) **trenn, -i, -i, -e**

tram **tramm, -i, -i, -e**

travel (verb) **reisi/ma, -da, -n**

trolleybus **troll, -i, -i, -e**

trousers (of sports uniform) **dressi/püksid, -pükste, -pükse**

try (verb) **proovi/ma, -da, -n mida?mida teha?**

try to **püüd/ma, püüd/a, püüa/n mida teha?**

Tuesday **teisi/päev, -a, -a, -i**

turn (verb) **pööra/ma, -ta, -n**

turn around **ümber pööra/ma, ümber pööra/ta, pööra/n ümber**

turn to, talk to **pöördu/ma, -da, -n kelle poole?**

TV (set) **teler, -i, -it, -eid**

TV (slang) **tele/kas, -ka, -kat, -kaid**

TV show, programme **saade, saate, saadet, saateid**

two **kaks, kahe, kaht**

two-room(ed) (apartment) **kahetoali/ne, -se, -st, -si**

understand **aru saa/ma, aru saa/da, saa/n aru kellest?**

unemployed **töötu, -, t, -id**

unfortunately **kahjuks**

university **ülikool, -i, -i, -e**

up to, until **kuni**

use (verb) **kasuta/ma, -da, -n mida?**

valid **kehtiv, -a, -at, -aid**

vegetarian **taimetoitla/ne, -se, -st, -si**

very **väga**

view **vaade, vaate, vaadet, vaateid**

visitor **külasta/ja, -, -t, -id**

visitor, guest **külali/ne, -se, -st, -si**

wait (verb) **oota/ma, ooda/ta, oota/n**

waiter **kelner, -i, -it, -eid**

waitress **ettekandja, -, -t, -id**

wake up **ärka/ma, ärga/ta, ärka/n**

walk (verb) **jaluta/ma, jaluta/da, jaluta/n**

want, wish **taht/ma, -a, taha/n keda? mida?**

wardrobe, closet, cupboard **kapp, kapi, kappi, kappe**

warranty repairs **garantii/remont, -remondi, -remonti**

wash **pese/ma, pes/ta, pese/n**

washing machine **pesumasin, -a, -at, -aid**

watch (verb) **vaata/ma, vaada/ta, vaata/n**

we **me (meie), me (meie), meid**

we **meie (me), meie, meid**

weak **nõrk, nõrga, nõrka, nõrku**

wear, put on **selga pane/ma, selga pann/a, pane/n selga**

wear, put on (used for footwear and trousers) **jalga pane/ma, jalga pann/a, pane/n jalga**

wear, put on (used for gloves) **kätte pane/ma, kätte pann/a, pane/n kätte**

wear, put on (used for hats) **pähe pane/ma, pähe pann/a, pane/n pähe**

wear, put on (used for shirts) **seljas ole/ma, seljas oll/a, on seljas** *(blouses, coats, jackets etc.)* **kaela pane/ma, kaela pann/a, pane/n kaela**

weather **ilm, -a, -a**

Wednesday **kolma/päev, -a, -a**

weekend **nädalavahetus, -e, -t, -i**

weigh **ära kaalu/ma, ära kaalu/da, kaalu/n ära**

welcome **tere tulemast**

wet **märg, märja, märga, märgi**

what **mis, mille, mida**

what kind of **milli/ne, -se, -st, -seid**

what? **mida?**

when? **millal?**

where? **kus?**

which one **kumb, kumma, kumba, kumbi**

who **kes, kelle keda**

why? **miks?**

window **aken, akna, akent, aknaid**

wireless **traadita**

wish (verb) **soovi/ma, -da, -n mida? mida teha?**

without **ilma**

witty **vaimukas, vaimuka, vaimukat, vaimukaid**

woman **nai/ne, -se, -st, -si**

wooden house, building **puu/maja, -, -, -maju**

woollen **villa/ne, -se, -st, -seid**

work (verb) **tööta/ma, tööta/da, tööta/n**

(workmen's) sick fund **haigekassa**

worry (verb) **muretse/ma, -da, -n kelle pärast ? mille pärast?**

wrap up, pack **ära pakki/ma, ära pakki/da, paki/n ära**

wrap, turn **keera/ma, -ta, -n**

write **kirjuta/ma, kirjuta/da, kirjuta/n**

write down **kirja pane/ma, pann/a, pane/n kirja**

wrong **vale, -, -t, -sid**

wrong number (lit. *false connection*) **valeühendus, -e, -t, -i**

x-ray **röntgen, -i, -it, -eid**

year **aasta, -, -t, -id**

yeast **pärm, -i, -i**

yellow **kolla/ne, -se, -st, -seid**

yes **jah**

you (plural) **te (teie), te (teie), teid**

you (plural) **teie (te), teie (te), teid**

you (singular) **sa (sina), su (sinu), sind**

you (singular) **sina (sa), sinu (su), sind**

young lady, girl **neiu, -, -t, -sid**

young man **noor/mees -mehe, -meest, -mehi**

yourself **ise, enda, ennast**

zoo **looma/aed, -aia, -aeda, -aedu**

Taking it further

This section gives you some websites that may prove useful if you want to be in touch with authentic Estonian.

Päevalehed – *daily newspapers*

Eesti Päevaleht (**www.epl.ee**) and **Postimees** (**www.postimees.ee**) are the two biggest daily newspapers. For light reading and entertainment look at **SL Õhtuleht** (**www.sloleht. ee**). **Äripäev** (**www.aripaev.ee**) is a daily newspaper for people interested in business and economy. The biggest news site on the internet is **www.delfi.ee**.

Nädalalehed – *weekly newspapers*

An independent newspaper, **Eesti Ekspress** (**www.ekspress.ee**), has a variety of feature stories and articles of general interest. **Sirp** (**www.sirp.ee**) is a newspaper devoted to Estonian culture (literature, theatre, cinema, art etc.). **Õpetajate Leht** (**www.opleht.ee**) is the paper about education and is intended for teachers. **Maaleht** (**www.maaleht.ee**) claims its target group is farmers and people living and working in the countryside.

Ajakirjad – *magazines*

There is a variety of magazines for all kinds of target group. You will find the websites of the different Estonian magazines by going to **www.neti.ee**. Then type in **ajakirjad** – this opens a list of Estonian magazines.

Televisioon ja raadio – *TV and radio*

The website of Estonian Television is **www.etv.ee**. You will be able to view some broadcasts and there is a variety of DVDs available at the online shop there.

The website of Estonian Radio is **www.er.ee**.

If you would like to study further, a suitable study set for an independent learner is **Naljaga pooleks. Eesti keele õppekomplekt algtasemele** (Mare Kitsnik and Leelo Kingisepp, OÜ Iduleht and FIE M. Kitsnik, 2006).

There are several internet bookshops that you can use to find material about Estonia in either English or Estonian: **www.apollo.ee** and **www.rahvaraamat.ee** both sell new books. At **www.raamatukoi.ee**, you will also find second-hand books. **www.exlibris.ee** specializes in selling language-learning textbooks and dictionaries.

The Estonian Institute (**www.einst.ee**) has useful information about Estonia on its website and a list of links that someone wishing to visit Estonia might want to take a look at.

If you want to go on an Estonian course to further your knowledge of Estonian, look at the summer schools organized by Estonian universities: Tartu Ülikool: **www.ut.ee**, Tallinna Ülikool: **www.tlu.ee**. The website of the Estonian Ministry of Science and Education is **www.hm.ee**.

Grammar glossary

adjective word that gives more information about a noun, e.g. **kollane maja** *a yellow house*, **maja on kollane** *the house is yellow*. In Estonian, adjectives and nouns usually have the same case ending, e.g. **suures majas** *in the big house*. There are four case endings that behave exceptionally: *-ni, -na, -ta, -ga* are not added to the adjective and only the noun takes the case ending e.g. Minge kollase maja**ni**. *Go up to the yellow house.*

adverb word that gives more information about the time, place or manner of the action e.g. Mu pea valutab **kohutavalt**. *My head aches terribly.*

auxiliary verb olema *to be*, which is used to form the perfect and pluperfect tenses e.g. Ma **olen** eesti keelt õppinud kaks kuud. *I have been learning Estonian for 2 months.* Ma **olin** õppinud eesti keelt kaks kuud. *I had learnt Estonian for 2 months.*

auxiliary word see **compound verb**.

cardinal numbers the numbers 1 (**üks**), 2 (**kaks**), 3 (**kolm**) and so on.

case Estonian language has 14 cases, each of which has a different case **ending**. They frequently correspond to the use of prepositions with nouns in English. Most of the case endings are added to the so-called second form (genitive). See also Appendix 2.

comparative form of adjective special form of an adjective used when comparing things, e.g. **suurem** *bigger*, **kõige suurem** or **suurim** *the biggest*. We can add all case endings to these forms too, e.g. Palun andke mulle **suuremaid õunu**. *Please give me the bigger apples.*

comparative form of adverb special forms of adverbs used in comparing actions, e.g. **Auto sõidab kiiremini kui buss**. *The car drives faster than the bus.*

compound noun noun composed of two or more words, e.g. **võileib** *sandwich* = **või** *butter* + **leib** *bread*.

compound verb verb made up of two words, e.g. **aru saama** *to understand*, the main word (**saama**) and the auxiliary word (**aru**). The main word changes and the auxiliary does not. The auxiliary word frequently does not stand with the main word in the sentence, e.g. Ma **saan** sinust hästi **aru**. *I understand you well.*

conditional mood form of the verb indicating that you wish to do something or would do something, were it possible, e.g. **Kui mul oleks aega, ma läheks kinno**. *If I had time, I would go to the cinema.* This form is also in used polite questions, e.g. **Kas sa tahaksid teatrisse minna?** *Would you like to go to the theatre?* Past forms: **Kui mul oleks eile aega olnud, siis ma oleks kinno läinud**. *If I had had time yesterday, I would have gone to the cinema.*

conjugation forms forms of the verb that are used with different personal pronouns, names etc. e.g. mina **räägin** *I speak*, Peeter **räägib** *Peeter speaks* etc.

conjunction word that connects two parts of the sentence or two words, e.g. **ja** *and*, **kuigi** also etc.

consonant there are 14 consonants in Estonian words: b, d, g, h, j, k, l, m, n, p, r, s, t, v. There are a further nine that occur only in loanwords and foreign names: f, š, z, zˇ, c, q, w, x and y.

consonant change a feature of the language where certain consonants within the words change in different forms.

da-infinitive second basic form of the verb, which can end with either **-ta** e.g. vaada**ta** *to watch*; **-da**, e.g. luge**da** *to read* or **-a**, e.g. süü**a** *to eat*. This is the dictionary form of all verbs and is placed second after the ***ma*-infinitive** (the first basic form of the verb).

ending piece of grammatical information added to the end of the word, e.g. kohv koore**ga** *coffee with cream*, ma ela**n** *I live*.

first basic form of the noun form of the noun in the nominative case. This is the dictionary form and occurs in first position.

first basic form of the verb see **ma-infinitive**.

fourth basic form of the noun form of the plural partitive. This is the dictionary form and occurs in fourth position.

future tense no separate tense for the future in Estonian, instead, the present tense is used with an adverb of time, e.g. Ma **lähen** homme **Tartusse**. *I will go to Tartu tomorrow*.

gender no grammatical gender in Estonian, e.g. both *he* and *she* are translated with one word **tema/ta**.

imperative form of the verb used to tell or ask somebody to do something. There are two such forms: the singular (**Istu siia!** *Sit here!*) and plural (**Istuge siia!** *Sit here!*).

imperfect past tense used to talk about certain events that happened in the past, e.g. Eile ma **vaatasin** telerit. *Yesterday I watched the TV*.

indefinite adverb and **pronoun** a word used for talking about a person, thing, place or time that is not concrete, e.g. **keegi** *somebody*, **miski** *something*, **kuskil** *somewhere*, **kunagi** *sometime* in the appropriate form. These words can also take different case endings.

ma-infinitive first basic form of the verb, which ends with **-ma**, e.g. vaatama *watch*, luge**ma** *read*, söö**ma** *eat*. This form comes first in the dictionary.

mas-form special construction of the verb (**ma-infinitive + -s**) that is usually used to indicate repetitive or continuous actions, e.g. Ma käin iga päev **ujumas**. *I go swimming (for a swim) every day*.

mata-form special construction of the verb (**ma-infinitive + -ta**) that indicates that something is not done or is undone, e.g. **möbleerimata korter** *unfurnished apartment*, **korter on möbleerimata** *the apartment is unfurnished*.

mine-form noun constructed from a verb, indicating the name of an action, e.g. luge**mine** *reading*.

modal verb verb indicating possibility, intention or necessity, e.g. **saama** *to be able to*, **tohtima** *may, to be allowed to*, **pidama** *must, have to*.

negative adverb and **pronoun** word used for talking about negation of a person, thing, place or time, e.g. **Mitte keegi** ei taha süüa. *No one wants to eat.* Ma ei ole **mitte kunagi** Tartus käinud. *I have never been to* Tartu.

noun word used to refer to a person, thing or an abstract idea such as a feeling or quality, e.g. **õpetaja** *a teacher*, **maja** *a house*, **armastus** *love*.

object noun or a pronoun that refers to a person or a thing involved in or affected by the action of the verb, e.g. Ma söön **suppi**. *I eat soup.*

ordinal numbers numbers used to say in what position something is in a list or a set, e.g. **esimene** *first*, **teine** *second*.

past tenses forms of the verb used to indicate actions that took place in the past. There are three past tenses in Estonian. See also **imperfect**, **perfect**, **pluperfect**.

perfect (or **present perfect**) past tense used when we talk about past actions and make some summary about them, e.g. Ma **olen** Tallinnas **elanud** pool aastat. *I have been living in Tallinn for half a year.* The actions can continue in the future too.

personal pronoun pronoun that refers to the speaker, the person or people being spoken to or other people or things that have already been mentioned, e.g. **mina** *I*, **sina** *you*.

phrasal verb see **compound verb**.

pluperfect (or **past perfect**) past tense used when we talk about past actions and make some summary about actions that took place even earlier, e.g. Ma **olin** viis tundi **maganud**, kui äratuskell helises. *I had slept for 5 hours when the alarm clock rang.*

plural term used for a noun, pronoun, adjective or verb when it refers to two or more people, things or groups. See also Appendix 3.

possessive pronoun form of a personal pronoun that indicates possession or a link, e.g. **minu** *my*, **sinu** *your*.

postposition similar to a preposition but placed *after* the word it defines, e.g. teatri **juures** *near the theatre*, laua **taga** *behind the table*.

preposition word like **üle** tänava *across the street* that is followed by a noun.

present tense form of the verb used to indicate actions that take place at that moment, e.g. **ma söön** *I eat (I am eating)*.

pronoun word used instead of a noun or noun group to refer to someone or something, e.g. **mina** *I*, **siin** *here*.

second basic form of the noun form of the genitive case. See also Appendix 2.

second basic form of the verb see *da*-**infinitive**.

singular term used for a noun, pronoun, adjective or verb when it refers to only one person, thing or group, e.g. **kass** *a cat*, **puu** *a tree*.

tense form of the verb that shows whether you are referring to past, present or future time. See also **present tense**, **past tenses.**

third basic form of the verb form that indicates what is being done, e.g. **joon** *I drink*. This is the dictionary form and occurs in the third position.

tud-form special construction indicating that something is done, e.g. korter on möbleeritud *the apartment is furnished.*

verb word used to say what someone or something does or what happens, e.g. Ma töötan siin. *I work here.*

vowel there are nine vowels in Estonian: a, e, i, o, u, õ, ä, ö, ü.

Appendices

Appendix 1

THE ESTONIAN ALPHABET

The Estonian alphabet consists of 32 letters: A a, B b, (C c), D d, E e, (F f), G g, H h, I i, J j, K k, L l, M m, N n, O o, P p, (Q q), R r, S s, (Š š), (Z z), (Ž ž), T t, U u, V v, (W w), Õ õ, Ä ä, Ö ö, Ü ü, (X x), (Y y).

F, Š, Z and Ž occur only in loanwords and foreign names. C, Q, W, X and Y do not occur in Estonian words and are only used when writing foreign names.

There are nine vowels used in Estonian words: A, E, I, O, U, Õ, Ä, Ö, Ü and 14 consonants: B, D, G, H, J, K, L, M, N, P, R, S, T, V. Estonian words are written as phonetically as possible, which means that each letter usually corresponds to a sound and the words are pronounced exactly as they are written.

Appendix 2

CASES

case	question	ending of singular form	ending of plural form
nimetav	**kes?** *who?*	—	**-d**
nominative	**mis?** *what?*		
omastav	**kelle?** *whose?*	**-i, -e, -u, -a**	**-de, -te**
genitive	**mille?** *what?*		
osastav	**keda?** *whom?*	**-t, -i, -e, -u, -a, -d**	**-id, -i, -e, -u, -sid**
partitive	**mida?** *what?*		
sisseütlev	**kellesse?** *into whom?*	**-sse, no ending**	**-sse**
illative	**millesse?** *into what?*		
	kuhu? *where to?*		
seesütlev	**kelles?** *in whom?*	**-s**	**-s**
inessive	**milles?** *in what?*		
	kus? *where?*		
seestütlev	**kellest?** *about whom?*	**-st**	**-st**
elative	**millest?** *about what?*, *made of what?*		
	kust? *from where?*		

alaleütlev *allative*	**kellele?** *to whom?* **millele?** *to which?* **kuhu?** *where to?*	*-le*	*-le*
alalütlev *adessive*	**kellel?** *who has?* **millel?** *what has?* **kus?** *where?* **millal?** *when?*	*-l*	*-l*
alaltütlev *ablative*	**kellelt?** *from whom?* **millelt?** *from what?* **kust?** *from where?*	*-lt*	*-lt*
saav *translative*	**kelleks?** *to become who?* **milleks?** *to become what?, for what?* **missuguseks?** *to become what kind?*	*-ks*	*-ks*
rajav *terminative*	**kelleni?** *up to whom?* **milleni?** *up to what?, until what?*	*-ni*	*-ni*
olev *essive*	**kellena?** *as whom?* **millena?** *as what?*	*-na*	*-na*
ilmaütlev *abessive*	**kelleta?** *without whom?* **milleta?** *without what?*	*-ta*	*-ta*
kaasaütlev *comitative*	**kellega?** *with whom?* **millega?** *with what?*	*-ga*	*-ga*

Appendix 3

CONSTRUCTION OF PLURAL CASES

The plural nominative is constructed by adding *-d* to the singular genitive (the second form of the noun) e.g. koer, koera + *d* = koerad *dogs*.

The plural genitive is constructed on the basis of the singular partitive (the third form of the noun) i.e. if there is *-t* or *-d* at the end of singular partitive, **-e** is added e.g. õpetajat + **-e** = õpetajate, hea**d** + **-e** = hea**de**.

If the partitive singular (the third form of the noun) ends with a vowel, then **-de** is added e.g. maja + **-de** = maja**de**.

For construction of the plural partitive, see Unit 7.

All other plural cases (except nominative and partitive) are formed by adding the corresponding case ending to plural genitive i.e. koerte + **-ga** *with dogs*, inimeste + **-le** *to people.*

Appendix 4

THE SHORT FORM OF THE ILLATIVE CASE

I Short (one syllable) words. The short form is the same as the third form

Mis? *What?*	**Kuhu?** *Where to?*	**Mis?** *What?*	**Kuhu?** *Where to?*
kauss *bowl*	kauss**i** *into the bowl*	linn *town*	linn**a** *to town*
pott *pot*	pott**i** *into the pot*	saun *sauna*	saun**a** *to sauna*
kool *school*	kool**i** *into the school*	pank *bank*	pank**a** *to the bank*
kapp *cupboard*	kapp**i** *into the cupboard*	jaam *station*	jaam**a** *(in)to the station*
saal *hall*	saal**i** *into the hall*	mets *forest*	mets**a** *(in)to the forest*
klass *classroom*	klass**i** *into the classroom*	aed *garden*	aed**a** *(in)to the garden*
baar *bar*	baar**i** *into the bar*	külm *cold*	külm**a** *(in)to the cold*
restoran *restaurant*	restoran**i** *into the restaurant*	must *black, dirty*	must**a** *(in)to the black*
tass *cup*	tass**i** *into the cup*	õu *yard*	õu**e** *(in)to the yard*
kruus *mug*	kruus**i** *into the mug*		
klaas *glass*	klaas**i** *into the glass*		
karp *box*	karp**i** *into the box*		
pood *shop*	pood**i** *into the shop*		

II The letters *g, b, d* within the word change into *kk, pp, tt*

Mis? *What?*	**Kuhu?** *Where to?*	**Mis?** *What?*	**Kuhu?** *Where to?*
tu**b**a *room*	tu**pp**a *(in)to the room*	la**d**u *storey room*	la**tt**u *(in)to the storey room*
raamatuko**g**u *library*	raamatuko**kk**u *(in)to the library*	tööko**d**a *workshop*	tööko**tt**a *(in)to the workshop*

III The letters *l, m, n, r, j* in the middle of the word double

Mis? *What?*	**Kuhu?** *Where to?*	**Mis?** *What?*	**Kuhu?** *Where to?*
kü**l**a *village*	kü**ll**a (also in a meaning *to go to visit*)	me**r**i *sea*	me**rr**e *(in)to the sea*
lu**m**i *snow*	lu**mm**e *(in)to the snow*	ma**j**a *house*	ma**jj**a *(in)to the house*
ki**n**o *cinema*	ki**nn**o *(in)to the cinema*		

IV Irregular words

Mis? *What?*	**Kuhu?** *Where to?*	**Mis?** *What?*	**Kuhu?** *Where to?*
uus *new*	uude *(in)to the new*	suu *mouth*	suhu *(in)to mouth*
suur *big*	suurde *(in)to the big*	kodu *home*	koju *(in)to home*
keel *language*	keelde *(in)to the language*		
vesi *water*	vette *(in)to the water*		

Appendix 5

VERB FORMS

1 INDICATIVE

1.1 Present

Affirmative

ma õpin	me õpime
sa õpid	te õpite
ta õpib	nad õpivad

Negative

ma ei õpi	me ei õpi
sa ei õpi	te ei õpi
ta ei õpi	nad ei õpi

1.2 Imperfect

Affirmative

ma õppisin	me õppisime
sa õppisid	te õppisite
ta õppis	nad õppisid

Negative

ma ei õppinud	me ei õppinud
sa ei õppinud	te ei õppinud
ta ei õppinud	nad ei õppinud

1.3 Present perfect

Affirmative

ma olen õppinud	me oleme õppinud
sa oled õppinud	te olete õppinud
ta on õppinud	nad on õppinud

Negative

ma ei ole õppinud	me ei ole õppinud
sa ei ole õppinud	te ei ole õppinud
ta ei ole õppinud	nad ei ole õppinud

1.4 Past perfect

Affirmative

ma olin õppinud	me olime õppinud
sa olid õppinud	te olite õppinud
ta oli õppinud	nad olid õppinud

Negative

ma ei olnud õppinud	me ei olnud õppinud
sa ei olnud õppinud	te ei olnud õppinud
ta ei olnud õppinud	nad ei olnud õppinud

2 CONDITIONAL

2.1 Present

Affirmative

ma õpiksin (õpiks)	me õpiksime (õpiks)
sa õpiksid (õpiks)	te õpiksite (õpiks)
ta õpiks	nad õpiksid (õpiks)

Negative

ma ei õpiks	me ei õpiks
sa ei õpiks	te ei õpiks
ta ei õpiks	nad ei õpiks

2.2 Past

Affirmative

ma oleksin õppinud	me oleksime õppinud
sa oleksid õppinud	te oleksite õppinud
ta oleks õppinud	nad oleksid õppinud

Negative

ma ei oleks õppinud	me ei oleks õppinud
sa ei oleks õppinud	te ei oleks õppinud
ta ei oleks õppinud	nad ei oleks õppinud

3 Imperative

Singular	Negative	Plural	Negative
Affirmative õpi	ära õpi	Affirmative õppige	ärge õppige

Appendix 6

MA-**INFINITIVE,** *DA*-**INFINITIVE**

The *ma*-infinitive (first form) is used in the following cases:

1 with the word hakkama *to start*, **i.e.**

Ma **hakkan** lugema.   *I (will) start reading.*

2 with words indicating motion, like minema *to go*, **tulema** *to come*, **sõitma** *to drive* **etc.**

Ma **lähen** täna ujuma.   *I (will) go today to swim.*

Ma **tulen** sinu juurde telerit vaatama.   *I (will) come to you to watch TV.*

Kas te **sõidate** puhkama?   *Will you go (lit drive) to holidays?*

3 with some words expressing obligation

Mis kell ma **pean** kohal olema?   *At what time must I be there?*

Me **oleme kohustatud** seda tegema.   *We are obliged to do that.*

4 and also with some other words

Ma **ei ole harjunud** vara tõusma.   *I am not used to waking up early.*

Kas **olete valmis** kohe alustama?   *Are you ready to start at once?*

Ma **olen nõus** seda tegema.   *I agree to do that.*

Ma **õpin** eesti keelt rääkima.   *I (will) learn to speak Estonian.*

Kes **õpetab** mind tantsima?   *Who will teach me to dance?*

Ma **jään** veel töötama, minge teie koju.   *I (will) stay working here, you go home.*

Ma **jätan** teid töötama.   *I (will) leave you working.*

Ma **kutsun** teid sööma.   *I invite you to eat.*

The *da*-infinitive (second form) is used with:

1 with words and constructions expressing feelings and wishes

Ma **armastan** kaua magada.   *I love to sleep long.*

Mulle **meeldib** kirjutada.   *I like to write.*

Mida te **tahate** süüa?   *What do you want to eat?*

Ma **soovin** puhata.   *I wish to rest.*

Palume teil homme tulla.	*We ask you to come tomorrow.*
Soovitan teil natuke mõelda.	*I suggest you think a little bit.*
Me proovime kodus töötada.	*We try to work at home.*
Ansamblis **on tore** mängida.	*It is nice to play in a band.*

2 with words expressing probability

Ma **ei oska** hästi süüa teha.	*I can't cook well.*
Me **ei saa** väljas jalutada, sest vihma sajab.	*I can't walk outside because it is raining.*
Kas **võib** tulla?	*May I come?*
Siin **ei tohi** suitsetada.	*It is not allowed to smoke here.*
Ma ei **suuda** nii palju töötada.	*I am not able to work that much.*
Ma **ei jõua** seda kotti tõsta.	*I can't lift this bag. (Lit. I am too weak to lift this bag.)*

3 with words and constructions expressing obligation

Teil **ei ole vaja** süüa teha.	*You don't need to cook.*
Iga päev **tuleb** väljas käia.	*One has to go out every day.*

4 and also with some other words

Ma **aitan** teil CV-d kirjutada.	*I (will) help you to write the CV.*
Ma **püüan** teid aidata.	*I (will) try to help you.*
Lubame teil kodus töötada.	*We allow you to work at home.*
On aeg alustada.	*It is time to start.*
Kas teil **on aega** mind kuulata?	*Do you have time to listen to me?*
Mida siis teha?	*What to do then?*
Ma mängin kitarri, **et** raha teenida.	*I play guitar to make money.*

Index